Titles in ABC-CLIO's
Social History of the United States

The 1900s	Brian Greenberg and Linda S. Watts
The 1910s	Gordon Reavley
The 1920s	Linda S. Watts, Alice L. George, and Scott Beekman
The 1930s	Cecelia Bucki
The 1940s	Mark Ciabattari
The 1950s	John C. Stoner and Alice L. George
The 1960s	Troy D. Paino
The 1970s	Laurie Mercier
The 1980s	Peter C. Holloran and Andrew Hunt
The 1990s	Nancy Cohen

Social History of the United States

The 1930s

Cecelia Bucki

Series Editors
Daniel J. Walkowitz and Daniel E. Bender

Santa Barbara, California   Denver, Colorado   Oxford, England available, social history remains incomplete and contested; readers can benefit from studying this tension.

- The arguments in these volumes are supported by many tables and graphics. Social history has mobilized demographic evidence and—like its sister field, cultural history—has increasingly turned to visual evidence, both for the social history of media and culture and as evidence of social conditions. These materials are not presented simply as illustrations but as social evidence to be studied.
- Timelines at the head of every chapter highlight for readers all the major events and moments in the social history that follows.
- A series of biographical sketches at the end of every chapter highlights the lives of major figures more often overlooked in histories of the era. Readers can find ample biographical material on more prominent figures in other sources; here the authors have targeted lesser known but no less interesting and important subjects.
- Bibliographies include references to electronic sources and guide readers to material for further study.
- Three indices—one for each volume, one for the entire series, and one for all the people and events in the series—are provided in each volume. Readers can easily follow any of the major themes across the volumes.

Finally, we end with thanks for the supportive assistance of Ron Boehm and Kristin Gibson at ABC-CLIO, and especially to Dr. Alex Mikaberidze and Dr. Kim Kennedy White, who helped edit the manuscripts for the press. But of course, these volumes are the product of the extraordinary group of historians to whom we are particularly indebted:

The 1900s: Brian Greenberg and Linda S. Watts
The 1910s: Gordon Reavley
The 1920s: Linda S. Watts, Alice L. George, and Scott Beekman
The 1930s: Cecelia Bucki
The 1940s: Mark Ciabattari
The 1950s: John C. Stoner and Alice L. George
The 1960s: Troy D. Paino
The 1970s: Laurie Mercier
The 1980s: Peter C. Holloran and Andrew Hunt
The 1990s: Nancy Cohen

Daniel J. Walkowitz, Series Editor
Daniel E. Bender, Series Associate Editor

Volume Introduction

The 1930s was a momentous decade for the United States, as well as the world, since the international economic crisis of unregulated free-market capitalism transformed social relations and social conditions. The social history of the decade starts from this economic fact of the Great Depression. Work, family, culture and traditions, political beliefs, geographic and social mobility—all were affected. This volume will survey each of these themes. It will do so first through the lens of political changes and the emergence of the New Deal.

Americans responded in a variety of ways to the economic crisis, but two basic impulses were in tension with each other—individualist or collectivist actions, each of which took on unique American form. It may seem odd to mention individualist responses in a decade seemingly so defined by social movements and collective responses, but Americans still tended to see themselves in individual terms of success or failure. That tendency affected the early response to the economic crisis, as many initially saw it as a simple downturn in the economy, one that had happened many times before. It took some time for Americans to see themselves as united victims of an economic system gone awry rather than as individual failures. That process is outlined in the first chapter, which surveys the first two years of the decade, before the election of Franklin Delano Roosevelt in November 1932. The limited reach of the federal government in the first years of the decade, as well as the philosophical and political reluctance of President Herbert Hoover and his administration to use the potential power of the federal government, contributed to the social dislocation of many Americans. This created the pent-up frustrations that led to public pressure on local and state governments to respond. In turn, those local and state governments put pressure on Washington for a national solution to the crisis.

Thus the election of Franklin Delano Roosevelt was an indicator of Americans' hope for change. FDR had made only vague promises for a "New Deal" for Americans and given few details during his campaign. However, in the famous "One Hundred Days" of his first term, the New Deal emerged from the flurry of legislation proposed by his advisers and congressional supporters. First and foremost was a new role for the federal government. As will be reviewed in the next chapter, the so-called First New Deal (1933–1935) emphasized stabilizing the economy by regulating business sectors, while the Second New Deal (1935–1938) focused on guaranteeing people's purchasing power. These pieces of legislation placed the responsibility for repairing the economy in the federal government's hands. But this was neither apparent nor accepted at first, as the traditional roles of state and local governments placed economic development and people's welfare as their responsibilities. Institutional structures at the state and local level changed slowly, but by the end of the decade the federal government was deeply involved in affairs at these levels due to the enormity of the economic crisis. The federal government undertook responsibility for the state of the economy and people's welfare. Moreover, some key parts of the Second New Deal were explicitly created to allow greater power to weaker parties in the economic area. For example, the National Labor Relations Act of 1935 was established for the purpose of preventing disruptions of commerce because of labor disputes over economic inequities. The preamble of the act specifically put the federal government's protection on the side of the weaker party—workers—against large corporations, in order to provide for an equitable bargaining field. It did now, however, guarantee a favorable outcome for unions.

The shape of various parts of the New Deal depended on the contours of popular politics. Political agendas emerged from the grassroots as well as from the formal political parties and politicians. A *social history of politics* looks at the patterns of mobilization, the cultural bases for resonant political ideas in mainstream culture, along with a "history from the bottom up" focus, as one stream of social history has been described. For the 1930s, this perspective is vitally important, as the grassroots became mobilized as never before to demand certain social policies. On the electoral level, the "New Deal Coalition" of diverse social groups voting for the Democratic Party caused what political scientists call a *critical realignment* of the American electorate, one that continued to exist through the 1960s. The people making up this coalition—labor, urban, "new-ethnic," African American—did not always get what they asked for, since powerful conservative forces were also in motion at this time. A key point for any social survey of New Deal politics in this decade begins with the new-ethnics, those first- and second- generation immigrants who had diversified the American population during the Progressive Era and the 1920s. As native-born sons and daughters of the immigrants came of age to vote, they became more active in electoral politics. Their parents, many of whom had not taken steps to become citizens in the 1920s, generally took longer to get involved in politics, but the 1930s saw many of them beginning to participate in electoral politics. The 1928 presidential election, with Irish Catholic Al Smith of New York running on the Democratic ticket, electrified the new-ethnics, who gave Smith their votes. However, it took more than that for the new-ethnics to become loyal members of the Democratic Party. It took the politics of the New Deal to cement this group to the party, along with traditional Democratic groups like Irish Catholics and big-city voters, to create the New Deal Coalition in the presidential election of 1936. This story is also introduced in the chapter on the New Deal. They were joined by African Americans in the North, the legacy of the Great Migration of the 1920s, and by the newly created labor union members, the result of the new labor movement of the 1930s.

Social movements, whether of the right or left, are key to understanding the social history of the 1930s. The chapter titled "Social Movements" surveys these movements. They emerged from the bases of social and cultural networks in which people were enmeshed. Here the larger tensions in American society—between rich and poor, between rural and urban, between African American and white, between new-ethnic and old-stock Americans—played out in legal and extralegal ways. An important phenomenon of the first half of the decade that swayed American politics was the movements coming from the Midwest, the West, and the South that can be grouped under the populist label. Whether Huey Long's "Share Our Wealth" movement, Father Charles Coughlin's National Union for Social Justice, or Dr. Francis Townsend's Old-Age Pension Clubs—the ideas behind these movements captured the public imagination. Though they each had their own constituents and their own issues, commentators in 1934 called them collectively the "thunder on the left." Their leaders, their followers, and their positive and negative qualities are all reviewed. Another source of reform ideas were faith-based activists, arising out of various churches. Many merged their activities with other social movements, including leftist organizations and the labor movement.

Finally, there were the movements of various ethnic and racial communities, which had their own concerns and proposals. The foreign-stock communities, the first- and second-generation immigrant communities, were struggling to find their place in a United States that was alternately welcoming and hostile. The generation of European immigrants from earlier decades faced the eroding of their Old World culture and the loss of their children to a white, Anglo-Saxon Protestant American culture. The second generation faced difficulties being accepted in that same American culture and longed to create their own identities as ethnic Americans. Other groups of immigrants faced more particular hardships, such as Mexicans and Mexican Americans facing mass deportations or many industrial sectors. But in all cases, family members had to adjust their expectations, re-examine their social roles, and return to an earlier form of "family economy," as the pooling of individual incomes within the family unit is labeled. The gendered nature of the workforce in the 1930s, where jobs were rigidly labeled either "male" or "female," had some profound consequences for family dynamics. In many cases, women's jobs were less affected by the economic downturn. Thus, male breadwinners were often unemployed while women were able to eke out a living in the female sectors of the economy, causing changes in the internal psychological life of the nuclear family. Children were also profoundly affected by the economic crisis within their families, leading to new patterns of education and career path. One major change was the increase in high school attendance, but college attendance was down.

In conclusion, the social history of the 1930s is profoundly linked to the economic and political realities of this decade of depression. From this decade on, the federal government would be deeply involved in everyday life and the general welfare.

Useful Web Sites for the 1930s

New Deal Network
http://newdeal.feri.org
This site includes texts, images, documents, and other materials from the New Deal era.

The 1930s Project
http://xroads.virginia.edu/~1930s/front.html
This site maintained by the University of Virginia's American Studies program contains materials about the history and culture of the 1930s.

Franklin D. Roosevelt Library and Digital Archives
http://www.fdrlibrary.marist.edu/
This site contains documents, images, audio, and other primary source materials from the Franklin D. Roosevelt Library.

Franklin Delano Roosevelt
http://www.ipl.org/div/POTUS/fdroosevelt.html
This Internet Public Library site includes biographical information on Franklin Delano Roosevelt and his election to the presidency, and links to other resources about him.

A New Deal for the Arts
http://www.archives.gov/exhibit_hall/new_deal_for_the_arts/index.html

This National Archives site contains artwork, documents, photographs, and other materials from the New Deal programs that funded artists in the 1930s.

The following Web sites maintained by the Library of Congress include materials collected by or produced by various New Deal programs. More collections are added on a regular basis.

African American Odyssey: The Depression, New Deal, and World War II
http://lcweb2.loc.gov/ammem/aaohtml/exhibit/aopart8.html

American Life Histories: Manuscripts from the Federal Writers Project, 1936–1940
http://memory.loc.gov/ammem/wpaintro/wpahome.html

California Gold: Northern California Folk Music from the Thirties
http://memory.loc.gov/ammem/afccchtml/cowhome.html/

Florida Folklife from the WPA Collection, 1937–1942
http://memory.loc.gov/ammem/flwpahtml/flwpahome.html/

Farm Security Administration-Office of War Information Collection
http://lcweb2.loc.gov/fsowhome.html/

Southern Mosaic: The John and Ruby Lomax 1939 Southern States Recording Trip
http://memory.loc.gov/ammem/lohtml/lohome.html

Issues of the 20th Century

Rural/Agricultural

Urban/Suburban

Youth Culture

War and Society

Experiences of the Early Depression, 1929–1932

Overview

The 1930s have a distinct dividing line—the 1932 election—that makes it necessary to treat the early years of the Great Depression as a separate experience from the later years. In these early years, the economic catastrophe reached its nadir in 1933 when 24.9 percent (and probably more) of the nation's workforce was unemployed. There was no help from the federal government before 1933, and state and local charities did their best to cope with the emergency. By the summer of 1932, major cities were on the verge of declaring bankruptcy. Some general rhythms of social life for the decade can be found in these early years. For example, people enjoyed movies and radio programs. But the extensive displacement of "normal life" meant that the fear of losing one's job or, for immigrants, fear of being deported, the creation of shantytowns ("Hoovervilles"), the jobless and homeless traveling across the country "tramping," and political activism and demonstrations became commonplace. These conditions led to that portion of the decade, 1933–1939, collectively known as the New Deal, which will be covered in chapters 2, 3, and 4. During the Depression's early years Americans began to believe that the federal government was responsible for guaranteeing the American standard of living through its own actions in the economic arena. This chapter surveys the conditions that led to this belief.

Timeline

1929 The signal event of the Great Depression, "Black Tuesday," the stock-market crash, occurs on October 29.

1930 Sen. Robert Wagner (D-NY) introduces unemployment bills to Congress in January.

The first Unemployment Marches, organized by the Communist Party-led Unemployed Councils, gather on March 6 in major cities; in New York City, police clash with demonstrators in Union Square.

1931 President Hoover proposes moratorium on European war-debt payments to U.S. banks.

First National Hunger March converges on Washington, DC, on December 6.

1932 Congress approves Hoover's Reconstruction Finance Corporation in January.

On January 5, "Father Cox's Army" begins its march to Washington, D.C., from Pittsburgh.

During the Hunger March of laid-off Ford Motor Company workers to the Dearborn River Rouge Ford Plant on March 7, company guards shoot at unarmed demonstrators; five demonstrators are killed; event is dubbed the "Ford Massacre."

Congress passes Norris–La Guardia Anti-Injunction Act in March and Emergency Relief and Construction Act in July.

The Bonus Army March of World War veterans commences in May, culminating in their arrival in Washington, D.C., in July. Bonus Army is routed by regular U.S. Army troops commanded by Army Chief of Staff Douglas A. MacArthur.

The Farmers' Holiday movement acts during August harvest season.

In the presidential election in November, Franklin D. Roosevelt defeats the incumbent Herbert Hoover.

Great Crash and Financial Crisis

The stock-market crash of October 1929 revealed the weaknesses of the American economy and created panic and confusion among many. It did not cause

Table 1.1. Manufactures Summary, 1927–1939

Year	*Payroll (mill. $)*	*Value Added by Manufacture (mill. $)*
1927	13.1	26.3
1929	14.3	30.6
1931	—	—
1933	6.2	14.0
1935	9.6	18.6
1937	12.8	25.2
1939	12.7	24.5

Source: Historical Statistics of the United States: Colonial Times to 1970 (Washington, DC: GPO, 1975), 2:666.

the Depression. Nor did it directly impoverish the majority of Americans. Economist John Kenneth Galbraith calculated that only 1.5 million, out of a population of about 120 million, had *any* active participation in the stock market, contrary to the prevailing myth. Most astonishing to him was how the stock market had nonetheless permeated the culture of the nation (Galbraith 1961, 83).

The immediate repercussions were felt by investing and banking firms, which had been scrambling for much of 1929 to shore up the market. Charles E. Mitchell of National City Bank had saved the stock market in March 1929. Jitters had been calmed during the summer, but autumn witnessed a renewed downturn. After a meeting at J. P. Morgan and Company on Thursday October 24, 1929, Thomas W. Lamont, senior partner at Morgan's, announced to the public that the bankers had decided to stave off any further decline. That afternoon, Richard Whitney appeared on the floor of the New York Stock Exchange in his role as floor trader for Morgan's to buy stocks in steel and other major sectors at the morning's sale price. Trading stabilized that Friday and Saturday. But when Monday opened, sell-offs renewed, and this time the bankers did nothing. On Tuesday, October 29, the stock market was allowed to "adjust."

The myth of large numbers of ruined speculators committing suicide by jumping off buildings on Wall Street was not substantiated by fact, though a few dramatic suicides by prominent bankers did fuel the story. More important were revelations about embezzlements and other financial strategies, which were reported throughout the 1930s. Stories came out during an investigation by the Senate Committee on Banking and Currency in the spring of 1932. For example, it was discovered that Albert H. Wiggins of Chase National Bank had made stock purchases with unauthorized loans from his own bank's vaults; he quietly retired in 1932. In Chicago Samuel Insull's utilities empire, funded through holding companies that were really corporate shells, collapsed after the crash of 1929; Insull fled the country in 1932 to avoid indictment. Charles E. Mitchell of National City Bank was indicted on March 21, 1933, on income-tax evasion. Later

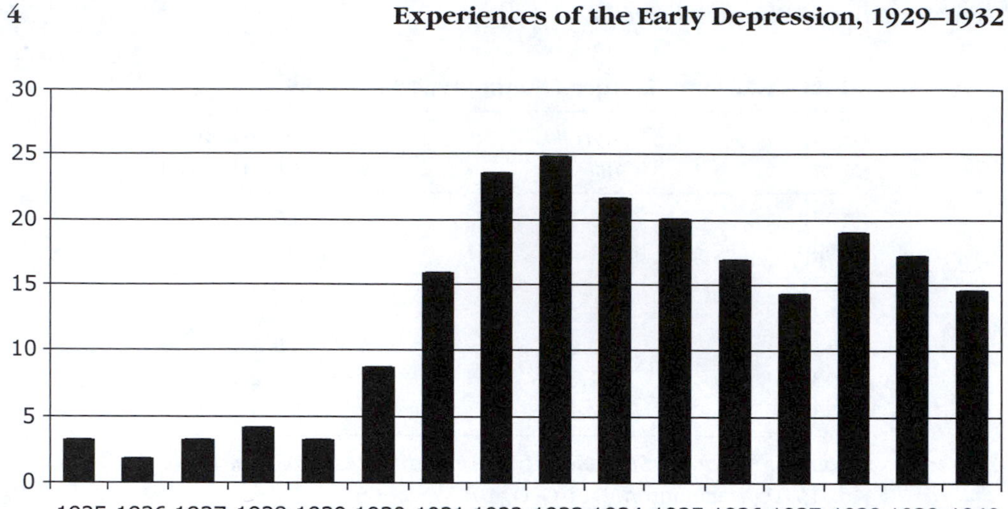

Figure 1.1 *Unemployment rate between 1925 and 1940 (in percentage).* Source: Historical Statistics of the United States: Colonial Times to 1970 *(Washington, D.C.: GPO, 1975).*

in the decade, Richard Whitney was arrested for grand larceny after he tried desperately to recoup his losses through increased speculation (Galbraith 1961, 133–165; Schlesinger 1957, 252–256).

Why Did the Depression Happen?

Economic historians have endlessly debated this question, and no one explanation seems to suffice. After the fact, economists have proposed explanations

Table 1.2. Bank Failures

Year	*Total Number of Banks*	*Total Assets (mill. $)*	*Bank Suspensions*	*Deposits of Suspended Banks (mill. $)*
1921	31,076	49,633	505	172
1925	29,052	62,282	618	168
1929	25,568	72,315	659	231
1930	24,273	74,290	1,352	869
1931	22,242	70,070	2,294	1,691
1932	19,317	57,295	1,456	725
1933	14,771	51,359	4,004	3,601
1934–1940	n/a	n/a	448	477

Source: Historical Statistics of the United States: Colonial Times to 1970 (Washington, DC: GPO, 1975), 1019, 1038.

that generally fit with their own perspectives on the free-market economy and its workings, as well as their policy recommendations. Milton Friedman, a monetarist, argued in 1963 that an unnecessary contraction of the currency, caused by the Federal Reserve's decision to raise interest rates, made an ordinary recession spin out of control into a major depression. His solution would have been to continue a sound monetary policy, not a fiscal solution such as taxing and spending. This is essentially what the Hoover administration did in 1930 to 1932. Economist Peter Temin in 1976 countered with an argument that the drop in investment and consumer spending caused a severe downturn. Thus a solution would have been to increase purchasing power, redistribute wealth, and increase government spending. This is essentially what the Second New Deal did between 1935 and 1937 (Friedman and Schwartz 1963; Temin 1976).

For our purposes in understanding the social history of the decade, some attention to the distribution of wealth and the health of various sectors of the economy is necessary. The international economy must also be factored into the situation. First, the so-called Prosperity Decade of the 1920s was enjoyed by only a segment of the American population. Indeed, when the Brookings Institution analyzed the U.S. Census data from 1929, it found that a third of nonfarm families were at or below the poverty line, and that fewer than 30 percent of all American families had incomes over $2,500, the entry level for an "American standard of living." Unemployment, including seasonal unemployment in industrial as well as farm work, was a constant menace. An estimated 10 percent of employable workers were unemployed at most times in the 1920s. These people were unable to participate in the new consumer economy of the 1920s. More important for many economists was the increasing gap between the rich and poor—during the 1920s, the share of national income going to the upper- and middle-income brackets increased steadily (Stricker 1983, 6–9, 21).

The economy underwent systematic changes in the 1920s. Even as productivity increased, some industries stagnated. The "sick" economic sectors of the 1920s included farming, coal mining, and textiles, along with soft spots in railroading, shipping and shipbuilding, and shoe and leather. The geographic regions of the South and New England were hardest hit by these declines. These factors meant that the Great Depression began slowly in the 1920s. After 1927 consumer spending declined, and in 1928 and 1929 manufacturers cut back production and began laying off workers, which further reinforced the decline. Then came the stock-market crisis. The heated market of 1929 consisted of inflated values on stocks, investors buying on margin where only 25 percent down was necessary to purchase stock, and an unregulated stock-market and banking environment. It was the Great Crash of October 29, 1929, where stock value declined nearly 40 percent overnight, which signaled the weakened state of the American economy.

The Great Crash did not cause the Depression, nor does it explain the severity or length of the economic crisis. Part of the problem was the international economic order. After World War I the international economic system relied on Germany's payment of high war reparations to the victors Britain and France, part of the 1919 Treaty of Versailles. Britain and France, in turn, needed those reparations to pay back the money they had borrowed from U.S. banks during and immediately after the war. When Germany proved unable to pay the reparations, a committee under the leadership of U.S. banker Charles Dawes produced a plan in 1924. The Dawes Plan stabilized Germany's currency, renegotiated Germany's repayment schedule, and put the world trading system back on the gold standard. The United States became the world's leading international lender. Most of the U.S. loans went to Germany to finance its rebuilding and reparations payments. Britain and France, in turn, used those dollars to repay their U.S. loans and to continue to buy American products, which were being produced in greater abundance due to the rising productivity of American manufacturing and farming. This led to further enthusiasm by American investors for the overseas securities market, matched by the overheated domestic stock market. The weight of European debt to U.S. banks by the end of the 1920s spelled disaster for European recovery and repayment. When the American stock market stumbled, it took down the European stock markets as well.

International trade was then further hampered by protectionist economic policies, first by the 1930 Hawley-Smoot Tariff passed by the U.S. Congress, and then by European powers retaliating by raising their own tariffs on American goods and produce. This economic nationalism prevented the international economy from rallying. Great Britain decided in 1931 to go off the gold standard and most European nations followed, thereby devaluing their currencies and thus lowering prices for their own goods relative to U.S. goods. In addition, since the United States remained on the gold standard, the U.S. Treasury was now transferring gold to countries that were selling their dollars back to the United States. President Herbert Hoover continued to blame foreign countries for the American economic difficulties in 1931 and 1932 (Kindleberger 1986).

The weakness of some portions of the U.S. economy, the legacy of the 1920s, exacerbated the domestic conditions. The farm crisis in 1930, brought on by bad harvests and low worldwide prices for key crops, caused farmers to declare bankruptcy and led to the collapse of rural banks, which then put enormous pressure on urban banks. Bank failures caused panic among depositors, leading to more runs on still-solvent banks, leading to more bank collapses. At this point the Federal Reserve ("the Fed") made some disastrous decisions, raising the discount rate (the interest rate that banks paid for loans from the Fed) and cutting back on the money it placed in circulation. The resulting limit on currency and credit hampered the banking system from meeting the economic crisis. These domestic decisions left the United States with little ability to stabilize its domestic economy, let alone the international order (Edsforth 2000; Fearon 1987).

Crowds of depositors gather outside of the Guardian Trust Company and National City Bank after the Clearing House Association announced withdrawals would be limited to 5 percent of deposits, February 28, 1933. The imposition of the withdrawal rule followed steady runs on the banks. Newly inaugurated President Franklin D. Roosevelt declared a "bank holiday," the temporary closure of banks, two weeks after this photo was taken. (National Archives)

Why Did the Depression Last So Long?

This question, too, has been debated and remains unresolved. There were short-run theories that started with the stock-market crash, such as a loss of "business confidence," and the unregulated banking and stock-market industries that had expanded credit too much. Working from a macro-economic level, the economist Joseph Schumpeter famously posited a theory of the Depression that argued that the coincidence of three major business cycles caused the Great Depression to last so long. Briefly, those cycles were: a Kondratieff (~50-year) cycle, which was associated with the introduction and widespread use of major inventions; a Juglar (~10-year) cycle, which was linked to population movements; and a Kitchin (~40-month) cycle of a typical inventory. Historian Michael Bernstein adds an additional explanation regarding timing: major industrial sectors (textiles, lumber, basic steel) were developmentally stagnant and potentially robust new sectors (consumer nondurables, aviation, petrochemicals, electrical appliances) were only beginning. Thus the economy could not pull itself out through its own powers of regeneration (Bernstein 1987). These economic debates, after the fact, had little effect on policymakers' understandings of the Depression while it was happening.

Response from the White House: "Prosperity is just around the corner"

The most significant post-crash economic indicator was falling industrial production and declining consumer spending. When the crash rattled the American economy, Treasury Secretary Andrew W. Mellon believed it was temporary, a "correction" in the economy. Mellon's famous quote, "Liquidate labor, liquidate stocks, liquidate the farmers, liquidate real estate," revealed his willingness to have the "natural" business cycle run its course. "It will purge the rottenness out of the system. High costs of living and high living will come down. People will work harder, live a more moral life. Values will be adjusted, and enterprising people will pick up the wrecks from less competent people," said Mellon (Hoover 1952, 3:30). Others in President Herbert Hoover's cabinet sided with the president who believed that the government should address the situation. But to Hoover that meant promoting confidence and encouraging voluntary efforts by business and individuals alike to stabilize the economy.

Hoover, as secretary of commerce during the Harding and Coolidge administrations, had been a progressive thinker on economic issues, though a strong believer in the free market. Progressive era reformers of his type had learned the lessons of previous economic downturns, including the postwar depression of 1920–1921, and rejected a strict laissez-faire attitude. They became convinced that a free-market system left to its own devices would spin out of control without some sort of regulating mechanism. However, that mechanism would be found in the private marketplace, not imposed by government. Hoover developed a model, which he called "constructive self-government of industry" (Wilson 1975, 86), which relied on the voluntary efforts of business trade associations to regulate their own market sectors; historians and political scientists call this concept "associationalism." As commerce secretary, Hoover encouraged trade associations to convene meetings where issues of product quality, standards, and relevant legislation were discussed. Hoover believed all this was necessary to prevent waste and inefficiency, as well as the unemployment that came from periodic downturns. However, these trade associations expanded their activities to include decision making about divvying up markets and deciding on prices, activities that Hoover did not publicly condone. This associationalism proved most useful to cartel-oriented sectors of the economy, producing oligopoly there, while having little effect on the weak sectors of agriculture, soft coal, and textiles.

Even though Hoover had encouraged this private economic planning, he would not cross the line to have the federal government intervene directly in the economy or to fund local relief efforts, given his antipathy to the "dole." He stood rigidly behind a balanced federal budget. Thus his legacy was negative. Indeed, in the early thirties, his name became synonymous with the Depression: "Hoovervilles" were the shanty towns outside of major cities where the poor and homeless lived, "Hoovercarts" were cars drawn by mules or horses because their owners could not afford gas, and "Hooverflags" were empty pockets turned inside out (Wilson 1975, 142).

The Hoover administration spent the next two years carrying out a delicate dance with congressional opponents and facing growing public unrest. Responding to legislative proposals by Democratic senator Robert F. Wagner of New York, Hoover in the fall of 1930 set up a President's Emergency Committee for Employment (PECE), chaired by Col. Arthur Woods. Woods had some experience in organizing unemployment relief in the postwar recession of 1921. But PECE's role was limited to investigating the problem and cooperating with industry, and had no relief funds. In August 1931 PECE was replaced by the President's Organization for Unemployment Relief (POUR), again with no funds for relief. Walter F. Gifford, president of American Telephone and Telegraph Company, became POUR's chairman. But Gifford, like Hoover, believed in local responsibility for relief, and POUR's mission was to encourage local charities and to promote local consumerism.

President Hoover's first bold legislative moves, in the summer of 1931, were aimed at strengthening the domestic and international banking order. He proposed a moratorium on all war-debt payments by European powers, especially Germany, reasoning that it would bolster American public confidence, relieve European nations of burdensome payments, and even stimulate trade. Congress approved the moratorium, though only after inserting a clause denying cancellation or reduction of those debts. No relief measures were debated in the fall of 1931. Hoover's next proposal to promote recovery was the Reconstruction Finance Corporation (RFC). The RFC was modeled after the War Finance Corporation of the war years. Hoover had approved this approach only after failing to get the nation's bankers to voluntarily set up a private credit pool. The RFC would use federal funds to provide loans to bankers and other financial institutions to put that economic sector, suffering from bank failures, back on solid ground. New York City mayor Jimmy Walker asked for an amendment to include loans for municipalities after bankers turned down his request for a loan to cover city relief payments, but the amendment was quickly defeated. By January 1932, Congress approved the RFC, budgeting it $500 million for loans to relieve banks, insurance companies, and railroads, to a maximum of $1 million

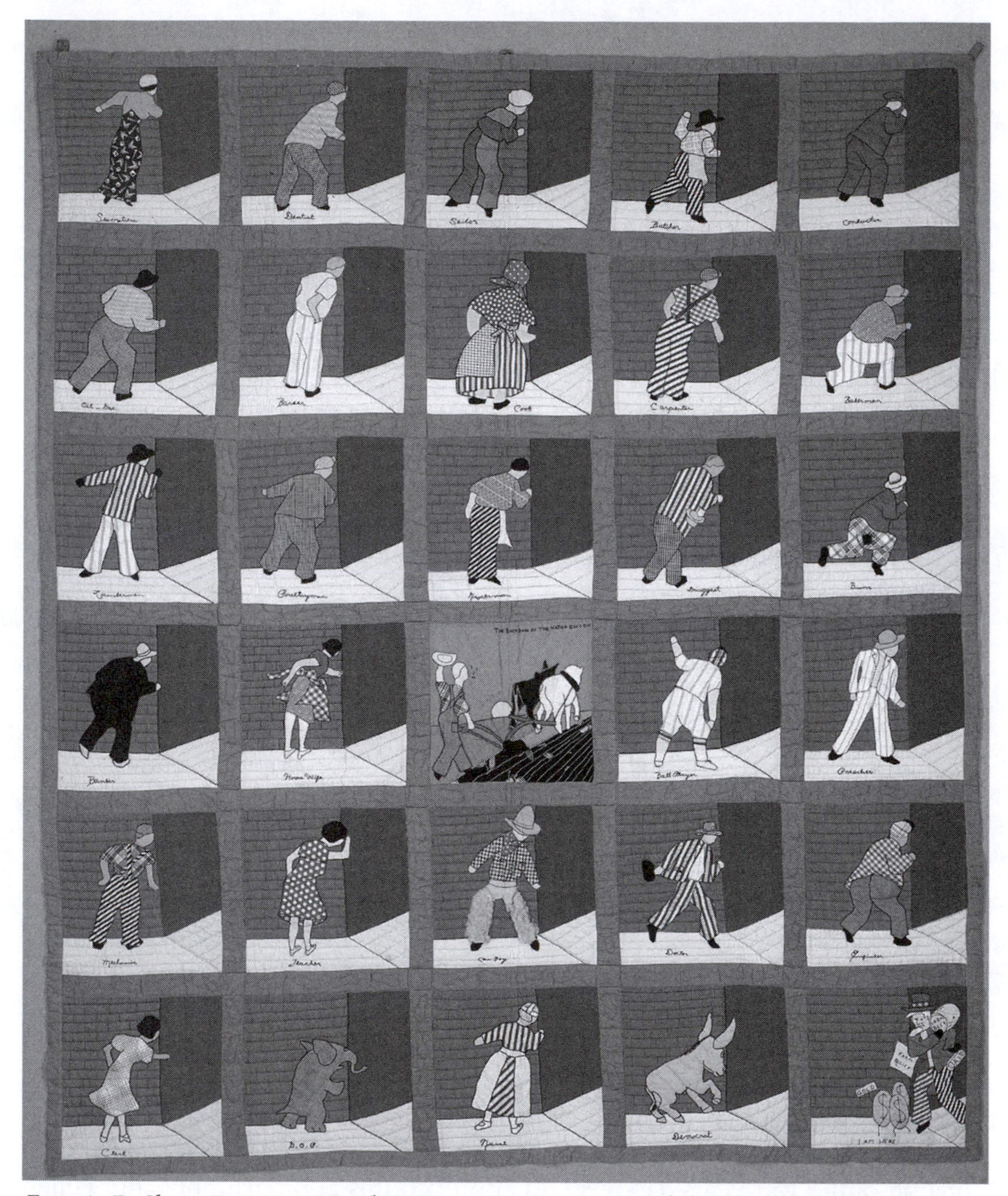

Fannie B. Shaw Prosperity Quilt, Prosperity Is Just Around the Corner, *1930–1932. This quilt, depicting citizens from a variety of walks of life, indicates a somewhat light-hearted approach to the economic crisis. (Mrs. Fannie B. Shaw, Cotton, Overall: 86 × 72 in. [2 m 18.44 cm × 1 m 82.88 cm], Dallas Museum of Art, anonymous gift)*

Historians' Perspective: Hoover's Presidency

Herbert Hoover had long been consigned to the list of failed presidents for his seeming lack of response to the Great Depression. But beginning with Joan Hoff Wilson's 1975 biography of Hoover, historians have discovered a more nuanced public servant. As Wilson noted, "Confronted by a welfare state based on federal coercion on his left and a welfare state based on government-sanctioned cartels on his right, Hoover rejected both extremes as violations of voluntary associationalism and cooperative individualism. Characteristically holding to a middle course, he was charged with doing nothing by both sides" (Wilson 1975, 152). Wilson used Hoover's memoirs, published in 1952, to reveal this other side of Hoover. The paradox was that Hoover's background as a Progressive-era reformer, with his long list of government relief accomplishments in the postwar era, did not fit his image as a do-nothing president in 1930–1932. Hoover had spent the 1920s as secretary of commerce, encouraging an "associative state." He was fearful, as many progressives were, of government control and yet also fearful of the wastefulness of market competition. His solution was to encourage trade associations and interest groups to share their information and needs, so as to carry out economic planning voluntarily. He had also been among the first politicians to see the potential in interest-group appeals (Balogh 2003). His own training as an engineer, as well as his grounding in Quaker principles of cooperation and consensus, had prepared him to view this model as the only possibility for success in an individualistic America. Indeed, he rejected Andrew Mellon's extreme laissez-faire approach. His first steps were unprecedented at the time: calling in over 400 business leaders to White House conferences where he coaxed the industrialists to maintain wage levels; encouraging the Federal Reserve System to ease credit by, among other things, lowering its discount rate to member banks; and, finally, calling on state and local governments to accelerate planned projects in order to pump up the economy. As historian David Kennedy has pointed out, the federal government was not geared at that time toward any large-scale action or spending on the scale that later critics said was needed (Kennedy 1999, 48–59). But caution must be used when consulting Hoover's memoirs, since they were often self-serving. As historian Jordan Schwarz pointed out in 1970, Hoover insisted that Democrats in Congress had thwarted all the president's proposals in 1931, but nothing was further from the truth (Schwarz 1970, 72–73).

each. No money was allocated for relief of the unemployed. The next step was a banking bill, which would lower the Federal Reserve's rediscount rate and aid bankers in their business. It passed quickly, with bipartisan support. Hoover's further legislative proposals included expansion of the capital of the federal land banks, a Home Loan Bank bill, and vague proposals for other banking supports (Schwarz 1970, 45–105).

Herbert Hoover (1874–1964), 31st president of the United States. (Library of Congress)

Democratic Party Response

The Democratic Party was divided, split between its traditional southern conservative wing and its newer urban ethnic constituency, a legacy of the 1928 Al Smith campaign. Moreover, when the Democrats regained a slight House majority after the 1930 election, there was some debate over whether it made sense to take over the leadership of the House when the Senate and the presidency were firmly in Republican hands. Why would the Democrats want to take any responsibility for the Depression before the presidential contest of 1932, some prominent Democrats reasoned. But responsible voices within the party prevailed and John Nance Garner (D-TX) assumed the Speaker of the House position in 1931. Garner had been in Congress since 1903 and, though a wealthy man in Texas, he championed a populist stance that one reporter characterized as "the demand of the common man for a larger portion of the profits of his toil" (Schwarz 1970, 65). With the exception of Henry T. Rainey of Illinois as floor leader, the rest of the House Democratic leadership was southern and generally fiscally conservative. This meant that they were of the same mind as GOP fiscal conservatives faced with this economic crisis.

It was Sen. Robert F. Wagner (D-NY) who became the prod to President Hoover's eventual activities. On January 9, 1930, Wagner introduced three bills that attempted to deal with unemployment. They were not motivated by the Depression, but were based on the results of the Senate Education and Labor Committee's hearings in 1928 on cyclical and technical unemployment. In essence, these proposed modest, federally funded public works projects when the unemployment rate reached a designated level and joint federal-state employment exchanges; the bills also directed the secretary of labor to gather monthly statistics on unemployment. Wagner's philosophy of government was based on what would later be labeled " welfare-state" principles, in which citizens' basic well-being was the ultimate governmental responsibility. Even as the Great Depression was becoming evident, Republicans in Congress were reluctant to endorse these bills, though the statistics bill was passed in the spring session. Wagner had, however, succeeded in bringing unemployment to the attention of the Congress.

The National Sales Tax Debate

President Hoover, the Republicans, and Democratic congressional leadership were all committed to the principle of balanced budgets; hence there was little revenue for the vast public works projects that many were clamoring for. The most debated new revenue source was a national sales tax, which was Speaker Garner's proposal, supported by his southern Democratic wing and most of the GOP. As Republican senator George H. Moses of New Hampshire explained, a sales tax was "based upon the surest foundation for one's ability to pay—namely one's ability to buy, and he who buys most, pays most—as he should. Under such a tax the rich are soaked, and the poor do not escape." But progressive politicians and some economists pointed out the uneven burden of such consumer taxes, falling most heavily on those who spend all their income on necessities. Or as socialist leader Norman Thomas put it in 1932, "It's a wonder they don't put a tax on tickets to the bread line" (Schwarz 1970, 110, 127).

A coalition of Democrats and progressive Republicans, led by Fiorello La Guardia (R-NY), defeated the sales tax bill in May 1932. Democratic speaker Garner, who had originally supported the sales tax, was overwhelmed by the negative response from both the public and his own party; he absented himself from most of the debate. The coalition responded to Hoover's proposed Revenue Act of 1932 by substituting a more progressive tax plan—a steeply graduated income tax; higher estate, gift, and corporate profits taxes; and a return to various excise taxes. This new revenue stream was not intended for relief, however, but to make up for the shortfall in tax receipts due to the business decline. State and local governments remained in charge of relief efforts (Leff 1984, 16, 49–90; Schwarz 1970, 106–141).

When Congress finally passed the Federal Employment Stabilization Act in January 1931, it committed the federal government to fund public works jobs as a means to control the business cycle. The president retained control, however, as only he had the power to invoke it. Wagner's final bill would have replaced the existing United States Employment Service (USES) with joint federal-state employment exchanges, or job centers, in each state to coordinate unemployed workers with available jobs. The National Association of Manufacturers (NAM) vigorously opposed such programs and the administration attempted to substitute a meaningless bill, but the House approved the Wagner bill. Hoover then acted with a pocket veto and vetoed twelve other bills in the lame-duck 1931 congressional session (Schwarz 1970, 23–44).

Employers' Responses

When economic hardship became apparent in early 1930, the national business community responded, like Treasury Secretary Mellon, with a faith in the self-

Welfare Capitalism

Gerard Swope, president of General Electric Company (GE), typified "welfare-capitalist" thinking in this era. In his widely known 1931 address, "The Stabilization of Industry," Swope called for the organization of cartels by industry associations with federal government oversight, private plans for life and disability insurance, pensions, and unemployment funds. But Swope's plan insisted on individual companies maintaining private control of these programs, thus easily complementing Hoover's insistence on private voluntary efforts. Moreover, GE's plan for unemployment insurance funds with "joint and equal" contributions by employee and employer the key to its success. Swope's speech was reprinted in Charles Beard's 1932 anthology, *America Faces the Future,* along with other business, labor, and political statements about the economic crisis (Beard 1932, 160–185; Schatz 1983, 53–61).

Welfare-capitalists were so named because they represented what was considered enlightened 1920s' management thinking. They were also a sophisticated management response to the labor upsurge of the 1915–1920 era. GE's employee welfare programs and its employee-representation plan (ERP) were established in response to labor organizing during and immediately after the war. They served as models for other companies who sought to curb the appeal of unions after 1919. The difference was that GE continued and even expanded its programs in the 1920s, while other companies discontinued theirs after the union threat diminished by mid-decade.

righting mechanism of the free market. Many business leaders argued that self-help and local boosterism were all that was needed. Chambers of commerce launched "Buy Now" campaigns, urging continued consumption for the sake of economic recovery, and promoted charity drives. Major industries promoted the "Share-the-Work" movement and a pledge not to reduce wages. This idea eventually received President Hoover's approval, and in 1932 he appointed Walter C. Teagle, president of Standard Oil of New Jersey, head of the national Share-the-Work movement. The idea was to put most workers on "short-time," that is, shorter hours, in order to spread the available work and to avoid layoffs; this was a new pattern from previous economic downturns. The larger and more stable firms were able to follow these guidelines for a time, finding advantage in keeping workers tied to their firms, a legacy of 1920s' sophisticated labor management. But major banking institutions attacked this "theory of high wages" which was based on the assumption that strong purchasing power would contribute to the recovery. This theory of high wages had been popular among consumer-goods manufacturers and retail employers. Finally, in October 1931, U.S. Steel broke the pact by announcing a wage cut of 10 percent, leading to wage reductions in all industries. By 1932 wage-cutting was the norm (Jacoby 1985, 212–215; Berkowitz and McQuaid 1988, 54–68; Bernstein 1960, 313–316).

Labor Proposals

Liberal Democrats, joined by progressive Republicans like congressman Fiorello La Guardia of New York and senators George W. Norris of Nebraska and Robert La Follette Jr. of Wisconsin, pressed for federal funds for unemployment relief. In 1930 and 1932 Senator Wagner had proposed his own unemployment relief plans. The La Follette–Costigan relief bill of February 1932 was defeated. More fruitfully, they sponsored legislation that had been part of organized labor's political agenda for some time.

Davis-Bacon Act

This 1931 piece of legislation, which required that contractors pay "prevailing wages" on federal construction projects, did not originate because of the Depression, but its effects meant that building craftsmen would have well-paid work when they had work at all. The American Federation of Labor (AFL), through its Building Trades department, had been trying since 1927 to regularize public construction work, insisting on the standard of "prevailing wages," which meant that construction contracts awarded by public entities like state and local governments had to pay the local standard wages. For building craftsmen who had retained union contracts throughout the 1920s and whose unions had lobbied successfully for the various state statutes that required this standard, this was one way to uphold union standards of living. In 1927, the problem came to the attention of Rep. Robert L. Bacon (R-NY), who noted that the construction of a federal hospital in his Long Island district had been awarded to an Alabama firm which brought in nonunion workers to work at very low wages. Bacon submitted a bill to the House to rectify this, and gained the support of the U.S. Department of Labor. In 1930 when James J. Davis, the long-time secretary

Drillers excavate for construction of the Hoover Dam in May 1933. The federal project provided jobs, housing, and social services for the thousands of workers and their families. (Library of Congress)

of labor, moved on to become a U.S. senator, his first act was to introduce prevailing wage legislation to the Senate, with Bacon submitting a companion bill to the House. Though the Associated General Contractors of America joined with some southern Democratic congressmen to oppose the bill, it was passed and signed into law by President Hoover in 1931. The act quickly came in for criticism, as labor deemed its threshold of $5,000 too high and contractors were unhappy that standards for deciding localities and wage rates were not delineated in the bill. In January 1932 Hoover signed an Executive Order laying out these procedures, thus briefly stopping attempts to amend the act. The passage of the act showed clearly the strength of some AFL affiliates in the halls of Congress. The act was successful in undergirding union wages in regions where building trades unions were already strong, but the principles came under pressure when unemployment relief projects got under way during the New Deal.

Anti-Injunction Legislation

The AFL had been working through much of the 1920s on legislation to curb state and federal courts' ability to stop organized workers' activities, such as strikes or even assembling; labor injunctions had become employers' favored weapons throughout the decade. Also related was the "yellow-dog contract," whereby employers forced new employees to sign a contract stating that they were not union members nor would they become union members for the duration of their employment. Sen. George Norris, as chairman of the Senate Judiciary Committee, committed himself to outlaw these practices, which he said violated due process and freedom of speech and assembly. The Norris Anti-Injunction Bill lay in committee from 1928 to 1930, before picking up support in 1931. Finally, in January 1932, it was reported out of committee, swiftly moving through the Senate, and on to the House. The Norris–La Guardia Act, prohibiting court injunctions against strikes and boycotts, was passed by the House by an overwhelming margin on March 8, 1932, and was signed by President Hoover two weeks later (Bernstein 1960, 393–415).

Shorter Hours

The 1930 AFL convention debated a proposal for shorter hours. Ever since 1886, the AFL had called for an eight-hour workday (thus a 48-hour week, with six working days), and some unions had won this shorter work-week during World War I. A few unions had struck for a Saturday half-holiday (a 44-hour week) in the early 1920s, and temporarily won. But now the issue seemed urgent. The AFL Executive Council endorsed a call for reduced hours and a five-day week. Of course, this dovetailed with Hoover's Share-the-Work program, which Hoover inaugurated in 1932, and of course, it came with a reduced pay envelope as well. In response, the AFL endorsed a six-hour day and five-day week, with no reduction in pay, at its November 1932 convention. In this move, the AFL repudiated the long-standing abhorrence of federal legislation that Samuel Gompers and his successors had stood for since the 1880s. This traditional philosophy was known as "voluntarism." The Thirty-Hours Bill was sponsored by Sen. Hugo L. Black of Alabama in December 1932 to a lame-duck Congress that was awaiting the inauguration of the new president, Franklin Delano Roosevelt. Congress put the matter into committee (Bernstein 1960, 476–484).

All these pieces of legislation broke new ground for industrial relations and paved the way for New Deal initiatives in a few years.

Poverty and Unemployment

While the federal government did little, the economy continued to contract. The downward spiral of low sales, leading to shutdowns of factories and growing numbers of unemployed, leading to fewer consumers being able to buy products, leading to more shutdowns, proceeded steadily, reaching a low in summer 1932. People coped as best they could.

Homelessness

In 1931 the number of unemployed and homeless using city shelters increased greatly from the previous year, for example, 280 percent in St. Louis, 421 percent in Minneapolis, and 700–750 percent in Detroit and Cleveland. Moreover, shantytowns sprang up in cities across the nation. The occupants of these "Hoovervilles" lived by scavenging and bartering for sustenance, relying on handouts from friendly local businesses, and using the charity services of local governments and agencies like the Salvation Army. More unemployed traveled in search of work by jumping on trains. As in previous eras, transients were disproportionately single men, under the age of 35, and from urban areas. But their population differed in some significant respects from the previous groups of homeless: a significant 12 to 16 percent were older, over age 44, and one Pennsylvania survey found some 10 to 14 percent were 55 or older. This reflected the employer practice of laying off older men in favor of younger, more vigorous workers. There were also more teenage boys riding the rails; some 20 percent were age 19 and younger. Women became a more noticeable part of the transient population in the 1930s, though most were members of families traveling together. These "auto-tramp" families, who used cheap automobiles to get around, were also a new feature of the 1930s. Sixty percent of transient women were married or separated. Unattached young women, however, were taking to the road in increasing numbers, where they faced sexual harassment and assault. These numbers were a reflection of the increased breakdown of family economies in 1930–1933 (Kusmer 2002, 193–209).

Meridel Le Sueur, "Women on the Breadlines"

Meridel Le Sueur wrote eloquently about the pain of the Great Depression through individual vignettes about women. She was born in Murray, Iowa, in 1900, granddaughter of an Iowa pioneer and one of the first white settlers of the Oklahoma territory, and raised by her mother, Marian Wharton, a feminist and socialist. Meridel grew up in a diverse Midwest and counted American Indian, Polish, Irish, and Scandinavian immigrant women as her friends, giving her a widely different view of women's lives than her own white middle-class Protestant culture. She imbibed the radical populist political culture of the early 20th century, as her mother and her stepfather, Arthur Le Sueur were teachers at the People's College in Fort Scott, Kansas. Her ideal activist was the radical worker-writer.

While pursuing her goal as an artist in Chicago, Hollywood, and San Francisco, Le Sueur married fellow radical and labor organizer Harry Rice in St. Paul, Minnesota, and bore two children. With the Great Depression, she began a new phase of her life as a writer, joining with other leftist writers in the Communist Party's John Reed Clubs where she met other writers like Jack Conroy and Richard Wright, and began writing for the *New Masses* magazine. Her first story for *New Masses,* "Women on the Breadlines," published in January 1932, captured the unique position of the unemployed woman, who rarely was noticed by the press.

> I am sitting in the city free employment bureau. It's the women's section. We have been sitting here now for four hours. We sit here every day, waiting for a job. . . . A girl we have seen every day all summer went crazy yesterday at the YW[CA]. She went into hysterics, stamping her feet and screaming.
>
> She hadn't had work for eight months. "You've got to give me something," she kept saying. The woman in charge flew into a rage, . . . because she is unable to give jobs, having none. . . . So they stood there, the two women, in a rage, the girl weeping and the woman shouting at her. In the eight months of unemployment she had gotten ragged, and the woman was shouting that she would not send her out like that. "Why don't you shine your shoes?" she kept telling the girl, and the girl kept sobbing and sobbing because she was starving.

The plight of the unemployed woman was very often unnoticed, because it was assumed that the most important person to help was the male breadwinner. As Le Sueur wrote, "It is one of the great mysteries of the city where women go when they are out of work and hungry. There are not many women in the bread line. . . . A woman will shut herself up in a room until it is taken away from her and eat a cracker a day and be quiet as a mouse so there are no social statistics concerning her." The alternative, prostitution, made any single woman or girl suspicious to a charity worker (Le Sueur 1982, 137–143).

Ethnic Communities

For the immigrant working class, it seemed just one more downturn to survive. Sociologist Ewa Morawska discovered this fatalism in her study of Johnstown, Pennsylvania, as elders remembered, "We were not surprised by hard times. . . . It was normal, it happened to us before in 1922 and 1923." She labeled this view of life as *morskoje plavanije,* "swimming at sea with an alternation of highs and lows" (Morawska 1985, 216). Ethnic households survived by pooling family members' incomes from odd jobs, buying on credit at the neighborhood store, and reducing expenditures. Some unemployed took decidedly less legal routes, as newspapers filled with arrest reports of stealing food or coal or peddling homemade liquor. Neighborhood ethnic grocers and butchers made a comeback from the loss of business to the chain stores of the 1920s, but only because they were willing to carry customers on credit—not a viable long-term condition.

Ethnic institutions tried to meet their communities' needs. Unemployed workers beseeched local parishes, the Catholic Charities, Jewish Charities, and nationality groups like the Polish National Alliance or the Slovenian, Lithuanian, or Slovak benefit societies for help. Fraternal organizations announced waivers of dues for unemployed members, while local chapters and churches held fundraisers to help their more unfortunate members. The fraternal organizations, which had originated as self-help societies at the beginning of their people's immigration to the States to provide sick and death benefits for members, had reorganized themselves during the 1920s when many state insurance regulators forced them to follow sound actuarial practices. But at the national level, ethnic fraternal organizations and banks were caught in the downward swing of the economy in the early 1930s. In Chicago, the failures of some ethnic banks—the Binga State Bank, the First Italian State Bank, the Slovak Papanek-Kovac State Bank, and the largest Polish bank, the Northwestern Trust and Savings Bank—caused a few fraternals to fail to cover their policies. Many of these banks had fallen because of heavy real estate investments, which were now largely unpaid mortgages and foreclosures. But by and large, ethnics did not abandon their institutions. Rather, those institutions remade themselves socially and politically during the decade (see "Social Movements" chapter) (Bucki 2001, 126–130; Cohen 1990, 213–238).

Immigrants

In 1931 Secretary of Labor William M. Doaks announced that there were 400,000 illegal immigrants in the United States taking jobs from needy Americans. He then ordered Bureau of Immigration agents to detain and deport persons who were in the United States illegally, as a simple solution to the unemployment problem. The 1924 Immigration Restriction Act had ended free entry into the United States, set up a quota system for Europeans (based on country of origin) whereby immigrants needed to obtain visas for entry, and barred entry of all Asians. Some 300,000 persons (compared to the million or more immigrating each year between 1905 and 1914) would henceforth be admitted annually, with the largest number of visas reserved for preferred northwestern European countries. The pre-1924 immigrants had to decide whether or not to stay in the United States, since they were no longer free to travel back and forth to their native lands. Thus they fortified their ethnic institutions while becoming Americanized. However, this process did not necessarily lead them to undertake naturalization procedures. In 1930, 35 percent of immigrants in the country had not taken steps toward becoming citizens.

The Western Hemisphere countries had unlimited entry, mostly due to pressure from agricultural interests and their labor needs. But these immigrants, especially Mexicans, had to enter at designated ports of entry and pay an $18 entry fee (an $8 head tax plus a $10 visa fee) to receive entry papers (Hoffman 1974, 30). In addition, the Immigration Act of 1929 made unlawful entry into the United States punishable as a misdemeanor. Moreover, the Bureau of Immigration tightened administrative procedures at the borders after 1929, especially those regarding contract labor and the literacy test, and reinforced the 19th-century ban on immigrants who were likely to become "public charges." Bureau agents first targeted workers on strike; next were ethnic clubs, where agents sent in teams to validate entry papers of members. Also, local relief agencies restricted their services to U.S. citizens only. Foreign nationals were no longer welcome. This became a spur for all immigrants to become citizens, a process that accelerated through the decade.

Mexican American Communities

The plight of Mexican Americans revealed the intense nativism of the 1930s. Mexican migrants had become reliable cheap labor in California and Southwest agriculture due to the day-laborer program established during World War I. They had also been enticed to come to industrial states when European immigration was curtailed by the war. They were exempt from the strict quota system established in the 1924 Immigration Restriction Act. But when the economy declined in the early 1930s, Mexican immigrants were particularly targeted, given their race and the nearness of their homeland. Mexicans who were common laborers were often denied entry visas to the United States beginning in mid-1930, unless they had resided previously in the United States. Historian Zaragosa Vargas claims that the Immigration Bureau began imposing a $1,000 bond for unskilled Mexican immigrants in 1930 (Vargas 2005, 48). Of course, many left when jobs were no longer available. In addition, as localities began to restrict relief to Americans only, there is ample evidence that U.S. citizens of Mexican descent were denied local relief. The federal government had a formal deportation policy, and those caught up in the deportation actions included Mexicans who were legal U.S. citizens, those who had entered the country before official measures

Cotton picker in the southern San Joaquin Valley, California, in 1936. Photograph by Dorothea Lange. (Library of Congress)

were in place to confirm their legal entry, and residents unable to show proof of their residency or legal status because of their poverty. The most notorious example in California was a sweep of the Los Angeles downtown public plaza on February 26, 1931. At three o'clock in the afternoon, immigration agents and Los Angeles city police detained the hundreds of persons there for over an hour, going through the crowd to ask each one for his or her papers. Eventually, eleven Mexicans, five Chinese, and a Japanese person were arrested and presumably later deported from the La Placita sweep (Hoffman 1974, 32, 59–63).

In Colorado, the Great Western Sugar Company persuaded county officials to give relief to Mexican families through the winter, but to cut them off when beet season started. In Texas, which held the largest number of Mexican nationals, the Catholic Welfare Council estimated that in El Paso alone, over 600 new welfare cases would be added to the relief rolls in 1931, due to families losing their breadwinner to deportation (Balderrama and Rodriguez 1995, 60). In Detroit, the Mexican consul Ignacio Batiza established relief programs for local Mexicans. His office aided the U.S. Repatriation Program by facilitating group departures by train to the Mexican border, where the Mexican government had trains waiting for the returnees. The Mexican government initially welcomed

Table 1.3. Deportable Aliens Located and Expelled, 1929–1940

Located		*Aliens Expelled*	
Year	*Number*	*Formal Removal*	*Voluntary Departure*
1929	32,711	31,035	25,888
1930	20,880	24,864	11,387
1931	22,276	27,866	11,719
1932	22,735	26,490	10,775
1933	20,949	25,392	10,347
1934	10,319	14,263	8,010
1935	11,016	13,877	7,978
1936	11,728	16,195	8,251
1937	13,054	16,905	8,788
1938	12,851	17,341	9,278
1939	12,037	14,700	9,590
1940	10,492	12,254	8,594

Source: Adapted from *Historical Statistics of the U.S.,* Millennial ed., Table Ad1072–1075, pp. 1–648.

Table 1.4. Mexicans "Repatriated," 1929–1937

Year	*Number of Repatriated*
1929	79,419
1930	70,127
1931	138,519
1932	77,453
1933	33,574
1934	23,943
1935	15,368
1936	11,599
1937	8,037
Total	458,039

Source: Hoffman 1974, 174–176.

Note: The author used numbers reported by the Mexican Migration Service, which he claimed were more accurate than U.S. Immigration Bureau records.

back its citizens, planning public works projects and offering land through "colonization" projects on the country's west coast. But by the end of 1932, the Mexican government was no longer enthusiastically welcoming back migrants, as its own unemployment problem had grown and the colonization projects were beset with health problems due to the tropical climate. In any event the new Roosevelt administration reorganized the Immigration Bureau and discontinued the repatriation program in 1933 (Vargas 2005, 39–61; Vargas 1993, 169–94).

Table 1.3 indicates the numbers of aliens who were discovered and removed from the United States in the 1930s. It does not reflect the large numbers of Mexicans who were "repatriated"; that number is estimated to be between 300,000 and 450,000. Note that the government figures in Table 1.3 do not jibe with official policy and indicate the coercion applied to foreign-born residents; more aliens left than were actually deportable. Table 1.4 represents one researcher's findings of numbers of Mexicans repatriated.

Local Relief Efforts

Cities responded to the economic crisis as they had always done, by ratcheting up their charity departments for the larger-than-usual numbers of the temporarily needy. Traditionally, charity (in the 1930s also called relief, assistance, the dole; only some large cities called their departments Public Welfare) was based on the preindustrial tradition of Christian responsibility, where localities were charged with aid for the poor and unfortunate. In the 1930s many smaller cities and towns still retained "poor farms" for housing the indigent and elderly; larger cities also maintained other public welfare institutions like orphanages and city hospitals. Cities and towns provided "outdoor" relief in the form of a food basket and delivery of coal or wood to needy families staying in their own homes. Homeless people used municipal shelters. Some cities still used "tramp rooms" in police stations. Local soup kitchens and breadlines were run by city charity departments, though many localities depended on religious groups, such as the Salvation Army, to provide these services.

Towns and cities were required by law to care for their own indigent, and as needs increased so did the bureaucracy to confirm the appropriate residency for each person. Residency status was defined by state statute, specifying the days or months in residence in a particular locality in order to qualify for relief in that place. Some states attempted to set up a state-level agency to oversee the certification of the indigent and to send them back to their city or state of residency or else bill that city. The immensity of the need in the early 1930s soon overwhelmed this system.

Cities in Bankruptcy

The city charity departments were geared only for sporadic neediness, not the large-scale impoverishment of the early 1930s. Most city budgets were strained to the limits by early 1931, as the downturn seemed to have no end in sight. By statute, state and local governments had to balance their budgets each year, and borrowing money through bond issues became difficult during the downturn of 1930–1933. In addition, cities found that their property tax collection was ineffective; tax delinquency was an average 12.2 percent (Ridley and Nolting 1935, 2). By early 1932 many cities were on the verge of bankruptcy.

In many cities, "Citizens' Emergency Committees" had been erected to deal with the crisis but only the Philadelphia Committee for Unemployment Relief and the Detroit Mayor's Unemployment Committee received national attention,

Table 1.5. Relief Expenditures (mill. $)

	Detroit	*Milwaukee*	*Hamilton County (Cincinnati)*
1930	0.2	0.9	0.5
1931	10.8	2.7	2
1932	8.7	7.3	4.2
1933	7.4 (6 mo.)	8.2	6.1

Source: C. E. Ridley and O. F. Nolting, eds., *What the Depression Has Done to Cities* (Chicago: International City Managers' Association, 1935), 16.

providing examples of what public agencies could do in such a situation. Coordinating with the private charity organizations was one important task, though disputes over whether public or private officials should be in charge provoked stormy meetings.

Clarence Ridley and Orin Nolting's account, *What the Depression Has Done to Cities,* reported in late 1934 on various examples of urban difficulties from 1930 to 1933. They found that funding for police and fire protection had to be diverted to relief. One in four cities reported to the U.S. Commissioner of Education that they had shortened their school year. Most cities reported that they had decreased teacher salaries (on average by 10 percent), laid off teachers, and increased the teaching load for the remaining, reduced appropriations for books and supplies, and deferred maintenance on school facilities. Some deficits were hard to measure: Robert and Helen Lynd reported that in mid-1930s "Middletown," the slowly accumulating health debits resulting from cuts in school health and food programs—malnutrition, "rachitic children," abscessed teeth, digestive disorders, respiratory infections—were generally not recorded (Lynd and Lynd 1965, 400; Ridley and Nolting 1935).

Regional Perspective: Detroit

Detroit is a good example of both the difficulties of the old charity system and the initiatives taken by forward-thinking public servants in the early Depression. After Detroit citizens had voted on July 22, 1930, to recall their mayor, Charles Bowles, a four-way nonpartisan race took place, which led to the election of Frank Murphy in September 1930. He had run a campaign for a "new deal" in the city's political life, one free of patronage and corruption and committed to the "common people." Murphy pledged to care for the unemployed and homeless. Indeed, historian Sidney Fine called Murphy "a New Dealer before there was a New Deal" (Fine 1975, 226). He was re-elected, for a full two-year term, in 1931. Murphy became close to the activist priest Father Charles Coughlin in the early 1930s, with Murphy writing some of the priest's speeches and developing a Catholic social-justice philosophy to suit the times. The economic situation in the Detroit area was dire. By January 1931 32.4 percent of the city's gainful workers were unemployed. The city of Detroit had the worst relief crisis of any major American city; the average monthly caseload of Detroit's Department of Public Welfare (DPW) increased from 5,029 during late 1929 to 49,314 in early 1933. Jane Addams reported that 50,000 homeowners in the Detroit area lost their homes within one 60-day period in 1931. Black inhabitants fared worse, since they were last hired, first fired, and had twice the unemployment rates of whites; though making up only 7.6 percent of Detroit's population, they made up 30–35 percent of those on relief rolls when Murphy was mayor (Fine 1963, 19; Fine 1975, 247).

As mayor of Detroit from 1930 to 1933, Frank Murphy distinguished himself by giving extraordinary attention to the unemployed of the city. Murphy later served as U.S. governor-general and then high commissioner of the Philippines (1933–1936), governor of Michigan (1936–1938), U.S. attorney general (1939–1940), and finally was appointed associate justice of the U.S. Supreme Court in 1940 and served until his death in 1949. (Library of Congress)

The main culprit was the drastic decline in the auto industry. The auto industry usually operated on a seasonal basis, so the fall 1929 layoffs occurred with little comment. But auto production was headed downward. From a high of 5,300,000 vehicles in 1929, production dropped to 2,389,738 in 1931 and 1,331,860 in 1932. Annual autoworker wages in 1931 averaged $757, according to the Labor Research Association, and in 1934 the Department of Labor estimated annual wages at less than $900 (Peterson 1987, 131). Henry Ford had originally responded to the downward swing in the economy by raising his minimum wage to $7 a day and declaring: "If every one will attend to his own work, the future is secure." But even Ford could not succeed; by 1932, he had been forced to cut the minimum to $4 (Fine, 1963, 20).

Noting by early 1931 that the relief situation was spreading beyond the capabilities of the DPW, Murphy instituted a Mayor's Unemployment Committee (MUC). With a much broader responsibility to attack unemployment "from every possible angle" (Fine 1975, 261), the MUC was able to move beyond the red tape binding the DPW and provide guidance for the public and private charity agencies in the city. With little city funds, the MUC carried out fund-raising activities of its own, raised some $250,000 in its first year, established a Clothing

Bureau (the DPW by custom did not distribute clothing), coordinated distribution of food baskets to the hungry who were not receiving relief aid, and carried out legal aid to those facing eviction. Mayor Murphy declared his opposition to evictions, though the committee was ultimately unable to stem the tide of evictions. The MUC instituted centralized lodging facilities for the homeless in December 1930 when the General Motors Company offered its Fisher Body plant on West Fort and Twenty-third streets as a lodging house for men and boys. The MUC equipped it, and the Salvation Army ran it. The Studebaker Company did the same in January 1931 when it offered its Plant 10 on the same terms as the Fisher Body plant. The sleeping quarters were racially segregated. Of course, this revealed the dearth of auto production in the city at this time. At the same time the city offered feeding stations around the city for those homeless men for whom it did not provide lodging. All these efforts meant the reduction of panhandling and disorderly conduct during the winter of 1930–1931.

Nonetheless, the city's Common Council grew concerned that the city was being taken advantage of by "foreigners" or recent arrivals to Detroit, and that the lodges were becoming "hotbeds" of communist agitation. The Common Council voted to close the lodges as of June 30, 1931, and transfer the needy to the Wayne County Infirmary in Eloise, about 15 miles from the city. But the Eloise facility, once the county's poorhouse, had more recently been a facility for the aged and infirm, the handicapped and feeble-minded, not the able-bodied unemployed. Moreover, Eloise was prison-like, with an iron fence around it and strict policies on coming and going. Most unemployed men refused to transfer. The consequence was homeless men sleeping around the city in flophouses or the parks, or roaming the streets. In September the mayor and the MUC decided to reopen the lodges as dormitories alone, without meals, as a cheap alternative. On November 2, 1,200 lodgers led by the local Unemployed Council representatives demonstrated for meals. The Common Council relented. But in May 1932, the Common Council closed the lodges once again. The author John Dos Passos reported in the *New Republic* in July 1932 that in Detroit homeless men were "everywhere, all over the vast unfinished city, the more thrifty living in shacks and shelters along the waterfront, in the back rooms of unoccupied houses, the others just sleeping anyplace . . . a sluggish, drowsy, grimy life of which the Grand Circus Park is the social center and the One Cent Restaurant operated by some anonymous philanthropist on Woodward Avenue is the Delmonico's" (quoted in Fine 1975, 280).

Other initiatives of the MUC included the oversight of homeless women's needs, which were carried out by various religious and secular agencies devoted to women's issues; a "thrift-garden" program using vacant lots; and a school-lunch program that used both city funds and those of the Children's Fund of Michigan, a private foundation established in 1929. The MUC ran out of funds again and again. The city got embroiled in a dispute with the Ford Motor Company, which did not pay any taxes to the city of Detroit since its giant River Rouge plant was located outside the city limits in Dearborn. But former Ford employees made up over 15 percent of Detroit relief recipients in the winter of 1930–1931 (Fine 1975, 310). Murphy called on Ford to set up its own welfare department. Ford resisted, claiming that Detroit's relief expenditures were poorly managed.

Mayor Murphy came in for criticism from afar—the *Chicago Tribune* noted, "The mayor's enterprise is glorious in sympathy and irresponsibility. Mr. Murphy radiates kindness and buns, short order steaks and ice cream cones and may soon have all the taxpayers and property owners in Detroit reduced to the line with tin cups waiting their turn at the handouts" (quoted in Fine 1975, 312).

Tax Revolts

An influential political backlash against the high cost of government, and of relief, brought a series of taxpayer revolts across the country in these early years of the Depression. The traditional unpopularity of taxes, combined with the dire economic situation in which individuals and businesses found themselves, sparked a massive tax revolt on the local level during 1930–1932. According to historian David Beito, some 3,000–4,000 taxpayer groups sprang up nationally in the early 1930s, organized to lower taxes on the state and local level. In 145 cities over 50,000 in population, tax delinquency rose from 10.8 percent in 1930 to 25.2 percent by 1933 (Beito 1989, 6–7). While some of this was the result of homeowners' inability to pay, it was aided and abetted by large real estate holders who agitated for tax reassessments, tax freezes, or spending constraints.

The most notorious tax strike took place in Chicago in the early 1930s, where legal challenges to the city's property assessment had resulted in a delay in levying of property taxes from 1928 to 1930 while the county carried out a complete reassessment. When taxes were finally levied, major real estate holders banded together to challenge the assessments. When these challenges lost in court, the Association of Real Estate Tax Payers (ARET) urged all taxpayers to resist paying the new taxes. By offering free legal representation on threatened foreclosures, ARET gained a considerable following of small homeowners, as did other groups like the Polish United Home Owners of Illinois, but small homeowners were not the driving force behind the organization. ARET conducted its campaign as an attack on what it called "tax eaters," those political machines with their padded budgets and patronage games. These attitudes and the widespread problem of tax delinquency alarmed municipal experts, bankers, and civic leaders, who mounted a "Pay Your Taxes" campaign throughout the country.

The Socialist Party (SP), with a number of municipal governments at this time, challenged the notion that cities were spendthrift and that the best city was the city with the lowest tax rate. Daniel Hoan, the Socialist mayor of Milwaukee,

Historians' Debate: Tax Revolts

David Beito's study, *Taxpayers in Revolt: Tax Resistance during the Great Depression,* is the fullest account of this issue. But his stated thesis that tax delinquency tapped a widespread "anti-big-government" sentiment is open to question. From his evidence, "anti-big-government" sentiment was clearly apparent among large real estate interests, but not necessarily among small property owners. Small property owners, working class or middle class, may have been moved by anti-"machine" sentiment, but this does not mean that they rejected an expanded government role. Mark Leff also points out that taxes in this era fell most heavily on real estate property owners, with additional "personal property" taxes on manufacturing equipment and inventory. State chambers of commerce led the drive in many state legislatures to reform the tax base in order to "broaden the base of taxation" (Bucki 2001, 143–144, 231n26; Leff 1984).

The "serviceability of organized government," to use Mayor Hoan's phrase, was the key ideological issue underlying much political debate in this era between business interests who wished no state interference and the liberal business leaders and the public who wanted government intervention in the economy to solve an economic collapse. On the state and municipal front, the former wanted lowered government expenditures, period. The latter two wanted full-service government but battled over who should pay for it and how it should be run. At the root of the contest for control over city budgets and relief funds was the elite perception that city politics were dominated by patronage politics. Elite hostility to urban "machines" had its roots in the Gilded Age and had animated Progressive Era municipal reform movements. Indeed, some analysts have contended that it was the inability of social and economic elites to eliminate or regulate patronage politics that derailed the beginnings of a welfare state in the Progressive Era (Orloff and Skocpol 1984). Elite reformers had been unwilling to place social spending in the hands of the political parties before 1930. In the Depression era, even as business leaders were conceding that private charity could not meet the crisis, they tried both limiting their own tax burden and controlling disbursement of relief funds.

Finally, in July 1932, the federal Emergency Relief and Construction Act was passed, making $300 million available for distribution to the states by the Reconstruction Finance Corporation (RFC). Governors could apply to the RFC for loans if they could prove that their relief needs were greater than their resources. These supplemental funds would have to be repaid eventually. By March 1933 the $300 million had been completely disbursed (Fearon 1987, 143; Romasco 1975).

addressed the issue in his 1933 pamphlet, *Taxes and Tax Dodgers,* where he argued that government service was cheaper than a comparable private service. The solution, he claimed, was "not lower taxes, but fairer taxes." The SP favored steep income and inheritance taxes, and deplored the taxpayers' leagues who used "the bogey of 'high taxes' for no other purpose than to undermine public confidence in the serviceability of organized government, and to keep the tax burden falling on the poor instead of the rich" (Hoan 1933, 3–4, 16).

Organizing in Community and Workplace

All was not quiet in workplaces and communities around the country. In local communities, both local self-help organizations and union organizations sprang up. Seattle's Unemployed Citizens' League started in 1931, organized around Hulet M. Wells and Carl Brannin of the Seattle Labor College, which was an offshoot of A. J. Muste's Brookwood Labor College in New York. With the ideal of the "republic of the penniless" (Bernstein 1960, 416–425), the League set up producers' co-ops, bartering exchanges with local farmers and fishermen. In March 1932 Seattle voters elected one of the leaders of the League, John F. Dore, as mayor; unfortunately, Mayor Dore then turned his back on the League. Other groups emphasized self-help in the form of consumers' co-ops. The Dayton (Ohio) Association of Cooperative Production Units used the utopian ideals of Ralph Barsodi to return to the land, where cooperating families would raise their own food and fabricate goods by hand.

Sometimes, the unemployed would take direct action against big stores. In the summer of 1932 in Detroit, it was reported that "grown men, usually in twos's and three's, enter chain stores, order all the food they can possibly carry, and then walk out without paying" (Rosenzweig 1976, 45). Unemployed coal miners dug "bootleg coal" from idle anthracite mines. Some of these efforts were the result of organizing by the Communist Party and later the Socialist Party. But many of these efforts were founded on experiences of community organizing in earlier eras, especially in the Progressive Era, and the burst of union activity during World War I and the general strikes of 1919.

Communist Party and the Third Period

The Communist Party USA (CP) had about 18,000 members at the beginning of the Great Depression. It was on the threshold of a dramatic expansion in membership and influence, which would become apparent in the mid-1930s with the industrial unions drives of the CIO and a change in its theoretical understanding of the world economic and political crisis (see the "Social Movements" chapter). But the party began the 1930s with a militant fervor that garnered significant notoriety. Since the early 1920s the CP had been working to define itself as the premier American revolutionary party, using the Bolshevik revolution as its model of historical change. By combining its regional and ideological variations into a cohesive organization, the CP fused Communist International (Comintern) directives with American-born initiatives on industrial unionism

Chicago communists parade on Roosevelt Road and Jefferson Street, on March 6, 1930, as part of the national Hunger March campaign. (Library of Congress)

and farmer-labor party efforts. The "Third Period" analysis had been proclaimed at the Sixth Congress of the Comintern in 1928. It analyzed the eras since the Russian revolution into three periods: first, the postwar revolutionary movement, which ended in 1923; second, the growth phase of world capitalism, ending in 1928, which restored the economies to their prewar levels and put the revolutionary movement on the defensive. The Third Period of capitalist development, since 1928, was characterized by the increase of industrial output due to rapid technological development and the incapacity of markets to absorb this great output. The Comintern's prediction was that this would lead to an economic crisis, a rapid disintegration of capitalism, and the consequent radicalization of the working class. When the economic crisis did come in late 1929, the CP was convinced that its prediction of a revolutionary era was at hand.

Consequently, their methods of organizing emphasized militant confrontation with authorities at the workplace through Trade Union Unity League (TUUL) unions, and in the neighborhoods through Unemployed Councils. In trade union activism, the CP's Trade Union Educational League (TUEL) had been formed in the mid-1920s to work within existing AFL unions. But in 1929, TUEL was replaced by the TUUL, which established independent industrial unions to organize the mass of industrial workers outside of the AFL. This was a new dual unionism, sure to earn the wrath of the AFL, but the CP had decided to move to the revolutionary stage. The TUUL attracted what was left of the 1919 amalgamation efforts and 1920s' industrial-union efforts within and independent of the AFL, and thus they were ready to organize when economic conditions became severe in 1930 and after. The TUUL's militancy was signaled by its slogan "Class Against Class" (Ottanelli 1991, 21). The TUUL metalworkers' union, the National Miners Union (NMU), and the Auto Workers Union (AWU) carried out local strikes over conditions, but most lost in that inhospitable economic climate. TUUL's greatest organizing achievement in the early 1930s was through its Unemployed Councils (Lorence 1996, 15–21).

Unemployed Councils

Unemployed Councils were created first by the Communist Party USA (CP). The CP's TUUL declared in July 1930 that TUUL would sponsor Unemployed Councils in localities to protest unemployment and to demand relief. Standard slogans included "Fight! Don't Starve" and "Work or Wages!" Steve Nelson, an unemployed carpenter who headed the Unemployed Councils of Chicago, noted that some councils rose up spontaneously in some neighborhoods and others were formed out of a nucleus of existing ethnic clubs. As an integral part of the neighborhood, they would mobilize when families were being evicted, calling on local aldermen or sympathetic priests to help confront the authorities. Nelson remembers that policemen, who had been ordered to evict a family, sometimes saw the crowds and hesitated or walked away; other times they roughed people up (Nelson, Barrett, and Ruck 1981, 77). Often, the crowd would allow the police to evict the family and move their possessions to the curb. Then once the police had padlocked the house and gone away, the Unemployed Council would break the padlock and put the family's furniture and possessions back in the house. Unemployed Councils also helped people fill out the applications for city aid and demonstrated at City Hall for more adequate relief.

The CP put a special emphasis on organizing among African Americans, given the CP's analysis of the African American community as special victims of American society. As St. Clair Drake and Horace Cayton reported in their classic 1945 work, *Black Metropolis,*

> It was these [Unemployed] Councils that led the fight against evictions, and hundreds of non-Communists followed their lead. When eviction notices arrived, it was not unusual for a mother to shout to the children, "Run quick and find the Reds!" Through the spring and summer of 1931 small groups of Negroes under Communist leadership skirmished with the police at the scene of evictions. Then, one August day, several thousand people decided to march *en masse* to a home in a poverty-stricken neighborhood to replace some furniture. When the police arrived there was some scuffling, and then shooting. Three Negroes lay dead on the pavement when it was over and scores were wounded. (Drake and Cayton 1945, 87).

Hunger Marches

From 1930 to 1936, the Unemployed Councils organized local, state, and national "hunger marches." The first Hunger March took place on March 6, 1930: some 2,000 in San Francisco; in Chicago "tens of thousands"; in Flint, Michigan, over 15,000 participated. Thousands in Washington, D.C., Los Angeles, Detroit, Boston, Cleveland, and Milwaukee were attacked by local police. The most violent demonstration took place in New York City, where an estimated 35,000 gathered in Union Square and then attempted to march on Mayor Jimmy Walker's office. New York City police attacked, and many demonstrators and bystanders were injured. Four CP leaders were arrested. William Z. Foster, Robert Minor, and Israel Amter served six months in jail; Harry Raymond served ten months.

The Unemployed Councils became very visible advocates for the dispossessed at this point, and delegates met in national convention in Chicago in early June 1930, forming an independent national organization, Unemployed Councils of the United States, and electing a CP member, Bill Mathieson, as national secretary. In February 1931 a delegation from the Unemployed Councils arrived in Washington, D.C., to lobby in favor of an unemployment insurance bill, which they claimed had been endorsed by 1.5 million workers and a number of AFL unions. When that failed to gain any attention in Congress, a national Hunger March was organized for December 6, 1931, where 1,200 delegates marched down Pennsylvania Avenue to the Capitol (Ottanelli 1991, 30–33).

The final report described thousands of protesters who filled the streets for the funeral procession for these three African American "martyrs."

Father Cox's March

Father James Cox, a Roman Catholic priest in Pittsburgh, did what he could to alleviate the problems of unemployment and homelessness. He became pastor of Old St. Patrick's Church in the Strip District between downtown and the Lawrenceville neighborhood of his youth, the poorest parish in the city. When the Great Depression hit, Cox established a soup kitchen, using donated produce from the Strip District warehouses, and arranged a deal with a local coal company to donate one ton of coal for every twenty tons of coal bought by the parish. In this way Cox distributed 2,120 tons of coal to the needy between 1930 and 1934. Cox threw himself into support for union organizing. By building homeless shelters on the church grounds with wooden packing crates, Father Cox found himself proclaimed the "Mayor of Shantytown, Pennsylvania." Cox was alarmed by the violence with which the Unemployed Council Hunger Marches

More than 10,000 American citizens march to the Capitol under the leadership of Father James R. Cox, of Pittsburgh, January 7, 1932. (Library of Congress)

had been met in New York City and Dearborn, Michigan, and was displeased with the rhetoric of the CP-influenced Unemployed Councils. He decided to form his own march on Washington. He was inspired by the 1894 example of Social Gospeler Jacob Coxey, who had led a similar march of the unemployed to Washington during that earlier depression. Father Cox announced that the march would begin on January 5, 1932, from Old St. Patrick's Church. A larger-than-expected crowd assembled that morning, with 600 trucks and cars, along with two brass bands; they had come from Catholic parishes around the region, mostly from steel towns. Father Cox made it clear that no women would be allowed on the march, to avoid any semblance of impropriety. Six thousand men set off, picking up marchers along the way in Johnstown and Huntingdon, for Harrisburg, where they were met by Gov. Gifford Pinchot, who offered them food and shelter. They marched on to Washington, D.C., where their numbers were estimated between 12,000 and 25,000. A local detective reported to President Hoover that at least 20 percent of Father Cox's army had fought in the World War, and another 10 percent had served in the Spanish-American War. Hoover finally relented and agreed to meet with Father Cox, who told him that "the administration was acting like an ostrich that sticks its head in the sand, believing that if he cannot see the hunter pursuing him or the trouble that is nearby, that the hunter or the trouble does not exist" (Heineman 1999, 24). Cox demanded federal funds to care for the hungry and the ill children, to construct more roads and schools, and to provide cheap electrical power to the nation's rural areas. He proposed that the costs be covered through increased taxes on corporations and wealthy individuals.

Upon his return to Pittsburgh, Father Cox set up an organization called the Blue Shirts, which quickly spread to Chicago, Cleveland, and New York and claimed 200,000 members. Cox claimed it was modeled after a Gaelic Blue Shirt movement in Ireland, and the organization embraced the Sermon on the Mount as its ideology. The Blue Shirts organized the new Jobless Party. The Jobless Party met with the new Liberty Party (a southwestern populist movement started by William "Coin" Harvey) in convention in St. Louis in August 1932. The two parties proved incompatible—the Protestant populists were unable to embrace the overwhelmingly Catholic Blue Shirts—and Father Cox turned to the new Democratic Party candidate Franklin D. Roosevelt and gave him a ringing endorsement. Father Cox spent the fall of 1932 campaigning for Roosevelt (Heineman 1999, 16–30).

The Ford "Massacre"

In Detroit, the AWU-TUUL and the Detroit Unemployed Council organized a diverse group of 3,000 demonstrators to march on Henry Ford's Dearborn headquarters on March 7, 1932, to present a list of demands, which included unemployment relief, rehiring, guarantees against racial discrimination, a moratorium on foreclosures against Ford workers, and the right to organize. The marchers were met at the Dearborn town line by Dearborn police and Ford Service Department guards, all armed. In the ensuing melee, five demonstrators were killed. Accusations flew: charges in the local press that Communists were to blame for the incident; statements from the company that they had nothing to do with it; and accusations from the left of police and company brutality. The investigation by the President's Organization for Unemployment Relief (POUR) announced that the difficulty was the "stupidity of the Dearborn police. . . . All those hit by bullets were among the paraders or bystanders." Of course, POUR investigator Roland Haynes concluded that the incident "had nothing directly to do with unemployment" (Lorence 1996, 41).

Rural Poverty

The agricultural sector of the economy had never rebounded from the postwar depression of 1920–1922. It continued to be the weakest sector throughout the 1920s and into the 1930s. The majority of farm families in the 1920s lived under the poverty line, and this represented one-quarter of the U.S. population. The collapse of agricultural prices after 1929 was quite extreme: cotton had sold for 17 cents in 1929, but the price was under 6 cents in 1931, while corn dropped from 60 cents per bushel in 1930 to 32 cents in 1931. Average net farm income in 1929 was $945; by 1932 it was $304. Farm families consequently cut expenditures, like consumption of manufactured goods, and substituted unpaid family labor for paid farm hands. Thus farm laborers' daily wages fell from $2.30 in 1929 (in itself an example of the stagnation in this economic sector, as this was the same as wages in 1914) to $1.33 in 1933. Taxes went unpaid. Mortgage and loan payments went unmet, putting rural banks under great stress. Many large landlords could not obtain credit for themselves and thus could not extend needed loans to their tenants and sharecroppers.

Furthermore, after 1929, there was a curious reversal of the rural-to-urban migration process that had been common in the 1920s. By 1933 urban dwellers without jobs were migrating to the country to eke out a living on abandoned farms. This back-to-the-land movement, especially noticeable in New England, created a subsistence economy, unconnected to marketplace, as people moved to abandoned land in order to grow food for themselves.

President Hoover's legislative attempts to regulate the farm market came from his campaign promises in 1928. The Agricultural Marketing Act of 1929 sought to prevent speculation and promote cooperative marketing associations, and created the federal Farm Board to offer loans to farmers; it was only moderately successful when the market changed dramatically in 1930. Both the Cotton Stabilization Corporation and the Grain Stabilization Corporation, established in 1930, were modeled after World War I agencies designed to support prices, but what was now needed was production control. Finally the Smoot-Hawley Tariff Act of 1930 was a protectionist act that raised import duties to their highest levels ever. The reaction worldwide was negative, as other countries retaliated with their own high tariffs against American goods, and did little for American farmers (Fearon 1987, 101–106) (see "Rural Life" chapter).

The Dust Bowl

The Dust Bowl of the 1930s was not a new, natural phenomenon, but a man-made ecological disaster. The plains had experienced drought on a regular basis, usually an extreme one every 20 years and lesser ones every few years. During the spring and summer of 1930, little rain fell on most of the eastern United States, a condition that continued for much of the 1930s. By 1931 the center of drought moved to the Great Plains. Added to that were record high temperatures. The rains did not return on an adequate basis until 1941.

What made the 1930s' drought different from previous instances was the great expansion of farming during the World War which brought under cultivation marginal land that had never been farmed before. Prairie sod had been plowed up to grow wheat for the European market and for the U.S. military. Farmers were encouraged to buy more land and equipment to meet the growing demand, and at the end of the war in 1918 farmers were heavily mortgaged to bankers. When drought came, there was no more sod to hold the soil down, and winds blew it away (Worster 1982, 3–25). The Dust Bowl phenomenon was only beginning in this period of the early 1930s and will be covered more thoroughly in the chapter titled "Rural Life."

The Farmers' Holiday Movement

What did happen in the early 1930s was that upper-Midwest farmers, squeezed between the cost of production and the lowering market prices for their goods, began to organize against these market conditions and the banks that held their mortgages. Farmer organizations had been numerous since the early part of the century, though only some retained a vestige of the Populist decade of the 1890s. The Farmers' Union, organized in 1902, was one of them. The Iowa Farmers' Union, with Milo Reno at its head, was the core of the cornbelt rebellion. Reno's philosophy was: "If the Farmers' Union means anything on earth, it means the right of you and me to determine the value of the products of our labor, just as organized labor, organized manufacturing, or organized banking" (Shover 1965, 26). Agricultural prices tumbled from April 1931 until June 1932, cutting the average farmer's income in half. In Cedar County, Iowa, the first action took place, when farmers protested an attempt by state veterinarians to enforce Iowa's law on compulsory testing and inoculation of dairy cattle against tuberculosis. Farmers converged on the state capital to demand the law's repeal. This "Cow War" was based on farmers' grievances over the potential unreliability of the test as well as state intrusion on private property. Though the Iowa Farmers' Union did not actively sponsor this protest, it tried to channel farmers' anger into more organized directions.

Farmers were caught in a cost-price squeeze as the costs of production through mechanization increased while prices for the product decreased. Mortgage pressures added to farmers' difficulties. Foreclosures spread across the Midwest. The Iowa Farmers' Union presented a resolution to the National Farmers' Union convention in 1931 calling for a farm strike to begin January 1, 1932. Though the resolution was defeated, the Iowa organization went ahead with plans. Senators from agricultural states—Lynn Frazier, the former Non-Partisan League governor of North Dakota, together with Elmer Thomas of Oklahoma—sponsored farmers' bills in Congress: first, to support refinancing of farmers' mortgages at 1.5 percent yearly payment of principle and 1.5 percent yearly interest; second, to abolish the Farm Board and to secure "cost of production" in the selling price of produce. These bills were defeated (Shover 1965, 33–35).

The movement for a strike, or "farmers' holiday," gathered momentum. As one farmer-poet for the *Iowa Union Farmer* put it:

> We can't continue longer now
> Upon our weary way—
> We're forced to halt upon life's trail
> And call a "holiday."
> Let's call a Farmers' Holiday
> A Holiday let's hold
> We'll eat our wheat and ham and eggs
> And let them eat their gold. (Shover 1965, 36)

The term "holiday" mimicked that of bankers who claimed a "bank holiday" to prevent runs on their banks (Mooney and Majka 1995, 77). With the upsurge gathering in Iowa, Reno contacted farmers' unions in Wisconsin, South Dakota, and Minnesota. On May 2, 1932, some 2,000 farmers assembled at the Iowa Fair grounds in Des Moines and launched the Farmers' Holiday movement. The idea was to stay home and sell nothing and buy nothing, and thus bring the nation to the realization of the farmers' importance. Borrowing tactics from the North Dakota Non-Partisan League of two decades earlier, the organizers, as they traveled, asked farmers to sign pledges to support the forthcoming holiday.

The farm strike began in Sioux City, Iowa, on August 11 (four days before its announced target date) as farmers in Plymouth and Woodbury counties began patrolling highways and threatening farmers who were trying to bring their produce to market. Dairy farmers were in the vanguard, as they had tried to form a producers' cooperative to negotiate prices with the biggest distributor in the area, the J. R. Roberts Dairy Company. The Roberts Company had refused to deal with them, fueling the anger of the dairy farmers. Newsreel footage of farmers dumping milk from stopped trucks out on the road shocked the nation. The AFL and the Railway Brotherhoods sent messages of sympathy to the farm strikers, while other farm organizations like the American Farm Bureau were decidedly hostile. After a week or so of standoff between roaming pickets and state police, Iowa confrontations were peacefully settled as the milk distributors agreed to an increase in price on August 20. The milk stoppage was a success since it was a highly perishable product and the farmers' cooperative was well organized.

But farmers in other sectors had a more difficult time. On the outskirts of Omaha, Nebraska, police and farmers clashed; farmers stopped an interstate freight train and uncoupled cars. The movement called a truce on September 1, as the state governors called a conference to hear Farmers' Holiday leaders on September 9. An estimated 5,000 farmers marched through Sioux City, where the governors of Iowa, South Dakota, Wisconsin, and North Dakota heard Milo Reno lay out a four-point program: (1) state mortgage moratoriums putting a temporary stop to all foreclosure proceedings; (2) a special session of Congress to enact the Frazier inflationary farm credit bill; (3) voluntary action by farmers to

Table 1.6. Number of Farms Changing Ownership by Foreclosure of Mortgages and Bankruptcy (per 1,000 of all farms)

Year	*1931*	*1932*	*1933*	*1934*
United States	18.7	28.4	38.8	28.0
West North Central	25.8	43.8	61.5	44.4
Minnesota	31.2	42.9	59.1	37.5
Iowa	24.8	52.5	78.3	54.3
Missouri	23.7	42.1	51.2	36.1
North Dakota	34.1	54.0	63.3	31.3
South Dakota	33.2	49.2	78.0	64.2
Nebraska	21.8	34.4	58.2	45.8
Kansas	20.0	36.0	52.7	48.0

Source: Adapted from J. L. Shover, *Cornbelt Rebellion: The Farmers' Holiday Association* (Urbana: University of Illinois Press, 1965), 16.

withhold goods from market; and (4) a demand for state-enforced embargoes against the sale of farm products at less than the cost of production. The governors' conference produced only vaguely worded resolutions to President Hoover, while Reno declared himself somewhat satisfied but disappointed at the lack of an embargo. The Holiday movement petered out in Iowa, picked up momentum in Minnesota in late September, and, most important, became an issue in the presidential election campaigning that fall. Roosevelt's victory over Hoover in November left the Farmers' Holiday movement, which had supported FDR, hopeful that their grievances would be listened to (Shover 1965; Mooney and Majka 1995).

Bonus Army

A final phenomenon that seemed to indicate the organizing potential in the population was the Bonus Army March to Washington in the summer of 1932. The "bonus" had been promised to veterans of the World War who had protested their loss of income during their stint in the armed services; Congress passed the Bonus Bill in 1924 over President Coolidge's veto. This so-called bonus, formally an "Adjusted Service Certificate" pegged to days in the service, was really a 21-year endowment life insurance policy, payable to every World War veteran in 1945 (or to his family at his death). Its value averaged about $1,000 per veteran at maturity. The bonus issue got new life when in 1928 veteran Wright Patman of Texas was elected to Congress on a platform of a "square deal" for veterans, an issue he reiterated in his 1930 re-election campaign. He introduced a bill for immediate payment of the bonus in 1931. The bill's supporters included the Veterans of Foreign Wars (VFW). It passed with an amendment that

Bonus Army veterans from Chattanooga, Tennessee, parade past the White House on a truck in May 1932. (Library of Congress)

the payment would be a loan, deductible from the 1945 payment; the interest rate, noted an angry Patman, would eat up the entire payment.

His proposal gave veterans an idea. The VFW organized a rally in Washington in early April 1932, when 1,200 vets carried boxes of petitions, said to contain over 2 million signatures, to the Capitol building, calling for an immediate bonus payment. On the other side of the country in May, former sergeant Walter W. Waters of Portland, Oregon, organized a march of veterans from Portland, where they hopped trains or hitched rides on trucks headed to Washington, D.C. This Bonus Expeditionary Force (BEF) was joined by thousands coming from all parts of the country. Estimates vary on the number—between 20,000 and 45,000 veterans and their families converged on the Capitol by late May. Pelham D. Glassford, former Army general and now Washington, D.C., police chief, prepared a camp in the Anacostia Flats section of the city, furnished with Army tents and bed sacks. Glassford arranged meals as well. Like the Hoovervilles throughout the country, this encampment was racially integrated, in contrast to the military. Veterans quickly moved to lobby Congress for a new Patman bill. Controversy soon erupted over the accusation by Army Military Intelligence that the BEF harbored Communists and other "red" agitators.

A ditty circulating through the camp revealed the political mood of the men, and it was definitely antibanker but hardly "red."

Mellon pulled the whistle,
Hoover rang the bell,
Wall Street gave the signal
—And the country went to hell!
(Waters and White 1933, 127)

While Patman's bill passed the House (211 for, 176 against), it failed in the Senate. Only 28 of the 96 senators were in favor, even as some liberal-progressive senators went to great lengths to explain their negative vote. These senators, fearing a run on the U.S. Treasury, thought that any federal money should be put toward a more general relief measure. Congress adjourned on July 16 (Daniels 1971, 116–122).

At this point, the DC police commissioners ordered the veterans to move on. Most veterans refused to leave Washington—many had no homes to go back to—and even more veterans poured into the city to join the protest. The eviction order, set for July 28, was carried out first by Glassford's police department, who panicked and fired into a building, killing two Bonus Marchers. Federal cavalry troops, led by Army Chief of Staff Douglas A. MacArthur with assistance from Maj. Dwight D. Eisenhower and Maj. George S. Patton Jr., pushed veterans away from the Capitol. MacArthur then ignored President Hoover's order not to enter the camp and ordered his troops across the river to storm the camp with bayonets drawn and tear-gas grenades tossed. After routing the encampment, the soldiers set the camp on fire. The negative publicity hit Hoover hard as he was campaigning for re-election. This incident haunted not only Hoover, but also Roosevelt and the New Deal, until the Patman bill was finally passed by Congress in January 1936. Its most important consequence, arguably, would come in World War II, when Congress passed the GI Bill of Rights in 1944 (Dickson and Allen 2004).

The 1932 Presidential Election

The election of 1932 was a referendum on Hoover's popularity. Democratic candidate Franklin Delano Roosevelt agreed with Hoover on some issues, as he was committed to economy in government and to a balanced budget. He sounded a new note when he addressed the Democratic Convention in Chicago in June 1932 with the ringing promise: "I pledge you, I pledge myself, to a new deal for the American people." But he had few specifics on the campaign trail.

Roosevelt had generated policy innovations in his four years as governor of New York, and these could be taken as a model of what might be done to address the crisis. In 1929 he began his tenure in Albany with two projects: cheaper electric power and conservation of natural resources. He favored public power, and continued and broadened the Al Smith administration's plan for the St. Law-

"Brother, Can You Spare a Dime?"

It is alleged that the 1932 hit song "Brother, Can You Spare a Dime?" was inspired by the Bonus March. Bing Crosby and Rudy Vallee each recorded this song in October 1932, and both versions went to number one on the charts before the presidential election of 1932.

> They used to tell me I was building a dream
> And so I followed the mob
> When there was earth to plow or guns to bear
> I was always there, right on the job
> . . .
> Once I built a railroad, made it run
> Made it race against time
> Once I built a railroad, now it's done
> Brother can you spare a dime?
> . . .
> Once in khaki suits, gee we looked swell
> Full of that yankee doodle dum
> Half a million boots went sloggin' through hell
> And I was the kid with a drum.
> Say, Don't you remember they called me Al?
> It was Al all the time
> Say, don't you remember, I'm your pal
> Buddy can you spare a dime? (Harburg and Gorney 1931)

rence River power plants. Moreover, he pressed for the strict regulation of private utility companies and urged the development of public power plants in order to give state regulators a benchmark for private power company rates. In addition, the new governor returned to his avocation as a gentleman-farmer by advocating natural resource conservation, through abandonment of marginal lands, reforestation, and other forms of land management.

After the stock-market crash, FDR turned his attention to the issues of human want. He was encouraged by being re-elected as governor in 1930, with an overwhelming plurality. His industrial commissioner, Frances Perkins, had been a pioneer in labor legislation since her involvement with the 1911 Triangle Shirtwaist Fire investigation. Perkins had already been working on a system of old-age pensions for the state and now turned to the issue of unemployment. In August 1931 FDR created the Temporary Emergency Relief Administration (TERA), stating "modern society, acting through its Government, owes the definite obligation to prevent the starvation or dire waste of any of the fellow men and women who try to maintain themselves but cannot." He called it a "matter of

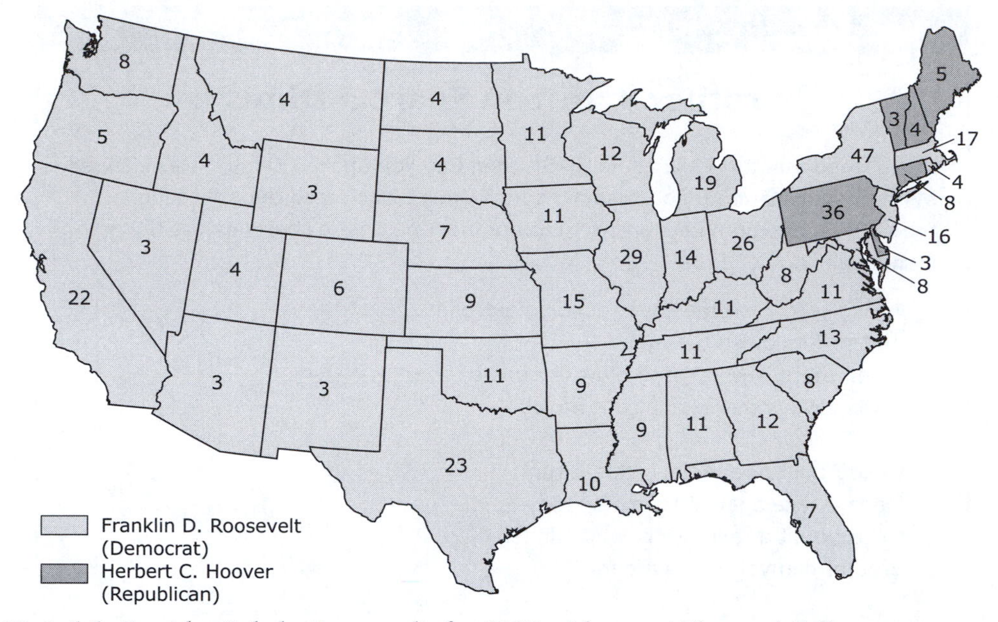

Map 1.1 *Presidential election results for 1932 with states' Electoral College votes*

social duty" (Schlesinger 1957, 392). He appointed New York City social worker Harry L. Hopkins as TERA's executive director. This emphasis meant that the state of New York, unlike most other state governments, pledged to aid the cities and towns struggling with relief expenditures. Roosevelt even called a meeting of northeast governors in 1931 to encourage them to act likewise.

As Roosevelt prepared himself for a presidential run, he gathered a group of experts who would become his "brain trust" in the White House: Professors Raymond Moley and Rexford G. Tugwell of Columbia University and Adolph A. Berle Jr. of Columbia Law School. Together with his advisers Sam Rosenman and Basil O'Connor, Roosevelt began casting about for possible solutions to the economic crisis. He had already struck a chord in a radio speech in April 1932, when he called for "the building of plans . . . that put their faith once more in the forgotten man at the bottom of the economic pyramid" (Bird 1966, 92). This phrase would recur throughout the campaign season. After his acceptance speech to the Democratic Convention—itself an innovation as no presidential nominee had done so before—Roosevelt set out to attract the progressive political forces in the country behind him, mobilizing dissident Republicans and independents to his side, politicians like Burton K. Wheeler of Montana, George W. Norris of Nebraska, Hiram Johnson of California, Robert La Follette Jr. of Wisconsin, and Bronson Cutting of New Mexico. He began criticizing Hoover's economics and proposed various remedies that seemed to waver between old-fashioned trust-busting and economic planning, those same alternatives from the Progressive era. Yet President Hoover, hitting the campaign trail, attacked Roosevelt as a dangerous radical whose Democratic Party principles reeked of "the fumes of the witch's caldron [*sic*] which boiled in Russia" (Schlesinger 1957, 437). The contrast was clear: Hoover's Treasury secretary, Andrew W. Mellon, insisted that the dismal economic conditions of 1930–1931 were simply a traditional downturn that would right itself in due course. Nothing Hoover could say would restore people's faith in him. Roosevelt was elected by an overwhelming 57.7 percent of the popular vote, and three million more voters had participated in the election than four years before.

The new Roosevelt administration would focus on, first, regulating business sectors, and, second, boosting consumer spending to stimulate the economy. These programs became known as the New Deal, reviewed in the next chapter.

Biographies

James R. Cox, 1886–1951

Roman Catholic Priest

Father Cox led a march of thousands of unemployed men to Washington, D.C., in January 1932, dubbed "Father Cox's March." Cox was born the son of a millworker in the working-class neighborhood of Lawrenceville in Pittsburgh. He worked his way through college as a steelworker and a taxicab agent, attending Holy Ghost College (now Duquesne University) in Pittsburgh and then entering the diocese's seminary school, St. Vincent's, in Latrobe. He was ordained in 1911. After serving in the war ministering to casualties at a western front hospital, Cox returned to Pittsburgh, earned a master's degree in economics from the University of Pittsburgh, and took up his duties as pastor of Old St. Patrick's Church in the lower-class Strip District near Lawrenceville. During the Depression, Father Cox threw himself into organizing hunger relief and supporting unionization efforts in the area. He served on the Pennsylvania Civil Liberties Committee, which defended organizers from arrest and students and faculty who were denied free speech at the University of Pittsburgh. His ministry to the unemployed is what led to his plan for a march to Washington. After brief activity in an alternative party, Cox enthusiastically supported FDR for president, campaigning for him in western Pennsylvania in 1932. President Roosevelt soon appointed him to the state recovery board of the National Recovery Administration. Cox continued his active support for the New Deal throughout the 1930s.

William Z. Foster, 1881–1960

Radical Activist

An important leader of the Communist Party USA in the 1930s, Foster carried out a rather narrow sectarian line of the "Third Period" in 1928 through his leadership of the Trade Union Unity League (TUUL), a revolutionary dual-union federation. Born to an Irish working-class family in Philadelphia, Foster amassed a great deal of political experience through socialism, syndicalism, and communism in the early years of the 20th century. Through the TUUL, he was instrumental in creating the Unemployed Councils in the early 1930s. He was the CP's presidential candidate in 1924, 1928, and 1932, though he suffered a severe heart attack during the 1932 campaign. Replaced by Earl Browder as general secretary of the CP in 1934, Foster returned to active politics in 1935 and clashed with Browder over the latter's implementation of the Popular Front and then the Democratic Front in the mid-1930s. The Comintern sided with Browder in 1937 and 1938, and Foster was isolated within the Party for the remainder of the 1930s.

Milo Reno, 1866–1936

Leader of the Farmers' Holiday Movement

Born in Wapello County, Iowa, Reno was educated in a log cabin and briefly studied for the ministry at Oskaloosa (Iowa) College. He became an ordained Campbellite minister. His family had been active in the Greenback Party in the 1880s. He voted the Populist ticket in 1892 and campaigned for Bryan in 1896. Reno joined the Farmers' Union in 1918, was elected secretary-treasurer of the Iowa Farmers' Union, and in 1921 was elected president of the Iowa organization. He resigned the presidency in 1930 to take a job in the union's insurance business (for a salary of $9,600), but he continued to dominate the organization. Continuing his Populist past, he believed that an expanded currency was the answer to farmers' marketing problems; thus he was an inflationist. With his trademark flaming red tie and extravagant ten-gallon hats, Reno gave speeches that carried the Farmers' Holiday to its height in the summer of 1932. After 1932 Reno continued to lobby Congress and the state legislatures on farmers' behalf. Disillusioned with New Deal agricultural plans, he supported third-party efforts in 1935–1936. However, he was uncomfortable with the left-wing adherents of the Farmer-Labor Party movement, and gravitated toward the rhetoric of Huey Long and Father Charles Coughlin. As

Milo Reno, national leader of the Farmers' Holiday Movement, 1932. (Bettmann/Corbis)

the Farmers' Holiday Association got caught up in the wrangles over which party formation and which political leader to support, Reno died of influenza on May 5, 1936.

Walter W. Waters, 1898–1959

Leader of the Portland, Oregon, Bonus Army

Born in 1898 in Burns, Oregon, Waters soon moved with his family to Idaho. Leaving school in 1916 at the age of 18 , he enlisted in the Idaho National Guard. His regiment was called up to join the U.S. Army's pursuit of Pancho Villa in Mexico until February 1917. When his enlistment with the Idaho Guard finished, he joined the Oregon National Guard, which then became part of the Infantry Division that sailed to France in late December 1917. Promoted to sergeant in April 1918, he participated in many of the famous battles of that war. His division then became part of the army of occupation, and he did not return to the United States until June 1919. After his honorable discharge, Waters tried various business ventures in the Pacific Northwest, finally settling into a cannery superintendent's job and marrying a cannery worker, Wilma Anderson. That cannery shut down in the early Depression, and he and Wilma headed to Portland, where he got a job in another cannery. By 1932 he was again jobless. Obsessed with a veterans' march to Washington, he began making speeches in March 1932. When the idea finally clicked with Portland veterans, Waters found himself at the head of a band of veterans headed to Washington. The events of summer 1932 made Waters a recognizable figure. He returned to Washington in January 1935 to take a clerical job in the War Department, through the intercession of Gen. Douglas MacArthur (Dickson and Allen 2004, 299). Less than a month later he resigned to form the National Soldier's Bonus League of America to lobby for Patman's bill. He later took a job as adviser to Governor Ernest W. Marland of Oklahoma, then joined the Navy after the outbreak of World War II.

References and Further Readings

Balderrama, F. E., and R. Rodriguez. 1995. *Decade of Betrayal: Mexican Repatriation in the 1930s*. Albuquerque: University of New Mexico Press.

Balogh, B. 2003. "'Mirror of Desires': Interest Groups, Elections, and the Targeted Style in Twentieth-Century America." In *The Democratic Experiment: New Directions in American Political History*, ed. M. Jacobs, W. J. Novak, and J. E. Zelizer, 222–249. Princeton, NJ: Princeton University Press.

Beard, C. A., ed. 1932. *America Faces the Future*. Boston: Houghton Mifflin.

Beito, D. T. 1989. *Taxpayers in Revolt: Tax Resistance during the Great Depression*. Chapel Hill: University of North Carolina Press.

Berkowitz, E., and K. McQuaid. 1988. *Creating the Welfare State: The Political Economy of Twentieth-Century Reform*. 2nd ed., rev. and expanded. New York: Praeger.

Bernstein, I. 1960. *The Lean Years: A History of the American Worker, 1920–1933*. Boston: Houghton Mifflin.

Bernstein, M. 1987. *The Great Depression: Delayed Recovery and Economic Change in America, 1929–1939*. New York: Cambridge University Press.

Bird, C. 1966. *The Invisible Scar*. New York: D. McKay Co.

Bucki, C. 2001. *Bridgeport's Socialist New Deal, 1915–1936*. Urbana: University of Illinois Press.

Cohen, L. 1990. *Making a New Deal: Industrial Workers in Chicago, 1919–1939*. New York: Cambridge University Press.

Daniels, R. 1971. *The Bonus March: An Episode of the Great Depression*. Westport, CT: Greenwood.

Dickson, P., and T. B. Allen. 2004. *The Bonus Army: An American Epic*. New York: Walker and Co.

Drake, S. C., and H. R. Cayton. 1945. *Black Metropolis: A Study of Negro Life in a Northern City*. New York: Harcourt, Brace.

Edsforth, R. 2000. *The New Deal: America's Response to the Great Depression*. Malden, MA: Blackwell.

Fearon, P. 1987. *War, Prosperity and Depression: The U.S. Economy, 1917–1945*. Lawrence: University Press of Kansas.

Fine, S. 1963. *The Automobile under the Blue Eagle*. Ann Arbor: University of Michigan Press.

Fine, S. 1975. *Frank Murphy: The Detroit Years*. Vol. 1. Ann Arbor: University of Michigan Press.

Friedman, M., and A. J. Schwartz. 1963. *A Monetary History of the United States, 1867–1960*. Princeton, NJ: Princeton University Press.

Galbraith, J. K. 1961. *The Great Crash, 1929*. Boston: Houghton Mifflin.

Harburg, Yip, and Jay Gorney. 1931. "Brother Can You Spare a Dime?" The Authentic History Center. http://www.authentichistory.com/1930s/music/1932-Brother_Can_You_Spare_a_Dime.html.

Heineman, K. J. 1999. *A Catholic New Deal: Religion and Reform in Depression Pittsburgh*. University Park: Pennsylvania State University Press.

Hoan, D. W. 1933. "Taxes and Tax Dodgers." Chicago: Socialist Party of America.

Hoffman, A. 1974. *Unwanted Mexican Americans in the Great Depression: Repatriation Pressures, 1929–1939*. Tucson: University of Arizona Press.

Hoover, H. 1952. *Memoirs: The Great Depression, 1929–1941*. Vol. 3. New York: Macmillan.

Jacoby, S. M. 1985. *Employing Bureaucracy: Managers, Unions, and the Transformation of Work in American Industry, 1900–1945*. New York: Columbia University Press.

Kennedy, D. M. 1999. *Freedom from Fear: The American People in Depression and War, 1929–1945*. New York: Oxford University Press.

Kindleberger, C. P. 1986. *The World in Depression, 1929–1939*. Rev. and enl. ed. Berkeley: University of California Press.

Kusmer, K. L. 2002. *Down and Out, on the Road: The Homeless in American History*. New York: Oxford University Press.

Leff, M. H. 1984. *The Limits of Symbolic Reform: The New Deal and Taxation, 1933–1939*. New York: Cambridge University Press.

Le Sueur, M. 1982. *Ripening: Selected Work, 1927–1980*. Ed. E. Hedges. Old Westbury, NY: Feminist Press.

Lorence, J. J. 1996. *Organizing the Unemployed: Community and Union Activists in the Industrial Heartland*. Albany: State University of New York Press.

Lynd, R. S., and H. M. Lynd. 1965. *Middletown in Transition: A Study in Cultural Conflicts*. New York: Harcourt Brace Jovanovich, Harvest/HJB Book.

Mooney, P. H., and T. J. Majka. 1995. *Farmers' and Farm Workers' Movements: Social Protest in American Agriculture*. New York: Twayne Publishers.

Morawska, E. 1985. *For Bread with Butter: The Life-Worlds of East Central Europeans in Johnstown, Pennsylvania, 1890–1940*. New York: Cambridge University Press.

Nelson, S., J. R. Barrett, and R. Ruck. 1981. *Steve Nelson, American Radical*. Pittsburgh: University of Pittsburgh Press.

Orloff, A. S., and T. Skocpol. 1984. "Why Not Equal Protection? Explaining the Politics of Public Social Spending in Britain, 1900–1911, and the United States, 1880s–1920," *American Sociological Review* 49 (December): 726–750.

Ottanelli, F. M. 1991. *The Communist Party of the United States: From the Depression to World War II*. New Brunswick, NJ: Rutgers University Press.

Peterson, J. S. 1987. *American Automobile Workers, 1900–1933*. SUNY series in American labor history. Albany: State University of New York Press.

Ridley, C. E., and O. F. Nolting, eds. 1935. *What the Depression Has Done to Cities*. Chicago: International City Managers' Association.

Romasco, A. U. 1975. *The Poverty of Abundance: Hoover, the Nation, the Depression*. New York: Oxford University Press.

Rosenzweig, R. 1976. "Organizing the Unemployed: The Early Years of the Great Depression, 1929–1933," *Radical America* 10 (4): 37–60.

Schatz, R. W. 1983. *The Electrical Workers: A History of Labor at General Electric and Westinghouse, 1923–60*. Urbana: University of Illinois Press.

Schlesinger, A. M., Jr. 1957. *The Age of Roosevelt: The Crisis of the Old Order, 1919–1933*. Boston: Houghton Mifflin.

Schwarz, J. A. 1970. *The Interregnum of Despair: Hoover, Congress, and the Depression*. Urbana: University of Illinois Press.

Shover, J. L. 1965. *Cornbelt Rebellion: The Farmers' Holiday Association*. Urbana: University of Illinois Press.

Stricker, F. 1983. "Affluence for Whom? Another Look at Prosperity and the Working Classes in the 1920s," *Labor History* 24 (1): 5–33.

Temin, P. 1976. *Did Monetary Forces Cause the Great Depression?* New York: Norton.

Vargas, Z. 1993. *Proletarians of the North: A History of Mexican Industrial Workers in Detroit and the Midwest, 1917–1933*. Berkeley: University of California Press.

Vargas, Z. 2005. *Labor Rights Are Civil Rights: Mexican American Workers in Twentieth-Century America*. Princeton, NJ: Princeton University Press.

Waters, W. W., and W. C. White. 1933. *B.E.F.: The Whole Story of the Bonus Army*. New York: John Day Co.

Wilson, J. H. 1975. *Herbert Hoover, Forgotten Progressive*. Boston: Little, Brown.

Worster, D. 1982. *Dust Bowl: The Southern Plains in the 1930s*. New York: Oxford University Press.

The New Deal and American Society

Overview

A social history of the 1930s must recognize that one of the distinguishing features of this decade is the increased power and presence of the federal government over the lives of ordinary people. Before the 1930s, the average citizen had little to do with the federal government, other than at the post office. Now with the greatest economic catastrophe ever experienced and local and state governments unable to deal with the human suffering, only the federal government had the resources to assume responsibility

Franklin Delano Roosevelt was decisively elected in November 1932, not because he had articulated a clear plan but because Hoover had proven that he could not respond adequately. Roosevelt's campaign, though with few specifics, was deeply committed to giving the American people hope. FDR's inaugural address reassured the nation, as he stated, "The only thing we have to fear is fear itself." He lashed out at financiers:

> the rulers of the exchange of mankind's goods have failed, through their own stubbornness and their own incompetence, have admitted their failure, and abdicated. . . . The money changers have fled from their high seats in the temple of our civilization. We may now restore that temple to the ancient truths. The measure of the restoration lies in the extent to which we apply social values more noble than mere monetary profit.

He also warned that if Congress did not act speedily on his proposals, he would ask Congress for "broad executive power to wage war against the emergency as great as the power that would be given me if we were invaded by a foreign foe" (Rosenman 1938).

Congress was as eager to act as the president was. Roosevelt had first used the phrase "New Deal" in his acceptance speech at the 1932 Democratic National Convention. The First New Deal, as the 1933–1935 legislative agenda came to be known, focused on economic recovery. Even given the president's inaugural rhetoric, he focused first on business solutions, as well as providing some individual relief. The inadequacy of that phase led to the Second New Deal, 1935–1937, which focused on economic recovery through raising consumer spending power, supporting unionization, and enacting social-provision programs such as old-age pensions and unemployment insurance. The Second New Deal laid the foundation for the contemporary American welfare state. The New Deal, however, did not solve the economic crisis of the Great Depression; only the defense spending of World War II did that.

Timeline

1932 In November, Franklin D. Roosevelt is elected president, winning 472 votes in the Electoral College to Hoover's 59. Democrats gain 90 seats in the House and 13 in the Senate.

1933 FDR is inaugurated on March 4

On March 5, FDR declares a four-day bank holiday to stop runs on banks and to stabilize the banking system.

FDR's first "fireside chat" is broadcast over the radio on March 12; in it the president explains the bank holiday that has just been announced.

Congress convenes on March 9 and starts the "One Hundred Days" of the First New Deal legislative package, ending June 16.

In November elections, Fiorello La Guardia is elected mayor of New York City on a Fusion ticket; Arthur Mitchell of Chicago is the first African American elected to Congress as a Democrat.

The Twenty-first Amendment to the Constitution is adopted in December, repealing the Eighteenth Amendment (Prohibition).

1934 Upton Sinclair publishes his book, *I, Governor of California, and How I Ended Poverty,* as part of his run for governor of

California. Sinclair, with his EPIC (End Poverty In California) campaign, is narrowly defeated by incumbent Republican Frank F. Merriam.

1935 The "Second New Deal" begins in the January congressional session.

On May 27, in the decision *Schechter Poultry Co. v. U.S.*, the Supreme Court declares the National Industrial Recovery Act unconstitutional.

Sen. Huey Long of Louisiana is assassinated on September 8 by a disgruntled constituent.

1936 First Lady Eleanor Roosevelt begins publishing her syndicated column, *My Day,* in January.

The U.S. Supreme Court declares the Agricultural Adjustment Act unconstitutional in January

On November 3, FDR is re-elected president in a landslide victory over Republican Alfred M. Landon of Kansas. Democrats have strong control over Congress, with only 89 Republicans in the House and 16 in the Senate.

1937 In his Inaugural address on January 20, FDR declares his intention of pursuing economic fairness: "I see one-third of a nation ill-housed, ill-clad, ill-nourished."

In February, FDR asks Congress to increase the number of justices on the Supreme Court to as many as fifteen (using forced retirement combined with a penalty for justices over 70). The plan is quickly labeled "court-packing" by critics.

In the April Court decision *NLRB v. Jones & Laughlin Steel Company,* the Supreme Court upholds the constitutionality of the National Labor Relations Act.

In May, the Supreme Court upholds the Social Security Act.

The economy takes a downturn in the summer, and the stock market tumbles between August 1937 and March 1938.

1938 In May the House Committee on Un-American Activities (HUAC) is established.

In September the Munich Pact, signed by Hitler and Prime Minister Chamberlain of Great Britain, cedes the Sudetenland to Germany.

In the November election, Republicans regain some congressional seats, seven in the Senate and eighty in the House, due to dissatisfaction over the "Roosevelt Recession" of 1937–1938.

1939 In his January State of the Union message, Roosevelt stresses the ominous international situation.

In May, the U.S. Department of Agriculture introduces food stamps, which needy people can redeem for surplus agricultural goods.

On September 1, Germany invades Poland; World War II begins; American Communists reverse their antifascist stand in order to support the Hitler-Stalin Pact declaring neutrality between Germany and the Soviet Union.

On September 5 FDR officially declares U.S. neutrality and bans the export of weapons to warring nations.

The First New Deal

When Congress convened on March 9, 1933, ready to do the president's bidding, FDR's advisers had already been busy preparing pieces of legislation to revive the economy and provide some relief for individuals and families. The Roosevelt administration was confronted with the rise of conservatism elsewhere in the industrial world. France and Britain were ruled by conservative governments, and Germany had embarked down the road to Hitler's fascism. Italy had been ruled by the fascist Mussolini government since 1924. Only the Soviet Union, under the increasingly harsh rule of Joseph Stalin, seemed to have escaped the worldwide economic crisis. FDR and his "brain trust" hoped to construct an alternative that would fashion a middle way between communism on the left and fascism on the right. It would preserve the free market and individual liberties, but it would rein in the free market's excesses.

Banking and Finance

The first move of the administration came in response to the bank panic of 1933. Roosevelt ordered a national "bank holiday" in which all banks would close. FDR used his first "fireside chat" on March 12 to explain to the American people what he was doing. The estimated one-half of the country that tuned in that Sunday evening was reassured that the federal government would reopen sound banks and reorganize the system to create more sound banks. The Emergency Banking Act of March 9 granted the federal government the power to reopen

FDR's Fireside Chats

The brilliance of Roosevelt's communications skills with the American public was very much in evidence in his use of the new medium of radio. FDR addressed the nation 27 times (some authorities list 28, some 31, including more formal speeches) in a calm, informal style that explained his actions, his legislation, and his thoughts on the crisis confronting the American people. The term *fireside chat* was coined by Harry Butcher of CBS in his network press release before the speech of May 7, 1933 (the second speech). However, Roosevelt's first fireside chat was broadcast on Sunday evening, March 12, 1933, eight days after his inauguration. It was on the banking crisis, and its opening lines give an indication of FDR's style.

"My friends, I want to talk for a few minutes with the people of the United States about banking—to talk with the comparatively few who understand the mechanics of banking, but more particularly with the overwhelming majority of you who use banks for the making of deposits and the drawing of checks. I want to tell you what has been done in the last few days, and why it was done, and what the next steps are going to be. . . . I can assure you, my friends, that it is safer to keep your money in a reopened bank than it is to keep it under the mattress" (Buhite and Levy 1992, 12–15). In this way, Roosevelt built up his political support, which became known after 1936 as the New Deal Coalition.

those solvent banks, which it did on March 15. Only one-half of the nation's banks were judged sound and allowed to reopen. Forty-five percent of the remaining banks were put under conservatorship, to reorganize their finances and eventually return to solvency. The remaining 5 percent, some 1,000 banks, were closed permanently (Wicker 1996).

The Banking Act of 1933, also known as the Glass-Steagall Act, was a sweeping reform of the banking system proposed in 1932, but Hoover had refused to act on it. Sponsored by Sen. Carter Glass of Virginia and Rep. Henry Steagall of Alabama, the Banking Act of 1933 formally separated investment banking from commercial banking and prohibited individual banks from engaging in both arenas. Each bank would have to declare itself one or the other, and commercial banks had one year to divest themselves of securities activities. To forestall depositors' runs on banks, the act set up the Federal Deposit Insurance Corporation (FDIC), which guaranteed individual bank accounts up to $5,000. All national banks were required to sign up for FDIC insurance, and all state banks that wanted to enroll had to become part of the Federal Reserve System, thus insuring their stability. The insurance program would be financed by federal appropriations ($150 million in the first year) and premium payments by member banks. When the insurance program went into effect on January 1, 1934, the FDIC sign on a bank window quickly was accepted by the general public as

President Franklin D. Roosevelt gives a fireside chat "On the Works Relief Program," April 28, 1935. He gave 27 of the popular national radio addresses in all. (Franklin D. Roosevelt Presidential Library)

a guarantee that the bank was sound. The system stabilized the banking system; only 34 banks failed in 1934 (Olson 1988).

Work-Relief

Like many of his advisers and contemporaries, FDR preferred work-relief to direct government payouts to the needy, fearing that the "dole" would undermine self-reliance. With nearly a quarter of the workforce unemployed, however, and states and cities having exhausted their resources, something needed to be done by the federal government.

The Civilian Conservation Corps

The president's proposed relief measures on the national level stemmed from what had worked for him as governor of New York. He proposed to put unemployed young men to work in the national forests and other federal and state properties to preserve natural resources. This new program, the Civilian Conservation Corps (CCC), proved highly popular and successful. At its peak in September 1935, the CCC had stationed some one-half-million young men between the ages of 17 and 25 in 2,500 camps around the country built by the Army. The military ran these camps, where CCC workers were paid $30 a month plus room and board, though the "CCC boys" were required to send at least $22 back to their families. For most of those from impoverished rural areas, the camps were a large improvement over their previous situation, as they now received adequate food and benefited from night classes that taught literacy and job skills. The country benefited from the CCC's work of reforesting, building roads, bridges, and trails in state and national forests, and improving public parks and campgrounds. It remained so popular that when FDR proposed funding cutbacks in 1936 a majority of congressmen rose in defense of the program, and it continued until 1942.

The CCC was not without controversy, however, as racial segregation prevailed in most regions, and in the South state officials protested the "high" wages paid to African American youth. After the 1936 election and a strong Democratic majority, especially from African American districts of northern cities, pressure built to enroll more African American youth, so that by the end of the program nearly 11 percent of enrollees were African American. By the late 1930s Labor Secretary Frances Perkins and Interior Secretary Harold Ickes succeeded in getting CCC camps integrated outside the South (Edsforth 2000, 137–139).

Federal Emergency Relief Administration

Another important relief measure for the unemployed was the Federal Emergency Relief Administration (FERA), a program that made federal grants to state agencies to dispense to the needy in local areas. Initially $500 million was made available to states as grants, rather than loans as had been true under Hoover's Reconstruction Finance Corporation. Administrator Harry Hopkins developed a rigid formula for states to apply for funds, with $250 million available to states on a matching basis of one dollar of federal money for every three dollars they had spent on unemployment relief in the previous three months. The rest of the funds ($250 million) could be disbursed by Hopkins on a discretionary basis. Hopkins held states to high standards of professional social work in their administration of relief funds and preferred useful work projects. Each state had to create a State Emergency Relief Administration to account for its distribution of funds to the localities, and state administrators and arrangements had to be approved by Hopkins. This new emphasis on federal-state cooperation, as well as the very fact of relief funds coming from the federal government, set a new model for dealing with unemployment on a vast scale.

One final relief program of the First New Deal was the Civil Works Administration (CWA), which took over FERA's works projects from November 1933 to April 1934, and rapidly provided work for four million unemployed. When FERA returned to work-relief programs in early 1935, it implemented four special relief programs to suit specific group needs: Rural Rehabilitation, Relief for Transients,

College Student Aid, and Emergency Education. But it quickly became apparent that only some of the able-bodied were being put to work; others were simply receiving cash relief payments. When FDR reiterated his belief in work projects alone, the FERA was phased out in late 1936 in favor of a new agency, the Works Progress Administration (WPA). Between 1933 and 1935, $4.1 billion had been expended on relief, with 71 percent coming from federal funds (Fearon 1987, 243).

Tennessee Valley Authority—Debates over Public versus Private Interests

The Tennessee Valley Authority (TVA) exemplifies the struggle between private profit interests and public needs, as it decisively set up a government-owned power plant in a poor section of the South. The TVA began as a project during the World War to produce weapons-grade nitrate plants and a hydroelectric support facility on the Tennessee River at Muscle Shoals, Alabama. In the 1920s, the reigning Republican Party wanted to divest the federal government of any public-power capacity in favor of private utility companies. Only the diligent efforts of progressive congressmen, led by Sen. George Norris of Nebraska, kept the Muscle Shoals facility from being shut down. When public support for government ownership of utilities returned in the early Depression, the Muscle Shoals project provided President Roosevelt with an opportunity to showcase public power, planning, and economic development for a region, ideas he had implemented on a smaller scale while governor of New York. Congress rapidly approved the TVA in May 1933 and established an agency that would both develop hydroelectric dams on the Tennessee River and plan the development of industry, agriculture, flood control, and conservation within the river's watershed. Roosevelt appointed Arthur E. Morgan, president of Antioch College, Harcourt Morgan, president of the University of Tennessee, and David E. Lilienthal, leader of the Wisconsin Public Service Commission, to the three-person board of the TVA.

The TVA faced a host of difficulties from the beginning, not the least of which was the fierce hostility of private utility companies led by Commonwealth and Southern (C&S) holding company which served Tennessee, Georgia, Mississippi, and Alabama. Its president, Wendell Willkie (in 1940 to become the Republican candidate for president), initially suggested that TVA sell its power at the source to private companies, and TVA chairman Arthur Morgan agreed. David Lilienthal, however, was adamant that TVA be allowed to sell its own power to the public, thereby fulfilling its stated role as providing a yardstick for utility rates and forcing private utilities to lower their rates. The Morgan-Lilienthal dispute continued over the next six years, until the U.S. Supreme Court ruled that TVA

Building Dams

Both the Boulder Dam on the Colorado River on the Arizona-Nevada state line and the Grand Coulee Dam along the eastern Columbia River in Washington State had been originally proposed for flood control and irrigation projects before the Great Depression, and served as massive work-relief projects once they got under way in the early 1930s. The Boulder Dam (renamed the Hoover Dam in 1947 because of Hoover's contribution to the project) had been approved by President Coolidge in late 1928, with $165 million in federal funds to be administered by the Bureau of Reclamation. It was meant to address the competing water-rights claims of the previous decade, to control flooding, and to generate electricity for the region. When President Roosevelt dedicated the dam in September 1935, it became the largest hydroelectric facility in the world, producing over 700,000 kilowatts, and remained the largest until the Grand Coulee Dam exceeded that level in 1949.

The Grand Coulee Dam along the eastern Columbia River in Washington State had originally been proposed decades earlier as an irrigation system for the semi-arid region. The final project, as a New Deal economic development project coupled with a work-relief project, created the largest concrete structure in the world, built one of the most productive hydroelectric generating plants, and created the 151-mile-long Lake Roosevelt. Along with its sister dams along the Columbia, notably Bonneville Dam which opened in 1938, it provoked controversy for its large size, for destroying the natural beauty of the river, and for disruption of salmon fishing. The latter problem was partially solved by building fish ladders. President Roosevelt's words at the dedication of the Bonneville Dam in 1938 addressed the other criticisms when he extolled the project as providing for "the widest possible use of electricity [to create] more wealth, better living and greater happiness for our children" (Billington, Jackson, and Melosi 2005, 191; www.usbr.gov/history).

had the right to produce and market power. C&S then gave up and sold its area holdings to TVA.

The extensive TVA agricultural programs were coordinated with the area's land-grant colleges, with the other board member, Harcourt Morgan, in charge. TVA's main focus, however, remained electricity production, an emphasis that only grew stronger after World War II. The principle of local citizens' participation remained part of the project's rhetoric, though that too faded during the World War II era. Nonetheless the TVA remained a strong example of what government could do in the economic arena that would improve people's lives, as the history of the Rural Electrification Administration later in the decade would prove. Along with the Columbia River dam projects, TVA produced the lowest utility costs in the country (www.tva.gov/heritage).

Grand Coulee Dam on the Columbia River, Washington. (Library of Congress)

National Industrial Recovery Act

This legislation summed up the thrust of the First New Deal. The essence of the National Industrial Recovery Act (NIRA) was an attempt to regulate business by promoting government-sanctioned cartelization of economic sectors. This attempt at economic planning borrowed from the Associationalism of Herbert Hoover and added the federal government and labor as counterbalances to business power. Associationalism had developed in the 1920s as Secretary of Commerce Hoover encouraged private business trade associations to regulate themselves within their own sectors and avoid cut-throat competition (see previous chapter). The NIRA economic planning also borrowed from the tripartite boards of the World War I era, in which Roosevelt had himself participated (Himmelberg 1976; Hawley 1966).

The NIRA legislation contained three titles. Title I implemented the program of self-regulation of economic sectors by permitting industries to draft codes regulating business and labor practices that were exempt from antitrust laws and had the force of law if the codes were signed by the president. Section 7 required codes to include provisions for maximum hours, minimum wages, and the right of workers to organize and bargain collectively. Other sections gave the president the power to license industries and to remake any code that he

A woman hangs a "Blue Eagle" National Recovery Administration (NRA) poster in a restaurant window to show support for the government program. (Franklin D. Roosevelt Presidential Library)

felt was necessary to impose on an industry. Title II authorized a $3.3-billion public works program, and Title III provided for new taxes on capital stock and excess profits to finance the system.

The NIRA was based on the idea that the economic debacle had been caused by overproduction and destructive competition. The combination of business, government (representing the public), and labor would ideally be able to negotiate fair standards of conduct and parcel out production quotas to businesses in their sectors. Thus the economy would be stabilized, labor wages and conditions would be standardized, and the quality of goods produced would be guaranteed. The National Recovery Administration (NRA), headed by retired general Hugh S. Johnson, had oversight of each code authority in each industry. These code authorities, made up of representatives of business, labor, and government, would negotiate Codes of Fair Conduct in each industry and then oversee the codes. Every business that adhered to the codes would be allowed to display the NRA Blue Eagle, as a public signal that "We Do Our Part!"

The NRA quickly fell into dispute as small companies complained that large companies in their sector were dominating the code boards and ruling in favor of the larger firms, consumers complained that price-fixing was undermining their purchasing power, and labor unions complained that their concerns were being ignored. Moreover Section 7(a), which stated the principle of collective bargaining, motivated a wave of labor strikes to implement union recognition across the nation. Finally, the NIRA was declared unconstitutional by the U.S. Supreme Court in *Schechter Poultry Company v. United States* in May 1935.

National Labor Board of the NRA

NIRA Section 7(a) was not expected to produce any unmanageable activity on labor's part. Indeed, so the thinking went, if the NRA code authorities did their jobs appropriately, there would be no reason to strike. So the NRA was given no mechanism for dealing with labor disputes or even to interpret Section 7(a). However, strikes were an immediate response. The year 1933 witnessed the largest number of strikes since 1921, and the biggest issue was the right to bargain collectively (see "The Labor Movement" chapter). Basic industry corporations, where few unions had survived the antiunion 1920s, refused to deal with the newly formed unions and responded by forming or reinvigorating company unions. By mid-summer 1933, a National Labor Board (NLB) was set up within NRA to deal with the explosive situation. This tripartite board, modeled on the War Labor Board arrangement of World War I, had three labor members—economist Leo Wolman, chairman of the Labor Advisory Board of NRA, William Green of the AFL, and John L. Lewis of the United Mine Workers (UMWA)—and three industry members—Walter C. Teagle of AT&T, chairman of the Industrial Advisory Board, Gerard Swope of GE, and Louis E. Kirstein of Filene's Department Store. Its one public member was Sen. Robert Wagner (D-NY). William M. Leiserson, its executive secretary, arranged for labor mediators from the U.S. Mediation and Conciliation Service of the Department of Labor.

The NLB began by intervening in the hosiery strike in the Philadelphia area. It worked out an agreement between the employers and the Federation of Full-Fashioned Hosiery Workers–AFL. The "Reading Formula," as the agreement became known, had these four elements: the union called off the strike; the employers agreed to rehire all the strikers; the NLB would conduct a secret-ballot election for workers to choose their representatives; and those representatives would then negotiate with employers regarding wages, hours, and working conditions. Finally, if the parties were unable to agree on any issues, those issues would then be returned to the NLB for a final decision. The representation election became the main means of implementing Section 7(a), and the NLB used its many decisions that summer to create a basic set of procedures and principles of labor relations that would have a longer life than the agency itself (Bernstein 1969, 172–175).

But with no real enforcement mechanism, the NLB was challenged in the fall of 1933 by strong-minded executives like Weirton Steel's Ernest T. Weir, and the Edward G. Budd Manufacturing Company of Philadelphia, which made auto parts. Both companies refused to abide by rulings of the NLB. The trend continued in early 1934 when autoworkers in Flint, Michigan, threatened to strike unless their AFL federal local was recognized by General Motors. But the auto manufacturers did not need the NRA, as they were enjoying a major economic boom that would be untouched by the little strike that the AFL could muster. This forced the NLB's hand, and President Roosevelt agreed to set up a special Automobile Labor Board to mediate disputes. On the main points, the president deferred to the company's insistence that company unions be given the same voice as independent unions and that proportional representation be acceptable. So, according to historian Irving Bernstein, by March 1934 "the labor provision of the Recovery Act was verbiage; the Reading Formula, majority rule, and exclusive representation were repudiated; and the National Labor Board was in ruins" (Bernstein 1969, 185). It was at this point that Senator Wagner's staff began drafting what would become the National Labor Relations Act in spring 1935. In the 1934 congressional session, a preliminary version of the bill was debated in Congress. But as a national steel strike threatened, President Roosevelt asked for, and got, a noncontroversial labor bill that would allow him to create labor boards for various industries as needed. This expedient action was not sufficient, as the strike wave of summer 1934 was just starting (see "The Labor Movement" chapter).

Public Works Administration of the NIRA

Title II of the NIRA established a $3.3-billion public works program, to be overseen by Secretary of the Interior Harold Ickes and named the Public Works Administration (PWA). Its mandate overlapped with that of the FERA, headed by Harry Hopkins, and rivalry between the two agencies and men persisted for the rest of the decade. PWA's orders were to spend its money quickly on necessary public works projects, while FERA was a more deliberative work-relief program. PWA's federal projects division was dominated by two agencies, the Army Corps of Engineers and the Bureau of Reclamation. Massive dam-building projects were their most visible work. PWA offices quickly employed some 3,700 people with offices in every state and with 10 regional offices to provide a larger planning perspective. The construction industry and construction unions benefited most from these projects, which aided economic recovery.

Nonfederal projects were in the second division of PWA, where states and localities could propose projects that they needed. Each proposed project had

Public Works Administration (PWA) construction site in Washington, D.C., 1933. (Franklin D. Roosevelt Presidential Library)

to survive a detailed screening process through an engineering, a financial, and a legal division, before undergoing scrutiny by Ickes and finally Roosevelt himself. As Ickes reported in his 1935 book, *Back to Work: The Story of PWA,* more than 19,000 projects had either been completed or were under way in all 48 states (Ickes 1935). However, the criticism remained that the tight-fisted Ickes failed to infuse the economy with money and reduce unemployment sufficiently.

Saving Agriculture

The Agricultural Adjustment Act, formulated in the midst of farm strikes and mortgage foreclosure protests in the Midwest and enacted in May 1933, was the First New Deal's answer to the plight of rural America. Secretary of Agriculture Henry A. Wallace led the administration's focus on voluntary production controls with farmers' cooperation. In its final form, the law authorized the secretary of agriculture to create a production control board for eight major commodities —wheat, cotton, corn, rice, potatoes, tobacco, hogs, and milk and milk products—

The Roosevelt "Brain Trust"

The brain trust, or "brains trust" as it was called in 1932 before being shortened by newspaper reporters, was the name given to FDR's circle of advisers. It included academics like Columbia University political scientist Raymond Moley, who then recruited his Columbia colleagues Rexford G. Tugwell and Adolf A. Berle Jr. They helped draft speeches for FDR during his election campaign. Tugwell, an economist, had written extensively on the causes of the Great Depression with a specific focus on agriculture. Berle was a legal expert who had analyzed the modern corporation. Moley's contribution was political advice, while Tugwell drafted agricultural policies. Berle instructed FDR on finance and corporations. All three had agreed in 1932 that big business was inevitable and the key to dealing with big business was regulation, not antimonopoly as the Wilson administration had emphasized during the Progressive Era. Thus some form of economic planning seemed the only solution. Both Tugwell and Moley continued in the first Roosevelt administration, while Berle returned to New York to advise Mayor Fiorello La Guardia in dealing with the New York City fiscal crisis. Others who figured large in Roosevelt's early circle included: Harold Ickes, lawyer, social worker, and political activist who became secretary of the Interior; Harry Hopkins, a social worker whose stint in the New York City charity, the Association for Improving the Condition of the Poor, and then with the New York Tuberculosis Association, was noticed by then-governor Franklin Roosevelt who asked Hopkins to head up the new New York Temporary Emergency Relief Administration and then the federal relief agencies; retired general Hugh S. Johnson, who took over the NRA; agricultural businessman Henry Wallace, who became secretary of agriculture; and Frances Perkins, the new secretary of labor who had been FDR's labor adviser in Albany.

A considerable new group came to Washington in the middle years, young and highly aggressive reformers compared to the original brain trust, and the term *New Dealers* began to refer to this latter group alone. As George Peek, the first administrator of the Agricultural Adjustment Administration and by 1937 a serious critic of the New Deal, noted, "A plague of young lawyers settled on Washington. They all claimed to be friends of somebody or another, and mostly of Jerome Frank and Felix Frankfurter, They floated airily into offices, asked for papers, and found no end of things to be busy about" (Brinkley 1995, 51). These new protégés of Frankfurter from his days teaching at Harvard Law School included Thomas G. Corcoran ("Tommy the Cork") and Benjamin V. Cohen. Corcoran and Cohen collaborated on many bills and drafted many of FDR's 1936 campaign speeches. Along with Secretary of the Interior Harold Ickes, the larger group included William O. Douglas, Robert Jackson, Thurman Arnold, Jerome Frank, Mordecai Ezekiel, and Isidor Lubin. Their antimonopolist inclination rang out clearly during the 1937 recession when Jackson, who headed the antitrust division of the Justice Department, lashed out at business, blaming the downturn on "a strike of

Continued on next page

The Roosevelt "Brain Trust," Continued

capital . . . a strike against the government—a strike to coerce political action" (Brinkley 1995, 58). Here Jackson revealed his own (and Thurman Arnold's) passion for breaking up monopoly, which they pursued through a very active antitrust division. On the other hand, there was another approach to big-ness. Many New Deal liberals argued for regulation of bigness, which "required a strong and constant public presence in the private economy, an elaborate system of regulation that would enable the state to monitor corporate behavior continuously and, when necessary, to change it. Antitrust efforts would not be an alternative to the growth of a regulatory state; they would be part of that growth" (Brinkley 1995, 62).

and financed by a tax on the processors of these commodities. The Department of Agriculture committed itself to raising farm prices to a level such that farm families could enjoy the same purchasing power they had between the years 1909 and 1914. This ideal was known as "parity." Another section of the act created the Emergency Farm Mortgage Act, which provided emergency mortgage loan financing for farmers.

The act created the Agricultural Adjustment Administration (AAA), which fundamentally changed the agricultural sector since it established a permanent system of price and income supports for American farmers. Participation in the program was voluntary for farmers, who would agree to reduce acreage according to AAA orders and in return receive benefit payments. It was hoped that curtailing production would raise prices. Bankrupt farmers would receive an immediate cash payment (see "Rural Life" chapter). The program was controversial from the start, since creating artificial scarcity meant plowing up already planted crops, spilling out milk, slaughtering hogs and dumping them when so many of the country's citizens were going hungry. More controversy ensued when southern cotton producers began evicting sharecroppers rather than sharing AAA benefits payments with them. Black and white tenant farmers in Arkansas, Oklahoma, Mississippi, and Missouri organized the Southern Tenant Farmers Union to deal with this situation (see "The Labor Movement" chapter). When Jerome Davis, chief of the AAA legal division, tried to impose a more equitable system in 1935, he and his staff were abruptly fired by the AAA chief administrator, Chester Davis. The issue was never fairly resolved.

Commodity processors, angered over having to pay the tax to fund this program, brought a suit before the U.S. Supreme Court, challenging the AAA's constitutionality. The Court ruled in their favor in the *U.S. v. Butler* decision of January 6, 1936. By the time of its demise, the AAA had paid $1.1 billion in benefits payments to the farm sector.

Housing

Housing construction, regarded by Roosevelt as "the wheel within the wheel to move the whole economic engine" (Radford, 179), received significant attention in the early New Deal. Part of the One Hundred Days included the creation of the Home Owners Loan Corporation (HOLC) in June 1933. Answering FDR's call for legislation to protect small home owners from foreclosure, the HOLC was capitalized with $200 million from the U.S. Treasury. The HOLC did not deal directly in individual mortgages, but gave money to lending institutions by purchasing defaulted mortgages (or those in danger of default) with government bonds paying 4 percent interest (this was later reduced to 3 percent). Thus by the time its authorization came up for renewal in June 1936, HOLC had made over one million loans and become the owner of about one-sixth of the home-mortgage debt in the country. This program was seen as a godsend to ordinary home owners at the time, and scholars since have generally agreed with this positive assessment. HOLC reduced the rate of foreclosures and allowed payment of delinquent taxes to states and cities across the land. Most important, HOLC introduced the long-term self-amortizing mortgage, presently still the major way to buy a home, and made home ownership possible for middle-income families who had not been able to afford the short-term, high-interest mortgages available before this time. But some scholars have criticized HOLC for propping up mortgage lenders by legitimating the inflated housing prices of the 1920s. HOLC was also responsible for developing the practice of a neighborhood mortgage ratings system, where less desirable neighborhoods, usually with high concentrations of racial minorities, were "redlined" as too risky for government mortgage assistance. Private lenders adopted this practice, thus leaving some neighborhoods and racial groups outside the circle of home ownership. The practice also reinforced the segregated pattern of housing that would become problematic for cities in the postwar era (Jackson 1980).

The National Housing Act of 1934 established the Federal Housing Administration (FHA) to promote the ideal of private single-family home ownership through increases in the national housing stock. This aimed at reviving the construction industry and expanding home ownership. The agency did this by providing federal insurance for private mortgages to protect creditors from default and thus encourage banks to loan more money for housing construction. Working alongside HOLC, the FHA made mortgage lending less risky and home ownership more secure. Within the decade, nearly half of all mortgages were secured by FHA insurance (Edsforth 2000, 193). The two programs together brought into being the American middle class, as home owning now became a reachable goal for many families (Jackson 1985).

But as historian Gail Radford notes, these programs created a "two-tiered" federal housing policy. On the one hand, the FHA, HOLC, and its later progeny, the Federal National Mortgage Association (Fannie Mae), put the wealth of the federal Treasury behind individual home ownership and propped up financial markets which were heavily invested in home mortgages. On the other hand, public housing, authorized by the United States Housing Act of 1937, "created a form of directly assisted housing that was stingy, physically alienating, and means-tested" (Radford 1996, 197–98). Public housing in the First New Deal was created through the PWA's Division of Housing in 1933–1934, which offered low-interest loans to some limited-dividend housing corporations for the construction of urban housing. Philadelphia's Carl Mackley Houses, built in 1934–1935 by the Hosiery Workers' Union with PWA loans, became a model community in the eyes of housing critic Catherine Bauer, who praised the integration of living and family services with an emphasis on fostering community. This, of course, was due to the spirit of the Hosiery Workers rather than the PWA. However, in 1934 the PWA discontinued the loan program and began constructing public housing directly (Radford 1996, 111–144).

The Demise of the First New Deal

In spite of the resistance of many Republicans and the overt hostility of the newly organized American Liberty League, which accused the New Deal of destroying the free market and delaying recovery, popular support for Roosevelt's policies were registered in the 1934 congressional elections, where Democrats gained an even bigger majority. What undid the First New Deal was the unworkability of some key legislation. Most important, the NRA code authorities had not succeeded in their goal of economic planning, as squabbling among business elements in each market sector as well as the massive labor unrest seemed to doom it. The Supreme Court decisions of 1935 which declared key portions of the One Hundred Days legislation unconstitutional were thus not entirely surprising or necessarily unwelcome. FDR's advisers were already working on new legislation with a new approach. The administration was moving to answer its radical critics, the so-called thunder on the left (see "Social Movements" chapter) with a new emphasis on increasing individual purchasing power and larger social-welfare programs.

The Supreme Court, dominated by the conservative "Four Horsemen"—Willis Van Devanter, James Clark McReynolds, George Sutherland, and Pierce Butler—also included two moderates, Owen Roberts and Chief Justice Charles Evans Hughes, and three liberals, Louis D. Brandeis, Harlan Fiske Stone, and Benjamin Cardozo (who replaced Oliver Wendell Holmes in 1932). The justices' problems with some early New Deal legislation came from concerns over regulation of interstate commerce, as well as the due process clauses of the Fifth and Fourteenth amendments. These clauses limited the regulatory powers of state and federal governments. In January 1935 the Court invalidated a section of the NIRA dealing with regulation of the oil industry as an improper delegation of congressional authority. In early spring, the Court declared the Railroad Retirement Act of 1934 unconstitutional, stating that creating a pension system for railroad workers lay beyond the power of Congress to regulate interstate commerce. In May, in *Schechter Poultry Company v. U.S.*, the Court invalidated the remainder of Title I of the NIRA, rejecting the administration's use of the Constitution's commerce clause to extend its regulatory powers. The case involved the Live Poultry Code Authority fining Schechter's Poultry Company for violating its code by selling uninspected and diseased chickens in its kosher practice, as well as falsifying records and violating the wage and hour provisions. It became known as the "sick chicken case." Schechter's appeal, however, was financed by the Liberty League and the Iron and Steel Institute, which together aimed to demolish the NRA. The Court's final ruling in this case turned on the definition of "interstate commerce," in which Schechter's business was not involved, as well as the unconstitutional delegation of congressional authority, in that Congress had delegated code-drafting authority not to a government agency, but to nongovernmental trade associations. The NRA code authority was now shattered. In his response, President Roosevelt chose to focus on the first charge, famously quipping that the Court had used a "horse-and-buggy" definition of interstate trade (Irons 1982, 100–107).

The Second New Deal

The term *Second New Deal* includes all of the legislation passed by the 74th Congress in 1935, but it usually refers specifically to the new social-welfare provisions that placed a safety net under all American citizens. These include the extensive public work-relief program of the Works Progress Administration (WPA), the Social Security Act, and the National Labor Relations Act (NLRA), all passed in spring and summer 1935. The thrust of the First New Deal was based on an "overproduction" theory of the causes of the Depression. In that thinking, cutting back production and planning output were the keys to recovery. The Second New Deal, broadly speaking, was based on the theory of "underconsumption." The economy could not yet revive itself because people had no money to buy the goods produced. Thus emphasis was placed on reviving the general public's purchasing power.

Work Relief

FDR's annual message in January 1935 had made it very clear that the unemployment rate was still too high. The House quickly passed the Emergency Relief Appropriation Act, with nearly $4.9 billion and few details, while the Senate drafted a number of amendments stating a preference for private over public jobs and setting the wage level below prevailing local minimums. When the law was finally enacted in April, it took months to get all the projects ready to go. The administration consolidated rural relief programs, which had been scattered in the FERA, the AAA, and the Department of Interior, and regrouped them in a new agency, the Resettlement Administration with Undersecretary of Agriculture Rexford Tugwell as administrator. The Works Progress Administration (renamed the Works Projects Administration in 1939) was created by Executive Order 7034 in May 1935, with Harry Hopkins as its administrator.

Works Progress Administration

The Works Progress Administration (WPA) replaced the FERA relief system with a much bigger, better-funded, but now wholly work-relief-based system. WPA was funded by the omnibus Emergency Relief Appropriation Act of 1935, and FDR declared that the intent was to help able-bodied workers "preserve their self-respect, their self-confidence, courage, and determination," through work, not the dole. Harry Hopkins administered this massive agency, which averaged $2.1 million on its monthly payroll from 1935 through 1941. Hopkins emphasized "useful projects" and tried to match projects to the talents and skills of WPA workers.

The Washington staff, with Aubrey Williams as Hopkins's aide, ran the program, with field representatives monitoring the projects in the localities. Though Hopkins tried to keep local politics out of WPA, his office was inundated with complaints from Republicans that they were being slighted in the disbursement of funds, and with complaints about waste and inefficiency. Nonetheless, WPA workers built or refurbished much of the U.S. infrastructure—hospitals, schools, courthouses, libraries, roads, bridges, and airports, many still in use today. Much of this construction work employed able-bodied men. A key Washington staffer, Ellen S. Woodward, headed the Women's Division and saw to it that over half a million women received WPA jobs, in such varied programs as public health, sewing, and school lunch preparation.

Unfortunately, relief and labor reforms shortchanged women. In the First New Deal, NRA wage rates had set differential wages between men's work and women's work, even for the same job. Women's Bureau head Mary Anderson argued that the actual effect of the code was to institutionalize low wage rates for women. Nonetheless, NRA wages were sufficiently above what industries were paying at the time, so women's wages generally increased. In the Second New Deal, the differential continued: male WPA workers got five dollars a day, women, three dollars. Widows with children got 30 cents an hour, while unmarried teenage boys got 50 cents an hour for similar work (Kessler-Harris 1982, 263). African Americans and other minorities were often passed over for desirable jobs for which they qualified, especially in the South.

Mural funded by the Works Progress Administration (WPA) on the Coit Tower in San Francisco reveals a humorous take on the urban scene of the 1930s. (Carey Mack Weber)

Actors, artists, writers, and musicians, including many women, were employed as part of Federal One, the WPA arts program that included the Federal Art Project, the Federal Music Project, the Federal Theatre Project, and the Federal Writers' Project. Modern and experimental arts were included, and the WPA creations embodied the zeitgeist of the era. The hundreds of murals painted on school and post-office walls revealed the talents of the many artists employed, as did the resulting immersion of an approving general public in the arts. Hallie Flanagan, Hopkins's classmate at Grinnell College, ran the theater program, which produced many plays with political themes. However, political controversy dogged it, as the Theatre Project became the target for the newly formed House Committee on Un-American Activities, which condemned the WPA for hiring Communists. Roosevelt ended the Theatre Project on June 30, 1939. One project that produced a wide array of books and pamphlets was the Federal Writers' Project, in which state committees determined what theme the writers would investigate. Teachers and historians, as well as journalists, roamed throughout their states, gathering newspaper clippings, interviewing residents, surveying historic sites, and writing state guides, some of which were published before the program's end in 1943. One spectacular addition to the historical record was the slave narratives, where WPA writers took up the task first started by African American scholars in the 1920s and interviewed thousands of former slaves in 17 states. Though that project ended in 1939, project director Benjamin Botkin's book, *Lay My Burden Down,* published in 1945, prompted the Library of Congress to microfilm its collection for greater accessibility. The interviews were neglected by historians, however, until the civil rights movement in the 1960s sparked renewed interest. Though problematic as historical records, they remain important evidence to this historical experience, as well as providing linguistic and narrative evidence of contemporary African American life in the 1930s (Berlin, Favreau, and Miller 1998, xiii–xlvii) (see "Culture of the 1930s" chapter).

Resettlement Administration

Under the Emergency Relief Appropriation Act, the Resettlement Administration (RA) was established in May 1935. The president appointed Rexford G. Tugwell, the undersecretary of agriculture, as administrator of RA. As the AAA was being reorganized, RA consolidated programs from the Department of Agriculture (USDA), AAA, and the National Resources Planning Board, as well as taking over rural relief activities from the now-discontinued FERA. RA now became agriculture's antipoverty agency, giving out rehabilitation loans which farmers used to underwrite their operations and improve their farms. The largest project it carried out in the mid-1930s was its resettlement program, with 150 projects in the lower Mississippi Valley. Many of these involved the federal government leasing government-owned land to resettled farmers, with varying levels of cooperation in the communities. Many farmers were being settled from the Dust Bowl (see "Rural Life" chapter). Many of the projects came under fire from congressional conservatives as communistic. RA also tried to get funds to assist tenants in buying farms of their own, but when the Bankhead-Jones Act was finally passed in July 1937, it was very limited. The RA was renamed the Farm Security Administration (FSA) at that time. The FSA documentary "The Plow That Broke the Plains," produced in 1937 by director Pare Lorentz to explain the origins of the Dust Bowl and government efforts to reverse the ecological disaster and resettle farmers on better land, also came under fire for allegedly insulting the Midwest farmer. One important program that assisted refugees from the Dust Bowl was building FSA camps for migratory agricultural workers in the west, as depicted in John Steinbeck's book (and later the film) *The Grapes of Wrath* (Worster 1982; Baldwin 1968).

National Labor Relations Act

Sen. Robert F. Wagner of New York, the strongest supporter of labor in the Senate, had been drafting labor legislation to overcome the obvious flaws in NIRA

Section 7(a), and had introduced his National Labor Relations Act (NLRA) in spring 1935, before the Supreme Court invalidated most of the NIRA. Roosevelt reluctantly supported Wagner's labor bill only after it had gained enough support in Congress to pass. The Wagner Act, as it came to be known, was a major statement on the part of the federal government that workers had the right to organize, and that the government had the responsibility to protect that right. The act also outlawed "unfair labor practices" on the part of employers, such as threatening or firing of workers who joined unions, company spy rings, yellow-dog contracts (which made workers pledge not to join a union as a condition of their hiring), and company unions. It set up a neutral National Labor Relations Board (NLRB) to define collective-bargaining units, to supervise secret-ballot elections by workers to choose their "collective-bargaining agent," and to certify the results. The act called for employers to "bargain in good faith" with such duly certified representatives of the workers. It could not compel the acceptance of a contract by the employer.

Sen. Robert F. Wagner (D-NY) guided so many key New Deal bills through the U.S. Senate that he was dubbed the "legislative pilot of the New Deal." (Library of Congress)

The NLRB was a reactive agency, however—workers themselves had to begin the process by gathering the signatures of half of the proper bargaining unit, at which point the NLRB would gear up to create and supervise an election. The next few years were a trial-and-error process of deciding administrative case law to build a structure for collective bargaining, often borrowing from the earlier NRA practice. Workers, by their actions, helped shape the procedures of the NLRB.

The NLRA put the weight of the federal government on the side of the weaker party, labor, and defined antagonistic industrial relations as an unhealthy economic element preventing a stable economy. It is instructive to see the language of the preamble of the bill in order to appreciate lawmakers' reasons for this decision:

> The denial by employers of the right to organize and the refusal by employers to accept the procedure of collective bargaining lead to strikes and other forms of industrial strife or unrest. . . .

> The inequality of bargaining power between employees who do not possess full freedom of association or actual liberty of contract, and employers who are organized in the corporate or other forms of ownership association substantially burdens and affects the flow of commerce, and tends to aggravate recurrent business depressions, by depressing wage rates and the purchasing power of wage earners in industry and by preventing the stabilization of competitive wage rates and working conditions within and between industries.
>
> Experience has proved that protection by law of the right of employees to organize and bargain collectively safeguards commerce from injury, impairment, or interruption, and promotes the flow of commerce by removing certain unorganized sources of industrial strife and unrest, by encouraging practices fundamental to the friendly adjustment of industrial disputes arising out of differences as to wages, hours, or other working conditions, and by restoring equality of bargaining power between employers and employees.
>
> It is hereby declared to be the policy of the United States to eliminate the causes of certain substantial obstructions to the free flow of commerce and to mitigate and eliminate these obstructions when they have occurred by encouraging the practice and procedure of collective bargaining and by protecting the exercise by workers of full freedom of association [and] self-organization. (U.S. Statutes)

These words illustrate the new Second New Deal's emphasis on expanding the purchasing power of the ordinary consumer in order to boost the economy. Thus the NLRA proposed creating a government agency to support the weaker partner in the industrial-relations sphere, the worker, in order that a strong labor movement could redistribute profits from industry and commerce more equitably through union contracts with employers. (see "The Labor Movement" chapter).

Social Security Act

Another key social-welfare legislation, the Social Security Act (SSA) of 1935, was a broadly conceived and complicated bill that provided old age pensions, mandated unemployment insurance, and gave aid to low-income families with children. After a year of study and heated debate, FDR's Committee on Economic Security, headed by economist Edwin Witte, who had been responsible for designing Wisconsin's pioneering unemployment insurance law, decided on a plan that favored social insurance rather than a government pension, based on worker contributions rather than general government revenues. Various components of this bill had all been lobbied for in the past, and its provisions were

New York City postal workers wave Social Security applications as they begin to deliver the forms in November 1936. More than 3 million forms were distributed in New York City alone. (Library of Congress)

the result of history, compromise, and good politicking. Each provision had a different constituency, a specially crafted appeal, and different funding. As President Roosevelt declared in signing the SSA on August 14, 1935,

> Today a hope of many years standing is in large part fulfilled. The civilization of the past hundred years, with its startling industrial changes, has tended more and more to make life insecure. . . . We can never insure one hundred per cent of the population against one hundred per cent of the hazards and vicissitudes of life but we have tried to frame a law which will give some measure of protection to the average citizen and his family against the loss of a job and against poverty-ridden old age. This law, too, represents a corner stone in a structure which is being built but is by no means complete—a structure intended to lessen the force of possible future depressions, . . . a law that will take care of human needs and at the same time provide for the United States an economic structure of vastly greater soundness. (Rauch 1957, 144–145)

Old-Age Pensions

The old-age pension provision had been the goal of a number of groups since the 1920s, when old-age relief bills drafted by economist Abraham Epstein (who had organized the American Association for Old Age Security in 1927) received wide support in reform circles and in such groups like the Fraternal Order of Eagles as well as some labor unions (Epstein 1931). The popularity of the Townsend movement (see "Social Movements" chapter) of the early 1930s accelerated the passage of some form of old-age pension. The SSA old-age pension would be administered by a federal agency, funded by a special tax on wages and salaries, and matched by employer contributions of the same amount, to go into a separate Social Security Trust Fund, from which benefits would be paid out to eligible retirees starting in 1942. Once a worker had paid this tax for a specified number of months over several years, the federal government would guarantee a level of benefit based on the recipient's recent annual income. Thus this pension would be seen as a political right by recipients, rather than a dole, insulating it from the political criticism targeted at other welfare programs. Funded by what economists today label a regressive tax system, it favored the upper-income wage-earner; a flat tax is laid on all workers regardless of income level, and that level is capped off at a set amount, with income above that level not subject to taxing. Several key flaws and gaps were the result of successful lobbying by powerful economic groups. For one, domestic servants, agricultural workers, educational, charitable, and hospital workers, and government workers were not eligible to participate due to strong opposition from those employers. This eliminated many women, African Americans, and other minority workers who were concentrated in these jobs. Moreover, the system depended on having had a qualifying job for a certain number of months, something that due to Depression conditions was difficult to achieve. Finally, it was envisioned to be only one part of an old-age retirement plan and was meant to be combined with individual savings and an employer's pension to reach a standard of living comparable to one's working days. An important additional program in Title I was needs-based Old-Age Assistance programs, where the federal government would provide funds to states, and states were mandated to construct a system for welfare to those already old or with too low an income to qualify for Old-Age Insurance. The state systems varied.

Unemployment Insurance

The second important provision of SSA was unemployment insurance, whose rules were laid out in the federal legislation but whose operation was put in the hands of the states. Each state was responsible for establishing an Unemployment Fund financed by taxes laid on every employer over a certain minimum size. Each state had to create an Unemployment Fund agency to oversee the operations of the system and impose a variable tax rate on each employer based on the size of its workforce as well as its record of labor-force hirings and layoffs. This provision, which penalized those companies who engaged in seasonal hiring and firing or had large labor turnover for other reasons, was designed to encourage employers to reform their hiring practices and to regularize employment. The old system, which put the social costs of their employment (or unemployment) practices on state and local government and private charities, had proved disastrous after 1929. The plan was based in the individual states to overcome criticisms that the federal government was controlling too much of the social-insurance system.

Public Assistance

The final program in SSA was the public assistance program, Aid to Dependent Children, based on the precedent already set in most states with "mothers' pensions" of the Progressive Era and 1920s (Skocpol 1992; Lubove 1968). This emphasis on providing relief for single, mostly widowed, mothers and their children was the result of "maternalist" reformers from earlier decades who wished to support low-income women who had no male breadwinner. But reformers' attempt to mandate uniform standards and adequate benefits was defeated in Congress, and the programs were placed in the hands in individual state governments. In this needs-based relief system, racial discrimination and inadequate funds marked this program from the very start and gave "welfare" a stigma that would prove difficult to overcome in succeeding decades.

Criticism and Revision of the Social Security Act

Controversy over SSA began almost as soon as it was passed, with critics charging that since the plan was to build the old-age pension fund with no payments going out until 1942, it was draining wages from workers' pockets and the economy. Moreover, the Old-Age Assistance program was growing rapidly and draining funds from federal coffers. So Congress amended the SSA in 1939 by transforming it in fundamental ways. First, it changed from an individual retirement plan to a family support system by adding spousal and survivor benefits, making the benefit more favorable to low-income workers in that lower-income workers received a slightly higher benefit, relative to their smaller contribution, than more highly paid employees, and moving the payout date to start in 1940. The most important shift was to adopt a "pay-as-you-go" system, where worker contributions were not held in reserve for their own retirement but were used to finance benefits for current retirees. One overlooked dimension of this move to a family-support system was that it reinforced traditional gender roles by assuming that the male breadwinners were the income providers and wives were dependent on their husbands. Thus spousal benefits were made available to wives and not to husbands (Kessler-Harris 1995).

The Workers Unemployment and Social Insurance Act (aka the Lundeen Bill)

To measure how the Social Security Act was constructed and approved, it is useful to compare it to another bill that vied with it in 1934 and 1935. Sen. Ernest Lundeen, Farmer-Labor Party of Minnesota, introduced the Workers Unemployment and Social Insurance Act in February 1934. Drafted by Mary van Kleeck, director of industrial studies at the Russell Sage Foundation, the bill owed its genesis to an AFL Trade Union Committee for Unemployment Insurance and Relief. That committee, originally made up of rank-and-file activists from 18 union locals in New York City but now national in scope, had drafted such a bill to present to the national AFL convention in 1933 for endorsement and was rebuffed. At its peak in early 1935, the committee had collected endorsements from 3,000 locals, five international unions, six state federations, and 33 central labor councils. The AFL's president, William Green, embroiled in his fight with industrial unionists (see "The Labor Movement" chapter), dismissed the bill as communist-inspired. Nonetheless, after printing the contents of the Lundeen bill, the Townsend bill, and the Wagner-Lewis (SSA) bill, a poll of readers of the *New York Post* taken in April 1935 showed that the vast majority preferred the Lundeen bill.

What differentiated the Lundeen bill from the SSA was the Lundeen bill's insistence that all categories of the needy be treated the same. Van Kleeck explained that the vagary of the modern industrial system "suggests the necessity for *social* insurance as opposed to *individual* insurance, and it makes necessary the *integration* of insurance against 'unemployment' . . . whether the cause of unemployment be located . . . in a general industrial depression; or whether it be due to the recognized general hazards to security, namely, industrial accidents, sickness, maternity, and old age. . . . *Social insurance should not be split into categories* [emphasis in original]" (Casebeer 1992, 250). Moreover, the plan would be funded out of general tax revenues, not individuals' paychecks. Recent debates over welfare and Social Security have made similar criticisms of the way the relief system has been structured (Skocpol 1988).

Why No Health Insurance?

One major hole in this legislation was health insurance. New Dealers, fearing that the overwhelming disapproval of the American Medical Association (AMA) and state medical societies would scuttle the entire bill, went forward with the SSA without the inclusion of health insurance. Some health care was already being provided by various relief programs of the New Deal; FERA and WPA funded some public health services. The AMA had organized its most influential members to oppose government involvement in the health-care field. Some dissent to this position came in 1936–1937 from a group of liberal academic physicians who organized the Committee of Physicians for the Improvement of Medicine. Their 1937 "Principles and Proposals," which were signed by over 400 doctors, declared that health was a "direct concern of the government" and called for a national health policy, something short of a call for a compulsory health insurance program (Starr 1982, 274). Labor and community groups would continue to lobby for the rest of the decade for the inclusion of health insurance under the rubric of "social security" (Berkowitz 1991; Gordon 1994b; Kessler-Harris 2001; Klein 2003, 116–161; Quadagno 1988; Rubinow 1934; Witte 1963).

"Little New Deals" in the States

A number of states with progressive governors and legislatures proceeded to pass what came to be called "Little New Deals" to augment the programs emanating from Washington, D.C., or simply to quell violence in their respective states. Governors such as Floyd B. Olson (Farmer-Labor Party) of Minnesota, Philip La Follette (Progressive Party) in Wisconsin, Frank Murphy in Michigan and George H. Earle III of Pennsylvania (both Democrats) promoted state legislation to provide greater tax equity, farm-debt moratoria, small business protections, new welfare benefits like public health services, and prohibitions on employer unfair labor practices. In Pennsylvania, for example, Earle, a former Republican and now a strong supporter of FDR, won election in 1934 and became the first Democratic governor in Pennsylvania in 40 years. With his running mate, Thomas Kennedy, a long-time officer of the UMWA, Earle created a firm alliance between the Democratic Party and organized labor. Earle campaigned hard for FDR and the state Democratic ticket in 1936, and in the FDR landslide that resulted the Pennsylvania state legislature was now in Democratic hands. One of Earle's first acts was to call a series of public meetings in the bootleg coalfields (see "The Labor Movement" chapter), and he appointed the Pennsylvania Anthracite Coal Industry Commission to document conditions and make recommendations for state action. He was generally sympathetic to bootleg coal miners (Dublin and Licht 2005, 79–80).

The biggest "Little New Deal" was in New York State, where Franklin Roosevelt had paved the way during his four years as governor. Herbert Lehman, FDR's lieutenant governor from 1928 to 1932, was elected governor in 1932 and held that position until 1942. New York enacted unemployment insurance and a minimum wage law before the federal government did, and expanded on federal welfare programs for the residents of the state. Lehman, himself from a wealthy family as son of a founder of the investment firm Lehman Brothers, impressed the *New York Times* in 1938; it described him as a "modest, hard-working and undramatic governor . . . [who created] a labor and social program transcending any ever executed in America" (Ingalls 1975; Patterson 1969).

Urban Policy

The New Deal marked a major transformation in federal-city relations, as "the Hundred Days" of Franklin D. Roosevelt's first term attempted to intervene in the workings of a national economy gone awry. The New Deal set a precedent for the federal government's intervention in local affairs. General issues for cities were the level of home rule (or cities' ability to control the federal programs that were available to them) and the persistent public-good versus private-marketplace tensions that accompanied the entire New Deal. The New Deal did not have a distinct urban policy, but many of its programs touched the cities at critical points. It was the plight of the major cities that placed urban issues high on the 1933 congressional agenda. The first item was unemployment relief, since the cities were responsible for the well-being of their inhabitants and the three long years of the Depression had led to the near-bankruptcy of major cities. Moreover, dependent as they were on local property taxes to fund their activities, cities faced a decline in assessed valuation of properties and a rising tax delinquency rate from property owners unable to pay their taxes. Tax revolts, often organized by local real estate interests, further threatened local government financing, while state legislators were slow to provide funds. Chambers of commerce and other business groups lobbied state governments with old Progressive Era accusations about city "machines" and "bosses," and painted the urban budget crises of the early Depression as a continuation of municipal corruption and spending profligacy. Business organizations were focused on reducing their own taxes, and this business emphasis stiffened many state governments' resolve against cities. But cities were places with volatile populations, and the growing demonstrations by the unemployed put mayors, not governors or congresspeople, on the front lines of unrest.

The U.S. Conference of Mayors (USCM) was initiated in early 1933 by Detroit mayor Frank Murphy to obtain needed operating funds for relief. As a result, the Federal Emergency Relief Administration (FERA) made block grants to the states, which then distributed funds locally. This raised municipal fears of states' prorural biases in the disbursement of FERA funds, where politicking might favor one area over another. Indeed, Roosevelt had early made his antiurban bias clear by encouraging shifts in population from urban to rural areas through the Resettlement Administration's idea of Greenbelt Towns. Such concerns were later found to be baseless, as urban areas received a fair share of funds, though states could bypass a local elected government in setting up the local FERA committee. In early 1934 the federal government was supplying 73.9 percent of all urban relief funds (Ridley and Nolting 1935, 2).

Congress then established the Civil Works Administration (CWA), which funded work-relief jobs for a short time. Big-city mayors' calls for public works projects were met by PWA grants and loans (some $4.5 billion) to build schools, water and sewage plants, bridges, and the like. Finally, the federal Works Progress Administration (WPA), beginning in 1935, provided a large amount of work-relief dollars directly to municipalities. However successful the WPA projects were ($11 billion), they provided jobs for only an estimated one-third of the unemployed. The significant change was the increase in federal grants to subfederal governments, which by the end of the 1930s had leveled off at some $1 billion annually, five times what it had been at the beginning of the decade (Kleinberg 1995, 97).

Another key point where federal action benefited urban areas was in housing policy. With housing construction at a standstill in the early 1930s, the resulting unemployment in the building trades called out for remedy. As discussed above, housing received significant attention in the early New Deal. The National Housing Act of 1934 established the FHA to promote the ideal of private single-family home ownership through increases in the national housing stock. This, along with the Home Owners Loan Corporation, meant help for middle-income families. HOLC redlining, however, placed many urban neighborhoods in undesirable categories and led to their decline.

Affordable housing had long been a concern of municipalities. Social reformers' push for large public-housing projects met resistance in this atmosphere of private real estate imperatives. Public-housing advocates and architects created a coalition with representatives of the AFL state councils in the Northeast to lobby for an expanded public housing program. When Sen. Robert Wagner of New York introduced a public housing bill into Congress in spring 1935, couched in terms of slum clearance and economic recovery as well as providing housing for the poor, it met serious resistance from commercial and financial interests. Finally, when a newly revised Housing Act was introduced in 1937, it included labor's wish for moderate-priced housing assistance with a vision of group sponsorship and control of housing developments. When the bill was finally passed, these more innovative cooperative provisions and moderate-price focus had been stripped away and the bill funded housing only for the poor and explicitly tied projects to slum clearance. The funding levels of the new U.S. Housing Authority (USHA) mandated an even lower physical standard of housing than had been provided

U.S. Housing Authority poster promotes better housing as a solution for high rates of infant mortality in the slums, by showing a blueprint of new housing next to existing tenement buildings over which stands the figure of Death, 1936. (Library of Congress)

Greenbelt Towns

An example of an antiurban impulse in the New Deal was the creation of the Greenbelt Towns program, whose goal was to build entire communities outside of some major cities. This early planned suburbanization aimed at taking excess population out of cities, providing the unemployed with jobs building the towns, and providing housing for low- and moderate-income families. It was established within Rexford Tugwell's Resettlement Administration (RA). The RA's Suburban Division built three towns: Greenbelt, Maryland (outside of Washington, D.C.); Greendale, Wisconsin (outside of Milwaukee); and Greenhills, Ohio (outside Cincinnati). Tugwell idealized cooperatives and made economic and social cooperatives a central feature of each town. Planners used Clarence Perry's concept of the neighborhood unit, which centered around a small shopping district, a park, and an elementary school that also served as a community center, with a street design that limited auto traffic in its interior. Everything was in walking distance. Surrounding each town was a greenbelt that would be used for parks or farming. All three towns were completed by 1938. The program and Tugwell attracted negative criticism from anti–New Deal congressmen and from the business community which called it communistic. Tugwell, who had been nicknamed "Rex the Red" for his emphasis on economic planning, was controversial and was forced to resign in 1936 and the RA was dismantled; the Farm Security Administration finished building the towns (Knepper 2001).

through PWA. Thus New Deal housing policy helped develop a "two-tiered" housing market: the top tier promoted private home ownership through institutional support for financial markets; the bottom tier promoted public housing for the poor that was miserly and unattractive (Radford 1996, 194–198).

The New Deal did not attempt to remake the cities, either structurally or financially. However, in focusing on cities as separate entities, the New Deal succeeded in loosening control of cities by state governments. At the same time, by encouraging states and cities to enact local administrative authorities, such as the PWA authorities or housing authorities, the New Deal fostered a new intergovernmental arrangement (federal-state-local) that structured all future programs of the twentieth century.

Political Realignment—the 1936 Election

The 1936 election crystallized the New Deal Coalition. With the First New Deal largely rejected by the business community as well as the Supreme Court, and with the "thunder on the left" of quasi-populist movements (see "Social Movements" chapter), FDR chose to play up the class conflict that now defined the Democrats from the Republican Party. The economy had rebounded and the federal government was providing some sort of assistance to approximately 35 percent of the population. Though the Supreme Court still had to rule on the constitutionality of Second New Deal legislation, the New Deal seemed to be working.

FDR started the campaign year of 1936 with a strongly worded acceptance speech at the Democratic convention in Philadelphia in June 1936. With an opening warning that "clouds of suspicion, tides of ill will and intolerance gather in many places [in the world]," he went on to compare the events of Philadelphia in 1776 to "reaffirm the faith of our fathers" to the situation in 1936. He once again charged "economic royalists" with threatening the freedoms that the Minute Men of 1776 fought to achieve.

> These economic royalists complain that we seek to overthrow the institutions of America. What they really complain of is that we seek to take away their power. Our allegiance to American institutions requires the overthrow of this kind of power. . . .
>
> Governments do err— . . . Better the occasional faults of a government that lives in a spirit of charity than the consistent omissions of a government frozen in the ice of its own indifference.
>
> There is a mysterious cycle in human events. To some generations much is given. Of other generations much is expected. This generation of American has a rendezvous with destiny. (Rauch 1957, 148–152)

His campaign theme was "Four Years Ago and Now" (Leuchtenburg 1963, 193).

The Republican nominee, Alfred "Alf" M. Landon, the governor of Kansas, was mild-mannered and had worked well enough with the first Roosevelt administration to receive more federal funds for his state than other midwestern states received. His moderate campaign course, however, was overwhelmed by the fierce attacks on Roosevelt from conservative Republicans and business leaders in the American Liberty League. What especially drove FDR to fury were the businesses who stuffed anti–New Deal literature in their workers' pay packets, claiming, for example, that the new Social Security system would require them to wear stainless-steel identification dogtags around their necks and that they would never see their Social Security taxes paid back to them. FDR's fall campaign tour took him around the industrial Northeast, where he ended it with a massive rally at Madison Square Garden in New York City on October 31, 1936. There he unleashed his final accusations against the business leaders who opposed him, those beneficiaries of "business and financial monopoly, speculation, reckless banking, class antagonism, war profiteering." He ended this point with the line: "Never before in all our history have these forces been so united against one candidate as they stand today. They are unanimous in their hate for me—and I welcome their hatred" (Kennedy 1999, 281–282). FDR was concerned with the appeal of so-called populists like the Union Party, the party hastily put together by Father Charles Coughlin, the Townsendites, and the successor to Huey Long's Share-the-Wealth clubs, Gerald L. K. Smith, who were running North Dakota congressman William Lemke for president. (see "Social Movements" chapter.)

Labor's Non-Partisan League

The CIO organized Labor's Non-Partisan League (LNPL) to campaign for FDR. LNPL had no direct affiliation with the Democratic Party. With its state companion the American Labor Party (ALP) in New York, LNPL drew together a much more formidable labor base than the rather ineffective Labor Division of the Democratic Party, which was headed by the Teamsters leader Daniel J. Tobin of the AFL. The antagonism between the AFL and CIO leaders was nearing a breaking point. Moreover, LNPL was designed to "channel rebellious sentiments into the safe harbor of New Deal democracy," bringing into mainstream politics the thousands of voters who had previously supported Socialist or Communist candidates and could not bring themselves to support the Democratic Party fully (Fraser 1991, 362–369). Labor donated more than $800,000 to Roosevelt's campaign, nearly 16 percent of the total, with the largest contributions coming from the UMWA, the International Ladies Garment Workers (ILGWU), and the Amalgamated Clothing Workers (Webber 2000, 113–120). Of course, in comparison, the du Pont family alone donated $385,000 to the Republican Party in 1936, after having supported Democrats in 1928 and 1932 (Burk 1990, 244).

The election results were stunning: with a high turnout of voters (61 percent), Roosevelt received 60.8 percent of the vote (27,752,869 votes) compared to Landon's 16,674,665. FDR received the Electoral College votes of all states except Maine and Vermont (523 to 8). Moreover, congressional elections returned the same wildly lopsided results, with Democrats now firmly in control of both houses. The Roosevelt vote of 1936 has been exhaustively analyzed: FDR won 76 percent of the lower-income voters, 80 percent of union members, 84 percent of northern African Americans, between 70 and 81 percent of Catholics, and 86 percent of the Jewish vote. He won 104 of the cities with over 100,000 population, compared to 2 for Landon. Political scientists called this a "critical realignment" election, in that it cemented the loyalties of particular socioeconomic, ethnic, and regional groups to one particular party, with loyalties that carried on for a generation. Debate continued over whether these new Democratic voters were converted Republicans or were newly mobilized first-time voters.

Thus, on January 20, 1937, FDR was riding high when he made his inaugural speech, noting that "I see one-third of a nation ill-housed, ill-clad, ill-nourished," and pledged to continue the Second New Deal. "The test of our progress is not whether we add more to the abundance of those who have too much; it is whether we provide enough for those who have too little" (Kennedy 1999, 287). This New Deal ascendancy would be short-lived, however.

New Deal Political Stalemate

The political misstep that FDR took with his so-called Court-Packing Scheme in 1937 had an effect on political opinion at the time, but only the downturn in the economy in late 1937 rippled the political waters so that the 1938 midterm election returned a more conservative Congress to Washington. The Court proposal that Roosevelt introduced in February 1937, without laying any political groundwork, was to add one new justice to the Court for every current justice over the age of 70 who declined to retire. The average age of the current Supreme Court justices was 71. In addition, he asked for authorization to name up to 44 more justices to the lower courts, ostensibly to clear up crowded dockets. The proposal met with fierce opposition in Congress, with conservatives accusing FDR of trying to "pack" the courts with liberals. It was a fact that Roosevelt was at that time the only president since Andrew Johnson who had *not* made an appointment to the Supreme Court, and he had been frustrated by the unfavorable rulings on his One Hundred Days of legislation. He characterized the Court as filled with "aged or infirm judges" whose thinking he described: "Little by little, new facts become blurred through old glasses fitted, as it were, for the needs of another generation, older men, assuming that the scene is the same as it was in the past, cease to explore or inquire into the present or the future" (Kennedy 1999, 326).

A political cartoon satirizes the court-packing plan proposed by President Franklin D. Roosevelt in 1937. Roosevelt's plan represented an attempt to influence Supreme Court decisions related to his New Deal legislation. (Bettmann/Corbis)

The president's timing could not have been worse, as public opinion was already being swayed negatively by the sit-down strikes occurring in Michigan (see "The Labor Movement" chapter) and by his proposed Executive Reorganization Act. Accusations of dictatorship were being heard. The president's advisers, Tom Corcoran and Ben Cohen, who had prepared the legislation along with the attorney general, had to

Fair Labor Standards Act

The last piece of New Deal legislation was the Fair Labor Standards Act (FLSA), which FDR signed into law on June 25, 1938. It was a compromise bill and fell short of the goal of many New Dealers who wanted to guarantee a "living wage." New Deal lawyers Tom Corcoran and Ben Cohen had prepared the original version, which was introduced in May 1937 by Sen. Hugo Black and Congressman William Connery. The Black-Connery bill called for fixing a national minimum wage and a maximum work-week for workers engaged in interstate commerce, though no specific numbers were attached to the bill. It also provided for a five-person Labor Standards Board, which could set higher wages and lower hours requirements for individual industries that were judged to have "inadequate" collective bargaining. It also included a ban on child labor. For 14 months, Congress argued over this bill, as business leaders were opposed, and the bill failed to win the support of the AFL, which returned to its old fear of government involvement in the setting of wages. When the FLSA finally emerged from committee, it had an initial minimum wage of 25 cents, to go up to 40 cents an hour in seven years. It also set an initial work-week at 44 hours, with a reduction to 40 in three years; overtime work would be paid at time-and-a-half. Child labor was proscribed. Agricultural labor, domestic workers, and supervisory jobs were exempt. The Labor Standards Board was scrapped, and jurisdiction for enforcement was placed in the Department of Labor. While FLSA was a path-breaking law in that it raised the wages for some 300,000 workers while reducing hours for an estimated one million, its standards were so low that a full-time worker receiving these standards could still be in poverty (Paulsen 1996). By continuing the exclusion of agricultural workers and domestic workers, the law failed to provide benefits to many minority and women workers. The surge of Republican victories in the 1938 midterm elections meant that the New Deal legislative plans came to an end.

scramble for legal support for the plan, and got the newly formed National Lawyers Guild as well as Yale Law School dean Charles Clark and Henry Edgerton of Cornell to testify (Emerson and Emerson 1991, 83–84). Although this legislation did not pass, Roosevelt got his message across, and soon the Supreme Court was ruling favorably on the constitutionality of Second New Deal legislation, or at least that was what pundits were saying. But legal historian Peter Irons notes that the justices, particularly Justice Owen Roberts who deserted the conservative bloc, had heeded the 1936 election returns and were already changing their minds. In their vote on *West Coast Hotel v. Parrish* in December 1936, Roberts voted to uphold Washington State's minimum wage law for women and thus to demolish the "freedom of contract" argument (Irons 1982, 272–289). Positive rulings on the National Labor Relations Act and the Social Security Act followed in the spring of 1937.

It was the stumbling of the economy in late 1937 and 1938 that caused public doubts. Farm prices and industrial production fell and unemployment was increasing again. Robert Jackson of the Justice Department cried foul play and accused the business sector of a "strike of capital." FDR called Congress back into special session to take up more New Deal programmatic legislation, but he had not clearly decided what countercyclical economic measures to take. By 1939, he would be calling for deficit spending again, but this time military preparation for a future European war would be at the top of his agenda.

The Anti–New Dealers

Organized opposition to the New Deal began in August 1934 when Jouett Shouse, who had been appointed executive chairman of the Democratic National Committee by Chairman John J. Raskob in 1929, announced the establishment of the American Liberty League. Shouse declared that the League would "defend and uphold the Constitution . . . teach the necessity of respect for the rights of persons and property as fundamental to every successful form of government . . . to foster the right to work, earn, save and acquire property, and to preserve the ownership and lawful use of property when acquired" (Wolfskill 1962, 21–22). He declared that it would not be hostile to the administration or to Roosevelt, but would lobby in Congress. It had its genesis in an informal discussion in March of that year after a du Pont Corporation board meeting, at which Raskob was present. Raskob was also on the board of General Motors. Subsequent conversations led these corporate men to form an organization to combat what they perceived as dangerous trends in the New Deal. In particular, southern business leaders had complained about high CCC and CWA wages that drew off African American labor from the harvest and other tasks. Moreover, the 1934 national strike wave was troublesome (see "The Labor Movement" chapter). Careful to appear bipartisan, the board of directors of the League were two prominent Democrats, John W. Davis and Al Smith; two Republicans, James J. Wadsworth Jr. and Nathan Miller of U.S. Steel; and Irénée du Pont, who had been a Republican but had supported Smith in 1928 and Roosevelt in 1932. Shouse was asked to be president of the League. Raskob and Smith had the leadership of the Democratic Party taken from them at the 1932 convention by Roosevelt, but more than this bound the two men. In early 1919 they had constructed a lobbying group, the Association Against the Prohibition Amendment (AAPA). Though they had often proclaimed a "wet" perspective, their main objection was that the Eighteenth Amendment was an unconstitutional intrusion of the federal government into state affairs. Thus they were traditional conservatives. Historian George Wolfskill also noted that they invariably added an argument about income taxes, which the AAPA carefully calculated could be lowered if the beer tax were reinstated along with the beer (Wolfskill 1962, 37–55).

President Roosevelt, asked to comment on the new Liberty League at his press conference on August 24, 1934, was at his rhetorical best when he noted:

> An organization that only advocates two or three out of the Ten Commandments, may be a perfectly good organization in the sense that you can't object to the two or three of the Ten Commandments, but that it would have certain shortcomings in having failed to advocate the other seven or eight Commandments. . . . Teach[ing] the necessity of respect for the rights of persons and property . . . and that government should encourage enterprise . . . [leaves many other things out]. There is no mention made here in these two things about the concern of the community, in other words the Government, to try to make it possible for people who are willing to work, to find work to do. For people who want to keep themselves from starvation, keep a roof over their heads, lead decent lives, have proper educational standards, those are the concerns of government . . . [as well as] the protection of the life and liberty of the individual against elements in the community that seek to enrich or advance themselves at the expense of their fellow-citizens. They have just as much right to protection by government as anybody else. (Buhite and Levy 1992, 127–128)

Roosevelt's secretary of the Interior, Harold Ickes, observed that the establishment of the League would draw the political lines between right and left more sharply than ever before. He was correct. The American Liberty League's approach to the New Deal was argued along constitutional lines similar to the approach to the Prohibition Amendment. It failed to gather a large public following, but it did not lack funds from its millionaire directors. During its six years of existence it spent nearly $1.2 million, with over half a million spent on the 1936 election to defeat Roosevelt (Wolfskill 1962, 63–64). The du Pont family was the largest contributor (Burk 1990).

The American Liberty League's key activities from 1934 through 1936 were to issue a series of pamphlets (135 in total), often based on speeches and radio addresses by key directors on key issues of New Deal legislation, and to distribute the five reports of its Lawyers' Committee on the constitutionality of the National Labor Relations Act, the Bituminous Coal Conservation Act, the Potato Control Act of 1935, the Social Security Act, and the Agricultural Adjustment Act. After Democratic victories in the 1934 midterm elections, the Liberty League launched "the most intense and concentrated campaign to propagate conservative political and economic thought. . . . To a philosophy that was at once a combination of Social Darwinism, laissez-faire economics, Old Testament apocalypse, and Constitution and ancestor worship, the Liberty Leaguers now often added a savage hatred of the man who had come to symbolize their torment and frustration" (Wolfskill 1962, 102). The New Deal was increasingly characterized as a Marxist conspiracy, and FDR was labeled a Communist as well as a megalomaniac. The 1936 campaign season resonated with Al Smith's anti–

Historians' Debate: Did the New Deal Solve the Great Depression?

The simple answer is *no.* The Great Depression was not overcome until government spending for war preparations in 1940 and then World War II itself brought the national economy out of its doldrums. But beyond this simple observation, there are a myriad of debates and questions. Like the debates over the causes of the Great Depression (see "Experiences of the Early Depression" chapter), answers to parts of this question are tied to the economic theories that analysts hold.

For example, the balanced-budget perspective of Treasury Secretary Henry Morganthau Jr., who feared inflationary pressures from the modest recovery of late 1936 and early 1937, persuaded FDR to cut back on federal expenditures in late 1937 to make federal bonds more attractive to investors and to have the Federal Reserve raise reserve requirements for member banks, thus reducing the funds banks could use for loans. This choked the fragile recovery, and FDR quickly reversed himself in early 1938 to resume the fiscal spending policy that would soon become known as Keynesianism. This would seem proof that such federal deficit spending was a crucial part of the recovery that was based on the Second New Deal's underconsumption theory. Roosevelt's advisers even accused big business of a "strike by capital" to undermine the New Deal in summer 1937, an accusation made plausible by the Liberty League's rhetoric at that time. However, historian Gary Dean Best has made the contrary argument that FDR's New Deal, by ignoring the needs of business, stifled the recovery and continued to do so until the 1938 congressional elections, which returned many more Republicans to Congress and reduced federal spending (Best 1991). This argument, however, ignores the ways in which many business sectors depended on government intervention to regulate the economy, a perspective that predated the 1930s. A less condemnatory, yet critical, perspective on the New Deal and its tendency toward increased federal intervention and welfare-state building is Paul Conkin's *The New Deal,* first published in 1967 and in its third edition in 1992 (Conkin 1967). In contrast, Colin Gordon's *New Deals* (Gordon 1994a) argues that the shape of the New Deal, with its many policy limitations and contradictions, was indeed a product of business demands, but one that business was ambivalent in supporting, thus leading to the political backlash of the 1938 elections.

For our purposes, the ever-expanding role of the federal government in economic regulation and in supporting a basic standard of living for the average American family is key to understanding the social history of the decade.

New Deal speech of January 25, 1936, delivered to a prominent gathering of Liberty League supporters and also broadcast on radio. The League was sorely disappointed by the landslide victory for Roosevelt in 1936.

At this point, Liberty Leaguers blended with other conservative congressmen in general opposition to the New Deal. That congressional bloc represented white, rural traditional constituencies, and consisted of Republicans allied with southern Democrats who disapproved of the urban, ethnic, and pro-labor bent of their party under Roosevelt. Senators Carter Glass and Harry Byrd (D-VA) were key opponents, with Glass voting against the Roosevelt administration a record 81 percent of the time, according to historian James T. Patterson (Patterson 1967, 348). In the "Conservative Manifesto" of December 1937, mostly written by North Carolina Democrat Josiah Bailey, the anti–New Deal bloc attacked sit-down strikes, endorsed states' rights and private property rights, and demanded lower taxes and a balanced budget. The only pieces of New Deal legislation that were passed were the Wagner-Steagall National Housing Act of 1937 and the Fair Labor Standards Act of 1938 (see above). The Wagner-Costigan antilynching bill was filibustered by southern Democratic senators. When FDR tried to intervene in state party politics to purge conservative Democrats from Congress, he raised the ire of local party leaders, and in the 1938 election those conservative southern Democrats returned to Congress along with new Republicans from other areas. At this point, conservative congressman Martin Dies of Texas led a new House Committee on Un-American Activities (commonly abbreviated HUAC) to investigate alleged Communist infiltration of New Deal programs and the labor movement. HUAC proceeded in 1938 and 1939 to investigate the American League for Peace and Democracy, the American Youth Congress, the National Maritime Union, and the League of Women Shoppers, among others (Ottanelli 1991, 205). Congress also passed the Hatch Act, prohibiting federal employees, including relief workers, from participating in political campaigns. Finally, with war already begun in Europe, Congress passed the Smith Act in 1940, making it a crime to advocate the overthrow of the U.S. government. The postwar Red Scare was being shaped.

The Contours of Popular Politics

One thing that set electoral politics in the 1930s apart from earlier decades was the high level of citizen involvement and action. New parties were born, new coalitions were forged, and a new sense of engagement with government animated many Americans. Though old concerns about government intrusion still could be heard, especially in business circles, the average citizen ended the decade with a vast appreciation for what the federal government, embodied by Franklin D. Roosevelt, could do on behalf of the people.

The "New Deal Coalition"

Political analysts at the time pointed out that the electorate was growing, and that those new voters were flocking to the Democratic Party. The party attracted

Woman wearing a Roosevelt campaign button standing before a banner, "Board of elections meets here," 1935. (Louise Rosskam/Library of Congress)

the allegiance of those who benefited from the New Deal. But it was more than that. Writing in 1951, political scientist Samuel Lubell pointed out "a little matter of birth rates," that the children of the 13 million immigrants settled in the United States before World War I had reached adulthood just as the Depression came crashing down on them. Combined with the steady influx of Americans from the countryside, over 6.5 million, to the cities in the decade of the 1920s, the "revolt of the city" seemed an obvious political event (Lubell 1965, 43–68). The electoral change had begun with the 1928 presidential election, when Al Smith grabbed the new-ethnic vote. But it was the Great Depression and the New Deal that cemented the loyalties of these urban, ethnic voters. The Democratic Party welcomed these new ethnic voters, moving well beyond its Irish base on the local and state levels. In addition, organized labor was now an important participant in electoral politics, especially the CIO which broke with old AFL voluntarism to champion FDR. John L. Lewis set up Labor's Non-Partisan

Table 2.1. Electoral and Popular Votes Cast for President, 1932–1940, by Party

			Votes Cast	
Year	*Candidate*	*Political Party*	*Electoral*	*Popular*
1932	Franklin D. Roosevelt	Democrat	472	22,809,638
	Herbert C. Hoover	Republican	59	15,758,901
	Norman Thomas	Socialist	-	881,951
	William Z. Foster	Communist	-	102,785
	William D. Upshaw	Prohibition	-	81,275
	Verne L. Reynolds	Socialist Labor	-	33,276
	William H. Harvey	Liberty	-	53,425
1936	Franklin D. Roosevelt	Democrat	523	27,752,869
	Alfred M. Landon	Republican	8	16,674,665
	William Lemke	Union	-	882,470
	Norman Thomas	Socialist	-	187,720
	Earl Browder	Communist	-	80,159
	D. Leigh Colvin	Prohibition	-	37,847
	John W. Aiken	Socialist Labor	-	12,777
1940	Franklin D. Roosevelt	Democrat	449	27,307,819
	Wendell Willkie	Republican	82	22,321,018
	Norman Thomas	Socialist	-	99,557
	Roger Q. Babson	Prohibition	-	57,812
	Earl Browder	Communist	-	46,251
	John W. Aiken	Socialist Labor	-	14,892

Source: U.S. Bureau of the Census, *Historical Statistics of the United States, Colonial Times to 1970* (GPO, 1975), Series Y.

League (LNPL)—though it was hardly "nonpartisan"—to rally voters for New Deal candidates at all electoral levels during the 1936 election, but specifically promoting the re-election of FDR. The Democratic Party Women's Division mobilized tens of thousands of women at the grassroots who supported what the New Deal had done locally. A broad group of middle-class voters also supported the New Deal, since they too had benefited from New Deal programs. The unemployed were an important voter bloc for the Democratic Party. An early Gallup poll reported that 84 percent of those on relief voted the Democratic ticket in 1936. This electoral coalition would continue to support the Democratic Party for decades.

The African American community became a solid part of the New Deal Coalition. Robert L. Vann, the African American leader and editor of the influential *Pittsburgh Courier*, had urged his community to abandon the Republican Party and vote Democratic in 1932, famously saying, "I see millions of Negroes turning the pictures of Abraham Lincoln to the wall" (Weiss 1983, 28). That did not happen in 1932, but it became the reality in 1936 and after. According to George Gallup, 76 percent of northern African Americans voted for FDR in 1936 with large majorities in Harlem (80 percent, a 20 percent increase over 1932) and other major cities. Even in Chicago, where the Republican machine had long nurtured the African American vote, FDR captured 49 percent (up from 23 percent in 1932). This was the largest switch of any voting bloc in the 1930s. After the election, *The Crisis* observed that African Americans voted "for Roosevelt *in spite of* the Democratic Party . . . [because of] a feeling that Mr. Roosevelt represented a kind of philosophy of government which will mean much to their race" (Sitkoff 1978, 95–97). Of course, in the South, few African Americans could vote, even though the Black Cabinet (see "Social Movements" chapter) denounced the white primary and the poll tax. The National Association for the Advancement of Colored People (NAACP), along with the United Mine Workers, led a voter-registration drive in Birmingham, Alabama, in 1938 and 1939, with minor results.

Table 2.2. Voter Participation in Presidential Elections, 1924–1940

Year	*Percentage of Eligible Voters*
1924	48.9
1928	56.9
1932	56.9
1936	61.0
1940	62.5

Source: U.S. Bureau of the Census, *Historical Statistics of the United States, Colonial Times to 1970* (GPO, 1975), Series Y.

The contradiction in the New Deal Coalition was that the Democratic Party nationally still depended on the "Solid South," those white southern voters who had dominated the party for so long, and whose senators and congressmen had the seniority to control the major committees in Congress for the New Deal era. It was this political reality that FDR considered when he declined to challenge the Jim Crow laws and lynching practices of the southern states, as some of his party wanted him to do (see "Social Movements" chapter). This internal schism weakened the New Deal coalition even as it was being formed, and would continue to do so for decades.

Electoral Alternatives

In 1936, for those who felt the Republican and Democratic parties were too compromised by the failed capitalist system, there were parties on the left, like the Socialist Party of America, the Communist Party, state variants of Farmer-Labor Parties, as well as the Union Party which was a merger of Huey Long's Share-the-Wealth Club and Father Charles Coughlin's National Union for Social Justice. Each had an influence on the evolution of the New Deal, and many had local and state impact (see "Social Movements" chapter).

Upton Sinclair and the End Poverty in California (EPIC) Campaign

One example of an independent leftist electoral campaign that merged with a mainstream party was novelist Upton Sinclair's run for governor of California in 1934. As a prominent Socialist who had been active in California Socialist Party campaigns since 1914, Sinclair was compelled by the Depression to switch to the Democratic Party to try to implement his ideas. Publishing a 60-page book, *I, Governor of California, and How I Ended Poverty,* Sinclair proposed a program of "production-for-use" that would end unemployment and poverty. The EPIC campaign proposed turning over idle land to the unemployed and an old-age pension that would provide persons 60 years of age or older with $50 a month, financed by higher income and inheritance taxes. With support from hundreds of EPIC clubs from all over the state, he won the Democratic primary and seemed poised to win the general election. In the first instance of a modern electoral campaign, the Metro-Goldwyn-Mayer film studio, the Southern California citrus growers, and the *Los Angeles Times* orchestrated a smear attack on Sinclair's personal and political life, including newsreels that depicted a flood of transients planning to overrun the state if Sinclair was elected. After FDR refused to endorse Sinclair's campaign, state Democratic Party leaders ultimately made a deal with incumbent Republican governor Frank Merriam to support Merriam in the election, with a promise that Democrats would share power after the election. Merriam won handily. The legacy of the EPIC campaign, like the Townsend and Long movements (see "Social Movements" chapter), was to pull the New Deal to the left (Mitchell 1992).

Movement toward a Labor Party

The League for Independent Political Action (LIPA), formed in the late 1920s by Paul H. Douglas, Sherwood Eddy, and Norman Thomas, was one more attempt to develop a program for a new farmer-labor party that would steer a middle course between the corporate-based Democratic and Republican parties and the Marxist left. Third parties, such as the Minnesota Farmer-Labor Party, had success in the Midwest, and LIPA hoped to build on that model. With the onset of the Depression, LIPA tried to rally progressive Republicans and Democrats as well as independent candidates around a "Cooperative Commonwealth" plan of a consumer-controlled, planned economy based on "production-for-use, not profit," a Socialist slogan. In July 1932, a small National Progressive Conference endorsed the Socialist ticket of Norman Thomas and James H. Maurer. LIPA was responsible for organizing the Farmer-Labor Political Federation in 1933 and the American Commonwealth Political Federation in 1935. Wrangling with Communist Party activists in 1935 led to a Communist-dominated Farmer-Labor Party effort

American Labor Party in New York City

One successful 1930s' third party formation took place in New York City, where two pro-FDR labor leaders, Sidney Hillman of the Amalgamated Clothing Workers Union and David Dubinsky of the International Ladies' Garment Workers Union, formed the American Labor Party (ALP) to appeal to their members who were traditionally opposed to the Tammany Democratic machine and who were more likely to vote for the Socialist Party ticket or even vote Republican. Indeed, liberal New York City politicians had often run on these other lines: Fiorello La Guardia, a liberal Republican, formed his own fusion movement to win the mayoral office in 1933, with Vito Marcantonio as his campaign manager. Marcantonio himself ran as a Republican for Congress in 1934 and won; he became a outspoken supporter of the New Deal in his first term in Congress, but was defeated for re-election in the Democratic landslide of 1936. But the Hillman-Dubinsky tactic succeeded in 1936, as Roosevelt received over a quarter million votes on the ALP line. La Guardia was cross-listed on the ALP line in his re-election bid in 1937, and the ALP votes provided his margin of victory. Marcantonio followed suit in 1938 and was successfully elected again to his seat in 1938 and continued to be re-elected until 1950. The ALP solidified its hold on its constituency by providing community service, replacing the Tammany machine's usual politics, and La Guardia cleaned up the traditional corrupt political practices in the city. The ALP also was instrumental in bringing African Americans and Latinos into political office, as it championed racial and ethnic equality. The ALP's uneasy alliance between Communists and non-Communists broke apart during the Nazi-Soviet Pact in 1939. While Marcantonio and his pro-Communist supporters retained power in the ALP, the anti-Communists broke away and formed the Liberal Party in 1944 (Meyer 1989).

in 1936, but the movement collapsed in the face of FDR's popularity and the CIO's decision to create Labor's Non-Partisan League to campaign for Roosevelt in 1936 (Davin 1996; Gieske 1979; Miller 1979; Valelly 1989; Waltzer 1980).

Biographies

Vito Marcantonio, 1902–1954

Congressman from East Harlem

Born the oldest child of a working-class Italian immigrant family, Marcantonio got his start in politics by being chosen as Fiorello La Guardia's aide after La Guardia won the 1922 congressional election in East Harlem. Intimately familiar with the district, Marcantonio soon built up the most effective political organization; in 1930, the Fiorello La Guardia Political Association had 5,000 members who formed a "political center for progressive Italian activity" (Meyer 1989, 17). Soon after La Guardia's 1926 campaign, Marcantonio became a law clerk in the congressman's firm. Following in La Guardia's wake as La Guardia won the mayoral race in 1933, Marcantonio campaigned for the congressional occupied at one time by La Guardia and now by an inept Democrat, James Lanzetta. As a Republican, Marcantonio was endorsed by major labor leaders in the city and parlayed his long history of activism in the district to win over the incumbent. In 1936 he was defeated, for one time only, by the Democratic Party landslide for FDR, as well as a rising pro-Mussolini sentiment in his Italian district. Marcantonio, who continued his antifascist position and his friendship with both Socialists and Communists in his district, received the endorsement of the new American Labor Party in 1938. He was elected and continued to serve in Congress until 1950. His record in Congress remained a radical one, which eventually led to his defeat in the postwar Red Scare.

As President Franklin D. Roosevelt's secretary of the treasury from 1934 to 1945, Henry Morgenthau Jr. worked to stabilize the value of the dollar during the Great Depression and oversaw the raising of the capital necessary to win World War II. (Franklin D. Roosevelt Presidential Library)

Henry Morganthau Jr., 1891–1967

FDR's Secretary of the Treasury

Known as a fiscal conservative since he favored restraint in federal spending, Morganthau nonetheless supported tax reform to shift the burden of taxes to the wealthy and was the author of the 1935 Revenue Bill that was labeled a "soak the rich" measure. Born to German Jewish immigrant parents in New York City, he married well and prospered in real estate. In 1913 he bought several hundred acres in Dutchess County, and he spent the 1920s involved in agricultural affairs and politics in Dutchess County, befriending his neighbors Franklin and Eleanor Roosevelt. When FDR became governor in 1928, he appointed Morganthau to agricultural affairs, and when FDR became president, he appointed Morganthau the chairman of the Federal Farm

Bureau and then the Farm Credit Administration. In 1933 FDR asked Morganthau to help negotiate recognition of the Soviet Union and to arrange large sales of grain. When Morganthau was appointed acting Secretary of the Treasury in November 1933, he succeeded in stabilizing the price of gold and managing the international exchange rate for the dollar. Though he initially resisted Keynesian economic theory and opposed FDR's plan to start a spending program to counter the deepening recession in 1938, he soon advocated spending on defense, which restored full employment. He was the first cabinet member to raise concerns about the State Department's blocking of Jewish refugees fleeing Nazi persecution in the early 1940s.

Frances Perkins, 1882–1965

FDR's Secretary of Labor

Graduating from Mount Holyoke College in 1902, Frances Perkins became active in settlement-house work and other reform movements. But it was her experience on the state commission to investigate factory conditions after the 1911 Triangle Shirtwaist fire that clarified her life-long goal of alleviating bad labor conditions through legislation and government enforcement. She married in 1913 and had one daughter, but in the spirit of that era's feminism, she kept her maiden name and continued to work. She entered government service in 1918 when the newly elected governor Alfred E. Smith appointed her to the New York State Industrial Commission. She became the state industrial commissioner in 1928 under Smith's governorship and then continued under Roosevelt's. When Roosevelt was elected president, he appointed her secretary of labor, the highest-ranking woman in the federal government. Her strong personal rapport with the president helped her become the strong voice for labor and women's concerns throughout the 1930s.

Frances Perkins served as U.S. secretary of labor from 1933 to 1945. As the first woman cabinet member, she was also the first woman to be in line for succession to the presidency. (Library of Congress)

John Jakob Raskob, 1879–1950

Founder of American Liberty League

Born in Lockport, New York, to a Catholic immigrant (Irish and Alsatian) family, Raskob trained at a local business college in accounting and bookkeeping. Pierre du Pont hired him as a bookkeeper in 1907 and soon made him his personal secretary. He accompanied Pierre du Pont in the takeover of the family firm, the E. I. du Pont de Nemours explosives company, and helped transform it into a modern, vertically integrated company. World War I made the company, and Raskob, wealthy. Also at this time, he persuaded the du Ponts to invest in General Motors Company and landed a seat on the GM board. He associated with a group of New Yorkers, including Al Smith, who like himself were Catholic and the successful sons or grandsons of immigrants. He became Democratic Party chairman in 1928 when Smith ran for president and remained close to Smith after the campaign. He allied with Smith to attempt to block FDR's nomination in 1932. He famously gave an interview to Samuel Crowther in the August 1929 issue of *Ladies' Home Journal,* entitled "Everybody Ought to Be Rich"; the Great Crash was only two months away. In 1934 he helped found the American Liberty League to combat the alleged radicalism of the New Deal.

Rexford G. Tugwell, 1891–1979

Adviser to FDR

In 1932, Rexford Tugwell joined FDR's brain trust, where he provided the economic policy regarding agriculture. Tugwell had earned the nickname "Rex the Red" as a result of his 1927 trip to the Soviet Union as part of a trade delegation; he was ever after identified with radical ideas and communist solutions. After FDR's election, Tugwell left Columbia University to work for the administration in the Department of Agriculture, assisting Secretary Henry Wallace in a number of projects. But it was his tenure in the Agricultural Adjustment Administration (AAA) that proved his undoing, as he did not agree with the policies of AAA director George Peek or his successor, Chester Davis. Roosevelt then put him in charge of the Resettlement Administration, an independent agency established in 1935 to run the administration's rural antipoverty program. He lasted one year on that job, in which time he oversaw the resettlement of Dust Bowl victims on better land and implemented the Greenbelt Towns project. By 1936 he had become a political liability and Roosevelt accepted his resignation. After trying his hand at business, Tugwell returned to New York City where he became chairman of Mayor La Guardia's New York City Planning Commission from 1937 to 1940. He remained highly committed to economic planning.

Mary van Kleeck, 1883–1972

Social Activist

Mary van Kleeck was the long-time director of the Department of Industrial Studies of the Russell Sage Foundation, where she got her start conducting research on child labor in New York City, after her graduation from Smith College in 1904. Born into an Episcopal minister's family in Glenham, New York, she had a life-long affiliation with the Episcopal League for Social Action. Though she served a short stint in the First New Deal, she quickly became frustrated and evolved a political philosophy strongly opposed to the private ownership of the means of production and envisioning a modified economic collectivism with a strong labor movement. She drafted the basic points of the Lundeen bill, which was debated alongside the Social Security Act in 1935.

Robert L. Vann, 1879–1940

Publisher of the *Pittsburgh Courier*

Vann was born in Ahoskie, North Carolina, and traveled north for his college education. He earned his law degree from the Western University of Pennsylvania (today the University of Pittsburgh) in 1909, and in 1910 he became the treasurer of the African American newspaper the *Pittsburgh Courier*. Shortly thereafter he became the editor of the paper—a position he held for 30 years until his death in 1940. Under Vann's leadership the *Pittsburgh Courier* became the second most influential black newspaper in the country—second only to the *Chicago Defender*. The *Pittsburgh Courier* was a crucial chronicler of black life in the 1930s, including Joe Louis's boxing career, Negro league baseball teams like the Homestead Grays, the Italian invasion of Ethiopia, the careers of jazz musicians and singers, and daily life in Pittsburgh as captured by the prolific *Courier* photographer Teenie Harris. Vann initiated a number of influential campaigns in the 1930s, including the unsuccessful boycott of the radio program *Amos 'n' Andy*, a campaign for more black doctors in Pittsburgh, and a call for African Americans to turn away from the Republican Party in favor of the Democrats. His support for the Democratic Party earned him a position as the special assistant to the U.S. attorney general by FDR.

Robert F. Wagner, 1877–1953

U.S. Senator

Born in Germany, Wagner immigrated with his Methodist family to the Yorkville section of New York City at age nine. His family lived in the basement of a tenement building, where his father was the janitor. He attended City College and

New York Law School, where he graduated with a law degree in 1900. He began his political career giving speeches for Tammany Hall candidates in 1898, was elected to the New York State Assembly in 1904, and then elected to the New York Senate, where he became president pro tem in 1911 and showed his reformist bent. In 1911 he was on the New York Factory Investigating Commission investigating the Triangle Shirtwaist fire, and along with Alfred E. Smith sponsored more than 60 bills to help labor and improve working conditions. After serving for eight years as a judge on the New York First District Supreme Court, he won the U.S. Senate seat in 1926. Wagner used his influence to introduce new issues like the increasing unemployment rate of the late 1920s and urged support for countercyclical federal spending to stabilize employment and consumption. Thus he was a key shaper of Roosevelt's New Deal welfare state after 1932. Particularly attuned to labor issues, Wagner got his National Labor Relations Act passed by the Senate in 1935, capturing the attention of FDR, who was little interested in labor legislation.

References and Further Readings

Baldwin, S. 1968. *Poverty and Politics: The Rise and Decline of the Farm Security Administration*. Chapel Hill: University of North Carolina Press.

Berkowitz, E. D. 1991. *America's Welfare State: From Roosevelt to Reagan*. Baltimore: Johns Hopkins University Press.

Berlin, I., M. Favreau, and S. F. Miller, eds. 1998. *Remembering Slavery: African Americans Talk about Their Personal Experiences of Slavery and Freedom*. New York: New Press in association with the Library of Congress, Washington, DC.

Bernstein, I. 1969. *The Turbulent Years: A History of the American Worker, 1933–1941*. Boston: Houghton Mifflin.

Best, G. D. 1991. *Pride, Prejudice, and Politics: Roosevelt versus Recovery, 1933–1938*. New York: Praeger.

Billington, D. P., D. C. Jackson, and M. V. Melosi. 2005. *The History of Large Federal Dams: Planning, Design, and Construction in the Era of Big Dams*. Denver: U.S. Department of the Interior, Bureau of Reclamation.

Braeman, J., R. H. Bremner, and D. Brody, eds. 1975. *The New Deal,* vol. 1: *The National Level*. Columbus: Ohio State University Press.

Brinkley, A. 1995. *The End of Reform: New Deal Liberalism in Recession and War*. New York: Knopf.

Buhite, R. D., and D. W. Levy, eds. 1992. *FDR's Fireside Chats*. Norman: University of Oklahoma Press.

Burk, R. F. 1990. *The Corporate State and the Broker State: The Du Ponts and American National Politics, 1925–1940.* Cambridge, MA: Harvard University Press.

Burns, J. M. 1956. *Roosevelt: The Lion and the Fox, 1882–1940.* New York: Harcourt Brace Jovanovich.

Casebeer, K. 1992. "The Workers' Unemployment Insurance Bill: American Social Wage, Labor Organization, and Legal Ideology." In *Labor Law in America: Historical and Critical Essays,* ed. C. L. Tomlins and A. J. King, 231–59. Baltimore: Johns Hopkins University Press.

Cohen, W. J. 1986. *The Roosevelt New Deal: A Program Assessment Fifty Years After.* Austin: Lyndon B. Johnson School of Public Affairs, University of Texas.

Conkin, P. K. 1967. *The New Deal.* New York: Thomas Y. Crowell Co.

Davin, E. L. 1996. "The Very Last Hurrah?: The Defeat of the Labor Party Idea, 1934–36." In *"We Are All Leaders": The Alternative Unionism of the Early 1930s,* ed. S. Lynd, 117–171. Urbana: University of Illinois Press.

Dublin, T., and W. Licht. 2005. *The Face of Decline: The Pennsylvania Anthracite Region in the Twentieth Century.* Ithaca, NY: Cornell University Press.

Edsforth, R. 2000. *The New Deal: America's Response to the Great Depression.* Malden, MA: Blackwell Publishers.

Emerson, T. I., and J. Emerson. 1991. *Young Lawyer for the New Deal: An Insider's Memoir of the Roosevelt Years.* Savage, MD: Rowman and Littlefield Publishers.

Epstein, A. 1931. "The Older Worker," *Annals of the American Academy of Political and Social Science* 154 (March): 28–31.

Fearon, P. 1987. *War, Prosperity and Depression: The U.S. Economy, 1917–1945.* Lawrence: University Press of Kansas.

Fraser, S. 1991. *Labor Will Rule: Sidney Hillman and the Rise of American Labor.* New York: Free Press.

Fraser, S., and G. Gerstle, eds. 1989. *The Rise and Fall of the New Deal Order, 1930–1980.* Princeton, NJ: Princeton University Press.

Gamm, G. H. 1989. *The Making of New Deal Democrats: Voting Behavior and Realignment in Boston, 1920–1940.* Chicago: University of Chicago Press.

Gieske, M. 1979. *Minnesota Farmer-Laborism: The Third Party Alternative.* Minneapolis: University of Minnesota Press.

Gordon, C. 1994a. *New Deals: Business, Labor, and Politics in America, 1920–1935.* New York: Cambridge University Press.

Gordon, L. 1994b. *Pitied but Not Entitled: Single Mothers and the History of Welfare, 1890–1935.* New York: Free Press.

Graham, O. L., Jr. 1967. *An Encore for Reform: The Old Progressives and the New Deal*. New York: Oxford University Press.

Hawley, E. W. 1966. *The New Deal and the Problem of Monopoly: A Study in Economic Ambivalence*. Princeton, NJ: Princeton University Press.

Himmelberg, R. F. 1976. *The Origins of the National Recovery Administration: Business, Government, and the Trade Association Issue, 1921–1933*. New York: Fordham University Press.

Ickes, H. L. 1935. *Back to Work: The Story of PWA*. New York: Macmillan.

Ingalls, R. P. 1975. *Herbert H. Lehman and New York's Little New Deal*. New York: New York University Press.

Irons, P. H. 1982. *The New Deal Lawyers*. Princeton, NJ: Princeton University Press.

Jackson, K. T. 1980. "Race, Ethnicity, and Real Estate Appraisal: The Home Owners Loan Corporation and the Federal Housing Administration," *Journal of Urban History* 6 (August): 419–452.

Jackson, K. T. 1985. *Crabgrass Frontier: The Suburbanization of the United States*. New York: Oxford University Press.

Kennedy, D. M. 1999. *Freedom from Fear: The American People in Depression and War, 1929–1945*. New York: Oxford University Press.

Kessler-Harris, A. 1982. *Out to Work: A History of Wage-Earning Women in the United States*. New York: Oxford University Press.

Kessler-Harris, A. 1995. "Designing Women and Old Fools: The Construction of the Social Security Amendments of 1939." In *U.S. History as Women's History: New Feminist Essays,* ed. L. K. Kerber, K. K. Sklar, et al., 87–106. Chapel Hill: University of North Carolina Press.

Kessler-Harris, A. 2001. *In Pursuit of Equity: Women, Men, and the Quest for Economic Citizenship in Twentieth-Century America*. New York: Oxford University Press.

Klein, J. 2003. *For All These Rights: Business, Labor, and the Shaping of America's Public-Private Welfare State*. Princeton, NJ: Princeton University Press.

Kleinberg, B. 1995. *Urban America in Transformation: Perspectives on Urban Policy and Development*. Thousand Oaks, CA: Sage.

Knepper, C. D. 2001. *Greenbelt, Maryland: A Living Legacy of the New Deal*. Baltimore: Johns Hopkins University Press.

Lash, J. P. 1988. *Dealers and Dreamers: A New Look at the New Deal*. New York: Doubleday.

Leuchtenburg, W. E. 1963. *Franklin D. Roosevelt and the New Deal, 1932–1940*. New York: Harper and Row.

Louchheim, K., and J. Dembo, eds. 1983. *The Making of the New Deal: The Insiders Speak.* Cambridge, MA: Harvard University Press.

Lubell, S. 1965. *The Future of American Politics.* 3rd ed., rev. New York: Harper and Row.

Lubove, R. 1968. *The Struggle for Social Security, 1900–1935.* Cambridge, MA: Harvard University Press.

McElvaine, R. S. 1993. *The Great Depression: America, 1929–1941.* New York: Times Books.

Mangione, J. 1972. *The Dream and the Deal: The Federal Writers' Project, 1935–1943.* Boston: Little, Brown.

Meyer, G. 1989. *Vito Marcantonio: Radical Politician, 1902–1954.* Albany: State University of New York Press.

Miller, D. L. 1979. *The New American Radicalism: Alfred M. Bingham and Non-Marxian Insurgency in the New Deal Era.* Port Washington, NY: Kennikat Press.

Mitchell, G. 1992. *The Campaign of the Century: Upton Sinclair's Race for Governor of California and the Birth of Media Politics.* New York: Random House.

Olson, J. S. 1988. *Saving Capitalism: The Reconstruction Finance Corporation and the New Deal, 1933–1940.* Princeton, NJ: Princeton University Press.

Ottanelli, F. M. 1991. *The Communist Party of the United States: From the Depression to World War II.* New Brunswick, NJ: Rutgers University Press.

Patterson, J. T. 1967. *Congressional Conservatism and the New Deal: The Growth of the Conservative Coalition in Congress, 1933–1939.* Lexington: University of Kentucky Press.

Patterson, J. T. 1969. *The New Deal and the States: Federalism in Transition.* Princeton, NJ: Princeton University Press.

Paulsen, G. E. 1996. *A Living Wage for the Forgotten Man: The Quest for Fair Labor Standards, 1933–1941.* Selinsgrove, PA: Susquehanna University Press.

Quadagno, J. 1988. *The Transformation of Old Age Security: Class and Politics in the American Welfare State.* Chicago: University of Chicago Press.

Radford, G. 1996. *Modern Housing for America: Policy Struggles in the New Deal Era.* Chicago: University of Chicago Press.

Rauch, B., ed. 1957. *The Roosevelt Reader: Selected Speeches, Messages, Press Conferences, and Letters of Franklin D. Roosevelt* New York: Holt, Rinehart and Winston.

Ridley, C. E., and O. F. Nolting, eds. 1935. *What the Depression Has Done to Cities.* Chicago: International City Managers' Association.

Rosen, E. A. 2005. *Roosevelt, the Great Depression, and the Economics of Recovery.* Charlottesville: University of Virginia Press.

Rosenman, S. I., ed. 1938. *The Public Papers and Addresses of Franklin D. Roosevelt.* Vol. 2. New York: Random House.

Rubinow, I. M. 1934. *The Quest for Security.* New York: H. Holt.

Schlesinger, A. M., Jr. 1959. *The Age of Roosevelt: The Coming of the New Deal.* Boston: Houghton Mifflin.

Schwartz, B. F. 1984. *The Civil Works Administration, 1933–1934: The Business of Emergency Employment in the New Deal.* Princeton, NJ: Princeton University Press.

Schwarz, J. A. 1993. *The New Dealers: Power Politics in the Age of Roosevelt.* New York: Knopf.

Sitkoff, H. 1978. *A New Deal for Blacks: The Emergence of Civil Rights as a National Issue,* vol. 1: *The Depression Decade.* New York: Oxford University Press.

Skocpol, T. 1988. "The Limits of the New Deal System and the Roots of Contemporary Welfare Dilemmas." In *The Politics of Social Policy in the United States,* ed. M. Weir, A. S. Orloff, and T. Skocpol, 293–311. Princeton, NJ: Princeton University Press.

Skocpol, T. 1992. *Protecting Soldiers and Mothers: The Political Origins of Social Policy in the United States.* Cambridge, MA: Harvard University Press.

Starr, P. 1982. *The Social Transformation of American Medicine.* New York: Basic Books.

Tennessee Valley Authority Web site, www.tva.gov/heritage.

U.S. Department of the Interior, Bureau of Reclamation Web site, www.usbr.gov/history.

Valelly, R. M. 1989. *Radicalism in the States: The Minnesota Farmer-Labor Party and the American Political Economy.* Chicago: University of Chicago Press.

Waltzer, K. 1980. "The Party and the Polling Place: American Communism and an American Labor Party in the 1930s," *Radical History Review* 23 (Spring): 104–129.

Webber, M. J. 2000. *New Deal Fat Cats: Business, Labor, and Campaign Finance in the 1936 Presidential Election.* New York: Fordham University Press.

Weiss, N. J. 1983. *Farewell to the Party of Lincoln: Black Politics in the Age of FDR.* Princeton, NJ: Princeton University Press.

Wicker, E. 1996. *The Banking Panics of the Great Depression.* New York: Cambridge University Press.

Witte, E. E. 1963. *The Development of the Social Security Act*. Madison: University of Wisconsin Press.

Wolfskill, G. 1962. *The Revolt of the Conservatives: A History of the American Liberty League, 1934–1940*. Boston: Houghton Mifflin.

Worster, D. 1982. *Dust Bowl: The Southern Plains in the 1930s*. New York: Oxford University Press.

Social Movements

Overview

Social movements of various kinds defined the ethos of the 1930s and influenced informal community organization as well as politics on all levels. This chapter covers these kinds: the "populist" movements that emerged during the First New Deal, which commentators at the time called the "thunder on the left," though it was unclear exactly where they were on the political spectrum; the movements that were decidedly on the conservative political spectrum, whether anti-immigrant, anti-African American, anti-Catholic, or anti-Semitic; faith-based movements to address the economic calamity; and the ethnic and racial movements for self-defense and self-expression. Ethnic Americans, that foreign-stock population that made up 31.1 percent of the population, were going through the difficult process of Americanization. Their second generation, claiming its place in the political order, became a prominent component of the New Deal Coalition. They accomplished this task through different social movements and political parties, and these are reviewed in this chapter. The electoral roles of left-wing political movements were covered in the previous chapter, but their social bases are considered in this chapter. Also covered are those community movements that sprang up in minority populations, which provided a concrete expression of those people's hopes and desires for their futures. Finally, the labor movement, the largest and most influential social movement, will be covered in the next chapter.

TIMELINE

1930 The Association of Southern Women for the Prevention of Lynching is established in November, the first white women's group to tackle this issue.

The Scottsboro case begins in Alabama, and causes an international movement for racial justice through trials until 1937.

1931 Bishops of the Episcopal Church in America, as well as the Federal Council of Churches of Christ, publish statements calling for a rethinking of the profit-motive and attention to "justice, not charity" in dealing with the economic catastrophe.

Pope Pius XI issues his encyclical *Quadragesimo Anno,* emphasizing social justice and calling for a cooperative relationship between capital and labor.

1932 On November 8, Franklin D. Roosevelt is elected by a wide margin, winning 472 votes in the Electoral College to Hoover's 59. Democrats gain 90 seats in the House and 13 in the Senate.

1933 Dr. Francis E. Townsend of California designs his Old Age Pension Plan and Townsend Clubs spring up throughout the nation.

Italian immigrant Joseph Zangara fires six shots at President-elect Roosevelt in Miami, Florida, on February 15. Though Roosevelt is not hurt, several others are wounded, and Chicago mayor Anton J. Cermak dies of his wounds a few days later.

Dorothy Day and Peter Maurin publish the first issue of *The Catholic Worker* on May Day.

In New York City, the Chinese Hand Laundry Alliance is formed.

The Socialist Party of American sponsors the Continental Congress of Workers and Farmers in Washington, D.C.

The American Federation of Labor (AFL) begins a boycott of German-made goods in October in response to the rising antiunion sentiment in Nazi Germany.

On Election Day, November 7, Fiorello La Guardia is elected mayor of New York City on a Fusion ticket; Arthur Mitchell of Chicago is the first African American elected to Congress as a

Democrat; Socialist Jasper McLevy wins the mayoralty of Bridgeport, Connecticut, along with most of his Socialist slate.

1934

Huey P. Long, U.S. senator from Louisiana, announces his Share Our Wealth Society; by spring 1935, it had 7.5 million members.

Father Charles E. Coughlin of Detroit, the "Radio Priest," establishes a new national organization, the National Union for Social Justice.

The Indian Reorganization Act (Wheeler-Howard bill) returns control of land to Indian tribes.

Congressman Martin Dies of Texas renews his call for immigration restriction.

1935

The unemployed organizations of the three major leftist groups merge to form the Workers Alliance, with a goal of lobbying for national unemployment insurance.

Mussolini's Italian government invades Ethiopia in February, claiming colonial rights dating from the late 19th century; Italian American communities rally in support of his efforts, while African Americans demonstrate in support of Ethiopian independence.

In March, after an incident involving an African American child at a store in Harlem, the Harlem Race Riot breaks out, and ends with 75 people arrested, 57 civilians injured, and 626 windows broken.

The National Negro Congress is formed in May.

Sen. Huey P. Long is assassinated in September.

1936

First Lady Eleanor Roosevelt begins publishing her syndicated column, *My Day,* in January.

The Federal Council on Negro Affairs is established.

Mary McLeod Bethune is appointed head of the Division of Negro Affairs in the National Youth Administration in June.

During the fall campaign season, Catholic priests deliver radio broadcasts on political topics, Father Coughlin against the New Deal, and Father John Ryan of Washington, D.C., for the New Deal.

On November 3 FDR wins a landslide victory over Republican Alfred M. Landon of Kansas. Democrats win strong majorities in Congress.

In the late fall, 20,000 American volunteers form the Abraham Lincoln Battalion to join the international forces fighting alongside the Loyalist government in the Spanish Civil War.

1937 In early January, Congress outlaws supplying weapons to either side in the Spanish Civil War.

1938 The Stock market tumbles between August 1937 and March 1938.

The House Committee on Un-American Activities (commonly abbreviated HUAC), headed by Congressman Martin Dies, is established in May.

In July, the Christian Front is organized in New York City.

The Munich Pact, signed by Hitler and Prime Minister Chamberlain of Great Britain, cedes the Sudetenland to Germany in late September.

On November 8, Republicans regain some congressional seats, seven in the Senate and 80 in the House, due to dissatisfaction over the "Roosevelt Recession" of 1937–1938.

After the Kristallnacht ("night of broken glass") in Germany in November, the German government imposes new restrictions on its Jewish citizens; the United States recalls its ambassador from Germany in protest over the treatment of German Jews; the German ambassador is recalled to Germany a few days later.

1939 In his State of the Union message on January 4, Roosevelt stresses the ominous international situation.

Sen. Robert Wagner of New York introduces a new refugee bill to admit 20,000 German-Jewish refugee children; the measure is defeated.

In April, the founding convention of El Congreso de Pueblo de Hablan Español (the Spanish-Speaking Congress) is held in Los Angeles.

Marian Anderson sings on the steps of the Lincoln Memorial on Easter Sunday, after having been barred from performing at the DAR Hall because of her race.

On April 1, the United States recognizes the government of Francisco Franco in Spain.

On September 1, Germany invades Poland; World War II begins; American Communists reverse their antifascist stand in order to support the Nazi-Soviet Pact declaring neutrality between Germany and the Soviet Union.

On September 5, FDR officially declares U.S. neutrality and bans the export of weapons to warring nations.

In mid-October, the NAACP Legal Defense and Education Fund is established and declares an offensive against all racial discrimination.

Populism

"Populism" was a driving force behind such 1930s' social movements as Milo Reno's Farmers' Holiday Association, Huey Long's Share Our Wealth Society in Louisiana, and Father Charles Coughlin's National Union for Social Justice. The term *populist* has become attached to many social and political movements that actually share little in common. Like its predecessor, the Populist movement or the People's Party of the 1880s and 1890s, these movements shared one coherent strain, their antimonopoly stance, their fear of bigness in financial and corporate power. For them, the antimonopoly movement had a powerful moral and cultural rationale. They shared this attitude with many average American citizens and with some New Deal activists. It also animated some of the senior Republican and Democratic members of Congress from the South and Midwest. While many New Dealers rejected the populists' insistence on a moral or cultural justification against monopoly, certain voices in the Roosevelt administration, such as Robert Jackson, head of the antitrust division of the Justice Department, were strong advocates of this antimonopolist stance: "There is no practical way on earth to regulate the economic oligarchy of autocratic, self-constituted and self-perpetuating groups," Jackon wrote in 1937 (Brinkley 1995, 58–61). Thus for many antimonopolists of this decade, the solution was to continue to break up combinations by restoring free competition, not to promote economic regulation and planning. Their fear of monopoly was tied to an equal fear of a powerful government, a concern that many other New Dealers rejected. But even the political projects of many of these movements involved an enlarged national government role, a contradiction that was not resolved in the 1930s.

Dr. Francis Townsend and the Old-Age Pension Movement

The Old Age Pension movement got its 1930s momentum from physician Francis E. Townsend (1867–1960). Townsend, retired from the Midwest to the sunny climate of Long Beach, California, had a revelation in 1933 as he witnessed three old women rummaging for food in the garbage cans in his alley. Beginning with a letter to the *Long Beach Press-Telegram,* Townsend laid out his plan for an Old Age Revolving Pension Plan that he claimed would solve the crisis of the Great Depression as well as take care of the elderly. It was a simple plan: the federal government would provide everyone over 60 years of age with a monthly pension of $150 (it was soon increased to $200), on the condition that it be spent immediately. It would be funded by a nationwide sales tax (on all wholesale and retail transactions). Thus, it would pump new money into the economy, revive the consumer market, and ultimately end the Depression.

Though Townsend was not the first to suggest such a plan, he was the first to organize successfully around the idea. Starting with a few elderly volunteers and one high-powered salesman, Robert E. Clements, Townsend's mailings from the Long Beach office soon gained a flood of responses and Townsend Clubs were set up throughout the state. By mid-1935, the paid membership in Townsend Clubs around the nation was nearly one-half million. Congressional offices were inundated with letters and petitions. Yet, when California representative John S. McGroary introduced the Townsend pension bill in the House in early 1935, there was no congressional movement. The plan was denounced by many in Washington as unworkable and expensive. The administration strongly opposed the bill, and many representatives avoided the chamber when the bill came up for discussion. Ultimately, what came out of that congressional session was the Social Security Act, which fulfilled some of the goals of the Townsend Clubs (see previous chapter). The movement continued to exist as an insurgent force beyond 1935, and its constituency began mingling with those of the Long and Coughlin movements, though Townsend himself held back from endorsing either man. But the national news media began putting the three men together, and Hugh Johnson of the NRA denounced the Long and Townsend plans together as "dangerous Utopian folly" in a few highly publicized speeches in early 1935 (Brinkley 1982, 226).

Huey Long and the Share Our Wealth Movement

Huey Pierce Long (1893–1935), U.S. senator from Louisiana, came up with a plan that would promote his nationwide political ambitions. His Share Our Wealth Society was incorporated in 1934. Long's political career was built on the single issue of the maldistribution of wealth, which he insisted had caused the Great Depression. Getting little accomplished in the U.S. Senate, he brought his ideas to the Senate floor, delivered radio speeches, and published a book on what he would do in office, *My First Days in the White House*. The program of the Share Our Wealth Society was simple: confiscate all yearly incomes above $1 million and total assets above $8 million, and provide every needy family with a basic "household estate" of $5,000 which would provide a home, an automobile, and a radio, and guarantee each family an annual income of $2,500. Only millionaires would pay taxes.

Long, nicknamed "the Kingfish," had risen from a middle-class family in Winnfield, Louisiana, to become governor of the state in 1928. He had attracted the largely poor rural voters to his side by outpromising his political opponents. Once in office, he consolidated his power through nepotism, patronage, vote stealing, and the force of his personality. He made powerful enemies by attacking the Standard Oil Company, which dominated the state's economy. Facing resistance to his program from the legislature, he ran for U.S. senator in the 1930 Democratic primary, easily defeating the incumbent James E. Ransdell. With that, state legislative opposition crumbled and he got his program of free schoolbooks for the state's children, an improved road and bridge system, cheap natural gas to New Orleans, and increased funding for Louisiana State University. Unwilling to allow his lieutenant governor to rule the state, Long did not take his seat in Washington for two years, remaining both governor and senator-elect until 1932 when he took the oath as U.S. senator. While Long had campaigned for Roosevelt in 1932, he soon came to see FDR as an aristocrat whose promise to break up large fortunes had not been fulfilled. Moreover, Long planned to challenge Roosevelt in 1936.

There were no dues to join the Share Our Wealth Society; one only had to write to Long to gain membership. Members were encouraged to form local clubs to work to enact the plan. A Shreveport minister, Gerald L. K. Smith, was hired as national organizer. By spring 1935, the Society announced that it had 7.5 million members. The Kingfish moved toward an alliance with Father Charles Coughlin and Dr. Francis E. Townsend in 1935. Long was poised to challenge Roosevelt for the Democratic nomination when he was assassinated at the state capitol on September 10, 1935, by an aggrieved constituent, Carl Austin Weiss (Brinkley 1982; White 2006).

Father Charles Coughlin and the National Union for Social Justice

Charles E. Coughlin (1891–1979), a Catholic priest in Royal Oak, Michigan, a suburb of Detroit, and already known as the "Radio Priest" for his sermons broadcast over powerful Detroit radio station WJR, began commenting on the economic debacle and criticizing the Hoover administration in 1930. Given the closed auto industry and high unemployment in the Detroit area, his radio show quickly became even more popular and reached an estimated 30 million listeners in 1930. Using Catholic social-justice teachings, he denounced concentrated wealth and international bankers, supported the veterans' bonus in 1932, and condemned "International Communism." Coughlin was introduced into Democratic political circles by his growing friendship with then-mayor Frank Murphy

Father Charles E. Coughlin, a Michigan-based Roman Catholic cleric, whose extremely popular 1930s radio program routinely attracted about 30 million listeners. A one-time supporter of President Roosevelt, he turned away from FDR in 1936 to support the third-party candidacy of Congressman William Lemke of North Dakota. After 1938 Coughlin added increasingly vicious anti-Semitic comments to his already strident programs. (Library of Congress)

of Detroit, with whom he traveled to Washington for Roosevelt's inauguration in March 1933. Throughout 1933, Coughlin enthusiastically promoted FDR's New Deal, using phrases such as "Roosevelt or Ruin" and "The New Deal Is Christ's Deal!" (Brinkley 1982, 108).

In fall 1934, Coughlin established a new organization, the National Union for Social Justice (NUSJ), as a political vehicle to allow his followers to act on his 16-point Principles of Social Justice, and in 1936 he began publishing a weekly paper *Social Justice*. Mixing traditional populist rhetoric with the papal encyclicals *Rerum Novarum* (1891) and *Quadragesimo Anno* (1931), Coughlin railed against the injuries brought about by a financial elite ruling a system of "modern capitalism." But like the encyclicals, he preached class harmony rather than class conflict, and endorsed unionism only hesitantly, instead urging factory owners to "share the profits with labor" (Kazin 1995, 121). He nonetheless encouraged a new Automotive Industrial Workers' Association in early 1935, and blessed its merger into the growing United Auto Workers in 1936. Like Huey Long, Coughlin had grown impatient with the New Deal and criticized the NRA and other New Deal measures as consolidating power in the hands of a few. He did not distinguish among liberal bureaucrats, an international financial cabal, or Soviet communism.

The Union Party, 1936

To attract critics of the New Deal as well as to expand his political influence, Coughlin created a new political party, the Union Party (UP), as an alternative to a return to the Republican Party. Supported by Rev. Gerald L. K. Smith from the Share Our Wealth movement and Dr. Francis Townsend from the Old Age Pension movement, Coughlin and the NUSJ nominated a balanced ticket of a

Historians' Perspective: A Left or Right Movement?

Liberal and left-wing activists in the 1930s condemned both Long and Coughlin as demagogues leaning toward an American-style fascism. Socialist leader Norman Thomas challenged Huey Long to a public debate in 1934, where he criticized the Share Our Wealth scheme as a delusion: "It was that sort of talk, Senator Long, that Hitler fed the Germans, and in my opinion it is positively dangerous because it fools the people" (Brinkley 1982, 238). Historians since then have usually taken the same analytical path. But Alan Brinkley, in his influential 1982 study of Long and Coughlin, *Voices of Protest,* took another perspective, pointing out the common threads that ran from 19th-century American protest politics and placing both men within that tradition. Long and Coughlin were not the first, nor would they be the last, to combine populist rhetoric with cultural conservatism (Brinkley 1982, 269–83). Michael Kazin has expanded on that viewpoint in *The Populist Persuasion* (1995), casting an even broader net to place Coughlin's thought within a "producerist" ethic even as the man's actions fell short of these ideals.

In fact, when Coughlin returned to the airwaves in 1937, he often veered toward outright anti-Semitism (Jews as an international banking conspiracy), and his newspaper, following Henry Ford's example, reprinted the fictitious *Protocols of the Elders of Zion.* By the late 1930s he was expressing admiration for Hitler and Mussolini. His followers could be found in organized groups like the Christian Front. During 1940, he was most active in promoting American neutrality in the European war, and after Pearl Harbor he came under the scrutiny of the War Department. Under pressure from U.S. Attorney General Francis Biddle, Archbishop Mooney of Detroit silenced Coughlin in spring 1942.

What these populist movements had in common was the agitation at the grassroots of American society, where distraught people were trying to make sense of the economic calamity in the first half of the 1930s. The ways in which most agitation finally became absorbed by the New Deal or by the labor movement warrant further research and analysis. But clearly, there was a vast "middling rhetoric" that appealed to many (Kazin 1995, 11). Beyond this, there were clear right-wing movements, some allied to European fascist movements, that extended the traditional American nativism and racism into this new decade. There were also strong leftist movements like the Socialist Party, the Communist Party (CP), and assorted other Marxist groups. Within the labor movement, there were adherents of the Democratic Party, as well as those who wished an independent political voice for labor. Nascent labor parties, or farmer-labor parties, were eventually absorbed into the New Deal Democratic Party, but they left their mark on their region's electoral history.

farm-state Protestant, Congressman William Lemke of North Dakota, for president and a Boston Catholic, former prosecutor Thomas C. O'Brien, for vice president. Coughlin predicted 10 percent of the vote and staged rallies throughout the summer and fall of 1936. Calling the New Deal "anti-God," Coughlin whipped up enthusiastic audiences, such as the 40,000 NUSJ members who attended a rally at Cleveland's Memorial Stadium. Here he dramatically tore off his clerical collar before collapsing on the stage. But with every criticism of the New Deal and FDR, Coughlin lost supporters. The UP polled only 892,000 votes. Father Coughlin's supreme influence came to an end.

Who Were the Populist Followers?

Each of these movements attracted a slightly different constituency, but there were some commonalities. Many were from the elite of the white working class, those who had more to protect such as a home or a job outside of mass-production industry. They were joined as well by those middle-class elements who were threatened by or had been displaced by more modern business entities: local merchants, small businessmen, modest professionals, and family farmers. For example, one enemy was the chain-store phenomenon that was devastating local store owners, whether grocery stores or pharmacies. Predictably, Long's support was strongest in the South, though his Share Our Wealth Clubs soon began appearing in the Northeast and the West. Coughlin's support was mostly in the industrial Northeast and Midwest. Surprisingly for a Catholic priest, he had captured the imagination of farmers in the Midwest. A poll conducted by the Democratic National Committee in early 1935, in the infant days of sample polling, revealed that 54 percent of the respondents said they leaned toward Roosevelt, compared to 30 percent for an unnamed Republican. But Huey Long was named by 11 percent of the voters as their preferred candidate, a worrisome result for Democratic leaders. Long's supporters came fairly evenly from all corners of the nation. The only distinct difference was that Long supporters were most likely to be receiving some form of government relief. Historian Alan Brinkley notes that this result does not negate his conclusions that Long supporters tended to be "middle-class," since it was that group that was receiving the preponderance of New Deal programs in early 1935 (Brinkley 1982, 208). It should be noted that Brinkley uses the label "middle-class" in its broad post–World War II sense.

Faith-Based Movements

Protestant Churches

The major faith institutions responded to the economic crisis by urging members of their congregations to aid one another and to extend their charitable impulses beyond traditional outlets. Some churches went farther, engaging socially and politically with the social order.

Mainstream Protestant churches renewed the Social Gospel teachings of the Progressive Era, adapted now to the extreme economic crisis. In a statement in the fall of 1931, the bishops of the Episcopal Church in America exhorted their brethren to consider the underlying conditions and condemn the international arms race: "Unemployment, however, is but a symptom of underlying selfishness. The Church must insist that every financial question is essentially one of human relations. . . . The profit-seeking motive must give way to that of service." The statement went on to say:

> We covet for our country the courage to lead along the pathway of world peace by doing its utmost, even at the cost of risk and sacrifice, to achieve immediate substantial reduction of armaments and, above all, by more general and whole-hearted cooperation and conference with the nations of the world, especially through official participation in such existing international agencies as tend toward world peace. (Beard 1932, 22–23)

Also in fall 1931, the Commission on the Church and Social Service of the Federal Council of the Churches of Christ similarly laid out a call for economic security. But this statement distinguished itself with a more explicit call for economic planning and the redistribution of wealth. Noting that with wealth concentrated at the top, the vast majority of workers have "insufficient income to buy the goods which, with the help of modern machinery, they are now able to produce. Hence we have what is called 'overproduction,' but which, perhaps, should be called 'underconsumption.' Purchasing power has not been scientifically adjusted to production. Apparently it can be thus adjusted only as we move in the direction of a more equitable distribution of income which Jesus' principle of love and brotherhood also calls for." Calling for "justice, not charity," the statement went on to call for a living wage in the broadest sense ("we must extend the concept to cover all of a worker's life, including the two periods at the beginning and at the end—childhood and old age—when one cannot earn") and called for social provision such as health insurance, unemployment insurance, maternity benefits, and old-age pensions (Beard 1932, 27–28). These proposals would come to fruition during the New Deal.

One of the most significant Protestant theologians of the 1930s was Reinhold Niebuhr (1892–1971). Niebuhr, the son of an immigrant minister of the German Evangelical Synod of North America, grew up in Illinois and Missouri, and earned degrees from the Synod's Eden Seminary and Yale Divinity School, where he became a liberal and a modernist. In the 1920s, while serving as pastor of a middle-class church in Detroit, he condemned Henry Ford's labor practices and became a leading voice for social justice and racial tolerance from the pulpit and through writings in the national weekly magazine *The Christian Century*. Becoming a gradualist socialist, in 1928 he moved to New York to become a

Baptism near Mineola, Texas, 1935. Photo by folklorist Alan Lomax. (Library of Congress)

professor at Union Theological Seminary, where he threw himself into Socialist politics, writing for the socialist weekly *The World Tomorrow* and running for office on the Socialist Party ticket, for state Senate in 1930 and for Congress in 1932. His publications in the 1930s blended a "liberal hope for expanded justice and equality with the tragic sense of life," in an on-going argument with John Dewey. Niebuhr founded the Fellowship of Socialist Christians in 1931 and the Union for Democratic Action in 1941 (Fox 1996).

An additional important Protestant minister was Harry Emerson Fosdick (1878–1969), who was the first pastor of the new nondenominational Riverside Church on New York City's Upper West Side. A modernist and liberal, Fosdick nonetheless protested loudly the modernist tendency to water down religion and called for a renewal of ethical standards and faith in God. His popular radio broadcast on NBC, *The National Vesper Hour,* was estimated to reach the largest audience of any preacher on the airwaves in the 1930s.

On a more individual level, mainstream Protestant churches found themselves beset by evangelical and fundamentalist movements. In the southern states, including swathes of the Dust Bowl, evangelical Protestantism grew and spread westward to California with the Dust Bowl migrants. These white migrant communities found their own practice of religion—revivalism, scriptural literalism, piety, and commitment to individual salvation through Jesus Christ—less welcome in California churches of their denominations, and flocked to alternative sects on the fringes of evangelicalism, such as the Holiness and Pentecostal movements (Gregory 1989, 191–221). African American communities in the urban Northeast turned to a colorful religious personality, Father Divine (1879–1965), born George Baker, whose activities included distributing food to the needy, conducting healing services, and preaching racial tolerance. Father Divine's Peace Mission movement purchased hotels to provide housing for his followers, and by 1939 his congregation included 152 of these "heavens," mostly in the New York City area.

Roman Catholic Church

The Roman Catholic Church in the United States found itself in a new position of strength in the 1930s, given that the majority of its new-ethnic constituents were now participating in the political system and gaining influence. They were also key in the new labor organizations of the 1930s. Stirrings of labor solidarity meant that the grassroots were alive with new initiatives. Pope Pius XI built on his predecessor Leo XIII's encyclical *Rerum Novarum* (*The Condition of Labor*) (1891) with his own 1931 encyclical, *Quadragesimo Anno* (*After Forty Years*). *Quadragesimo Anno* laid out the basic church teachings on labor issues, emphasizing "social justice" and a cooperative relationship between capital and labor while condemning both individualism and collectivism. Responding to European political concerns, Pius XI went to great lengths to differentiate his statements from the system of Italian fascism, which he deplored for its overreliance on the state (O'Brien 1968, 21–22). Of course, the church in Italy did not overtly resist fascism in Italy, as its compliance during World War II would show.

The extreme poverty that came with the Great Depression fostered a new breed of Catholic, who was more prone to emphasize the corporate responsibilities of church members. Thus social responsibility became paramount. Catholic Action, promoted by Pope Pius XI, was a movement that would reinvigorate the laity's faith and moral compass in order to become active apostles in society, though that action was supposed to take place under the direction of the church hierarchy. Finally, the Catholic Revival, as it was called, made its appearance. This resurgence of Catholic thought and belief acclaimed by engaged novelists, poets, historians, philosophers, biographers, and theologians was brought to the United States by the publishing house of Maisie Ward and Frank Sheed, who established a bookstore in New York City in 1933. As one young visitor to the bookstore recalled,

> A sort of elation accelerated the heartbeat as one entered the shop: Frank or Maisie might be there while you browsed among the books. . . . And what books! . . . Sheed & Ward was attracting a stable of British and continental writers who were not only competitive or even top-notch in their various fields but who seemed to enjoy, to flaunt even, a no-nonsense, take-it-or-leave-it attitude about their faith—not the namby-pamby pap that passed for Catholic literature. (Dolan 1985, 409)

Sheed & Ward published such European Catholic authors as G. K. Chesterton, Jacques Maritain, and Paul Chaudel.

The American Catholic hierarchy continued its reluctance to establish separate ethnic parishes for its immigrant adherents and emphasized Americanization. But ethnic parishes thrived in the 1920s and 1930s, especially as new-ethnic congregants settled in and became citizens. Massive building projects signaled this intention, as, for example, in the case of the Polish Sacred Heart parish in New

Britain, Connecticut, which built its impressive church in the late 1920s and early 1930s (Buczek 1974).

Other Catholics became forceful activists for interracial justice. The Catholic policy toward African Americans moving into northern cities was to segregate them in their own parishes, where bishops would assign a religious order of priests to minister to this particular group. Thus as the neighborhood changed, so did the Catholic parish. This practice often led to the rifts between white and African American Catholics in the same neighborhood. Some Catholic priests became advocates for their African American parishioners. One such person was the Jesuit John LaFarge, who gathered African American Catholics in New York City to study the problem and suggest solutions to the Church. By the mid-1930s, the group formally established itself as the Catholic Interracial Council and committed itself to an educational and biracial approach to racial justice, and by the 1940s it had spread to many other northern cities and become the most important church organization to focus on racial justice. Another effort along these lines was the establishment of Friendship House in Harlem in 1938 by Russian émigré Catherine de Hueck to promote interracial justice, though this was run by the laity, not priests; within the next decade five more Friendship Houses were established in other major cities, along with farms that served as retreat houses (Dolan 1985, 364–369, 412–414).

The Catholic Worker Movement

Out of the Catholic Revival milieu came the Catholic Worker movement. It was established on May Day 1933 when Dorothy Day and her intellectual partner Peter Maurin began selling their new newspaper *The Catholic Worker.* From that newspaper came the movement. Dorothy Day (1897–1980) was nominally raised a Protestant of varying churches, but converted to Roman Catholicism in 1927 when she was 30 years old. This adult conversion had been influenced by her childhood fascination with the mysticism of the Catholic Church combined with her college-years' exposure to the lives of the immigrant poor on Chicago's West Side.

Day had spent the 1920s immersed in the bohemian life of New York City's Greenwich Village. Writing for the socialist *Call* and then *The Masses,* she gained a reputation as an activist journalist. Peter Maurin, an immigrant French cleric, sought her out in 1932 and persuaded her to join him in establishing his program for Catholic social reconstruction, which was a mix of primitive Christianity and agrarian utopianism. Given Maurin's rather eccentric personality, Day would become the main conduit for his ideas. She emphasized the plight of industrial workers and called her followers to suffer along with them, even as Maurin paid little attention to any aspects of industrial society (Piehl 1982; (Fisher 1989, 28–47).

Their goal was to make the Catholic Church the dominant social dynamic force, of greater influence than leftist organizations. The movement coalesced around "houses of hospitality," halfway houses that would feed and house the poor and unemployed. By 1942 32 houses of hospitality had been established around the country, joined by another dozen rural farms that became retreat houses and suppliers of produce for the urban houses. Catholic Worker activists lived in voluntary poverty, sold the paper for a penny, and engaged in acts of charity and intellectual debate over the issues of the day, especially labor issues. While Day and Maurin did not develop a systematic theory, they did enunciate principles that they expected others would follow: skepticism about government as a solution, faith in the community of worship, emphasis on spiritualism rather than materialism, and a deep belief in pacifism. This mixture of radicalism and Catholicism attracted people who were committed Catholics but weary of the old hierarchical Church. Most important, it was led by laypeople, and priests joined the movement only as advisers. Day's charisma kept the movement going and attracted people to it (Dolan 1985, 409–412).

Labor Priests

Father James Cox began his ministry to the unemployed in Pittsburgh in 1931 and led a march of the unemployed to Washington that year (see "Experiences of the Early Depression" chapter). Father Charles Coughlin of Detroit began his National Union for Social Justice. Other priests, notably Father John Ryan and his followers at Catholic University in Washington, D.C., threw themselves into the New Deal itself. A trained economist, Ryan headed the Social Action Department of the National Catholic Welfare Council from 1919 to 1944. His arguments regarding social justice emphasized the practical guarantees of living standards through government protection. Ryan analyzed the Great Depression as a crisis of underconsumption, and supported the New Deal's attempt to raise the standard of living, provide work for all, and stabilize the economy. He consistently supported expanded public works projects and urged a higher wage for WPA workers, to at least $50 a

Father John A. Ryan, outspoken proponent of the New Deal. (Library of Congress)

month (O'Brien 1968, 137). He made a notable early contribution as a member of the Industrial Appeals Board of the National Recovery Administration. In the campaign of 1936, Ryan was outspoken in his defense of the New Deal. He attacked the American Liberty League for its opposition to the New Deal. When Father Coughlin turned against Roosevelt, Ryan countered with his own broadcast on national radio on October 8, 1936, condemning Coughlin's "ugly, cowardly, and flagrant calumnies" against Roosevelt and the New Deal (Smith 1973, 49). He also was a strong supporter of the CIO, though he urged Catholics to become active so as to counter the Communist influences in the CIO.

Association of Catholic Trade Unionists

Many American Catholics became active in the labor movement, and some clergy were determined to both aid and direct that cause. The Association of Catholic Trade Unionists (ACTU) was founded in 1937 in New York by members of the Catholic Worker movement. It became far more influential in the hands of Pittsburgh-area priests Charles Owen Rice and Carl Hensler, whose connections to the growing CIO were greater than anything the New York Catholics could muster. They defined the goal of ACTU "to set Catholics working for the common good. . . . We propose to instruct Catholic employers, and others if they will listen to us, in their duties to us, in their duties toward labor and the common good. We propose to instruct the rich in their duties toward the poor and to emphasize that their wealth has been loaned them by God, Who will one day ask an accounting of it" (Heineman 1999, 151). They were influenced by Pope Pius XI's 1937 encyclical, *Atheistic Communism,* which condemned Marxist materialism. The Pittsburgh priests were concerned with the increased influence of the Communist Party in the Pittsburgh-area unions. Father Rice aligned himself with two devout Catholics in the CIO—Philip Murray, the head of the Steel Workers Organizing Committee, and James Carey, the young president of the United Electrical, Radio, and Machine Workers Union. Together they attempted to curb the CIO's leftward slant (see "The Labor Movement" chapter).

Jewish Community Concerns

Jews in the United States coped with a renewed wave of anti-Semitism brought on by the economic crisis of the Depression and by the rise of Hitler in Germany. The number of congregations grew during the 1920s and 1930s, but they suffered a loss of revenue during the 1930s' Depression. They were forced to raise their membership fees, which led to congregants dropping out of communal worship, while Jewish schools struggled to stay open. Jewish charity groups like the Hebrew Immigrant Aid Society opened their facilities to the homeless and unemployed.

Many Jewish professionals, discriminated against in their own professional fields, found work in New Deal agencies, which even brought labor-union and Socialist Jews into mainstream political life. This also had the effect of fueling anti-Semitism, as phrases like "Jew Deal" became common language in right-wing movements. One major effect of New Deal legislation on Jewish life was the creation of the five-day work-week, enshrined in the 1938 Fair Labor Standards Act (though the act called for a 40-hour week, most employers interpreted it as eight hours a day, five days a week). This allowed observant Jews to have Saturdays off without special arrangement.

There were a number of innovations in religious thought during the decade. One was the rise of Reconstructionism, promulgated by Rabbi Mordechai M. Kaplan (1881–1983). Reconstructionist Judaism was first proposed by Kaplan in 1920, and expanded in his 1934 book *Judaism as a Civilization: Toward a Reconstruction of American-Jewish Life*. This modernized attitude emphasized "Jewish civilization" rather than simply religious practice, and called upon American Jews "to reaffirm Jewish peoplehood, revitalize the Jewish religion, form networks of organic communities, strengthen Jewish life in the land of Israel, further Jewish cultural creativity, and cooperate with non-Jews in advancing freedom, justice, and peace" (Sarna 2004, 245). Kaplan hoped to hold on to the Americanized second generation by discarding the medieval traditions of Orthodox Judaism, yet holding on to elements of Jewishness that Reform Judaism had rejected. The rise of Zionism, the movement for a Jewish homeland, had accelerated after World War I and increased its appeal in the United States during the 1930s. A prominent leader in the 1930s was Stephen S. Wise, an independent-minded Reform rabbi who helped reorganize the American Jewish Congress in 1920 to rival the elitist and anti-Zionist American Jewish Committee. Rabbi Wise became the public spokesman for the plight of European Jews as their peril in the face of Hitler's regime was being chronicled by the American Jewish Year Book. However, the effort to loosen the immigration laws to allow European Jewish refugees into the United States, as in the 1939 Wagner-Rogers bill, failed, and American consuls in Europe were instructed by the State Department to "postpone and postpone and postpone" visa applications from European Jews (Sarna 2004, 260).

Ethnic Community Concerns

European immigrants and their families in the United States, as well as people of color, varied in their experience of the Great Depression, found themselves treated differently by the New Deal, and formed social movements based on their own histories in the United States. European immigrants found themselves on the defensive against strong nativist forces and responded by Americanizing and becoming involved in the political process. They insisted that the United

States was, or should be, a pluralist society. This meant that each ethnic group should "Americanize" or acculturate to the dominant Anglo-American society, but that each group should also be allowed to maintain cultural traditions, language, and self-identification. The question of the "hyphen" was one that many ethnic groups struggled with in the 1930s. Mexican Americans faced strong deportation movements, as well as economic competition from the white unemployed. African Americans, who were increasing their numbers in the North, built organizations around their new voting power in northern cities, all the while shining a light on southern racial violence. All became involved in the labor movement. All became part of the New Deal Coalition to varying degrees.

European Americans

Ethnics Facing Americanization

European immigrants and their American-born children had reached an important stage by the 1930s. This "foreign-stock" population now represented 31.1 percent of the U.S. population. They had been made to feel unwelcome in the xenophobic 1920s, had seen the cut-off of free migration to American shores with the 1924 National Origins Act, which discriminated against Eastern and Southern European countries, and had been subjected to increasing pressures to Americanize themselves and shed their "hyphens." But because of the creation of the New Deal Coalition, they experienced growing political power. Emboldened, many immigrants now became proud "ethnics," embracing their own culture while adapting to American ways.

At the same time, the second generation, those born in the United States, were already a conduit of American culture to their parents and immigrant relatives, and were in danger of being lost to the ethnic culture altogether. The American school system was assisting second-generation children in "learning to forget" their immigrant background (Lassonde 2005). Many ethnic fraternal organizations faced the problem of declining memberships by the late 1920s and had adapted by including English-language columns in their fraternal newspapers and substituting American sports like basketball for their old European soccer teams—anything to attract the younger generation.

But the older generation need not have worried too much. The Great Depression forced all working-class ethnics to reinvigorate the mutual ties that bound them together, for the sake of economic survival. People returned to neighborhood ethnic grocers, since they were the only ones who extended credit. These first- and second-generation Americans were already connected in a web of ethnic community organizations, such as religious institutions and fraternal societies. Though some fraternal organizations folded under the economic pressures of the Depression, these institutions tried mightily to attend to the needs of their members, waiving dues for the unemployed and holding charity fundraisers to aid their constituents in distress (Bucki 2001, 126–30). Historian Lizabeth Cohen argued that it was the failure of these institutions to overcome the effects of the Great Depression that united these ethnics in a "culture of unity" around the Democratic Party and the New Deal (Cohen 1990). But this is only partly true. First-generation ethnics remained attached to their Old World culture, even as their organizations underwent change.

International Workers' Order

One specific change in ethnic-fraternal circles in the 1930s was the rise of the Communist-oriented International Workers' Order (IWO), which used modern actuarial financial practices to offer cheap life and health insurance as well as a progressive, pro–New Deal ideological atmosphere. The IWO was established in 1930 from a left-wing split in the Workmen's Circle, a Jewish fraternal organization affiliated with the Socialist Party. The IWO leaders were open Communists, though the vast majority of the members were not. From its Jewish beginnings, the IWO expanded to become the largest ethnic fraternal organization in the nation in the 1930s. By the late 1930s, the Order had fourteen different nationality sections, including African American and Asian, something that distinguished them from all other fraternal benefit societies. Though the IWO was established before the CP's Popular Front era, it fit very well into the American framework of uniting ethnic groups around their culture and language, promoting "Americanization from the bottom up," organizing youth activities, and using a mild class rhetoric that seemed appealing to 1930s' working-class communities. These newer organizations flourished in the Popular Front era, along with some older ethnic fraternals that were swept along in their members' enthusiasm for the New Deal and the CIO (Keeran 1995). IWO members provided networks within working-class communities that supported union drives, for instance in the steel-workers' campaign of 1937 (see "The Labor Movement" chapter). In 1938 it reported 141,000 dues-paying members (Heineman 1999, 146).

Nativist Responses

Immigration restriction came up for debate immediately when the economic downturn became long-lasting. Congress debated an immigration-reduction bill in 1931, arguing for eliminating immigration entirely, except for a specified number of relatives of American citizens. It was the substance of the exceptions that caused debate, and Congress was unable to agree. Congressman Martin Dies of Texas renewed his fight for quota restrictions in 1934, stating, "If we had refused admission to the 16,500,000 foreign-born who are living in this country today, we would have no unemployment problem to distress and harass us" (Divine 1957, 86). He made no headway on his bills, though migration was already slowing due to the State Department's directive to American consuls to refuse visas to those "likely to become a public charge," as the language of the Immigration Act stated. Thus, in the entire decade, only 528,431 immigrants

Thomas Bell and Americanization

Americanization had different meanings for different classes within ethnic groups. In the 1930s working-class ethnics found a particular kind of Americanization within the new industrial labor movement. Nowhere was this more evident than in the Steel Workers Organizing Committee (SWOC) of the CIO. Thomas Bell, born Adalbert Thomas Belejcak in Braddock, Pennsylvania, in 1903, captured this ethos in his novel *Out of This Furnace* in 1941. In this fictional portrayal of the Pittsburgh area, strewn with examples from his own family's history, Bell told of the fate of two generations of Slovak steelworkers, ending with the triumph of SWOC at U.S. Steel Corporation in 1937. His hero, Dobie, muses near the end of the novel:

> And he realized now what it was that had once puzzled him about the C.I.O. men. Whatever their ancestry, they had felt the same way about certain things; and because Dobie had been born and raised in a steel town, where the word [American] meant people who were white, Protestant, middle-class Anglo-Saxons, it hadn't occurred to him that the C.I.O. men were thinking and talking like Americans. . . .
>
> Made in the U.S.A., he thought, made in the First Ward. But it wasn't where you were born or how you spelled your name or where your father had come from. It was the way you thought and felt about certain things. About freedom of speech and the equality of men. (Bell 1941/1976, 410–411)

An example of "Americanization from the bottom up" (Barrett 1992), this thinking reflected the experience of many ethnics in the 1930s who finally began to feel included through the labor movement or through the New Deal Coalition or both.

were admitted, and along with increased emigration, the net increase in the American population due to immigration was only 68,693 for the decade (Divine 1957, 89).

This issue would have profound effects when the problem of refugees in the increasingly volatile decade was considered. There was no category of "Refugee" in the Immigration Act of 1924, and there was little sentiment within the nation for making exceptions. The problem of Jewish refugees from Hitler's regime dominated immigration discussion from 1933 to 1938, as congressmen friendly to immigration, led by Rep. Samuel Dickstein, introduced a series of bills to liberalize immigration laws on behalf of German refugees. The second and more desperate stage was reached in 1938 with the anti-Jewish laws passed in Germany in the wake of Kristallnacht and with the German invasion of Austria. Finally, in 1939 Sen. Robert Wagner introduced a new refugee bill that would admit 20,000 German-Jewish refugee children over a two-year period outside of the quota system. It failed to pass (Wyman 1984).

Ku Klux Klan

The Ku Klux Klan (KKK) spread in the 1920s and 1930s beyond the South because of its rejection of the new ethnic pluralism that seemed to be defining American society, and it became the vehicle for a revived nativism. The Klan in the 1920s focused on immigrants and Catholics, as well as its traditional role in suppressing African Americans. But in the 1930s, the Klan's traditional attention to defending American ideals and traditions was superseded by more extreme terrorist groups which often borrowed from European fascist ideology.

Silver Shirts, Brown Shirts, and the Black Legion

These paramilitary groupings all shared the same radical nativist, racist, and antidemocratic stance that the KKK evinced, but were more informed by fascist movements in Germany and Italy. They rose in the early 1930s, and became more visible in the second half of the 1930s as their fears grew of the emerging labor movement and the left in general. The Silver Legion was founded in 1934 by William Dudley Pelley of California, a journalist and small businessman turned clairvoyant, who proclaimed that a dream had revealed to him his own spiritual mission coupled to the political mission of Adolf Hitler then unfolding in Europe. The Silver Shirts were most numerous in California and the Southwest, and the San Diego chapter formed a rifle club to safeguard their communities from an alleged impending Jewish-Communist takeover. More dangerous was the Black Legion of Detroit, set up in 1933 by unemployed semiskilled men who often were former Klan members. The chapter was known to have murdered a young Catholic WPA worker who had wrongly been accused of beating his pregnant wife (Smith 1973, 63).

By the late 1930s, with war clouds threatening in Europe, these groups came under increased scrutiny by Congress. In the House in 1934, the McCormack-Dickstein Committee's investigation of Nazi propaganda activities produced a large inventory of confiscated material and testimony on pro-Nazi sympathies in the United States and of linkages between the German-oriented groups and other domestic activists. A serious threat was posed by the German-American Bund, led by German immigrant Fritz Kuhn. Born in Munich, Kuhn (1895–1951) had been a German soldier in World War I, trained as a chemist after the war, joined the Nazi Party in 1921, fled to Mexico to dodge a larceny conviction, and finally arrived in Detroit in 1927. After working in Henry Ford's Dearborn plant for six years, he became a naturalized American citizen in 1933. He joined the Friends of the New Germany at that time and gradually took charge of that disorganized group. Kuhn streamlined organization, reinstated secrecy, and received propaganda directly from Berlin to spread in German American communities. In 1937 he verbally dueled with Mayor Fiorello La Guardia of New

German American Bund parade in New York City on East 86th Street, October 30, 1939. (Library of Congress)

York, responding to La Guardia's remarks calling Hitler "that brown-shirted fanatic now menacing the peace of the world." Kuhn defended Hitler, adding that the mayor was a cog in the Jewish-Communist world conspiracy that, along with President Franklin "Rosenfeld," would destroy the United States if given the chance (Smith 1973, 97). In 1938 Congressman Dies's Un-American Activities Committee investigated the German American Bund. La Guardia had the Bund's finances investigated, and U.S. District Attorney Thomas E. Dewey won a conviction of Kuhn for embezzling funds in 1939. Bund leaders were later interned for the duration of World War II.

In his detailed study of right-wing movements in Pennsylvania, historian Philip Jenkins notes that Congress shied away from investigating Italian pro-fascists or Catholic groups because of potential political fallout from Italian or Catholic voters. Jenkins also noted that some of these American groups rejected the authoritarian bent of their European counterparts and built their movement on the preservation of individual American rights being threatened by Communists and their followers. But other groups scoffed at democratic ideology, and Jenkins labeled as "fascist" those "extreme right-wing, authoritarian, anti-democratic, paramilitary, racist movements." He also noted that collectively they attracted at

Hollywood's "Black Legion"

An intriguing 1936 Hollywood film, *Black Legion,* starring Humphrey Bogart as a villainous bigot, put the Black Legion in the public eye. The screenplay was based on an actual Michigan incident where the ultrapatriotic Black Legion murdered a Works Progress Administration worker. Bogart's character, Frank Taylor, is a native-born autoworker whose economic woes lead him to seek a foreman's position. When the position goes to a Polish immigrant, Taylor falls in with the local Black Legion, who promise him revenge. In addition to the murder of the Polish worker, the audience witnesses the smashing of a downtown chain pharmacy that has just opened. Among the middle-class leaders of the gang is the local pharmacist, whose drugstore has folded from the competition (Zaniello 2003, 54–55). The film remarkably portrays the political *zeitgeist* of the time.

least the same number of followers as the better-known leftist movements of the 1930s (Jenkins 1997, 11–29).

Interethnic Conflicts in New York City

A case study of New York City reveals the interconnected cooperation and rivalry among Irish, Germans, Jews, and Italians during the 1930s. The economic crisis of the 1930s brought to the surface a variety of competitions, especially economic and political, between the large group of Irish Americans in control of political power and their rivals, Italians and Jews. The Irish-Jewish rivalry was especially fierce during the 1930s, noted historian Ronald Bayor. The election of Fiorello La Guardia (see the previous chapter) as mayor in 1933 resulted in changes to civil service appointments, increasing the number of non-Irish in city jobs. This increased Irish-Jewish hostilities in such neighborhoods as Washington Heights and the South Bronx, where Irish gang violence against Jews was encouraged by the Christian Front and Christian Mobilizers (Bayor 1978).

The "Old World" influences on ethnic groups in New York City were important. The German American community's response to Hitler's rise in Germany varied from outright disbelief in the resulting anti-Semitic violence to fear that the anti-German sentiment of the World War I years would re-emerge in American society. Some Germans proudly joined the German American Bund, organized in 1936 out of the factionalized German American organizations of the early 1930s. According to Bayor, the majority of these were recent Catholic immigrants, usually from the southern German states where anti-Semitism found fertile ground; more settled German Americans were not attracted to the Bund. But Nazi sympathizers soon took over prominent German American societies, such as the United German Societies of Greater New York, and rescinded their previous ban on flying the swastika flag at the annual German Day parade. A notable exception to this trend was the New York Steuben Society, whose president, Gustav W. M. Wieboldt, publicly attacked the Bund and in 1936 forbade membership in the society to any Nazis or others who were against the American form of government. Also, prominent German Americans like Sen. Robert Wagner (D-NY) began publicly criticizing the German government and its anti-Semitic activities in 1933 (Bayor 1978, 59–67).

Response from the Jewish American community was immediate, however. In March 1933 the Jewish War Veterans announced a boycott of German goods, which was soon taken up by the American Jewish Congress. As the decade progressed and Nazi intentions became more obvious, the boycott received great support from the American public. According to a Gallup Poll in late 1938, 96 percent of American Jews supported the boycott, as did 64 percent of American Catholics and 61 percent of American Protestants (Bayor 1978, 68). German Bundists retaliated with an anti-Jewish boycott. By 1937–1938, the German American community had awakened to the threat of Nazism, given international events such as the annexation of Austria and the Kristallnacht pogrom in November 1938, and began to resist the Nazi pressure within its ranks. In addition, Congress began investigating Nazi activities in the United States. With the creation of a committee in May 1938, headed by Congressman Martin Dies, the House Committee on Un-American Activities (HUAC) investigated both Nazism and Communism. New York Mayor La Guardia ordered an investigation of the Bund as well.

By the mid-1930s, German Bundists and Italian fascists began meeting together, as their homelands grew closer. In 1937 the Bund and the Italian Blackshirts met at Camp Nordland in New Jersey. But it was the German American Bund and the new Christian Front that raised the loudest voices in the late 1930s.

The Christian Front

Father Charles Coughlin grew more anti-Semitic in his broadcasts in the latter part of the 1930s, and reprinted in his newspaper *Social Justice* the fictitious *Protocols of the Elders of Zion,* which described a Jewish plot to rule the world. Irish American Coughlinites, in particular, found this mythical plot very appealing. Combined with the 1937 papal encyclical *Divini Redemptoris,* which stated that Communism was the greatest menace to the world, and the tendency to conflate Jews and Communism, Catholic communities witnessed a groundswell of anti-Jewish sentiment in their midst. One international point of confrontation was the Spanish Civil War. The Church rallied support for Franco's attempt to topple the elected government of Spain, while Communists, with many Jewish sympathizers among them, supported the Loyalists. Acting on Pope Pius XI's promotion of a Catholic Social Action movement to confront social problems, Coughlin called for a Christian Front, which while paying lip service to the pope's goal of bringing the world back to basic Christian concepts served in Greater

New York City to focus on the Jewish community and exacerbate tensions. Local rallies in Brooklyn and Manhattan led to a movement, and the Christian Front was born at the Church of St. Paul the Apostle in Manhattan in July 1938. According to Ronald Bayor, the Christian Front in New York City was dominated by Irish American professionals and some clergy, and attracted mostly blue-collar and lower white-collar Irish Americans. Their emphasis was on American patriotism and self-defense. As the New York City leader John Cassidy put it, "we are a militant group of men . . . determined to use every means at our command to guarantee to the Christian people of America, that they shall never be subjected to the misfortune that befell their Christian brothers in Russia, Mexico, and Spain" (Bayor 1978, 99). The Front focused on the imagined Jewish menace and organized boycotts against Jewish merchants, while also rooting out Communists from the labor unions and government. Many members were under the impression that the Roman Catholic Church supported the organization, since the Church had never made a public statement repudiating the Front and many prominent clerics in New York individually supported it.

In the Bronx and Manhattan, a more militant group, the Christian Mobilizers, was formed in July 1939 by former Fronters who thought the Front was being too timid in its methods. The Mobilizers had a brief existence while furthering the anti-Jewish boycotts and various incidents of street violence. But it was the Front that was targeted in a sweeping arrest by the Federal Bureau of Investigation in January 1940, charging 18 people with conspiracy to overthrow the government of the United States. In a complex case, the FBI accused the 18, most of whom belonged to the Front, of plotting the bombing of numerous buildings, including the Jewish *Daily Forward* and the Communist Party's *Daily Worker* publishing houses, a Russian-language movie theater, Jewish neighborhoods, and Jewish businesses. In the anticipated political chaos that would ensue, the Fronters hoped to stimulate an anti-Semitic movement and then a defensive response by Communists and Jews, which would then be crushed by a counterrevolution led by the Fronters who would set up a right-wing dictatorship. The long trial, which revealed the Fronters' penchant for organizing rifle clubs and accumulating ammunition, as well as their strident anti-Semitism, brought one of three outcomes for the defendants. Either the charges were dismissed, the defendants acquitted, or, in the case of the final five, a mistrial declared as the jury could not reach a unanimous verdict.

In the war atmosphere that was soon to follow, most of these groups that had not cut their ties with Nazi Germany were suppressed.

"Premature Anti-Fascists": The Abraham Lincoln Brigade

The Spanish Civil War became a touchstone for both the left and the right in the United States. When Gen. Francisco Franco rebelled against the newly elected Republican government of Spain in 1936, the Spanish Civil War quickly became a testing ground for the possibility of World War II, as a clash between

Italian Americans and Fascism

Italian Americans were never a secure part of the New Deal Coalition. Voting analyses from numerous cities showed that the Italian American community swayed between support for FDR and local loyalty to Republican Party leaders and their friends in fraternal organizational leadership (Maiale 1950). More important was their great ardor for Mussolini's Italy. Some analysts have pointed out that Mussolini was the first Italian leader to unite northern and southern Italians in a national political sense. This image crossed the Atlantic to Italian American communities in the United States. Radical Italian American community leaders had been silenced by the hostile antilabor and anti-immigrant atmosphere of the 1920s; the Massachusetts state execution of Italian anarchists Nicola Sacco and Bartolomeo Vanzetti in August 1927 was only the most potent reminder. Agents of Mussolini's fascist government working covertly with the FBI in the United States helped identify Italian nationals who were active radicals in their American communities. Of course, the American business community held Mussolini and his government in fairly high regard throughout the 1920s and into the late 1930s as well (Diggins 1972). The Italian government in the 1930s began using less overtly fascist and more nationalist appeals to the Italian American community, thus trying to convince them that antifascism was "un-Italian." The new Italian American organization, the Sons of Italy, organized to promote a unified all-Italian identification instead of the myriad regional- and local-identified fraternal societies dotting the Little Italies of American cities and town. The Sons of Italy supported Mussolini's programs. Historian Rudolph Vecoli bluntly stated, "Rather than speak of the Americanization of the Little Italies during the interwar years, it would be more accurate, then, to speak of their Fascistization" (Vecoli 2003, 54).

But there were a few voices in the Italian American community to counter the rising conservative tide. Long-time radical leaders like Carlo Tresca and Luigi Antonini continued to lead the antifascist movement in New York City. Antonini, president of Local 89–Italian Press and Waist Makers Union of ILGWU, was particularly influential. The influx of Italian radicals fleeing Mussolini in the mid-1920s provided a new cohort of radicals in Italian American communities, and bolstered the native-born Italian Americans who had come of age during World War I and who had had experiences in the labor movement and the Socialist Party. Many of them had joined the Communist Party in the 1920s (Ottanelli 2001). This second generation was more likely to be working, not in the traditional Italian jobs of building trades, needle trades, and the textile industry, but in maritime, auto, and steel. The CIO made inroads into the Italian working class, and leftist Italian Americans were prominent organizers for the garment, textile, steel, and auto unions. Liberal-labor coalitions in Italian Harlem provided the electoral base for congressmen Fiorello La Guardia (1922–1932) and Vito Marcantonio (1934–1950) (see previous chapter). However, Italians in the United States attended rallies in favor of Mussolini's invasion of Ethiopia beginning in February 1935 and enthusiastically gave up their gold wedding bands and other jewelry to the Italian military cause. Race relations in the United States worsened as African Americans rallied to the defense of Ethiopia, and the two communities often clashed.

Members of the American Ambulance Unit for Spain, part of the American Friends of Spanish Democracy, stand in front of their medical vehicles in Paris en route to Spain, 1937. (Library of Congress)

democracy and fascism. Nazis as well as Italian and Portuguese fascists rushed to the aid of Franco with troops and war materiel, while Western democracies remained neutral.

The North American Committee to Aid Spanish Democracy was founded in the fall of 1936 and acted as an umbrella for the many groups, such as ethnic organizations and labor unions, who contributed funds, medical supplies, food, and ambulances to Spain. Antifascist volunteers from many nations formed the International Brigades to defend the Spanish Republic. Guided by a Popular Front impulse, some 40,000 antifascists from Italy, Germany, France, Belgium, England, the Soviet Union, and Scandinavian and Slavic countries assembled battalions to assist the Loyalist army against the rebel army. In late fall 1936, some 3,000 American volunteers organized into the Abraham Lincoln Battalion (commonly referred to as the Brigade), and defied a U.S. State Department ban on travel to Spain. They saw their first battle at Jarama in February 1937. Their average age was 27, and they came from all walks of life, though many were from urban areas. Many were Communists, but there were also a mix of other leftists and antifascists. About one-third were Jews, which was not a surprise given Hitler's support of Franco. The largest occupational group, some 500–600, were sailors

Protesting the German Ship *Bremen* in New York Harbor

On the left, many grew concerned as Nazi Germany's plans for the world were becoming more apparent. One remarkable demonstration took place against the German oceanliner *Bremen* in July 1935, when it planned to sail into New York harbor flying the swastika flag of Germany. Many longshoremen in New York City had been radicals involved in organizing the Marine Workers' Industrial Union of the TUUL (see "Experiences of the Early Depression" chapter) and their antifascist sensibilities were high. Bill Bailey, who later volunteered for the Lincoln Brigade fighting in Spain, was one of the longshoremen who boarded the ship while other demonstrators massed on the dock. He remembered snatching the swastika from the flagpole and tossing it onto the shore before being knocked nearly unconscious by German sailors. Dragged off the ship by New York City policemen who were acting under the impression that all the demonstrators were Communists, he observed, "A white-haired police captain with a strong Irish brogue walked over to where we were sitting, and to each man he said 'And what would your name be?' Jotting down the names, he looked puzzled, then in a whisper that I could overhear, he told another policeman, 'Why they're all Irish! There's not a Jew amongst them'" (Bessie and Prago 1987, 52).

and longshoremen (Byrne 2007, 75). The Lincoln Brigade was centrally involved in the many fierce battles of 1937 and defended the city of Barcelona along the Ebro River in 1938. By the time the Loyalist forces surrendered on April 1, 1939, some 700 members of the Abraham Lincoln Brigade had died in Spain (Carroll 1994). Upon their return to the United States, members of the Brigade became the symbol for internationalism in a country that was undergoing a reversion to isolationism as World War II officially began in Europe. After the war, many were harassed by the emerging anti-Communist crusade in Washington, and they earned the nickname "premature anti-fascists" since they had volunteered to go to war against Hitler's allies before the United States was forced into World War II by Japan's attack on Pearl Harbor.

Youth Movements

American Youth Congress

The American Youth Congress (AYC) was the generational expression of a newly active cohort that lobbied Congress for expanded government assistance for low-income youth as well as rallying against war and fascism. The AYC was unique in its breadth of membership, uniting all races and ethnicities, urban and rural, student and nonstudent, and at its height in the late 1930s claimed to represent 4.5 million young Americans. Though its founder in 1934, Viola Ilma, was politically moderate, the organization quickly became dominated by a radical coalition of young Communists and Socialists who critiqued the New Deal, specifically the National Youth Administration, for not doing enough for the estimated five to eight million unemployed young people. The AYC wrote an alternative bill, the Youth Act, in 1935 and organized a march of 3,000 young people to Washington in 1937. Though the Youth Act was never passed, the activities of the AYC raised public awareness of the "youth problem" and caused Eleanor Roosevelt to champion their cause. In summer 1938, Eleanor played a prominent role in the AYC-sponsored World Youth Congress meeting, which organized around a progressive antifascist agenda. Unfortunately, in February 1940 at Youth Congress Citizenship Institute in Washington, the AYC Communist faction, now turned away from its antifascist position in the wake of the Nazi-Soviet Pact, turned the Institute into a demonstration against Roosevelt's foreign policies, to which President Roosevelt responded with an angry address to the Institute members gathered at the White House. The influence of the group dwindled from that point on (Cohen 1993).

American Student Union

The American Student Union (ASU) was the first mass protest movement of students in the United States. Between its founding in 1935 and the end of the decade, it claimed some 20,000 members and mobilized nearly half of the nation's college students in antiwar protests, as well as lobbying for federal aid to low-income students and unemployed youth. It was the culmination of two years of student agitation on the anniversary of U.S. intervention in World War I. On April 13, 1934, 25,000 students struck, and in 1935 nearly 150,000 students participated in one-hour strikes and peace rallies. Many of those activists were centered in New York City, but there was significant participation from the Midwest and California; over 130 campuses participated in the 1935 strike, including 20 in the South. Many students believed that World War I had not been a victory for democracy, and had led to the rise of Mussolini and Hitler. Many American college students adopted pacifism and isolationism, following the so-called Oxford Pledge. This resolution not to "fight for King and country" had been passed by the Oxford Union of students at Oxford University in England in February 1933. In the United States, the Oxford Pledge was translated into a refusal "to support the United States government in any war it may conduct" (Draper 1967, 169–172). The student strikes and rallies in 1934 and 1935 were organized by the Socialist-led Student League for Industrial Democracy (SLID) and the Communist-led National Student League (NSL). The two groups merged to form the ASU at a national unity conference of student activists in Columbus, Ohio, in December 1935. The ASU proceeded to make a large impact in 1936 and 1937 antiwar strikes and rallies, with more than 500,000 students participating each year, as college administrators became increasingly tolerant. Both the CP's Popular Front position and the leftward shift in college students' attitudes in the 1930s led to common ground between leftists and liberals on college campuses, as the ASU promoted solidarity with the labor movement and support for the New Deal. Franklin D. Roosevelt became the first Democratic presidential candidate in decades to win a plurality in the national student straw poll during the 1936 election season.

The organization was not without internal dissension between SP- and CP-affiliated factions over the CP's new emphasis on "collective security." This position had emerged as part of the Comintern's Seventh Congress in 1935 which approved the Popular Front, as well as approving increased defense spending as a way to halt fascism. This meant an uncomfortable transition for American Communists who had made antimilitarism an important part of the NSL. When FDR made his "quarantine the aggressors" speech on October 5, 1937, public opinion polls showed a negative response, as some 70 percent of the population favored even stricter neutrality laws and nearly three-quarters advocated a national referendum before the United States could go to war (Klehr 1984, 205). The CP, however, supported FDR's position. When the ASU got caught in the CP's swing to its antimilitarist position in 1939 as a result of the Nazi-Soviet Pact, the student movement withered. For bitter recollections of this transition, see Draper 1967; Draper was the SLID leader who continued to champion the Oxford Pledge. For a more balanced approach, see Robert Cohen's study (Cohen 1993).

Southern Negro Youth Congress

The Southern Negro Youth Congress (SNYC) was an outgrowth of the National Negro Congress (NCC, see below) and the leftist student movements of the day. Founded in 1937, SNYC focused on the special problems of African American youth in the south, for civil rights as well as economic advancement. Many of the 500 delegates to the 1937 founding conference in Richmond, Virginia, had experience in other leftist youth organizations like the American Student Union and the American Youth Congress. One of their first activities was to aid African American workers on strike at the Carrington and Michaux tobacco factory. The resulting independent union, the Tobacco Stemmers' and Laborers' Union (TSLU), won that strike and went on to organize other tobacco factories in the area; the TSLU later merged with the CIO's UCAPAWA (see the next chapter) (Korstad 2003, 149).

Mexican Americans

The 1930 U.S. Census revealed that for the first time the majority of Mexicans living in the United States were born in the United States. Like their Euro-American counterparts, these Mexican Americans would become part of the New Deal Coalition that placed "hyphenate-Americans" in the political arena. Mexican Americans, like other foreign-stock groups of this era, wrestled with the fierce anti-immigrant sentiment of the day. Mexican Americans, those who were born in the United States, created a new mindset, which historian Mario García has labeled the "Mexican-American Generation" (García 1989, 15). This second generation of Mexican Americans had its own character and historical understanding of its place in Anglo-America, even as it tried to claim its rightful American status. The immigrant experience of their parents was reinforced by proximity to the homeland and their continued migration across the border. Unlike European ethnics, whose entry to the United States was now regulated and restricted by the 1924 Immigration Act, Mexicans and other Latin Americans still had free access across the American border. However, the paperwork and fees surrounding that crossing meant that many were without documents and thus subject to deportation. The "Repatriation" movement of the early 1930s, fueled by the massive unemployment and relief needs of Americans, caught Mexicans unaware that their papers needed to be in order (see "Experiences of the Early Depression" chapter). This problem intimidated the Mexican American community throughout the 1930s.

Mexicans shelling pecans in a union plant in San Antonio, Texas, March 1939. (Corbis)

The second generation, García's Mexican-American generation, took two paths to address their political and material status during the 1930s. One path was pursued by middle-class professionals who aimed to become a political force within the American political process and to secure civil rights for their community. Working-class activists, on another path, aimed to raise the economic status of Mexican American workers in concert with the rising union movement of the 1930s, especially the Congress of Industrial Organizations (CIO).

League of United Latin American Citizens

The League of United Latin American Citizens (LULAC) became an important political entity promoting a new model of civic engagement for Mexican Americans in the 1930s. It was organized in 1929 in Corpus Christi, Texas, in response to increased discrimination against Mexicans and Mexican Americans in Texas as a result of changing economic conditions. In the 1920s, that state had experienced the onslaught of agribusiness, which displaced both Anglo and Mexican small farmers. Anglo farmers, in turn, blamed the Mexican Americans, along with the increased number of Mexican immigrants needed to pick these crops, for depressing economic conditions and wage rates. However, some Mexican Americans participated in the prosperity of the 1920s by becoming businessmen servicing this enlarged ethnic community, and they chafed at the continued segregation, discrimination, and racial violence that the Mexican community endured. Their answer was to found LULAC as a pressure group to demand equal rights as American citizens, and to raise the consciousness of their community to the need to adapt to American society while still retaining a Mexican cultural identity. Thus they championed bilingualism and ethnic pride. They revealed contradictions, however, since the founding constitution of the organization made membership open only to U.S. citizens of "Latin extraction" and declared English to be their official language. Leaders recognized the controversy about these decisions by explaining that their experience indicated that only an organization made up of U.S. citizens had a chance to be influential in Texas politics.

LULAC's stress on Americanization of their community led them to discourage their community from displaying Mexican nationalism such as the Mexican flag or joining "foreign" groups like the Mexican Chamber of Commerce in Corpus Christi. In this way, LULAC modeled a reformist, middle-class approach to solving their community's problems. They promoted acculturation, not assimilation, proclaiming they were Americans first but also retaining their ethnic culture, in keeping with their pluralist approach to American society. LULAC organized voter mobilizations, ran candidates for office, and protested discrimination against Mexican Americans in WPA projects in mid-decade. Throughout the 1930s, LULAC grew to more than 80 councils in Texas, New Mexico, Arizona, California, and Kansas.

One particular campaign that revealed both the aspirations and the contradictions of LULAC was the 1930 desegregation case in Del Rio, Texas. LULAC's strategy revealed the goal of improving Mexican American children's education by opposing the segregation of Mexicans in their own separate schools. Texas, in effect, had a three-part school system, one each for whites, African Americans, and Mexicans. The Del Rio school board defended its practice by noting the language difficulties of Mexican students, as well as their different school calendar, which had to be adapted to the harvest season; the court upheld the school board. The following year, LULAC in San Antonio, documenting the funding disparities between Mexican and Anglo schools, argued that this constituted illegal discrimination. They did not ask to break down the segregated school system, only to bring the Mexican schools up to Anglo funding standards. Some small progress was made.

Historian Mario García argues for understanding LULACers on their own terms (García 1989). In contrast, other historians point out the flaws in LULAC's strategy, as LULAC rejected the more radical labor-oriented activities of working-class Mexican Americans. Historian Neil Foley's complex study of the racial labeling of central Texas populations in the early 20th century documents this internal dynamic in the Mexican American community. LULAC tried to combat racial segregation by insisting that Mexicans should be classified as "white," which allowed them to separate themselves from African Americans, whose civil rights campaigns were also developing. In effect, middle-class Mexican leaders were attempting to put themselves on the white side of the color line (Foley 1997).

Mexicans and Labor Unions

Working-class Mexican Americans followed similar patterns of other American ethnic workers by enthusiastically joining AFL unions after the passage of the National Industrial Recovery Act in 1933, and again as the Congress of Industrial Organizations (CIO) pursued industrial unionism after 1935. From the Los Angeles Dressworkers strike of fall 1933 to the Cannery Workers organizing in 1933, to the furniture workers of Los Angeles and the International Longshoremen's Union in 1937, Mexican American workers participated in much of California industrial labor organizing. They also were key in agricultural unionization as well, participating in the sharecroppers' organizing in Texas (see the next chapter). Generally speaking, the Depression had begun to loosen the power of local ethnic elites over the Mexican American working class in Los Angeles (Sánchez 1993). In addition, the Mexican consulate had intervened in the late 1920s' labor disputes with efforts to moderate radical influences among Mexicans in California by forming La Confederación de Uniónes Obreras Mexicanas (CUOM), the Federation of Mexican Workers, connected to the Mexican labor movement. The Mexican government saw this as their role in protecting Mexican nationals and encouraging them to return to Mexico. However, as the Depression continued, more Mexican American workers came under the influence of American radicals such as the Communist Party USA. The Mexican consulate could do no more than denounce "red" unions.

Studies of cannery and packing workers revealed that greater numbers of Mexican American single women, many daughters still living at home, began entering the workforce as their male relatives were laid off. These young women became the backbone of the International Ladies' Garment Workers (ILGWU) in Los Angeles, organized by veteran East Coast ILGWU organizer Rose Pesotta. Even as older male Anglo cutters regarded the Mexican women as unorganizable, Pesotta signed up hundreds of Mexican workers through bilingual pamphlets and the use of a Spanish-language radio station. As she later recalled, "Some of the women quietly admitted to me that they, too, would like to be Americans. In Mexico, they said, women still had no freedom; a married woman could not vote nor hold a job without her husband's consent, and the father was still the supreme ruler over unmarried daughters until they reached the age of 30" (Sánchez 1993, 234). Thus the union drive meshed well with the aspirations of this Mexican American generation.

El Congreso de Pueblo de Hablan Español (The Spanish-Speaking Congress)

"El Congreso" was an important attempt to develop a Mexican American civil rights organization dedicated to advancing the rights of Mexican Americans and other Spanish-speaking people in the United States. It was tied to the emerging union movement and to left-wing elements within the Mexican American working class. The main organizer was Luisa Moreno. Born in Guatemala, Moreno had migrated to Mexico, and then to the United States. After working in a garment sweatshop in New York City's Spanish Harlem, she became active in the TUUL Needle Trades Workers Industrial Union (see the next chapter), and then with the AFL organizing Florida cigar workers. By 1937 she joined the CIO and organized Mexican pecan shellers in San Antonio into the militant United Cannery, Agricultural, Packing, and Allied Workers (UCAPAWA). Taking a leave from the UCAPAWA in 1938, she began traveling throughout the Southwest organizing what would become El Congreso. Moreno was most successful in organizing thousands of Mexican Americans in the Los Angeles area, and the first convocation of El Congreso's California organization was held in Los Angeles on December 4, 1938. Eighty-eight delegates representing 73 organizations with a combined membership of 70,000 attended this meeting, preparing for the national convention to be held in Albuquerque in March 1939. The goal was to create a nationwide movement unifying all Spanish-speaking people in the United States around jobs, access to land-ownership, education, and discrimination. In fact, it presaged the 1980s movement to create a Hispanic ethnic movement (García 1989, 148). Moreno got an impressive diversity of organizations and individuals to endorse the Albuquerque convention: LULAC, the Liga Obrera of New Mexico, the American League for Peace and Democracy, the Workers Alliance of America, the Women's International League for Peace and Freedom, the Mexican Methodist Church, the Amalgamated Clothing Workers of America, the Pecan Workers Union of San Antonio, the International Union of Mine, Mill, and Smelter Workers, the Mexican American Democratic Progressive Club of Los Angeles, Upton Sinclair, Herbert Biberman of the Screen Directors Guild, and John Bright of the League of American Writers. Various professors at the University of New Mexico were prepared to host the March 1939 convention of El Congreso at their campus, but red-baiting pressures from the local community caused the convention to be rescheduled for Los Angeles in April 1939. The Los Angeles venue proved more hospitable for a left-leaning group like El Congreso, and successfully opened with a reported 1,500 persons attending the opening ceremonies. Though the bulk of the delegates came from the southwestern states, there were scattered delegations from the Midwest and Florida.

The broad appeal was captured in some of the banners hung in the hall: "We Ask for Justice and Equality for La Raza Latina," "In Defense of Our Homes We Struggle Against Deportation," "Citizens and Non-Citizens Unite Together." Similar to the National Negro Congress, which had been formed in 1935, El Congreso followed CP's Popular Front strategy of encouraging wide organizations in defense of democracy and basic civil rights. Though there is no proof of the CP's direct influence in El Congreso, party publications gave the movement extensive press coverage. El Congreso had a left-wing secretary, Josefina Fierro de Bright, but a moderate, Eduardo Quevedo, as president. Quevedo was a popular leader among the L.A. *mutualistas* and had worked both for Upton Sinclair's EPIC campaign in 1934 and for Democratic candidates in California. El Congreso never reached its promised strength but for its existence remained mostly a California organization. After September 1939 it lost some of its attraction as it hewed to the new CP line, opposing the war in Europe as an imperialist war, not an antifascist conflict. El Congreso mobilized in 1939 to oppose proposed California legislation that would deny relief payments to non–U.S. citizens, to stop deportations, and to gain federally funded, low-cost housing for L.A. neighborhoods. It had a remarkable record of advancing women's issues and promoting women leaders; Fierro de Bright reported that some 30 percent of El Congreso's activists were women, unlike LULAC, which allowed women to participate only in women's auxiliaries.

Mexicans in the United States had a long history of radical thinking. As Dorothy Healey remembered in organizing the Cannery and Agricultural Workers Industrial Union in 1933, she had announced at the first meeting that the union organizers were Communists. When a later meeting was held for those who were interested in joining the Party, she addressed some two dozen workers crowded into one of the workers' homes. Their response was, "Of course, we're for the revolution. When the barricades are ready, we'll be there with you, but don't bother us with meetings all the time. We know what to do, we know who the enemy is!" (Healey and Isserman 1993, 45). These Mexicans had experienced the Mexican Revolution and were known for their anarcho-syndicalist orientation.

Asian Americans

The 1930 U.S. Census reported nearly 75,000 Chinese, 140,000 Japanese, 56,000 Filipinos, and a few thousands of Asian Indians and Koreans living in the United States. Most were on the West Coast. Corralled into specific economic niches such as agricultural laborers, small farmers, and entrepreneurs in service industries, Asian Americans were hard hit by the economic downturn. Asian Americans included many ethnic groups from Asia and the Pacific Islands; the two things all these groups had in common was that the majority came to the U.S.

mainland as cheap labor, just as European immigrants had done. All Asian immigrants suffered harsh racism, violence, and formal legal barring from the United States, beginning with the 1882 Chinese Exclusion Act. The 1924 Immigration Act specifically excluded all Asian immigration. The situation was different only on the island of Hawai'i, a U.S. territory, because of the majority population of Asian Americans there. Asians not born in the United States were not allowed to become citizens, a situation that did not change until 1943, when the restrictions were lifted for Chinese who now found themselves allies with the United States in the Pacific War. On the other hand, at that same time Japanese and Japanese Americans were interned and lost civil liberties as well as property for the duration of World War II.

San Francisco Chinatown

In the San Francisco Chinatown, the segregated nature of the Chinatown economy protected the community from some of the worst effects of the Depression (Yung 1995, 178–222). The Chinese were not scapegoated and attacked by white workers as they were in the depression of the 1870s. There were no bread lines or Hoovervilles in Chinatown. The district associations and kin networks in Chinatown provided resources for the needy in the early 1930s. As conditions worsened, a new organization, the Huaren Shiyi Hui (Chinese Unemployed Alliance) arose and challenged the Chinese merchant class of the Chinese Six Companies. The Huaren Shiyi Hui joined with the CP-influenced Unemployed Council at a large demonstration in the San Francisco financial district to demand city relief. The city finally began serving the Chinese community in mid-1932. With the advent of the New Deal, the Chinese, so marginalized throughout their history in the United States, became beneficiaries of federal relief programs for the first time, though one had to be a U.S. citizen to qualify. They were also welcomed into the growing labor movement. Yung noted that the Chinese took advantage of the repeal of prohibition to open bars and dance halls to attract tourists to Chinatown. By the mid-1930s, San Francisco Chinatown's economy was bustling.

In particular, Chinese women improved their circumstances, as they continued to have work even as men lost their jobs as cooks, seasonal laborers, and laundrymen. More Chinese American women began to escape the narrow strictures of traditional Chinese family customs, as their increased economic importance to their families grew throughout the decade. The Young Women's Christian Association (YWCA) and its programs in Chinatown, coordinated by local activist Jane Kwong Lee, became accepted and important for the women of Chinatown, who flocked to reading classes, lectures and plays on history and politics, and nutrition classes. She and other public-minded women became accepted by the Chinatown establishment, which had previously frowned on women's public roles. Second-generation Chinese American women also found that their job opportunities increased, as the tourist trade and nightclubs expanded, and as civil-service jobs opened up to those with training and professional schooling. Indicative of the changing mindset of women in Chinatown was the 1938 garment workers' strike against the National Dollar Stores, which involved over 100 first- and second-generation Chinese women (see the next chapter).

Chinatowns everywhere in the United States were concerned with Japan's military actions long before other Americans were. For Chinese Americans, World War II had started with the Japanese invasion of Manchuria in September 1931. The San Francisco Chinatown organized a Chinese War Relief Association to gather money and clothing for Chinese war refugees in the homeland. Most important, it organized a large demonstration on the San Francisco docks on December 16–20, 1938, to protest the loading of scrap iron bound for Japan's munitions industry. The resulting campaign eventually persuaded President Roosevelt to sign a presidential order halting the sale of war materials to Japan in 1941.

New York Chinatown

The social and political story in New York City's Chinatown was quite complex and seemingly contrasted with that of San Francisco (Kwong 2001, 61–91). The Chinese Unemployed Council of the early 1930s attracted large numbers of the unemployed in Chinatown, but was unable to make much headway in spite of the failure of the traditional organizations, particularly the Chinatown Chinese Benevolent Association (CCBA), to deal with the real needs of the community. Historian Peter Kwong blames the left-wing Unemployed Council's "dogmatic" approach to social problems for its lack of success. What did occur was a movement arising from the community itself. The Chinese Hand Laundry Alliance (CHLA), organized in 1933, brought together the many Chinese hand-laundry owners to oppose the new non-Chinese laundry association that set standard prices above the Chinese prices; when the Chinese laundries refused to abide by those rules, the non-Chinese laundries retaliated with a boycott of the Chinese laundries. In a typical scapegoating tactic, the non-Chinese laundry association blamed the cheaper Chinese laundries for their loss of business. The CHLA also fought against a proposed city ordinance, drafted by the city's non-Chinese laundry owners, which would require all laundries to pay an annual license fee to the city and post a $1,000 bond in order to do business. The Chinese laundries could not pay such costs, and this proposal was interpreted as an attempt to drive the Chinese laundries out of business. When the CCBA was unable, or unwilling, to fight the ordinance, the CHLA gained new power in the community. What set the CHLA apart from "old" organizations was that it was organized along trade lines, not family, clan, or geographical divisions. This "new" versus "old" organizational struggle defined the rest of the decade. The CHLA found allies within the Chinese and U.S. left movements, while the traditional elite received support from Chiang Kai-Shek's Kuomintang Party and conservative American political elements.

The CHLA was a harbinger of the modernization of Chinatown society. For example, the CHLA set up a very successful social club, the Quon Shar ("Mass

Four Chinese women of the Chinese Women's Patriotic League of New York march in the Easter parade, April 15, 1932. (Library of Congress)

Club"), for their members. These new types of organizations helped forge a new identity and break away from the traditional "sojourner" mentality, and toward settling in the United States. In addition, a new youth movement manifested itself. The Chinese Youth Patriotic Society was formed in the mid-1930s, for all Chinese men and women from 18 to 30 years of age. Though ostensibly set up to promote the anti-Japanese struggle of the homeland, it instead became a "new"-style recreational club with hobby groups and socializing, and it broke with tradition by admitting women. The International Workers' Order (IWO) established a Chinatown branch. One noteworthy failure was the unionization drive of the American Federation of Labor (AFL) in the early 1930s. The AFL's lackluster efforts failed to break into the traditional guild-association mentality of the small shops, where employer and employee were bound together for mutual survival. One union success was the strong union presence among Chinese seamen, who flocked to the new CIO-affiliated National Maritime Union, which pledged itself to racial equality. Chinese and Chinese American seamen, mostly cooks and stewards, supported the 1936–1937 NMU strike. In return, the NMU supported the Chinese seamen's protests against discriminatory rules on shore leave and summary layoffs of foreigners.

Japanese Community

In the 1930s the Japanese living in the United States became swept up in international affairs due to the aggressive nature of Japanese militarism in Asia. Japanese in the United States, like other Asian immigrants, had suffered severe discrimination, though they had a powerful home government that used diplomatic influence to lessen American nativism toward Japanese immigrants. Nonetheless, Japanese immigrants, or Issei, were aliens ineligible for citizenship, as were other Asian immigrants. The Japanese had previously built an economic niche for themselves on the West Coast by specializing in fruit and vegetable farming, and many Japanese families became prosperous (see "Rural Life" chapter). However, when the Japanese government invaded Manchuria in 1931 and began the Sino-Japanese War in 1937, it turned to the Issei and their American-born children, the Nisei, as a "bridge of understanding" to American society. It renewed its efforts to influence the Japanese American community. However, many Nisei were not enthusiastic about Japan's militarism, to the disappointment of Issei leaders. Some Nisei became prominent radicals, such as the Communist Karl Yoneda who participated in prolabor activities in California. But the Nisei generation's principal organization was the Japanese American Citizens League (JACL), which tended to be Republican, anti–New Deal, and antilabor. The JACL opted for a program of flag-waving, 100 percent Americanism in an effort to prove to the U.S. government that the Japanese American community was loyal, even reporting Issei pro-Japan enthusiasts to American military intelligence. However, this effort did not forestall the massive internment of Japanese Americans in 1942 in the midst of war. (Ichioka 2006, 10–52).

Filipino/a Communities

People from the Philippines were unusual Asians within the American immigration system, since they were U.S. nationals, though not citizens, who had unrestricted passage to the United States before the 1935 Repatriation Act. Yet the community was rather small, with some 60,000 Filipinos/as on the mainland, mostly in California, and 75,000 in Hawai'i. Because of their colonial relationship with the United States, they had been exposed to the English language and to the American education system in the Philippines itself. On the other hand, they found themselves in a parallel political situation with Mexican American groups after 1934. Filipinos/as found jobs in niches in the mainland economy, in agriculture, canneries, railroads, as well as in the U.S. military like the Merchant Marine. Filipinos/as generally went on a migratory path that took them from Alaska down the Pacific coast to Los Angeles, and Filipino/a communities sprang up in the major cities there, but especially in Seattle.

Filipinos/as were still subject to many of the anti-Asian prejudices that abounded on the West Coast. In one ugly incident in 1930, in Watsonville, California, tensions between a growing population of male Filipinos and the white townspeople erupted when the Filipinos opened up a club and hired white women from a nearly community as dance partners. White vigilante groups began harassing the Filipinos, and within a week, 22-year-old Fermin Tonera was shot and killed by a white raiding party. Eight people were sentenced as rioters and given minimal punishment. Filipinos/as began leaving the area, and others kept a low profile (Fujita-Rony 2003, 90).

In Hawai'i in 1932, 300 unemployed Filipino workers protested, asking the Philippine government for work, aid, and passage back to the Philippines. The Philippine government refused, citing problems at home. Indeed, labor unrest on the island was increasing in 1932 and 1933, and the independence movement was getting stronger as well. Congressional restrictionists had already been calling for excluding Filipinos/as from immigration by the late 1920s, though they were unsuccessful in convincing Congress to repudiate the perceived guardianship of the island that the United States had inherited when it annexed the Philippines in 1901. The issue, however, reinvigorated the cause of Philippine independence, which was accomplished in a bill passed by Congress in 1934 and accepted by the Philippine legislature on May 1, 1934. The Philippines would be given its independence after 10 years in a commonwealth status. At this point, a quota of 50 immigrants per year was placed on Filipino/a migration to the United States.

The repatriation bill that was finally passed by the U.S. Congress in 1935 gave Filipinos/as a federal program of travel back to the Philippines, but such repatriates were not allowed to re-enter the United States unless they received one of the 50 quota slots. Most Filipinos/as chose to remain in the States. Social clubs and fraternal lodges in U.S. cities provided a refuge for Filipinos/as against economic deprivation and American racism. In addition, Catholic churches established clubs; the Maryknoll church in Seattle was a particularly important parish for the Filipino/a community. In response to the racially segregated Knights of Columbus, Filipinos formed their own lodge, the Filipino Columbian Club. There was a strong left presence in the Filipino/a community: In the early 1930s Filipinos/as were key actors in the Fishermen and Cannery Workers' Industrial Union of the CP's Trade Union Unity League, and the International Labor Defense (ILD) took up the case of Filipino/a labor activists being imprisoned in the Philippines (Fujita-Rony 2003, 165).

African Americans

African Americans were hard-hit by the Depression, just as they found themselves at the bottom of the economic ladder in good times. Since over half of the African American population still lived in the rural South, their communities were very precarious economically even in the best of times. Those still engaged in agriculture in the South were devastated by the steep drop in cotton prices, which went from 18 cents per pound in 1929 to less than 6 cents a pound in early 1933 (Sitkoff 1978, 34–41). Sharecropper families struggled to survive, growing their own food, hunting and fishing, even as their crop yields forced them deeper in debt. Many chose to move to southern cities, where they joined earlier African American migrants in unemployment lines. Some moved to the North, following the Great Migration of the war years and the 1920s, but with little more success. African Americans made up a disproportionately large number of the unemployed and the homeless in northern cities. African American workers were the first to be laid off in steel, auto, and meat packing when those industries began contracting in 1928. African American women, mostly employed as domestic servants in the North, also were laid off. Consequently, the Depression impacted African American families in the North severely. There is ample evidence that African Americans, both North and South, were discriminated against in the receipt of public relief benefits, and in the South, even those able to get payments found that the sums were inadequate to live on. Moreover, in the South, according to the *New Republic,* white vigilantes organized in 1930 to defend white jobs, where "Ku Klux practices were being resumed in the certainty that dead men not only tell no tales but create vacancies" (Sitkoff 1978, 36). On the other hand, historian Kenneth Kusmer points out that Hoovervilles in the North were racially integrated, just like previous "hobo jungles" (Kusmer 2002).

The Great Migration to northern cities in the 1920s meant that many had escaped the plantation economy of the South. The African American population in the North had increased by 63 percent. While most were clustered into urban ghettos and faced racial tensions both on and off the job, the African American community did experience improvements in employment and income, health and education in the 1920s. Moreover, they could vote. By 1932, African American votes were sought after by both Republicans and Democrats in the North. In 1936, the majority of the African American vote went to Franklin D. Roosevelt (see previous chapter). In 1930, 40 percent of African Americans were living in cities, and the five largest urban populations were outside the South. This new vital concentration of African Americans meant that the movement for social equality could now take shape and be effective. There were three issues on which African Americans focused—equal opportunity within New Deal programs, a national antilynching campaign, and an end to discrimination in economic life.

African Americans and the New Deal

The First New Deal came under intense criticism from African American leaders for its silence on issues of racial injustice and its inability to promote equality within its programs. FDR's key political advisers, Louis Howe and James A. Farley, had warned him not to antagonize white southern Democrats. The vice president, John Nance Garner of Texas, was strongly opposed to antilynching laws and African American civil rights. Only Eleanor Roosevelt and Secretary of the Interior Harold L. Ickes raised concerns about the plight of African Americans. FDR, however, saw his duty in 1933 to deal with the economic crisis: "First things come first, and I can't alienate certain votes I need for measures that are more important at the moment by pushing any measures that would entail a fight" (Sitkoff 1978, 44). African American organizations were too weak in the early 1930s to press their case. Though Ickes initially issued a nondiscrimination rule on Public Works Administration projects, he soon had to relent in the face of opposition from southern contractors, unions, and politicians. The NRA did little to protect African American workers from employers' discrimination and allowed for wage differentials based on region, leaving southern workers, both African American and white, with lower pay. The AAA did not prevent landowners from cheating sharecroppers out of their fair share of payment benefits. African Americans received only 5 percent of the jobs in the CCC in 1933, and only 6 percent the following year, in spite of having an unemployment at twice the rate of white joblessness. The 1935 Second New Deal legislation retained the same bias against African Americans, though in some subtler ways. The National Labor Relations Act and the Social Security Act excluded agricultural workers and domestic servants, which were the majority of African American workers. Moreover, the decentralized nature of the relief system allowed southern administrators to set their assistance payments at lower rates than northern states.

The record of the second term, after FDR's landslide victory in 1936, showed improvement for African Americans. Public housing, though often still segregated, improved living conditions. Harry Hopkins insisted that there would be no discrimination in the Works Progress Administration (WPA). The WPA gave African Americans jobs on a greater scale than earlier relief programs had. The WPA Education program, the Federal Theatre Project, the Federal Music Project, and the Federal Art Project all supported African American themes and artists.

Traditional African American Organizations

The National Association for the Advancement of Colored People (NAACP) had become the premier organization for civil rights in its 20 years of existence, though it would be briefly overshadowed in the 1930s by more militant groups. Its traditional emphasis on investigation, lobbying, and legislative proposals fit well into the new environment in Washington. The NAACP focused on securing fair treatment for African Americans in the New Deal relief programs, as its national and local branches protested against discrimination. It also began emphasizing the importance of voter registration. As the NAACP's membership secretary noted, "We . . . began to try to build the image of the Negro as a voting personality, as a person who would influence his government by his vote" (Weiss 1983, 64).

More militant African Americans argued that economic issues should be the predominant focus, and this had some effect on the other traditional organization, the National Urban League. The League had always emphasized economic opportunity for African Americans and historically had made arrangements with friendly employers. This tactic had in the past earned the League the wrath of labor unions, since the Urban League sometimes aided strike-breaking. The League retorted that unions were to blame for barring African American membership. But now, in the New Deal, the League turned its attention to federal agencies and programs. Executive Secretary Eugene Kinckle Jones took a leave of absence in order to work for the U.S. Department of Commerce in 1933. Later in the decade, T. Arnold Hill, director of the National Department on Industrial Relations for the League, went to Washington as a consultant in 1939. Robert L Vann, editor of the *Pittsburgh Courier,* served as special assistant to the attorney general (Weiss 1974, 269). In addition, the new Negro Industrial League, created by African American graduate students from the Northeast, attended hearings on NRA codes to demand fair treatment. By late 1933, Walter White of the NAACP and George Edmund Haynes of the Federal Council of Churches created a new lobbying group, the Joint Committee on National Recovery, to channel all these efforts at lobbying from outside the government.

During the Second New Deal, both the NAACP and the Urban League tried to include amendments to the National Labor Relations Act that would end discrimination against African Americans by labor unions. Similarly, they attempted to modify the Social Security Act to include African American job sectors. Both efforts failed in Congress, as southern Democrats were inclined to resist New Deal measures if such amendments were included (Weiss 1974, 273–175).

Commission on Interracial Cooperation

Another strategy was to work within the government to address African American issues, a strategy that the so-called Black Cabinet would embrace in mid-decade. The first steps were taken by two white southerners, Will W. Alexander, director of the Commission on Interracial Cooperation (CIC), and Edwin R. Embree, president of the Julius Rosenwald Fund. They put together a proposal for an African American adviser in Washington to "look after the Negro's interests in all phases of the recovery" (Kirby 1980, 16). Alexander was a Methodist minister who had given up his pastorate in Nashville during World War I to create the Commission on Interracial Cooperation to promote better relations between the races. Its liberal influence in the southern states revolved around preventing racial violence; it did not challenge segregation. Embree, the great-grandson of an abolitionist preacher, had attended interracial Berea College in Kentucky and then Yale University. As a result of connections made at Yale, he was hired by the Rockefeller Foundation where he worked for a decade. When Julius Rosenwald, head of Sears, Roebuck and Company of Chicago, established his own philanthropic fund, Rosenwald asked Embree to become president of the Rosenwald Fund, a position he held until 1948. Rosenwald had been influenced by

Booker T. Washington and devoted his fund toward improving African American communities. Together with Charles S. Johnson, the African American sociologist and future president of Fisk University, Alexander and Embree created a series of conferences in 1933 on the "Economic Status of the Negro." Out of these meetings came the proposal for a race advisory post. The position was approved by the White House, and it was to be placed under Harold Ickes in the Department of the Interior and paid for by the Rosenwald Fund. Alexander and Embree made the decision that the most effective person would be a white southerner, and selected Clark Foreman, an Atlanta native with an economic background who had recently earned a Ph.D. in political science at Columbia University. Foreman had worked with the CIC and the Rosenwald Fund for the past three years. Foreman agreed to the post, but only until a qualified African American man could be found. This decision led to African American organizations' protests over this example of traditional white paternalism, though this attitude subsided as Foreman's activities became effective. Foreman chose as his assistant the young African American economist from the Joint Committee on National Recovery, Robert C. Weaver. Foreman and Weaver found the job to be too enormous and persuaded Ickes that the best solution was to have a race adviser appointed to every agency and department.

It should be noted that the Urban League and the Rosenwald Fund did not get along, ever since the late 1920s when the Fund tried to force a merger between the NAACP and the Urban League, in order to compel the League executive secretary, Eugene Kinckle Jones, to retire. Both of the organizations resisted this pressure (Weiss 1974, 160). But the attempt shows the influence that white philanthropies wielded, as well as the tensions between white and African American activists over philosophy and strategy.

The Black Cabinet

The Black Cabinet, sometimes called the Black Brain Trust, was the name given to the group of African Americans around the African American educator Mary McLeod Bethune and economist Robert C. Weaver, who were key to the formation in 1936 of the Federal Council on Negro Affairs. The influence of African American organizations began to increase in 1935, and Eleanor Roosevelt's public pronouncements and private persuasiveness led to a change in the White House. FDR began making public statements about racial equality. By mid-1935, the Roosevelt administration had appointed some 45 African Americans to Cabinet offices and New Deal agencies as race relations advisers. Bethune became adviser to the National Youth Administration, while Weaver served first in the Department of Interior and then the U.S. Housing Authority. Meeting at Bethune's house, African American civil rights leaders and government appointees forged a coalition between the New Deal and the civil rights movement during the 1936 election season. Wielding its influence in the African American press, the group succeeded in garnering the African American vote for Roosevelt.

Marian Anderson, Opera Singer, Breaks Color Bar

Marian Anderson (1897–1993), born in Philadelphia, was a classically trained opera singer who first gained recognition by winning the New York Philharmonic voice competition in 1924. Racism prevented her from performing in the United States, and she was forced to train and perform in Europe, where she met her future manager, Sol Hurok, who brought her back to the United States in 1935 for a successful concert tour. She gained further recognition by performing at the White House in 1936. But in 1939, the Daughters of the American Revolution (DAR) refused to allow her to perform at their Constitution Hall in Washington, D.C., saying the venue was for "white artists" only. Protest over this insult caused First Lady Eleanor Roosevelt to publicly resign her membership in the DAR. Finally, Secretary of the Interior Harold Ickes invited Anderson to perform at the Lincoln Memorial, where she sang on Easter Sunday, April 9, 1939. In addition to the audience of an estimated 75,000 at the Lincoln Memorial, a national radio audience heard the broadcast of the concert. Later in July at the NAACP conference in Richmond, Virginia, Eleanor Roosevelt presented Anderson with the Springarn Medal for her musical accomplishments. Anderson went on to break other color bars in the 1940s and 1950s, including performing at the inaugurations of presidents Eisenhower and Kennedy.

Bethune and Eleanor Roosevelt worked closely together to effect change in federal programs for African Americans. It became known that if something was needed, "Mary McLeod would tell Eleanor, and Eleanor would get somebody to get it done" (Weiss 1983, 146). Bethune organized two national conferences on the Problems of the Negro and Negro Youth in 1937, as well as a gathering of the National Council of Negro Women at the White House. Her visibility allowed her to preside over the Black Cabinet. On the whole, the Black Cabinet provided symbolic recognition of African American concerns at an unprecedented level, even if their concrete accomplishments were modest.

Antilynching Campaign

The antilynching campaign of the 1930s galvanized a nationwide interracial coalition that changed many whites' attitudes about racial violence and forged a movement that presaged the civil rights movement of the 1950s and 1960s. The NAACP, pressured by its young African American militants to embrace an economic agenda, decided to focus on lynching instead. In the early Depression, NAACP executive secretary Walter White needed an issue that would undermine the arguments of W. E. B. Du Bois, editor of the *Crisis,* who called for

Members of the National Association for the Advancement of Colored People (NAACP) New York City Youth Council picketing for antilynching legislation before the Strand Theatre in Times Square in 1937. (Library of Congress)

economic self-sufficiency through racial separation. This position was intolerable to White, who believed strongly in integration and full equality. Du Bois subsequently resigned from the NAACP in 1934. In the meantime, White had already spent the time since 1918 investigating over forty lynchings and eight race riots. His light skin allowed him to pose as a white reporter for the *Chicago Daily News* or the *New York Evening Post* and freely move about southern towns.

Racial violence flared during the early 1930s, especially in the South, as economic competition between the races increased. The Ku Klux Klan and Black Shirts forced African American workers out of jobs, and the numbers of lynchings began to rise. From a decrease to single digits annually in the late 1920s, there were at least 21 lynchings in 1930, followed by 21 each in 1931 and 1932, and 28 in 1933, according to the Tuskegee Institute (Sitkoff 1978, 269). The Commission on Interracial Cooperation (CIC) turned to the factual documentation of the region's problems, beginning with the problems of racial violence. In 1930 CIC leaders organized the Southern Commission on the Study of Lynching, which included established African American leaders and prominent white educators. The CIC published many case studies of racial violence and distributed its two key reports, Arthur Raper's *The Tragedy of Lynching* and James Harmon Chadbourn's *Lynching and the Law,* widely in the South. Reversing its caution on political matters, the CIC endorsed the Costigan-Wagner antilynching bill being promoted in 1935 by the NAACP.

The NAACP had first campaigned for a federal antilynching law after the riots of 1919. Now it renewed its efforts in 1933. Walter White persuaded senators Edward P. Costigan (D-CP) and Robert F. Wagner (D-NY) to sponsor a federal antilynching bill that brought federal sanctions to bear on local and county law officers who allowed lynchings and who failed to prosecute lynchers. To allay critiques by states'-rights advocates, the bill did not demand federal prosecution of lynchers. Nonetheless, southern congressmen protested the assault on states' rights and the threat of a filibuster kept the bill from the Senate floor in 1934. In the 1935 session, FDR had major economic-recovery legislation to pass and wanted to avoid any controversial topic; thus the antilynching bill languished. After FDR's landslide victory in 1936, the NAACP tried again. In the seventy-fifth session of Congress, an antilynching bill was brought to the House by Joseph A. Gavagan of New York (representing Harlem), and in the Senate by Wagner and Frederick Van Nuys of Indiana. A Gallup poll in January 1937 reported that 70 percent of those questioned favored antilynching legislation; even 65 percent of southerners felt that way. The bill passed the House by a vote of 277 to 120 (Weiss 1983, 241–242). But its fate in the Senate was caught up in debate over FDR's court-packing scheme, and consideration was delayed until the following session. In the 1938 session, a six-week filibuster by southern Democrats doomed it. In the course of these two years FDR was silent on the issue, disheartening those African American supporters who had voted for him in 1936. When Eleanor Roosevelt spoke publicly in favor of the Gavagan–Wagner–Van Nuys bill in 1939, it was too late; the administration now had the war in Europe to deal with. The record of FDR's administration on other race legislation in the 1930s was similarly reluctant; no action was taken on the issue of the white primary, the poll tax, or similar acts of disfranchisement. As FDR told his aide Aubrey Williams, "Politics is the art of the possible. . . . The administration had other bills before Congress" (Weiss 1983, 251).

Southern White Women and the Issue of Lynching

The CIC had excluded women from the Southern Commission on the Study of Lynching. Mrs. Jessie Daniel Ames, a white woman who had been CIC Director of Woman's Work since 1929, protested loudly. She organized a meeting of 26 white women to discuss the issue of lynching, and out of this meeting on November 1, 1930, came the Association of Southern Women for the Prevention of Lynching (ASWPL). The core of women were officials of Protestant church groups—southern Presbyterians, Baptists, and Methodists—along with members of Jewish groups, the YWCA, and some civic organizations like the Parent-Teacher Associations and the Southeastern Federation of Women's Clubs. Following in the footsteps of African American pioneers like Ida B. Wells and later NAACP efforts, the ASWPL was the first sustained effort by white women to combat the tradition that lynching was a defense of white womanhood and the only suitable punishment for any African American man accused of raping a white woman. Instead, the ASWPL published the facts of lynching, that only sometimes was the accusation of sexual assault a factor. Instead the ASWPL argued that mob violence undermined the economic and political interests of the United States abroad and advanced the appeal of radical movements within the African American community. Lynching "was rooted in poverty and the deprivation of the black and white rural poor, and, beyond that, in the presumptions and institutions of white supremacy" (Hall 1979, 221). As historian Jacqueline Hall has argued, by attacking the alleged tie between lynching and rape, these southern white women were challenging one basis of the southern way of life. But at the same time by placing emphasis on proper channels of law and order, the ASWPL statements did nothing to change the racist southern court system, as some African American critics charged. The first test of their approach became the Scottsboro case (see below). By the late 1930s, most ASWPL leaders could agree on the dangers of "legal lynching," but still concluded that "such corruption of the courts posed less 'danger to social institutions' than mob violence" (Hall 1979, 201).

By delving into the forbidden topic of interracial sex, Ames and the ASWPL explored with African American women the sexual double standard prevalent in the South, and indeed in the nation, and helped reveal the exploitation of African American women. The ASWPL supported the NAACP's federal antilynching legislative drive in 1933, though Ames remained convinced that education and state legislation were key to stopping racial violence in the South. The power struggle between Ames and the NAACP to define lynching and outline a role for white Southern women remained unresolved. Throughout the rest of the 1930s, the ASWPL continued to conduct investigations of lynchings and ASWPL speakers continued to approach their church organizations to sign petitions and pass antilynching resolutions. But Ames and the ASWPL held aloof from the new Southern Conference for Human Welfare, founded in 1938 by a coalition of labor leaders, New Dealers, and African American activists, which focused on economic democracy. The movement passed them by, and the ASWPL ceased to exist in 1942.

The Scottsboro Case

In March 1931, nine African American youths, aged 13 to 21, were accused of raping two white women in a boxcar aboard a train they were riding near Scottsboro, Alabama. All nine youths were convicted in a hasty trial and all but the youngest sentenced to death. While the NAACP ignored the case and the ASWPL

These nine African American youths, known as the Scottsboro Boys, were imprisoned in Scottsboro, Alabama, after being falsely accused of raping two white women in a freight car. Here, the young men are pictured conferring with civil rights activist Juanita Jackson Mitchell in 1937. The boys' convictions were overturned in Powell v. Alabama *(1932), when the U.S. Supreme Court declared that the defendants, who had not been given adequate time to prepare a defense, were denied due process. Subsequent trials, where they were defended by attorney Samuel Leibowitz, resulted in the acquittal of four defendants and jail sentences for the rest. (Library of Congress)*

tried to forestall a lynching solely through calming statements, neither was prepared to deal with the conviction. Only the International Labor Defense (ILD), a Communist-backed organization, stepped up to appeal the conviction and to prepare a defense. At this point the NAACP tried to wrest the defense from the ILD, and the CIC aided the NAACP by conducting its own investigations and discrediting the ILD. Jessie Daniel Ames of the ASWPL responded to appeals from northern liberals by arguing that the Scottsboro case was a distraction that was undermining the goal of antilynching legislation. Moreover, according to Ames, it was giving southern racists new ammunition for lynching, since they could point to interference in the southern courts by clever radical lawyers. The ILD arranged for a massive action campaign, organizing nationally and even internationally to "Save the Scottsboro Boys!" ILD-sponsored tours by mothers of the Scottsboro defendants raised money for legal defense; African American artists such as Langston Hughes composed works for the defendants, while white authors like Theodore Dreiser, Lincoln Steffens, and John Dos Passos wrote letters on their behalf. As a result, the ILD won recognition and support in African American communities, even forcing the NAACP to work with them for a time in 1933. Due to the ILD legal appeal, the U.S. Supreme Court decided in November 1932 that the Scottsboro defendants had received inadequate counsel and ordered a new trial. The ILD retained renowned New York attorney Samuel Leibowitz as defense counsel, but Leibowitz agreed only after carefully distancing himself from the "Communist" issue. Leibowitz carried out an aggressive defense, picking apart Victoria Price's testimony and causing Ruby Bates to recant her previous accusation. Nonetheless, the Alabama jury found the defendants guilty once again. In a surprise move, and one that cost him his judgeship at the next election, presiding judge James Edwin Horton granted the defense's motion for a new trial. The defendants were convicted once again in winter 1933. Here, the ILD made a fatal misstep and attempted to bribe Victoria Price to change her testimony.

With the ILD now discredited, mainstream civil rights groups returned to the defense effort, and the Scottsboro Defense Committee took over the case for the next round of trials in 1936 and 1937. The convictions had been overturned once again, but now, in the case of *Norris v. Alabama,* on the grounds that Alabama had systematically excluded African Americans from jury selection, thus depriving the defendants of a fair trial. Once again, the trials ended with convictions, though now only one man, Clarence Norris, received a death sentence. The others received sentences ranging from 75 to 90 years. Efforts to persuade Gov. Bibb Graves to pardon the Scottsboro defendants met with strong public resistance, and Graves only commuted Norris's death sentence to life imprisonment. The men were slowly paroled beginning in 1943, with the last paroled in 1950. The Scottsboro case remained a symbol of southern injustice and racism for the next decade (Carter 1971).

Negro Labor Committee

The Negro Labor Committee (NLC) was organized by African American labor leader Frank Crosswaith of the International Ladies' Garment Workers (ILGWU) and A. Philip Randolph of the Brotherhood of Sleeping-Car Porters in 1933. Some early gains were made among African American dress finishers, organizing them into the ILGWU Local 22. Crosswaith and Randolph were members of the Socialist Party, and their goals of organizing workers into CIO unions differed from that of the nationalist Harlem Labor Union (HLU). The HLU was willing to allow African American employers to sign contracts with lower wages because it felt that those merchants could not afford to pay the prevailing wage. Crosswaith and Randolph, in contrast, supported a strike by workers at the *Amsterdam News,* who had just organized themselves into the American Newspaper Guild, against their African American employers. They reasoned that even if Harlem had an all–African American economy, there would not be enough employment for all residents, and thus a strong unionized integrated working class movement was the solution. By 1938 the NLC claimed to represent or work closely with 73 unions in Greater New York City, both AFL and CIO. Between 1930 and 1940, African American trade union membership increased tenfold, but there was little progress in breaking into the skilled trades (Greenberg 1991, 110–13).

"Don't Buy Where You Can't Work" Campaign

In the midst of Harlem's union organizing campaigns, another sort of campaign united the African American community—one to win clerical jobs in white-owned Harlem businesses. The combination of mass protest and boycotts galvanized the church-based organizations and African American fraternal organizations, women's clubs, and political organizations. The movement was aided by the presence of a charismatic young minister, Adam Clayton Powell Jr. Few African Americans had been hired as clerks or in white-collar work, and those few "middle-class" clerks and professionals had often lost their jobs during the Depression. Here the approaches of traditional organizations became apparent. Both the NAACP and the National Urban League had doubts about the "Don't Buy" campaign. The NAACP was uncomfortable with direct action campaigns and preferred to challenge discrimination in the courts, as well as to promote city-wide job opportunities. The National Urban League was interested in promoting economic opportunities, as it historically had been, but it was fearful of antagonizing the white business leaders on whom it depended to support them. By early 1934, the New Deal had taken the edge off relief needs, and African American "progressive women" approached church and community leaders to organize the Citizens' League for Fair Play (CLFP). The broad-based League included the church activists, the Unity Democratic Club, the Fusion-Republican Club, the Cosmopolitan Social and Tennis Club, the Young West Indian Congress, and the Premier Literary Club. It also included African American nationalists of the Garvey movement and Sufi Abdul Hamid and his Negro Industrial Clerical Alliance of Chicago, where a successful movement had taken place a year before. This early effort was marred by clashes between the nationalists and the moderates, such that the organization was short-lived. Their first target was Blumstein's Department Store on 125th Street, Harlem's largest department store. Picket lines were a new phenomenon in this traditional boycotting, and an "honor roll" of picketers included 58 men and 83 women (Greenberg 1991, 122). When Blumstein finally relented and hired African American women as clerks, other stores like Woolworth's did the same. But because Blumstein had hired light-skinned women, nationalists protested this tendency. Since their members had not been hired, the nationalists split from the CLFP and resumed their picket line, now under the banner of the HLU. When violence ensued on the picket line, one store obtained an injunction. On October 31, 1934, the New York Supreme Court ruled that picketing was illegal because there was no labor dispute. Hamid's growing anti-Semitic remarks also alienated mainstream members of the community. Both the Harlem Merchants' Association and the Communist Party protested the anti-Semitic rhetoric. The HLU's rival, the

The Harlem Race Riot of 1935

On March 19, 1935, 16-year-old Lino Rivera stole a penknife from Kress's Store on 125th Street, was caught by a store clerk, and, after a scuffle, ran away. After police arrested a woman bystander for disorderly conduct, rumors quickly spread that the boy had been injured, or even killed. Leaflets later that evening embellished the rumors. A crowd gathered, reaching upwards of 1,000, and moved through 125th Street, breaking windows and looting foodstuffs. By the end of the night, 75 people, mostly African American, had been arrested, 57 civilians and 7 policemen were injured, and 626 windows were broken. The rioters carefully attacked white-owned stores and whites only at the beginning, but the action then became more generalized as frustrations grew. The police responded with excessive force. Mayor Fiorello La Guardia appointed a commission to investigate the incident, and their report concluded that pent-up grievances over job discrimination, the failure of the first phase of the "Don't Buy Where You Can't Work" campaign, and the continuing hardships of the Depression explained the riot. As the venerable pastor Adam Clayton Powell Sr. noted, "The Negro used to be the most lovable, forgivable [*sic*] being in America, but the white man's prejudice, hatred and lies have changed the Negro's psychology. He is just as full of hell, hatred and lies as the white man" (Greenberg 1991, 5). It was the first large-scale African American riot.

Negro Labor Committee, called the HLU "a terrorist campaign in Harlem against the Jews, against whites, and against the legitimate trade union movement" (Greenberg 1991, 127).

The racial and political climate had improved considerably by 1938, making a new effort possible. Some of this improvement came from both nationalist and integrationist efforts, the CIO advances and attention to race issues, and the U.S. Supreme Court decision, *New Negro Alliance v. Sanitary Grocery Company,* that ruled that since African Americans had suffered job discrimination they could make employment demands based on race and thus could picket. Adam Clayton Powell Jr., minister of the Abyssinia Baptist Church, held a mass meeting in March 1938 to form the Greater New York Coordinating Committee for Employment. It had the support of the New York Urban League, the NAACP, A. Philip Randolph, and the Communist Party, and soon after its founding claimed membership of 200 organizations and 170,000 members. Its goals included greater employment of African American workers in Harlem stores and public utilities like Consolidated Edison and the New York Telephone Company. Their most outstanding effort was to convince the World's Fair Corporation of 1939 to hire African American clerks and performers, by moving their pickets downtown to the Empire State Building where the World's Fair Corporation had its headquarters.

National Negro Congress

The National Negro Congress (NNC) was unofficially launched in May 1935 at a Howard University conference, under the auspices of the Joint Committee on National Recovery. Joint Committee leader John P. Davis gathered a broad cross-section of African American intellectuals, church activists, New Deal federal employees, and labor and civil rights activists. After the conference, Davis and Howard University professor Ralph J. Bunche invited a select group to form an organization to coordinate African American protest over deteriorating economic conditions. Key Socialists like A. Philip Randolph and Communists like James Ford, along with leaders from the Urban League and the NAACP, were at this meeting. Randolph was elected as president at its founding convention in Chicago in 1936. In Harlem, the CP was influential, though low-key, in its advocacy of this approach, as it moved toward a Popular Front approach. African American nationalists remained aloof and the NAACP national board eventually voted against participating. In New York, left-wing unions like the Teachers Union, the Musicians Union, the Newspaper Guild, the Fur Workers Union, and the Relief Workers Association endorsed the NNC. John L. Lewis and John Brophy of the new CIO also endorsed it (Naison 1983, 181). Active on a grassroots level, the NNC organized boycotts, rent strikes, and voting drives; the NCC took on international issues such as condemning imperialism in Africa, specifically Italy's invasion of Ethiopia, and fascism in Germany. Yet when the CP turned away from its antifascist activity because of the Nazi-Soviet Pact of 1939, most non-Communists left the NCC. In 1946 the NCC joined with the International Labor Defense and the National Federation for Constitutional Liberties to form the Civil Rights Congress; this organization succumbed to anti-Communist political pressure in the early 1950s.

Native Americans and the "Indian New Deal"

Indians on their reservations often were the poorest populations in their areas, and the Great Depression made little difference in their cycle of poor education, ill health, and minimal economic development. When the Roosevelt administration took office, the first relief expenditure, the Emergency Conservation Work Act, established the Civilian Conservation Corps (CCC) to protect the environment through reseeding and reforesting public land and developing recreation areas. Special funds were set aside for the Bureau of Indian Affairs to fund projects on Indian land. Unemployed Indians who passed the physical examination were eligible for these relief jobs, of which there were never enough to solve the unemployment problem. One example of a much-needed project for the Navajo reservation in New Mexico was a water-supply improvement project, tied to a soil-erosion reclamation effort to solve the Navajos' grazing problems.

John Collier, Indian Affairs commissioner, with Blackfoot Indian chiefs. (Library of Congress)

The New Deal for American Indians meant substantial reform legislation that reoriented the Office of Indian Affairs at the Department of the Interior. The federal legacy had been disastrous. Past practice, enshrined in the Dawes Act of 1887, included forcibly removing Indian children from their families and educating them in missionary schools, encouraging Indians to assimilate by moving off reservations and into farms and cities, and distributing Indian land to individual Indians as private property that could be sold. Nearly half of all Indian lands had been systematically seized or sold off after the Dawes Act. Franklin D. Roosevelt appointed John Collier as commissioner of Indian Affairs. Collier was a well-regarded reformer whose leadership of the American Indian Defense Association in the 1920s had improved Indians' legal and cultural status. A committed cultural pluralist, Collier was a major architect of the Indian Reorganization Act of 1934 (the Wheeler-Howard bill), which reversed decades of harmful federal practice. The 1934 Indian Reorganization Act recognized Native Americans as separate cultures, allowed Indian tribes to form their own autonomous governments and regain control over economic resources. Critics contemptuously called Collier's emphasis "return[ing] Indians to the blanket" (Parman 1976, 30). There was debate and dispute over the legislation among Indian tribes themselves, as traditionalists and modernizers clashed over economic and cultural issues. Of the 263 tribes and bands that voted on the Act, 174 approved it, while 73 opposed it. Those tribes that approved the Act and then drafted constitutions represented some 103,000 adults, while those outside the Act numbered 113,000 (Kelly 1975). Yet Collier continued as if all Indians had approved the Act and benefited from it. Collier's greatest achievement was to return to the principle of Indian autonomy, as well as garnering enough emergency funds from New Deal programs to help Indians survive the Great Depression and improve their educational system and job skills.

Leftist Alternatives to the New Deal

While conservatives from the pro-business lobby, as well as ultraconservatives such as the quasi-fascists described earlier, were lambasting the New Deal as communist, there existed a true "Left," the Communist Party USA (CP), the Socialist Party of America (SP), and other Marxist parties. They organized grassroots opposition to the deepening Depression during the Hoover years. When the First New Deal was underway, both the CP and the SP criticized it as moving toward fascism. Both parties engaged in grassroots organizing, as well as participating in the electoral process, but only the SP took the electoral tactic seriously. The SP did win some elections at the city and state level.

Communist Party USA

The Communist Party USA (CP), through its new strategy of the Popular Front, made a considerable mark on American culture and society, as well as in New Deal politics. The CP had maintained its existence quietly throughout the 1920s, and burst onto the political scene in 1930 with a vigor that surprised many. Spurred on by the devastation of the Great Depression, the CP pursued a multipronged approach through 1935 to rally Americans to its cause: first, to organize industrial workers by abandoning the AFL and establishing industrial unions in the Trade Union Unity League (TUUL); second, to defend and gain support for the unemployed through Unemployed Councils in cities large and small; third, to defend African Americans against Jim Crow violence through such famous cases as those of the Scottsboro Boys and Angelo Herndon. Herndon was a young African American Communist who was sentenced in Atlanta, Georgia, in 1932 to 18 to 20 years in prison for "insurrection," simply for leading a large interracial demonstration of the unemployed. That conviction was overturned in 1937 by the U.S. Supreme Court, which ruled the old "insurrection" law unconstitutional. Last and least important, the CP ran candidates for electoral office. Until 1935, its "Third Period" official ideology called upon members to denounce the Socialist Party as "social fascists" and the New Deal as a sham that was meant to prop up a failed capitalist system. But local organizing efforts had made this policy untenable and many local CP activists started implementing what would later come to be known as the Popular Front strategy.

The Popular Front

The Popular Front was most famously declared at the Seventh World Congress of the Communist International (Comintern) in Moscow in 1935, where General Secretary Georgi Dimitrov declared the immediate goal of preserving democracy against an increasingly powerful world fascist movement. The CP's official policy turned first in 1935 toward a United Front with the Socialist Party of America (SP), which the SP rejected, and then a Popular Front with all working-class elements of American society to defeat incipient world fascism. In this second phase, the CP achieved its greatest appeal and organizational strength by helping create the emerging industrial unions of the CIO. It still maintained, however, that the best political step was the formation of a Farmer-Labor Party, as it did not trust the Democratic Party with its conservative southern wing.

After Roosevelt's 1936 landslide re-election, the CP moved closer to the New Deal, especially as the New Deal was being challenged by conservative elements in American politics. Particularly, Roosevelt's "court-packing" plan in early 1937 was widely praised by CP leaders, who saw it as a break with conservative elements within the political structure. The results of the 1936 election, however, caused CP leader Earl Browder to rethink the standard line about the need for a Farmer-Labor Party. Since it was clear that the electoral realignment taking place was bringing the Democratic Party closer to being a party representing workers, it made sense to drop the Popular Front insistence on a Farmer-Labor Party. At its May 1937 CP convention in New York, Browder spoke of the "New Deal wing of the Democratic Party" which was an essential part of "the developing Democratic Front against monopoly capitalism" (Ottanelli 1991, 115). This Democratic Front then became the official policy of the CP until summer 1939. Historians continue to dispute whether this turn to the Popular Front and then the Democratic Front came solely from Moscow, or whether it had emerged from CP activities at the American grassroots. (For an example of the first argument, see Klehr 1984 and for an example of the latter, see Ottanelli 1991.)

Always internationalist in this period, the CP endorsed FDR's moves toward a collective-security foreign policy that advocated taking a stand against fascism abroad. This antifascist position of the CP, along with its strength in industrial unionism, enlarged its membership and its influence. But with the signing of the Molotov-Ribbentrop Pact (Nazi-Soviet Pact) by the Soviet Union and Germany in 1939, the CP turned away from its antifascist stance to oppose the impending European war as an "imperialist" war. With this brief turn toward American isolationism, the CP lost much of its popular backing. It continued to remain a force within the CIO, however, and when Hitler attacked the Soviet Union in 1941, the CP again returned to the national stage with significant influence and a strong antifascist message (see "Culture of the 1930s" chapter).

Socialist Party of America

The Socialist Party of America (SP) survived into the 1930s under the leadership of Norman Thomas, whose ministerial background fit with certain constituencies within the SP and whose emphasis on parliamentary socialism differed little from the days of Eugene Debs. What was missing now was a clear connection to the foreign-stock American industrial working class and a dynamic union base; that connection had died with Debs in 1926. Significant numbers of foreign-born members had split with the party at the famous SP 1919 convention and allied with the new Communist Party (CP) and the Soviet Union. The SP's trade union link in the 1930s was with AFL craftsmen, mostly native-born workers and some anti-Soviet Jewish unionists. The crisis of the Great Depression only reinforced Socialist doctrine about the inevitable decline of capitalism and the futility of the Democrats' New Deal to repair a broken system. Thus the SP repeated their argument for a society built on the economy of "production-for-use" rather than "production-for-profit." While CP activists gained organizing momentum in unemployed movements and among industrial workers, the SP concentrated on winning local electoral office. One prominent victory of the decade came in Milwaukee, where Socialist Daniel Hoan had been mayor for the previous decade, but in 1931 carried along others on his municipal ticket (Olson 1952; Shannon 1955). The Socialists also reaped municipal victories in small cities like Bridgeport, Connecticut, where slate-roofer Jasper McLevy rode into City Hall in 1933 on the public outrage over local Democratic malfeasance as well as solid labor support (Bucki 2001). Norman Thomas, SP presidential nominee in 1932, earned a small vote. The Socialist novelist Upton Sinclair ran on an independent platform of End Poverty In California (EPIC) in 1934, capturing the Democratic Party nomination (see previous chapter).

The SP nationally did have some early success organizing its own Unemployed Leagues, and successfully rallied thousands of local activists to a Continental Congress of Workers and Farmers in Washington, D.C., in mid-1933. From these sectors rose the so-called Militant bloc, made up of activists to the left of Norman Thomas, mostly American followers of Leon Trotsky (the Socialist Workers Party, SWP). The New Deal caused consternation in the SP, as many of its long-standing reforms were now being enacted. The Militants, whose slogan was "Socialism in Our Time!," argued for greater support for the emerging industrial-union movement, a more radical critique of capitalism and the New Deal, and for joining with the Communist Party in its call for a Popular Front in 1936. The Old Guard, including Bridgeport mayor Jasper McLevy, argued for support for

AFL strategies and against the United Front proposed by the CP in 1935. Daniel Hoan, also on the SP executive committee, remained neutral on this question, while Norman Thomas supported the Militants. The Militants won the vote for their Declaration of Principles at the SP 1936 convention, at which point many in the Old Guard left to form the Social Democratic Federation (SDF). The New York Old Guard was deeply conscious of new currents within the labor movement and was preparing to support Sidney Hillman and David Dubinsky when they placed their unions behind Roosevelt's 1936 campaign. The SDF thus affiliated with the new American Labor Party (ALP) in New York State, which followed the CIO Labor's Nonpartisan League in endorsing Roosevelt. Ironically, the anti-Communist SP Old Guard wound up in coalition with the Popular Front CP in the New York ALP (Hoan 1931; Swanberg 1976; Warren 1974).

Movements of the Unemployed

Once the New Deal got under way in 1933, the organizations of the unemployed moved more toward lobbying for national unemployment insurance. The CP-dominated Unemployed Councils, which had been successful in the early Depression (see "Experiences of the Early Depression" chapter), was followed in 1932 by the SP-oriented Unemployed Leagues, which had emerged from the youth wing of the SP. A newly invigorated SP and its League for Industrial Democracy (LID) restructured the Unemployed Leagues in early 1935, claiming to involve some 450,000 members, though it was estimated that activists numbered only some 40,000–50,000. It formed the Workers Alliance of America (WAA) in early 1935. The WAA invited other unemployed organizations to merge with it. A. J. Muste's Leagues of the Unemployed in cities and small towns of Ohio, Pennsylvania, and West Virginia quickly did, and the CP-led Unemployed Councils joined the WAA in spring 1936. This move was the result of the new CP strategy of the United Front which stood for an alliance of all leftist organizations to fight against the threat of fascism. The Workers Alliance was dominated by SP-Militant leadership, though there were also Communists in the leadership. It reflected the evolution of the unemployed movement, to a point where the *Saturday Evening Post* reported in 1938 that "the organized unemployed are no longer merely an undecorative and troublesome fringe on the body politic" (Rosenzweig 1979, 501). Because of the new opportunities for relief funds that came with the New Deal, the WAA focused its efforts on urging the federal relief programs to rectify injustices in the allocation of jobs and the inadequacy of relief vouchers. The 1936 convention of the WAA was held in the auditorium of the U.S. Department of Labor building, signaling its acceptance into New Deal politics. The WAA was recognized as the collective-bargaining agent for relief workers on WPA projects in the latter half of the 1930s. It also played a crucial role in assisting the CIO organizing drives of 1937–1938, especially among auto workers in Michigan (Lorence 1996).

Biographies

Jessie Daniel Ames, 1883–1972

Antilynching Activist

Born in Texas and raised in the Methodist tradition, Jessie Daniel Ames married late, bore three children, and became a widow by the age of 31. With a complex heritage of "frontier self-sufficiency and middle-class aspirations" (Hall 1979, 15), Ames threw herself into the women suffrage campaigns of the early 20th century, worked through Methodist women's circles on problems facing African American women, and confronted both the limitations placed on women by the church and Commission on Interracial Cooperation (CIC) and the racial tensions between African American and white women in the CIC. She was appointed to the position of director of woman's work in the CIC in 1929 and moved from Texas to Atlanta, Georgia, where she worked closely with Mary McLeod Bethune. Frustrated by the continuing subordination of women's work to the men within the organizational structure, Ames decided to focus on the one issue that needed a strong white woman's voice, the issue of lynching. Acting on the challenge to the CIC by Bethune to create a southern white women's organization, Ames founded the Association of Southern Women for the Prevention of Lynching in 1930.

Mary McLeod Bethune fought fiercely to achieve social, economic, and educational opportunities for African Americans, particularly for African American women. (Library of Congress)

Mary McLeod Bethune, 1875–1955

Founder of National Council of Negro Women

Born to former slaves in the farm-country of South Carolina, Mary McLeod Bethune was educated through a series of Christian schools and trained to become a missionary. When her application to a post was rejected, she founded the Daytona Educational and Industrial Training School for Negro Girls in 1904. In 1923 she merged her school with the Cookman Institute, a Methodist school for African American boys, creating Bethune-Cookman College. She was appointed to presidential commissions by presidents Coolidge and Hoover. She became a personal friend to Eleanor Roosevelt and was appointed to the National Advisory Committee of the new National Youth Administration in 1935. That same year she founded and became the first president of the National Council of Negro Women and established the Federal Council on Negro Affairs, informally known as the Black Cabinet, to influence New Deal programs regarding African American issues. As president of the NCNW, she spearheaded the fight against lynching and the poll tax, and pressed for the inclusion of African American history in public school curriculums.

Josefina Fierro de Bright, 1920–1998

Community Activist

Josefina Fierro de Bright became the first secretary of El Congreso at the age of 18, holding this post from El Congreso's inception in 1939 through the 1940s. Born in Mexicali, Mexico, she and her family fled the political persecution that accompanied her mother's support for the radical Ricardo Flores Magón during the Mexican Revolution and settled in Los Angeles. While her mother established a restaurant, the family moved constantly in the Los Angeles area, and for a time her mother joined the migrant farm worker ranks in the Central Valley. Josefina returned to Los Angeles in 1938 to attend UCLA, but met and married the young Hollywood screenwriter Joseph Bright instead. She was swept into Bright's radical world, and joined with other Mexican American activists to boycott the Eastside Brewery for refusing to hire Mexicans. Josefina broadcast a radio program for the boycott on a local Spanish-language radio program. When the boycott proved successful, Josefina continued the radio show and came to the attention of Luisa Moreno, who drew her into El Congreso movement. Josefina was instrumental in raising funds and support, including persuading friends like Orson Welles, Anthony Quinn, and Dolores del Rio to contribute to the movement. She eventually became a victim of the red-baiting atmosphere in late 1940s Hollywood.

Earl Browder, 1891–1973

Communist Party Leader

Elected in 1934, Earl Browder was the general secretary of the Communist Party USA throughout the 1930s. He then enthusiastically embraced the Popular Front and broke through the remaining sectarian tendencies of the CP to lead it in its most publicly accepted days. Browder, born to a poor farming family in Wichita, Kansas, had begun his organizing days as a bookkeeper in Kansas City, working with the Socialist Party and serving jail time for opposing World War I. Along with James Cannon, he led their Kansas City SP local into the left wing during the splits of 1919. He became a chief lieutenant to William Z. Foster, emphasizing trade union work, during the CP's 1920s factional years, and made a considerable impression on the Red International of Labor Unions (Profintern) in Moscow. In the early New Deal, he encouraged United Front activities in 1933–1934 in the areas of farm and unemployment organizing. When the 1935 Comintern convention proclaimed a Popular (People's) Front strategy to combat fascism, Browder was ready and seized the opportunity to connect with the revolutionary American past, promoting the slogan "Communism is the Americanism of the twentieth century" (Ottanelli 1991, 123). After the 1939 Nazi-Soviet Pact, as part of a general crackdown on Communists, Browder was arrested for a minor passport violation and sentenced to four years in jail.

Norman Thomas, 1884–1968

Leader of Socialist Party

Born in Marion, Ohio, the son of a Presbyterian minister, Norman Thomas graduated from Princeton University in 1905 and from Union Theological Seminary in 1911. His first post was as pastor of the East Harlem Presbyterian Church with its affiliated settlement house. In 1916, he joined the Fellowship of Reconciliation to oppose American entry into World War I, and worked with antiwar Socialists. He joined the SP in 1918. He became codirector of the League for Industrial Democracy, and when Eugene Debs died in 1926, he became head of the SP. He received wide notice, if little influence, for his attacks on Mayor Jimmy Walker and Tammany Hall graft and mismanagement, leading to the collapse of the Walker administration. From 1928 to 1948, he ran every four years for president on the SP ticket. He supported the SP's labor organizing,

The leader of the Socialist Party from the 1920s to the 1960s, Norman Thomas was an important critic of American society and politics. (Library of Congress)

especially the Southern Tenant Farmers Union, but could only observe as the New Deal enacted many of the reforms that the SP had been working for. The SP broke apart due to partisan wrangling under his watch in 1936.

Robert C. Weaver, 1907–1997

Leader in the Black Cabinet

Robert Weaver was born in Washington, D.C., to a middle-class family, his father a postal clerk and his mother a homemaker. He attended Harvard University, receiving his BA, MA, and finally his PhD in economics in 1934. He returned to work in Washington, in the Department of Interior's Public Works Administration as an adviser on minority problems for the TVA, the Advisory Committee on Education, and the National Youth Administration. He served as an informal leader of the Black Cabinet, along with Mary McLeod Bethune, in the Roosevelt administration. In 1938 he was appointed special assistant to the head of the National Housing Authority, which sought to provide housing for the nation's low-income families. After World War II, he left federal service to work on city issues in Chicago and then New York City. He became involved in Democratic politics again in the 1950s and was named the secretary of the newly created Department of Housing and Human Services (HUD) in 1966. He thus became the first African American to gain a Cabinet post in this later era.

Walter White, 1893–1955

National Secretary of the NAACP

Born in Atlanta, Walter White graduated from Atlanta University in 1916 and helped found the Atlanta branch of the National Association for the Advancement of Colored People (NAACP) that year. In 1918 he moved to New York City to become the assistant secretary of the organization. Blond-haired and blue-eyed, White could have "passed" for white but chose to identify himself with the African American community. In the 1920s he carried out investigations in the South of lynchings and race riots, where his complexion allowed him to pose as a white reporter. When lynching began to increase during the Depression, White and the NAACP made antilynching legislation a top priority. White directed the legislative battle on Capitol Hill, only to be defeated three times by filibusters by southern senators. He was the NAACP's national secretary between 1933 and 1955. Under his leadership the organization developed a strategy to target discrimination in education, working to win court cases mandating equal access to public higher education for African Americans and equalizing salaries for African American and white teachers. White was wary of left-wing involvement in African American affairs and also opposed W. E. B. Du Bois's call for African American economic self-help.

REFERENCES AND FURTHER READINGS

Barrett, J. R. 1992. "Americanization from the Bottom Up: Immigration and the Remaking of the Working Class in the United States, 1880–1930," *Journal of American History* 79 (December): 996–1020.

Bayor, R. H. 1978. *Neighbors in Conflict: The Irish, Germans, Jews, and Italians of New York City, 1929–1941*. Baltimore: Johns Hopkins University Press.

Beard, C. A., ed. 1932. *America Faces the Future*. Boston: Houghton Mifflin.

Bell, T. 1941/1976. *Out of This Furnace*. Pittsburgh: University of Pittsburgh Press.

Bessie, A. C., and A. Prago, eds. 1987. *Our Fight: Writings by Veterans of the Abraham Lincoln Brigade, Spain, 1936–1939*. New York: Monthly Review Press with the Veterans of the Abraham Lincoln Brigade.

Brinkley, A. 1982. *Voices of Protest: Huey Long, Father Coughlin, and the Great Depression*. New York: Alfred A. Knopf.

Brinkley, A. 1995. *The End of Reform: New Deal Liberalism in Recession and War*. New York: Knopf.

Bucki, C. 2001. *Bridgeport's Socialist New Deal, 1915–1936*. Urbana: University of Illinois Press.

Buczek, D. S. 1974. *Immigrant Pastor: The Life of the Right Reverend Monsignor Lucyan Bójnowski of New Britain, Connecticut*. Waterbury, CT: Heminway Corporation.

Byrne, J. 2007. "From Brooklyn to Belchite: New Yorkers in the Abraham Lincoln Brigade." In *Facing Fascism: New York and the Spanish Civil War*, ed. P. N. Carroll and J. D. Fernández, 72–83. New York: Museum of the City of New York, NYU Press.

Carroll, P. N. 1994. *The Odyssey of the Abraham Lincoln Brigade: Americans in the Spanish Civil War*. Stanford, CA: Stanford University Press.

Carter, D. T. 1971. *Scottsboro: A Tragedy of the American South*. New York: Oxford University Press.

Cohen, L. 1990. *Making a New Deal: Industrial Workers in Chicago 1919–1939*. New York: Cambridge University Press.

Cohen, R. 1993. *When the Old Left Was Young: Student Radicals and America's First Mass Student Movement, 1929–1941*. New York: Oxford University Press.

Diggins, J. P. 1972. *Mussolini and Fascism: The View from America*. Princeton, NJ: Princeton University Press.

Divine, R. A. 1957. *American Immigration Policy, 1924–1952*. New Haven, CT: Yale University Press.

Dolan, J. P. 1985. *The American Catholic Experience: A History from Colonial Times to the Present*. Garden City, NY: Doubleday.

Draper, H. 1967. "The Student Movement of the Thirties: A Political History." In *As We Saw the Thirties: Essays on Social and Political Movements of a Decade*, ed. R. J. Simon, 151–189. Urbana: University of Illinois Press.

Fisher, J. T. 1989. *The Catholic Counterculture in America, 1933–1962*. Chapel Hill: University of North Carolina Press.

Foley, N. 1997. *The White Scourge: Mexicans, Blacks, and Poor Whites in Texan Cotton Culture*. Berkeley: University of California Press.

Fox, R. W. 1996. *Reinhold Niebuhr: A Biography*. Ithaca, NY: Cornell University Press.

Fujita-Rony, D. B. 2003. *American Workers, Colonial Power: Philippine Seattle and the Transpacific West, 1919–1941*. Berkeley: University of California Press.

García, M. T. 1989. *Mexican Americans: Leadership, Ideology, and Identity, 1930–1960*. New Haven, CT: Yale University Press.

Greenberg, C. L. 1991. *"Or Does It Explode?": Black Harlem in the Great Depression*. New York: Oxford University Press.

Gregory, J. N. 1989. *American Exodus: The Dust Bowl Migration and Okie Culture in California*. New York: Oxford University Press.

Hall, J. D. 1979. *Revolt against Chivalry: Jessie Daniel Ames and the Women's Campaign against Lynching*. New York: Columbia University Press.

Healey, D. R., and M. Isserman. 1993. *California Red: A Life in the American Communist Party*. Urbana: University of Illinois Press.

Heineman, K. J. 1999. *A Catholic New Deal: Religion and Reform in Depression Pittsburgh*. University Park: Pennsylvania State University Press.

Hoan, D. W. 1931. *Socialism and the City*. Little Blue Book no. 1692. Girard, KS: Haldeman-Julius Publications.

Ichioka, Y. 2006. *Before Internment: Essays in Prewar Japanese American History*. Ed. G. H. Chang and E. Azuma. Stanford, CA: Stanford University Press.

Jenkins, P. 1997. *Hoods and Shirts: The Extreme Right in Pennsylvania, 1925–1950*. Chapel Hill: University of North Carolina Press.

Kazin, M. 1995. *The Populist Persuasion: An American History*. New York: Basic Books.

Keeran, R. 1995. "National Groups and the Popular Front: The Case of the International Workers Order," *Journal of American Ethnic History* (Spring): 23–51.

Kelly, L. C. 1975. "The Indian Reorganization Act: The Dream and the Reality," *Pacific Historical Quarterly* 44 (3): 291–312.

Kirby, J. B. 1980. *Black Americans in the Roosevelt Era: Liberalism and Race.* Knoxville: University of Tennessee Press.

Klehr, H. 1984. *The Heyday of American Communism: The Depression Decade.* New York: Basic Books.

Korstad, R. R. 2003. *Civil Rights Unionism: Tobacco Workers and the Struggle for Democracy in the Mid-Twentieth-Century South.* Chapel Hill: University of North Carolina Press.

Kusmer, K. L. 2002. *Down and Out, On the Road: The Homeless in American History.* New York: Oxford University Press.

Kwong, P. 2001. *Chinatown, N.Y.: Labor and Politics, 1930–1950.* Rev. ed. New York: The New Press.

Lassonde, S. 2005. *Learning to Forget: Schooling and Family Life in New Haven's Working Class, 1870–1940.* New Haven, CT: Yale University Press.

Lorence, J. J. 1996. *Organizing the Unemployed: Community and Union Activists in the Industrial Heartland.* Albany: State University of New York Press.

Maiale, H. V. 1950. *The Italian Vote in Philadelphia between 1928 and 1946.* Philadelphia: University of Pennsylvania Offset Press.

Naison, M. 1983. *Communists in Harlem during the Depression.* Urbana: University of Illinois Press.

O'Brien, D. J. 1968. *American Catholics and Social Reform: The New Deal Years.* New York: Oxford University Press.

Olson, F. I. 1952. "The Milwaukee Socialists, 1897–1941." PhD diss., Harvard University.

Ottanelli, F. M. 1991. *The Communist Party of the United States: From the Depression to World War II.* New Brunswick, NJ: Rutgers University Press.

Ottanelli, F. M. 2001. "'If Fascism Comes to America We Will Push It Back into the Ocean': Italian American Antifascism in the 1920s and 1930s." In *Italian Workers of the World: Labor Migration and the Formation of Multiethnic States,* ed. D. R. Gabaccia and F. M. Ottanelli, 178–195. Urbana: University of Illinois Press.

Parman, D. L. 1976. *The Navajos and the New Deal.* New Haven. CT: Yale University Press.

Piehl, M. 1982. *Breaking Bread: The Catholic Worker and the Origin of Catholic Radicalism in America.* Philadelphia: Temple University Press.

Rosenzweig, R. 1979. "'Socialism in Our Time': The Socialist Party and the Unemployed, 1929–1936," *Labor History* 20 (Fall): 485–509.

Sánchez, G. J. 1993. *Becoming Mexican American: Ethnicity, Culture, and Identity in Chicano Los Angeles, 1900–1945*. New York: Oxford University Press.

Sarna, J. D. 2004. *American Judaism: A History*. New Haven, CT: Yale University Press.

Shannon, D. A. 1955. *The Socialist Party of America: A History*. New York: Macmillan.

Sitkoff, H. 1978. *A New Deal for Blacks: The Emergence of Civil Rights as a National Issue*, vol. 1: *The Depression Decade*. New York: Oxford University Press.

Smith, G. S. 1973. *To Save a Nation: American Countersubversives, the New Deal, and the Coming of World War II*. New York: Basic Books.

Swanberg, W. 1976. *Norman Thomas: The Last Idealist*. New York: Charles Scribner's Sons.

Vecoli, R. J. 2003. "The Making and Un-making of the Italian American Working Class." In *The Lost World of Italian American Radicalism: Politics, Labor, and Culture*, ed. P. V. Cannistraro and G. Meyer, 51–76. Westport, CT: Praeger.

Warren, F. A. 1974. *An Alternative Vision: The Socialist Party in the 1930s*. Bloomington: Indiana University Press.

Weiss, N. J. 1974. *The National Urban League, 1910–1940*. New York: Oxford University Press.

Weiss, N. J. 1983. *Farewell to the Party of Lincoln: Black Politics in the Age of FDR*. Princeton, NJ: Princeton University Press.

White, R. D., Jr. 2006. *Kingfish: The Reign of Huey P. Long*. New York: Random House.

Wyman, D. S. 1984. *The Abandonment of the Jews: America and the Holocaust, 1941–1945*. New York: Pantheon Books.

Yung, J. 1995. *Unbound Feet: A Social History of Chinese Women in San Francisco*. Berkeley: University of California Press.

Zaniello, T. 2003. *Working Stiffs, Union Maids, Reds, and Riffraff: An Expanded Guide to Films about Labor*. Ithaca, NY: Cornell University Press.

The Labor Movement

Overview

The Great Depression wreaked economic and personal havoc on working people. The labor movement was the largest, and most influential, of the social movements to arise out of this turmoil. The actions of working people, not just officialdom in the already existing American Federation of Labor (AFL) unions, ultimately shaped the new industrial union movement, stirred the federal government to enact laws defending workers' rights to organize, and spurred the formation of the modern industrial-relations system. The complex maneuvering among government initiatives, activists in workplaces and communities across the nation, official trade unionists, radicals of various ideologies, and both anti-union and liberal employers shaped the emerging industrial-relations system. This industrial-relations system, though amended, exists today.

While craft unions in the AFL attempted to hold on to their niches in the economy and to expand their power, they resisted opening their doors to the mass-production workers that made up the majority of the American labor force. Historians continue to debate why the AFL did not seize this opportunity—anticommunism, institutional rigidity, nativism, and racism have all been raised as reasons. But the complexity of the situation does not allow for easy answers.

In the view of AFL leaders, industrial workers seemed difficult to organize, and it was even more difficult to gain recognition from employers. The variety of races and ethnicities in the American workforce boggled the minds of even the most ambitious union organizers. Nonetheless, the Depression focused the minds of workers everywhere, and New Deal political activities, ethnic organizations, and new labor organizations molded workers into communities of interest. Some historians have claimed that American consumer culture provided a common ground for American workers to clarify their aspirations and goals. This chapter lays out the successes and failures of the labor movement in this decade.

Activists in the 1930s debated whether it was better or worse to have government protection and be caught in legal entanglements. Historians more recently have disagreed about the effects of the so-called New Deal System on the labor movement. The union movement today has decried the failure of this system to stem the tide of labor losses over the last two decades. Some have called for ending the National Labor Relations Board—and the argument continues.

Timeline

1930–1932 In the early Depression, 1930–1932, the Trade Union Unity League (TUUL) begins industrial-union organizing.

1933 On June 16, the National Industrial Recovery Act (NIRA), with Section 7 (a), is signed into law by FDR.

The American Federation of Labor (AFL) charters "Federal Unions" to absorb industrial workers.

1934 The year is filled with so-called NRA strikes, in San Francisco in May, in Toledo in May and June, in Minneapolis in August, and a textile strike across the nation in September.

1935 On May 16, the National Labor Relations Act (NLRA or Wagner Act) is passed by the U.S. Senate.

On May 27, the Supreme Court, in *Schecter v. U.S.,* declares NIRA unconstitutional, but its labor provision, Sec. 7 (a), was not working anyway.

Industrial unionism becomes an issue at the American Federation of Labor convention in October, culminating in a fistfight between John L. Lewis and William Hutcheson.

John L. Lewis and like-minded industrial-unionists set up a Committee for Industrial Organization (CIO) within the AFL.

1936 In summer, the Remington Rand Strike leads to the infamous Mohawk Valley Formula.

Disagreements between craft unionists and the Committee for Industrial Organization lead the AFL Executive Council to suspend 10 CIO unions in September.

In late December, the new United Auto Workers–CIO begins a sit-down strike at a General Motors plants in Flint, Michigan.

1937 In late January, the Flint sit-down strike ends with a contract between GM and UAW.

The UAW victory in Flint prompts a wave of sit-down strikes across the nation in January through March.

In a stunning act in March, Myron Taylor, chairman of U.S. Steel Company, signs a contract with the Steel Workers Organizing Committee (SWOC).

Faced with recalcitrant employers, SWOC begins a "Little Steel" strike in late spring.

In April, the U.S. Supreme Court, in the decision *NLRB v. Jones & Laughlin Steel Company,* upholds the National Labor Relations Act as constitutional; the legal challenge had been brought by one of the "Little Steel" companies.

On Memorial Day in Chicago, strikers at Republic Steel Company, one of the "Little Steel" companies, rally and march to the plant; they are shot at by guards and Chicago police; 10 marchers die and the incident becomes known as the "Memorial Day Massacre."

1938 In November, the Congress of Industrial Organizations (CIO) is formally established as an independent union organization.

1939 WPA Relief workers, now organized by the Workers' Alliance, begin carrying out strikes against budget cuts.

Union Successes, 1933–1934

The earliest stirrings of union activity in 1933–1934 were the result of pent-up energy and frustration over three long years of the Depression. The inauguration of Franklin D. Roosevelt in March 1933 unleashed that energy. Social scientists have noted that labor activity, particularly strikes, tends to occur not at the nadir of any crisis, but when conditions seem to be improving, making success a possibility. This activity began even before the National Industrial Recovery Act was passed in June 1933, and foreshadowed the shape and texture of activities to follow during the rest of the year.

Table 4.1. Union Membership, 1935–1939

Year	*AFL*	*CIO*	*Unaffiliated*	*Total*	*Percentage of Nonagricultural Workforce*
1935	3,218,000		534,900	3,753,300	6.8
1936	3,516,000		590,700	4,107,100	7.4
1937	3,179,000	1,991,200	609,200	5,780,100	10.3
1938	3,547,000	1,957,700	575,400	6,080,500	10.7
1939	3,878,000	1,837,700	839,800	6,555,500	11.5

Source: Adapted from Leo Troy, *Trade Union Membership, 1897–1962* (New York: Columbia University Press, 1965), 2, 8.

Alternative Unions in the Early 1930s

The Trade Union Unity League (TUUL), affiliated with the Communist Party USA (CP), made some unsuccessful attempts to organize industrial workers in the Hoover years (see "Experiences of the Early Depression" chapter). As the new Roosevelt administration began its One Hundred Days of legislative action in Congress, the TUUL, as well as some AFL unions, acted.

TUUL unions laid the basis for future industrial unions in auto, metal-working, coal-mining, textiles, and western agriculture. In some cases, their Communist

Table 4.2. Work Stoppages, 1929–1940

Year	*Number of Work Stoppages*	*Number of Workers Involved*
1929	921	289,000
1930	637	183,000
1931	810	342,000
1932	841	324,000
1933	1,695	1,170,000
1934	1,856	1,470,000
1935	2,014	1,120,000
1936	2,172	789,000
1937	4,740	1,860,000
1938	2,772	688,000
1939	2,613	1,170,000
1940	2,508	577,000

Source: Adapted from U.S. Bureau of the Census, *Historical Statistics of the United States, Colonial Times to 1970* (Washington, DC: GPO, 1975), ser. D-970-971.

alliances became the justification for an extreme company response and local police hostility.

The Auto Workers Union (AWU-TUUL) had started organizing in Flint, Michigan, in 1930 and supported workers on a spontaneous strike at Fisher Body No. 1 in July of that year, marching through downtown Flint carrying a banner that said "in 1776 we fought for liberty; today we fight for bread" (Kraus 1985, 7). After local police broke up picket lines and arrested picketers, the strike disintegrated. Though the strike was not successful, the AWU recruited over 350 members during this action, and six years later Fisher Body No. 1 would lead the General Motors sit-down strike. The Briggs Manufacturing Company, the largest independent maker of auto bodies in Detroit, with its reputation for bad working conditions became the AWU's next concentration in late 1932. When in January 1933 Briggs announced a 20 percent wage cut, the AWU called a strike at their Waterloo plant, which was settled two days later with management's capitulation. That sparked a wave of auto strikes in the Detroit area. But when Briggs workers struck again for a broader list of demands, management hardened its stance. After two weeks on strike, the AWU came under attack in the press as a Communist-dominated union, and Briggs announced its refusal to deal with Communists. Rank-and-file sentiment soon turned against Communist strike-committee members, and they were removed from their posts. The strike, thus weakened from within, dragged on through February and even into May at the Mack Avenue plant, with no more success than had been achieved in the first week (Keeran 1980, 80, 94).

Also in 1930, Communists attempted to aid a strike by mostly Mexican and Filipino lettuce workers in California's Imperial Valley. They organized walkouts of cannery workers in the Santa Clara Valley, where their new union, the Cannery and Agricultural Workers Industrial Union (CAWIU)-TUUL, came under fierce attack by local authorities and vigilantes. Strikers soon returned to work, having gained nothing. Fifteen hundred Mexican, Filipino, and Puerto Rican pea pickers struck in Half Moon Bay in May 1932. From these failed strikes in agriculture came the CP leadership's stinging criticism of reliance on spontaneous uprisings. The CAWIU would learn from these mistakes and conduct an effective strike in 1933 (see NRA strikes, below) (Daniel 1981, 129–134).

The National Miners Union (NMU) emerged from the dissident wing of the United Mine Workers (UMWA), composed of those coal miners who were opposed to John L. Lewis's undemocratic leadership. When the CP decided to work in a dual union rather than provide the opposition within the UMWA, they could rely on between 300 and 400 members working in the mines. The NMU carried out a coal strike in 1931 in western Pennsylvania, eastern Ohio, and northern West Virginia. As in the 1930 lettuce workers' strike in California, the Communist union attempted to organize the workforce only after other unions had been defeated. According to William Z. Foster, leader of the TUUL, the total membership of the TUUL was 40,000 in 1932, and the NMU had fewer than 500 dues-

Mexican workers protest during the 1933 cotton strike led by the Cannery and Agricultural Workers Industrial Union in California. (Library of Congress)

paying members. They were usually defeated not by their own revolutionary rhetoric but by the same forces that defeated other organizations: legal and vigilante violence, weak finances, and a rising unemployment rate due to the deepening Depression (Ottanelli 1991, 27–28).

African American and White Women Nutshellers in St. Louis

In May 1933, nearly 1,400 women nutshellers in St. Louis struck to restore their wages, to demand equal pay for African American and white workers, and for union recognition. This strike, led by the Food Workers Industrial Union-TUUL, galvanized community support. Previous organizing work by the St. Louis Unemployed Council in the African American community emboldened African American women to stand up for themselves in the workplace. They were soon joined by the white women employees in another section of the Funsten Nut Company. What made this strike remarkable was the union's claim that the strike was a "municipal matter" because so many of the workers were on public relief due to the low wages paid by the company, and the union called on the mayor to arbitrate a settlement (Feurer 1996, 37). The strikers were accompanied by representatives from the Social Justice Commission, a newly formed mediation group of white ministers and academics. Within 10 days, the company agreed to most demands, except for recognition of the union. The African American community then used this impetus to organize other marginalized workers in the St. Louis area, underscoring the strong role of the Communist Party in adapting their workplace strategies to the needs of African American women in their neighborhood and community, just as Unemployed Councils were learning to do in this era. In St. Louis, as historian Rosemary Feurer points out, this community activity and the success of the Food Workers Industrial Union laid the basis for the 1934 campaign for a local "Bill of Rights for Negroes" that presaged the postwar civil rights movement, but in this era the movement was based in the African American working class.

AFL and the NIRA

The American Federation of Labor (AFL) met the challenge of the Depression with its traditional structures and methods intact and unquestioned. AFL President William Green and the AFL leadership met on June 6, 1933, to hammer out a set of principles guiding labor's participation in the National Recovery Administration's Code Authorities (see "The New Deal and American Society" chapter), demanding equal voice for unions in negotiation with trade associations over codes, and recommending administrative procedures in industries where no unions existed. Then President Green appealed to unorganized workers to join unions to take advantage of the National Industrial Recovery Act (NIRA) and warned against the company unions being promoted by the National Association of Manufacturers (NAM).

The three national unions that took immediate advantage of NIRA Section 7 (a) were the United Mine Workers of America (UMWA), the Amalgamated Clothing Workers of America (ACW), and the International Ladies' Garment Workers Union (ILGWU). These three unions, all industrial in organization, had survived the antiunion 1920s and were in a position to re-assert themselves in 1933. It should be noted that these industrial sectors needed the economic stability that unions provided, since standard labor conditions minimized the competitive atmosphere of these trades and benefited employers as well. Thus these employers were sometimes as eager as unions to cooperate with the NRA code boards.

United Mine Workers of America

President John L. Lewis, soon to become a vocal champion of industrial unionism, began rebuilding his union. The UMW had always been an industrial union, since its jurisdiction extended to all who worked in and around coal mines regardless of the specific job. The UMW had barely survived the unfavorable coal-industry economy of the 1920s by dint of Lewis's strong—some said dictatorial—leadership and his ability to make a deal with receptive coal operators. But by the early Depression, its ranks were torn by regional dissenting movements rebelling against Lewis's rule. The Progressive Miners of America were strong in Illinois, and the Communist-led National Miners Union (NMU) was vocal in the southern Appalachian coal fields.

The splits in the coal fields of Illinois among the mainstream UMW, the Reorganized United Mine Workers (RUMWA), and the Progressive Miners of America (PMA), rank-and-file democratic movements against Lewis, resulted in violence among miners' organizations from 1931 to 1933. Once the bituminous code was established in September 1933, the NRA sent Donald Richberg to mediate the dispute, which he did by declaring the UMW to be the union representing the Illinois miners during the length of the contract and ruling that the PMA had to wait until the expiration of the contract in 1935 before an election could be held.

The National Miners Union (NMU) was a TUUL union alternative to the UMW that had been created in the late 1920s. In 1931 they carried out strikes in western Pennsylvania, eastern Kentucky, and Ohio, and were met with violent company reprisal everywhere, especially in "Bloody Harlan" County, Kentucky. In keeping with Communist initiatives everywhere, the NMU organized demonstrations by unemployed miners with their families, as well as strikes by workers themselves. The NMU remained a presence that frustrated Lewis, even as the militancy that they and other miners' locals displayed compelled the coal companies and the White House to bargain a decent contract in the previously non-union southern Appalachian fields (Dubofsky and Van Tine 1986).

John L. Lewis solved the continuing dilemma of rival unions by having his vice president, Philip Murray, invite John Brophy back into the UMW. Brophy had led the "Save-the-Union" movement in the mid-1920s and had run against Lewis for the union's presidency in 1926. Brophy had left the union and the mines after his defeat. Upon his return to the UMW staff as an organizer, Brophy's job in 1933 was to seek rapprochement between the UMW and the PMA. His credibility with the PMA allowed him to approach them to hammer out an agreement. His report back to Lewis outlined the PMA demands for, among other things, representation in a constitutional convention in Illinois and a guarantee of district autonomy in Illinois. Lewis rejected these terms, and the stalemate continued until Lewis consolidated power in the union while using it as a springboard for founding the Committee for Industrial Organization (CIO) within the AFL in 1935. Brophy continued as a UMW organizer from 1933 to 1935, and then became national director of the CIO from 1935 through the rest of the decade (Bernstein 1969, 61–67).

Using the passage of the NIRA, the UMW distributed leaflets appealing to miners, with UMW organizers using the phrase, "The President wants you to join the union!" When questioned, the organizers admitted that it was President Lewis, not President Roosevelt, they were referring to. The response was overwhelming, as Ohio, West Virginia, Kentucky, Pennsylvania, and even Colorado and New Mexico coal fields reported near 100 percent success in the commercial mines, though the "captive" mines of the steel companies were a more difficult matter. Lewis then went on to attempt to negotiate a tough new contract for the entire bituminous coal industry with a nationwide standard wage rate, hours, and working conditions, thereby eliminating the ruinous regional competition. The NRA code board oversaw negotiations through the summer of 1933 and finally reached agreement in September. The Appalachian Agreement established the eight-hour day, the 40-hour week, and union dues check-off (but not the union shop), ended the employment of boys under 17, and ended the requirement to purchase supplies at the company store. The UMW compromised on regional wage rates, which varied from $4.60 a day in the Northeast to $3.40 in the Deep South.

Nonetheless, the steel companies refused to consider recognizing the UMW in their own mines and attempted to establish company unions instead. In response, the miners of H. C. Frick Coke Company, the supplier to U.S. Steel, went on strike in July, and bloody battles broke out in the Monongahela River valley and adjoining counties in Pennsylvania. Gen. Hugh Johnson of the NRA brokered a temporary agreement, but miners would not listen to Lewis's call to return to work. It was only when President Roosevelt sent his personal pledge that the union would be recognized that the miners went back to work. But as the steel industry continued to stall, miners struck again, and by mid-September some 30,000 pickets stood outside every captive mine in western Pennsylvania. At this point, the steel executives relented and signed an agreement similar to the NRA Appalachian Code but with no recognition of the UMW and no dues check-off. This caused a greater dispute than before, as miners in the U.S. Steel mines, called "captive mines" by the UMW, saw this as an attempt to impose a company union and they continued their strike. Finally President Roosevelt intervened personally with steel executives. NRA chief Hugh Johnson met separately with each party and signed identical agreements with both the steel companies and with the UMW. The National Labor Board held elections, and the UMW slate of Lewis, Philip Murray, Thomas Kennedy, and UMW District 4 representatives won elections in 20

John L. Lewis, president of the United Mine Workers from 1919 to 1960. (Library of Congress)

mines out of 30. But since the steel companies were unwilling to deal with the UMW, the NLB forced them to negotiate with the individuals named on the slate. Thus were collective-bargaining agreements reached in the captive mines, but without UMW recognition. The flaws in the NRA mechanism were becoming apparent (Bernstein 1969, 44–61).

Southern Coal

The miners' aspirations and success of this era were captured by the lyrics of a song from the Alabama coal fields. "This What the Union Done," written and sung by the African American miner George Jones, was recorded by folklorist George Korson at Trafford, Alabama, in 1940. Jones had been a member of the UMW since 1894.

> In nineteen hundred an' thirty-three
> When Mr. Roosevelt took his seat,
> He said to President John L. Lewis,
> "In union we must be.
> Come, let us work together,
> Ask God to lead the plan,
> By this time another year
> We'll have the union back again."
> *Chorus*
> Hooray! Hooray!
> For the union we must stan',
> It's the only organization
> Protect the living man.
> Boys, it makes the women happy,
> Our children clap their hands,
> To see the beefsteak an' the good po'k chops,
> Steamin' in those fryin' pans. (Library of Congress)

Anthracite Coal

Anthracite (hard) coal was a different economy and culture altogether. Confined to a small stretch of land in eastern Pennsylvania from Carbondale south through Schuylkill and Northumberland counties, anthracite was used mainly as home heating fuel, not for commerce and industry, and had been a declining market since 1920. The railroads that hauled the anthracite had gobbled up most of the coal properties by World War I and consolidated the industry thereafter. In a declining market, the owners began closing underground mines in the mid-1920s and adding strip-mining operations where possible. The Depression only exacerbated what was a dismal economy for miners' families in this region. Here, two developments in the 1930s were noteworthy: a large community movement in "bootleg coal," and a rebellion against John L. Lewis and the UMW.

Bootleg Coal

An estimated 20,000 independent miners and truckers began digging and selling coal from abandoned mines throughout the northern and southern anthracite regions. In the hard years of the early Depression, coal miners justified their actions. As miner Mike McCloskey put it:

> Illegal! Are we supposed to starve to death just 'cause the collieries are closed? These hills are full of coal and there's millions of people who wants it. We're miners, without jobs, and our bellies are empty. . . . God put that coal there—not the Philadelphia and Reading Coal Company. . . . I don't want nobody's charity . . . All I want is a chance so's our families can live. (Dublin and Licht 2005, 77)

Similar justifications came from the middle-class element of the area—local merchants, lawyers, doctors, and clergy—whose livelihoods were bound up with those of miners and their families.

Bootleg coal miners battled company guards in 1934 and 1935, and often sympathetic district attorneys declined to prosecute and local juries refused to convict the bootleggers. Neither Gov. Gifford Pinchot nor his successor, George Earle, intervened in the 1930s. By 1940, this illegal economy produced a significant portion of all anthracite coal. This movement, what Pennsylvania Governor Earle called "the greatest conflict between moral and property rights in the history of the state," revealed a communal loyalty that included a commitment to fundamental social change (Kozura 1996, 200). An organization of bootleggers, the Independent Miners and Truckers Association, formed in 1934, led mass demonstrations against proposed legislation to outlaw bootlegging in 1935, and finally negotiated an agreement in 1941 with coal companies to lease tracts to bootleggers on a royalty basis, in effect legalizing bootlegging (Dublin et al. 2005, 78). The community solidarity that carried out the equalization campaign (described below) and supported the bootlegging operation revealed a distinctly different sense of what "private property rights" meant in a time of economic crisis.

Insurgent Labor Movement in Anthracite Coal

Even more important was the insurgent labor movement within this community. Fed up with the UMWA's inability to address the plight of the hard-coal miners in the 1920s and the early 1930s, anthracite coal miners—mostly Polish,

Slovak, and Italian with a scattering of Welsh and Irish—struck in protest over the 1930 contract imposed by John L. Lewis. Lewis was attempting to extend the existing contract for another five and a half years, which would guarantee miners' basic wage rates but weaken local governance and force local union leaders to promote efficiency and conciliation with the mine owners. Fed up with Lewis's unwillingness to address local miners' issues, anthracite miners rejected the contract. The strike movement was strongest in the northern range, the Carbondale–Scranton–Wilkes-Barre area, where strikes against the 1930 contract led to the expulsion of strike leaders from the UMWA and to the creation of a dual union, the United Anthracite Miners of Pennsylvania (UAMP) (Bodnar 1983, 4–7).

In 1933, anthracite miners demanded from both the UMWA and the NRA Code Authority a plan for job "equalization" or work-sharing in the company-operated mines. This was an important demand since anthracite miners' unemployment rates were estimated to be at least 33 percent and working miners were employed only 50–60 percent of full time. Moreover, strip-mining operations caused even more unemployment, as machines replaced men. In the Panther Valley, the southeastern range of anthracite in Pennsylvania, a wide cross-section of the community, including the Lithuanian Catholic Action Convention and the local merchants association, supported the demand for equalization (work-sharing), since relief payments were straining local resources. Miners in the Panther Valley struck to enforce equalization while NRA negotiations continued in Washington. As labor consultant Jett Lauck reported, "there were about 10,000 men in this district who were in complete control of the situation having put up a large bell in the mountains and if there was any deviation from the policy which they had imposed upon the operators, the bell was rung and they mobilized and picketed the mines where the trouble took place and continued in a state of insurrection until matters were settled" (Dublin et al. 2005, 69). Though this may have been an apocryphal story, it illustrates the level of solidarity achieved in this southern range. Miners in the Panther Valley ignored national UMWA orders to go back to work, even under threat of revocation of their local charters. Local Equalization Committee leaders there negotiated directly with the Lehigh Navigation Coal Company (LNC), reached agreement on equalization, and returned to work on December 20, 1933. There were repeated, brief strikes against LNC in 1934 to reinforce the agreement. Equalization Committee leader James Gildea brought the equalization principle back into the UMWA, and equalization became the official policy of the UMWA in its 1936 contract. Gildea himself went on to be elected to two terms in Congress as a Democrat (Dublin et al. 2005, 70).

The northern anthracite-field miners had a more difficult time creating this united response on equalization, since their field was more spread out and had many more coal operators to contend with. In the northern field, the equalization demand was not uniformly supported by all miners, and the dual-union UAMP supported unemployed miners who picketed working miners in order to implement equalization. The dual-union UAMP and the UMW carried on a fierce internecine struggle in the northern fields until 1936, when UAMP leader Thomas Maloney and several others were killed opening package bombs sent through the mail. With the end of the UAMP, Lewis reorganized UMW District 1, readmitted former members who had participated in the dual-union movement, and smoothed over the disputes among anthracite coal miners. But the battle within the miners' union left a bitter taste in the mouths of many hard-coal miners, feelings that remained decades later.

Amalgamated Clothing Workers of America

Russian immigrant Sidney Hillman, its elected president since the ACW's founding in 1914, quickly took advantage of the NIRA in 1933 by striking the men's clothing industry in New York City over wages and succeeded in raising them some 10 to 30 percent. The ACW had been a renegade union outside the AFL in 1914 when it was founded from a split within the AFL's United Garment Workers, which represented only skilled tailors and cutters. The semi-skilled immigrant garment workers who had successfully struck the Chicago men's clothing company Hart, Schaffner and Marx in 1911 formed the nucleus of this new organization in 1914 and built a successful organization during and after the World War I years in the major markets of New York, Chicago, Philadelphia, Baltimore, Cleveland, and Rochester. The union had held on to agreements in the harsh 1920s by assisting willing manufacturers in modernizing operations and helping regulate the notoriously competitive market through standard contracts. But control gradually ebbed away, as corruption in the union and gangsterism in the industry allowed the spread of manufacturing into nonunion "out-of-town" contracting shops.

Sidney Hillman founded the Amalgamated Clothing Workers of America in 1914 and served as its first president from 1914 to 1946. (Library of Congress)

In 1931, Hillman acted to root out corruption and gangsterism in the New York City locals, and waged war on the out-of-town operations (Fraser 1991, 246–55). The ACW stopped the deterioration of conditions in NYC by calling strikes of 10,000 and 30,000 members during June and July 1932 to stop trucking of piecework to nonunion out-of-town contractors. The union proceeded to tackle the Baltimore market in 1932, where sweatshop conditions had grown enormously in the early Depression. Here the union was aided by a coalition of academics, and prominent rabbis and priests, including the labor priest Father Francis Haas. The strike was a qualified success. Even so, by early 1933 Hillman was deeply pessimistic about his union's ability to hang on since his major manufacturers were about to declare bankruptcy; he told his friend Felix Frankfurter that he was "fearful that before Mr. Roosevelt will do anything along constructive lines a great deal of disaster will overtake us" (Fraser 1991, 257).

Hillman proceeded to rely on governmental interventions in the economy and became an important architect of New Deal labor politics for the rest of the decade. After helping to draft the NIRA, Hillman was poised to strike other key markets in Boston, Philadelphia, Chicago, and other midwestern cities, asking for wage increases and union recognition. A dramatic confrontation in Rochester with manufacturers who chose to sign with the United Garment Workers (UGW-AFL) was mediated instead by NRA head Gen. Hugh Johnson. Finally, the ACW extended its influence in the cotton shirt industry which had spread outside New York City to small towns in Pennsylvania, New Jersey, and Connecticut. By the end of 1933, the Amalgamated had 125,000 members, an increase of 50,000 over the previous year. The NRA code in men's clothing was one of the first industry codes to take effect, with a 36-day week and minimum wages of 40 cents in the North and 37 cents in the South. The code in the cotton garments industry took longer to negotiate, but it finally established a minimum of 32.5 cents in the North and 30 cents in the South, with a 40-hour week.

With this success, Hillman was determined to join the AFL in order to consolidate labor's gains and extend its political influence. Petitioning to join the AFL on September 9, 1933, the ACW faced a jurisdictional challenge from the UGW and carefully proclaimed its jurisdiction over the men's clothing industry, excluding those workers already claimed by other AFL affiliates. Hillman even agreed to refrain from organizing more shirt factories without the UGW's permission, though he refused to hand over the shirt workers that the ACW had recently organized. Finally, the Amalgamated agreed that the only union label in men's clothing would be that of the UGW. With the ACW's petition supported by John L. Lewis and George L. Berry of the Printing Pressmen, the AFL council approved the application and the AFL convention in fall 1933 voted to admit the ACW.

Antisweatshop Campaign of 1933

The shirt industry had mostly deserted New York City for the cheaper hinterlands and kept only the skilled design and cutting operations in the city. This meant that the ACW needed to reach out to smaller towns in New Jersey, Pennsylvania, and Connecticut. The Pennsylvania shops were in anthracite coal country, where miners' wives and daughters found work in shirt-making. An "anti-Sweatshop Committee" was established in Allentown, headed by the mayor. A dramatic "children's strike" was called in Allentown, where Mrs. Gifford Pinchot, the governor's wife, joined the picket line. Hazleton was one town in which the UMW had great municipal influence, and the major shirt manufacturer there, S. Liebowitz and Sons, had connections to the Roosevelt administration. The company quickly agreed to arbitration. The Hazleton drive coincided with an organizing campaign among hosiery workers in nearby Reading, where the militant wing of the United Textile Workers under Emil Rieve had established itself (Bernstein 1969, 77).

In Connecticut, the New Haven shirt shops were quickly organized, aided by Yale students who joined picket lines (Fraser 1991, 291). In Bridgeport, where shirt shops had also relocated, strikes by 800 Italian, Polish, and Slovak women machine operators and Jewish male cutters organized the shirt shops by summer 1933. In Connecticut, the state's Department of Labor began a campaign against the "sweatshop scourge" by raiding "fly-by-night" contractors who were not adhering to the state's rather lenient labor hours for women and minors. By all accounts, the campaign was a success, helping the organizing efforts of both the ACW and the ILGWU, though the Republican-dominated General Assembly refused to pass any further labor regulations (Bucki 2001, 133–134).

International Ladies' Garment Workers Union

The ILGWU was presided over by Russian immigrant David Dubinsky, who was appointed president of the ILGWU in 1932 after the previous president's death. Dubinsky had been the union's national secretary-treasurer in the 1920s. The membership was decimated by the Depression, registering at some 40,000 in early 1933 (down from a peak of 105,000 in 1920), and it was broke (Bernstein 1969, 84). The women's garments industry was notoriously competitive, with many small contractors and subcontractors, and subject to fashion swings in ladies' clothing and its seasonality. The industry had become a huge sweatshop by 1933 in all the major cities. But the ILG successfully struck the Philadelphia dress industry in May of that year. The next step was in the coat and suit industry, where the ILG used the NRA code board to bring standard conditions to the industry. In this they were joined by the New York employer associations. The NRA code divided the country into the Eastern area (New England and the mid-Atlantic states) and the Western area (the rest of the United States), with a 35-hour week in manufacturing and 40 hours in nonmanufacturing, wage increases (though with regional differentials), and with acceptable guidelines for subcontracting. To the dismay of some of its members, the ILG accepted a piece-rate system in this industry, where it had not prevailed before.

Dubinsky's main victory was won in the New York dress industry where a complete strike was called in mid-August 1933, in the midst of code negotiations, and was answered by some 60,000 union and nonunion dress workers. This impressive display of solidarity caused the dress manufacturers to accept the closed shop, the major elements of the NRA coat-and-suit code, and wage increases. The great membership increase in the New York area caused the large locals to divide themselves into smaller branches, often by race and ethnicity. In addition, the ILG's great victories in these two sectors allowed the union to organize the many lesser trades like neckwear, embroidery, corsets, and brassieres. The union followed shops fleeing New York through the Out-of-Town Department, and scored victories in other major cities in Connecticut and New Jersey. The ILG also benefited from the antisweatshop campaigns carried on in these states in 1933. By mid-1934, the union had 200,000 members.

Other "NRA Strikes" of 1933–1934

Workers in other sectors of the economy, with less cooperative employers, also struck for wages and union recognition in 1933–1934, but were less successful. Their attempts revealed the weaknesses of the NRA overall, and its labor protections specifically. They also revealed the weaknesses in the AFL. Some well-placed AFL affiliates, like the Mine, Mill, and Smelter Workers (Mine-Mill), leaped at the chance to organize copper mines in the southwest and northwest. The Hotel Employees and Restaurant Employees (HERE) got a big boost from the repeal of Prohibition and the resurgence in their economic sector. President William Green of the AFL attempted to energize some affiliates, like the moribund Amalgamated Association of Iron, Steel, and Tin Workers, to organize the steel industry. He also opened the door to mass-production workers where the AFL did not have an industry union by authorizing Federal Labor Unions (FLUs) for those workers who were clamoring to be organized in rubber, auto, and electrical. FLUs were locals directly affiliated to the AFL, rather than to one of the international unions that made up the federation. In Green's mind, FLUs were to be temporary holding locals for these mass-production workers until the regular AFL affiliates could create categories of membership for these semi-skilled and unskilled workers who did not fit comfortably into a craft category.

Key to understanding the effects of the NRA on these industries was the fact that in industries where there was little union presence or strength, the NRA boards were often in the hands of company representatives who paid no attention to labor conditions as they tried to maximize their own revenues and markets. The NRA had set up the National Labor Board as a new entity to handle labor disputes, and the Board was struggling to bring a set of principles to a new labor relations system that could satisfy the labor unrest. Ironically, the labor legislation that was supposed to smooth out labor relations had the opposite effect of sparking labor protest. Recalcitrant employers blocked progress, and rank-and-file unionists were often in no mood to accept the compromises that their national leaders negotiated. And finally, these mass-production workers wanted to build unions of their own in their industry. This fueled the turmoil in the AFL that eventually led to the creation of the Committee for Industrial Organizations (CIO) led by the Mine Workers' president John L. Lewis. Key efforts in auto, steel, rubber, and electrical industries will be followed later in this chapter.

General Strikes of 1934

There were 1,856 work stoppages involving nearly 1.5 million workers in 1934. Three of them were important because of their expansion to general strikes in their cities: auto-parts workers in Toledo; truck drivers in Minneapolis; longshoremen in San Francisco. There was also a general industry strike, of cotton-textile workers of New England and the South. The strikes were born of a despair mixed with hope, along with anger over the continuing failure of Section 7 (a). These strikes proved a number of things: (1) workers who had been previously regarded by AFL officialdom as unorganizable could be staunch union members; (2) AFL craft unions were not equipped, either physically or psychologically, to deal with the mass of industrial workers who were flocking into their ranks; and (3) the federal government, in the form of the NRA, had failed to protect workers' interests. Thus, even as Sen. Robert Wagner was preparing his National Labor Relations Act, and before the NIRA was declared unconstitutional by the U.S. Supreme Court (see "The New Deal and American Society" chapter), workers and their unions had pushed far ahead of the NRA.

Toledo

Auto-parts workers had tried to organize during the summer of 1933, had formed an AFL federal union, No. 18384, and were trying to negotiate a contract. A partial strike in early 1934 resulted in the National Labor Board mediating a settlement by April 1. The Electric Auto-Lite Company, the largest independent supplier of auto parts, kept its market by cutting manufacturing costs through low wages and a high pace of production. It refused to negotiate, other companies followed, and FLU No. 18384 called a strike of all recalcitrant companies; this time, only a quarter of the workers responded. But Toledo had an independent Marxist party, the American Workers Party (AWP), led by minister A. J. Muste and surrounded by independent radicals of various political leanings (Bernstein 1969, 221). The AWP tried the unique move of bolstering the strike movement by organizing the jobless to prevent scabbing, as the companies were attempting to run their factories with strikebreakers. The AWP and its affiliate, the Lucas County Unemployed League, organized mass picket lines of the unemployed at factory gates. Ignoring a court injunction limiting picketing, FLU No. 18384 expanded its picket lines at the Auto-Lite Company. When the sheriff arrested the strike leader and four other picketers in front of a crowd of 10,000 and a deputy roughed up an old man in the crowd, the "battle of Toledo" began on May 23. Lasting all day and on until midnight, it was briefly stopped by the arrival of the Ohio National Guard at dawn. But later that afternoon, the Toledo crowd surrounded the troops, and in the melee the troops fired, first into the air and then into the crowd. Two were killed, and a score wounded. The International Brotherhood of Electrical Workers (IBEW-AFL), stymied in their negotiations with the power company Toledo Edison, then threatened a strike to move its own negotiations along, and the Central Labor Council voted to call a general strike in support of the IBEW. At this point Adjutant General Frank D. Henderson ordered four more militia companies to the city and ordered Auto-Lite to close. Mediator Charles P. Taft, son of the former president, was dispatched by President Roosevelt to the embattled city. Toledo Edison settled with the IBEW and Auto-Lite settled with FLU No. 18384, and peace settled on the city on June 1, 1934.

Minneapolis Truckers Strike

Minneapolis, like its twin St. Paul, had come upon hard times with the decline of its major industries—railroads, timber, iron ore, and agriculture. The city was polarized by income and ethnicity, with those of Anglo-Saxon stock successfully on top, with Scandinavians and some Irish and Jews and other new-ethnics on the lower rungs of society. The Minneapolis Citizens Alliance, organized in 1908, had been effective in thwarting unions, and now consisted of 800 Minneapolis employers willing to give a free hand to A. W. Strong, the Alliance leader. Minneapolis was widely known as an antiunion city, and the Citizens Alliance intended to keep it that way. The International Brotherhood of Teamsters (AFL) had only 1,000 members in Minneapolis, of whom some 200 were in an unusual local, General Drivers Local 574, which had a charter so broad that it allowed almost an industrial form of organization (Bernstein 1969, 231). Here an unusual confluence of forces—a cadre of militant Trotskyists assembled around the Dunne brothers in the De Laittre coal yard, the Local 574 charter, and the air of expectations provided by NIRA Section 7 (a)—led Local 574 to declare a strike of coal-yard workers in early February 1934. The vast majority of the city's coal yards were shut, and employers quickly capitulated. Local 574 was then emboldened to declare a unionization campaign for all the city's truckers and helpers. The Regional Labor Board was unable to mediate a settlement, given employers' unwillingness. Local 574's walkout began on May 15.

The city, virtually shut down, remained calm for the first three days, but then the Citizens Alliance laid plans to move trucks again and prepared their Citizens Army to confront strikers. Luring strikers into an ambush, the Citizens Army and the police beat them senseless. Retaliation by the union was assured, and the

The Dunne Brothers

The six Dunne brothers had been raised in Little Falls, Minnesota, by their Irish immigrant laborer father and French-Canadian mother. Raised Roman Catholic, they attended parochial school, where a dispute over the oldest, Bill, reading a Victor Hugo novel to his brothers caused them to be expelled from the parish. Four of the brothers turned to the left in young adulthood. Bill joined the Socialist Party in 1910, became an electrician, and moved to Butte, Montana, where he became a prominent labor leader. Taking the Butte Socialist Party into the Communist Labor Party in 1919, he stayed active in the CP throughout the 1920s and moved to a high rank in the Party as an editor of the *Daily Worker* and a representative to the Comintern in Moscow. His younger brothers, Vincent Raymond (Ray), Grant, and Miles, also made names for themselves as union activists, with Ray becoming known as a brilliant organizer. Ray had worked as a lumberjack, had joined the Industrial Workers of the World during World War I, and then joined the Communist Party when it was formed. He and his brothers Grant and Miles split with the CP in 1929, joining the Trotskyist Communist League (Left Opposition). Ray had worked at the De Laittre coal yard since 1921. When a subsidiary of the Ford Motor Company took over the yard in 1933, management fired him. He immediately decided that the coal yards needed to be organized. So he, along with fellow Trotskyists Carl Sköglund and Farrell Dobbs, approached the Teamsters. It was a decisive moment (Bernstein 1969, 231–234).

two sides clashed at the public market the following Monday. A few picketers and some 30 policemen were hurt. But the next day, some 20,000 people converged in the public marketplace to see if trucks would move the perishable goods that needed to be shipped. The "Battle of Deputies Run" then broke out, with the union forces outnumbering the police and Citizens Army. The union forces won control of the market and no trucks moved; 50 people were wounded, and two leaders of the Citizens Army were killed. Farmer-Labor Governor Floyd Olson then intervened, threatening to call out the National Guard, and arranged a truce between the two sides. An agreement was reached to abide by the NRA code for the industry, but no settlement was reached on union recognition. On May 26, trucking operations started again in Minneapolis.

But the unresolved questions and further discrimination against union members led to another strike declaration on July 16. Father Francis J. Haas arrived as the special mediator for the National Labor Board, to no avail as only the union would agree to its proposal. Instead the Citizens Alliance was determined to break the union. They set an ambush on July 20, whereby a decoy truck escorted by a police convoy picked up a shipment and proceeded to drive across town. When pickets attempted to stop the truck, the police opened fire. As more unionists rushed to the scene, they too were fired upon. After only a few minutes, two strikers were dead and 67 others were wounded, most shot in the back. Only one policeman was hurt. The funerals in the following days were attended by from 20,000 to 100,000 mourners, according to varying sources (Bernstein 1969, 244). The governor reluctantly declared martial law, which did allow trucks to begin moving again, just as the Citizens Alliance had planned. At this point the union protested, leading the governor reluctantly to order their leaders' arrest, setting off another round of violence, this time by enraged strikers who attacked trucks at random. Governor Olson finally had to declare that only essential trucks with foodstuffs would be issued permits to move, unless their employers had accepted the Haas proposal. More pressure from NRA officials and the White House finally caused employers to agree to a mediated settlement on August 21, putting an end to the 36-day strike. Local 574 won Labor Board elections in only 50 firms that August, but soon represented workers in 500 Minneapolis workplaces. As observer Charles Rumford Walker wrote, "the civil war had raged over far deeper issues [than the terms of the settlement], the first of which was the historic dictatorship over Minneapolis and the lives of its workers by the tightly organized camarilla of the Citizens' Alliance. The strike had challenged and broken that dictatorship" (Bernstein 1969, 251; Millikan 2001).

San Francisco General Strike

In the summer of 1934, San Francisco longshoremen determined to strike to win their demands for $1.00 an hour, a six-hour day and 30-hour week, and recognition of their union, the International Longshoremen's Union (ILA), an AFL affiliate that had been long moribund on the West Coast. Previously, in 1932–1933, the TUUL-affiliated Marine Workers Industrial Union had organized a nucleus of unionists in San Francisco, mostly old-time Wobblies along with Australian-born Harry Bridges. Bridges and the rest of his group decided to take charge of demands for the ILA local, adding abolition of the shape-up, the regular morning roll-call, and random choosing of the crews that would work that day. They wanted a union hiring hall, and they petitioned the NRA to make these demands part of the code. They also began organizing ports up and down the Pacific coast, from Seattle to San Diego. When the Waterfront Employers' Union refused to meet with the ILA or even to negotiate labor issues with the NRA board, President Roosevelt asked the union for a delay in the strike and ordered a special Federal Mediation Board to San Francisco. The forthcoming agreement was so worthless that it was rejected by the ILA locals. On May 9, longshoremen struck; almost 2,000 miles of American Pacific coast was shut down. Even though strikebreakers were immediately available to unload ships, they were incapable of loading cargo onto ships. On May 15, the Teamsters Union locals in San Francisco, Seattle, Oakland, and Los Angeles announced that they would not haul goods to and from the docks. Within a week, the shipboard workers—sailors, firemen, cooks, the Masters, Mates and Pilots Union, and the Marine Engineers—also declared a strike.

Finally, when ILA president Joseph P. Ryan arrived in San Francisco from the East Coast to negotiate a settlement, he found that the West Coast men were not willing to settle for his negotiated agreement. Ryan then started blaming "strong radical elements" in the local for the lack of a settlement. Employers picked up this theme and authorized the San Francisco Industrial Association, an organization similar to the Minneapolis Citizens Alliance, to conduct the business response to the strike. They embarked on a strong red-baiting campaign in the newspapers. At the bidding of the mayor, Ryan met once again with the Waterfront Employers, and signed an agreement without the input of Harry Bridges, now the elected strike leader. At local meetings that weekend, longshoremen at all the major ports except Los Angeles voted overwhelmingly against the agreement. Employers, however, were determined to reopen the docks. On July 3, trucks began to move, watched by thousands of spectators lining the San Francisco hills overlooking the port. Then after the Fourth of July holiday, on what came to be known as "Bloody Thursday," trucks began to move again, and violent clashes between police and picketers started once again, this time ending in gunfire. The afternoon clash became larger still, and it ended with two dead and at least 67 injured. Most were strikers, while a few were either bystanders or police.

Confrontation between a policeman wielding a night stick and a striker during the San Francisco General Strike in 1934. This city-wide movement was started by the longshoremen's union. (National Archives)

Gov. Frank E. Merriam declared a state of emergency and ordered the National Guard to the port. The San Francisco Labor Council declared a general strike, by a vote of 165 to 8 (Bernstein 1969, 279). The ILA arranged a massive funeral march on Monday, July 9, with thousands of men and women parading quietly on Market Street behind the caskets of the two slain strikers. No one watching that parade had any doubt that a general strike would be under way by the end of the week. Indeed, the Teamsters had begun picketing the roads to San Francisco from the South. The Labor Council created a Committee of 25 to handle the strike, giving them authority to issue permits for the movement of foodstuffs. The Bakery and Milk Truck Drivers were ordered not to walk out. The general strike lasted three days, after which conservative labor leaders caved in to the mounting red-baiting campaign of the newspapers and business spokesmen and called off the strike. On July 30, the ILA membership voted to end the strike after 82 days by accepting binding arbitration by the National Longshoremen's Board. The Board granted the ILA a contract, a hiring hall controlled by the union, a six-hour day and 30-hour week, and a hefty pay raise (Bernstein 1969, 295; Nelson 1988a, 210–249).

Cotton Textile Strike

Unlike other strikes in 1934, this one was geographically broad, in an industry that stretched from Maine to Alabama. The United Textile Workers (UTW), always internally divided between skilled and unskilled and by ethnicity, had never been able to hold on to its gains or members. As factories organized, textile companies pulled their mills out of the North and re-established them in non-union southern states, and they increased production through the old methods of "speed up and stretch out," where workers were expected to tend more and more looms. When the NRA was finally established, the industry-based Cotton Textile Industry Committee was ready with a draft code, which was quickly approved. The resulting code set a minimum wage of $12 in the South and $13 in the North, approved the 40-hour workweek, and prohibited child labor. One problem was that the NRA Code Board did not include a representative from the weak UTW; the labor representative was George L. Berry of the Printing Pressman. Moreover, the code board was dominated by the Cotton Textile Institute, an industry association. Nonetheless, the NRA code had the immediate result of improving the economy of the industry, and textile workers flocked to the UTW. However, it soon became clear that companies were ignoring the labor provisions of the NRA code, as reports of the firing of union members and the stretch-out continued. The Cotton Textile Code Board, commonly called the Bruere Board after its chairman, economist Robert Bruere, was powerless to enforce the labor codes. Moreover, the code board finally dealt with the excess inventories in late 1933 by ordering limitation of output, imposing a 25 percent reduction in machine hours, leading to unemployment and lost wages. The reduction was again imposed in summer 1934, and this time rank-and-file textile workers acted. The Alabama State Council of Textile Workers ordered a walkout on July 16, 1934, and 20,000 workers in 24 Alabama mills went out; they remained on strike for two months (Levinson 1938, 74). In the South, the main demand was for the NRA code board to end the stretch-out and to regulate machine load.

This forced the national union to act, and the UTW convention on August 14 voted a general strike of all cotton textile mills to begin on September 1. This was a reluctant move on the part of the UTW leadership, who had long been content to rely on cooperative liberal northern textile employers who were willing to sign contracts with the UTW. This arrangement benefited those remaining skilled craft workers within textiles, while often neglecting the unskilled, and the

Some of more than 10,000 textile workers on strike participate in a Labor Day parade in downtown Gastonia, North Carolina, 1934. (Library of Congress)

union acquiesced in employers' attempts to increase production. Now they were forced to deal with the workers' anger over NRA codes, even as they hoped that President Roosevelt would intervene. The White House instead acquiesced to Secretary of Labor Perkins's request that the recently created National Labor Board be allowed to settle the dispute, with little results.

The UTW had been pushed into the strike by the militancy of its new southern members, as historian Janet Irons argued (Irons 2000). The turnout for the strike on September 1 in both northern and southern mills was extraordinary, and extended to wool and worsted mills and silk mills. "Flying squadrons" of unionists spread the strike from one mill town to another. In the North, state governments in Connecticut and Rhode Island called out their National Guards. In the South, violence flared almost immediately, and four states called out their National Guards. The most notorious incident occurred on September 6, in Honea Path, South Carolina. The isolated village of 3,000 residents, all connected to the Chiquola Mill, was split over the strike, and a fistfight between two men flared into a gun battle that left six slain strikers and more than 20 wounded, most shot in the back as they were fleeing the picket-line battlefield. Most observers reported that gunplay had erupted from the management sympathizers.

The governor of South Carolina soon declared a state of martial law in effect for all mill properties.

But the large numbers of shut-down mills masked a simple truth. Many mills had simply closed, in effect locking out their workers, hoping to ride out the strike with their surplus stock stacked up in their warehouses. As historian John A. Salmond has argued, the strike support in many areas was weak, with many workers, especially in the South, too afraid of management and too intimidated by union flying squadrons, to wholeheartedly support the union cause (Salmond 2002, 56–63). Many public voices, and some private ones in the UTW, worried about the influence of outside agitators and "Un-American" influences, which could mean either Communists or simply foreign-born workers. As September wore on and the union, overwhelmed by the expanse of the strike, proved unable to assist strikers with foodstuffs and other material aid, workers slowly began drifting back to work. On September 22, at the urging of President Roosevelt, the UTW accepted the recommendations of the Labor Board and ordered its members back to work. Most strike issues had been left vaguely defined in the board report, and employers agreed only to give the Labor Board report "serious consideration." Many companies refused to rehire strikers, and most union demands were never acted upon. The strike was a clear defeat, and the southern textile industry remained unorganized until the 1980s.

Craft versus Industrial Organization

Industry had greatly changed its production process by the 1930s, when mass production of commodities through subdivision of labor and use of specialized machinery and the assembly line had become widespread. Mass production had created a new category of labor, the semi-skilled machine operative, who was trained to do one operation over and over again. Craft union structure had evolved from 19th-century labor practice, codified in 1886 with the creation of the American Federation of Labor. Many AFL craft unions had adapted to changing technologies by expanding their definitions of their jurisdictions. But often their distrust of "new" immigrants (those of the second great wave of immigration from 1895 to 1920) and their distaste for unskilled and semi-skilled workers led them to ignore these workers.

Fistfight at the 1935 AFL Convention

The dramatic climax to the debate within the AFL regarding what to do with the masses of industrial workers pouring into the federal locals came at the 1935 AFL convention in Atlantic City. On the last day, after days of debate and defeated motions to create industrial unions in auto, metal-mining, and rubber, a

Table 4.3. Membership Models, Craft and Industrial Unions

		Auto Industry		*Electrical Industry*
Machinists union—AFL	→	machinists	→	machinists
Molders union—AFL	→	molders	→	molders
Carpenters union—AFL	→	carpenters	→	carpenters
Federal union linked to AFL	→	semi-skilled operatives laborers	→	semi-skilled operatives laborers
		↑ United Auto Workers—CIO ↑		↑ United Electrical Workers—CIO ↑

lone delegate from a rubber local rose to describe the failure of the craft union to hold the rubber workers they had been given. At this, William H. Hutcheson, president of the carpenters' union, raised a point of order regarding the delegate's testimony, noting that the industrial union question had been decided on the previous day. As labor journalist Edward Levinson reported, John L. Lewis rose to defend the rubber worker, observing: "'This thing of raising points of order all the time on minor delegates is rather small potatoes.' Hutcheson was on his feet again, his face florid with anger. 'I was raised on small potatoes. That is why I am so small.'" As the two men passed each other, words were exchanged and then:

> the mine leader's right fist shot straight out. There was no swing to the blow, just a swift jab with 235 pounds behind it. It caught the carpenters' president on the jaw. Instantly other carpenters' officials rushed at Lewis and, as suddenly, the latter's colleagues sprang from their near-by seats. Hutcheson went crashing against his long table, which went over under the impact of ten or more delegates pushing, elbowing, punching. Others rushed to separate the fighters and in a few minutes the battle was over. Hutcheson was lifted to his feet. . . . Lewis casually adjusted his collar and tie, relit his cigar, and sauntered slowly through the crowded aisles to the rostrum. (Levinson 1938, 115–116)

Such were the moods of the craft and industrial unionists in the AFL. The break was not long in coming.

CIO Established within AFL

After the 1935 AFL convention, supporters of industrial unionism met on November 9, 1935, to discuss the future of industrial unionism and the organization of mass-production workers in the United States. The Committee for Industrial Organization was born at this meeting. Those present at this meeting were the leaders of the following unions: John L. Lewis, United Mine Workers; Charles Howard, Amalgamated Typographical Union; Sidney Hillman, Amalgamated Clothing Workers; David Dubinsky, International Ladies' Garment Workers; Thomas F. McMahon, United Textile Workers; Max Zaritsky of Hatters, Cap and Millinery Workers Union; Harvey C. Fremming of the Oil Workers; Thomas H. Brown of Mine, Mill, and Smelter Workers. Together these eight unions paid per capita dues on 828,000 members (compared to total AFL membership of 3,308,000) at the end of 1935. The ACW, UMW, and ILGWU each pledged $5,000 to the CIO to get it started. At this meeting the committee selected Lewis as president, Howard as secretary, and John Brophy as director. Analyst Walter Galenson also noted the ironic subsequent careers of some of these founders: Howard died a few years later, having failed to bring his union into the CIO; Dubinsky took his union out of the CIO after a few years of an uneasy alliance; Lewis repudiated the CIO in 1940 after a political dispute. Only the ACW stayed with the CIO through to its merger with the AFL in 1955 (Galenson 1960, 4–5).

The CIO, 1936–1938

The Committee for Industrial Organizations (CIO) within the AFL was an uncomfortable affiliation. After a series of failed negotiations between the AFL Executive Council and CIO affiliates, the groups split in September 1936 after the AFL Executive Board ordered the suspension of 10 national unions who failed to sever their affiliation with CIO. They were Amalgamated Clothing Workers (ACW), Amalgamated Association of Iron, Steel and Tin Workers; Federation of Flat Glass Workers; International Ladies' Garment Workers (ILGWU); International Union of Mine, Mill and Smelter Workers (Mine-Mill); United Automobile Workers (UAW); Oil Field, Gas Well and Refinery Workers; United Mine Workers (UMW); United Rubber Workers (URW); and United Textile Workers (UTW). It should be noted that though the officers of the United Hatters, Cap and Millinery Workers and the International Typographical Union participated in the early formation of the CIO, their unions were not involved and so escaped the AFL suspension notice. The 1936 AFL convention ratified the decision that fall, with only the Hatters and Typographical Union delegates opposed. What followed were aggressive AFL moves against CIO unions, including the February 1937 order to state federations of labor and to city central bodies to expel CIO locals from their organizations, and a May 1937 decision to levy one-cent-per-member dues to go directly to a national AFL fund to finance a campaign against the CIO. Subsequent negotiations stumbled over Lewis's insistence that the CIO unions could only rejoin the AFL if they were granted industrial-union jurisdictions, something that AFL unions were unwilling to countenance. Thus in February 1938, the AFL Executive Committee revoked the charters of the UMW, Mine-Mill, and the Flat-Glass Workers, followed a few months later by revocation of the charters of the UAW, Iron, Tin and Steel workers, ACW, UTW, and Oil Field Workers. It was only then that the move was made to transform the Committee into the *Congress* of Industrial Organizations. The constitutional convention of the Congress of Industrial Organizations was held in Pittsburgh, November 14–18, 1938. In spite of a February 1939 appeal from President Roosevelt to hold a peace conference to settle differences and unify labor, the AFL and CIO remained hostile and divided for the rest of the decade.

CIO unions arose in a variety of ways: top-down creations like the Steel Workers Organizing Committee (SWOC) or Packinghouse Workers Organizing Committee (PWOC); from various federal labor unions as in the Auto Workers (UAW); or from a combination of independent locals, federal locals, and renegade AFL locals, as in the United Electrical, Radio and Machine Workers Union (UE). Each had its own background, its own traditions, its own previous history of organization, its own management antagonists, so that the CIO as a whole defies reduction to just one model of union. A few industries will be profiled in order to highlight the contours of unionization in this era.

The CIO and FDR, the 1936 Campaign

John L. Lewis was determined that his labor movement would have a decisive influence on the 1936 election. He constructed Labor's Non-Partisan League (LNPL) as the political wing of the CIO, pledged to support Roosevelt and his New Deal. Unlike those labor-party advocates who insisted that labor have its own party, Lewis deeply believed that the re-election of Franklin D. Roosevelt was best for labor. Many workers apparently agreed with him. The LNPL had the effect of cementing the majority of industrial workers to FDR and creating a climate of hopeful organizing that allowed the CIO to flourish. The effect of FDR's landslide victory in 1936 energized and emboldened industrial workers everywhere.

The CIO Begins with Rubber

Rubber workers from Akron flocked into the Rubber Workers' federal labor unions (FLUs). The Big Four companies—Goodyear, Goodrich, Firestone, and U.S. Rubber—responded by setting up their company unions, patterned after Goodyear's Industrial Republic company union of 1919. The AFL stumbled over the concept of creating a Rubber Workers Union. The FLUs were being abandoned by the AFL national leadership, which had called off potential strikes against NRA codes. Green's reluctant presiding over a national convention to

Franklin D. Roosevelt's re-election campaign is supported by labor leader John L. Lewis (to right of FDR), and Marvin McIntyre (far right) in Wilkes-Barre, Pennsylvania, October 29, 1936. (Corbis)

organize the United Rubber Workers of America in September 1935 was undone by the 1935 AFL convention, which rejected the Rubber Workers' request for an industrial charter. It was this debate that sparked the Lewis-Hutcheson fight. The Rubber Workers, centered in Akron, decided to act alone. In November 1935, it was reported in the *Militant,* the Socialist Workers Party (Trotskyist) newspaper, that Goodyear workers had sat down in their department to protest a wage cut. A similar action appeared in January 1936 at Firestone. A full-scale strike by Goodyear developed, with mass picketing and a showdown with local police who backed down (Preis 1972, 44–45). In July 1936, the URW members withdrew from the AFL and received an industrial union charter from the CIO. The URW soon signed a contract with Firestone Rubber and subsequently won NLRB elections at Goodrich, Goodyear, and U.S. Rubber, though its existence in this industry remained precarious until 1940 (Nelson 1988b).

Organizing the Electrical Industry

The CIO union that eventually emerged in this industry, the United Electrical, Radio and Machine Workers Union (UE), grew out of a number of locally organized industrial unions that coalesced in 1936. One group was made up of workers from electrical factories, like those of the two giant companies, General Electric and Westinghouse, that dominated the industry. A second came from radio and home appliance factories. The final group, machine workers at nonelectrical factories, left the AFL's International Association of Machinists (IAM) and joined UE in mid-1937.

The electrical industry products ranged from durable goods like turbines and electric motors, down to consumer goods like light bulbs, radios, and toasters. GE workers had previously been successful in partial organizing during the world war. In Schenectady, machinists had led GE workers out on strike in 1918–1919, and were known for supporting the socialist municipal government in that city. That strike was ultimately unsuccessful. GE's management style in the 1920s became a sophisticated "welfare capitalism" built by GE's president Gerard Swope, which combined generous fringe benefits for long-time employees with a "works council" structure that allowed worker representatives to bring grievances to the attention of their management counterparts on the council (see "Experiences of the Early Depression" chapter). With the passage of the NIRA in 1933, GE restored its works councils as company unions in order to stave off independent union organizing, even as it began cutting back on the fringe benefits it had once guaranteed.

In 1930, when radical machinists founded the TUUL-affiliated Metal Workers Industrial Union (MWIU), the union built on the earlier legacy of organization in metal-working shops everywhere in the Northeast, with some outposts in the Midwest, such as Cleveland, Minneapolis, and Chicago. Other MWIU locals were organized in machine shops in industrial centers. When TUUL was dissolved in 1934 and its members instructed to work within AFL unions again, MWIU joined with other independent locals to create the Federation of Metal and Allied Unions, with James J. Matles as its secretary-treasurer. The Federation approached the IAM with a proposal for amalgamation into the IAM, with their industrial-union character intact, and their offer was accepted. They were given the right to choose their own grand lodge representative, and they chose Matles. At the same time, highly skilled mechanics at key shops like GE in Schenectady and Westinghouse in East Pittsburgh started organizing independent unions. In addition, since the AFL in 1933 decided to use federal locals (FLUs) as a solution to enroll industrial workers, radio and appliance factory workers at companies like the appliance plants of GE, Westinghouse, Philco, and King Colonial formed federal locals, and these workers made contact with each other.

In the meantime, the 1935 AFL convention took place, with the rejection of industrial-union proposals amid the famous Lewis-Hutcheson fistfight. The Committee for Industrial Organization was formed soon after. The AFL reaction was swift, and the AFL Executive Board soon ordered federal unions in radio and appliances to join the International Brotherhood of Electrical Workers (IBEW). The IBEW had no tradition of accepting semi-skilled or unskilled machine operatives and offered only Class B membership to the radio locals. Rejecting this ultimatum, the FLUs met in March 1936 to organize their own union, the United Electrical and Radio Workers of America. Balance was achieved within the two constituencies of the UE by electing a president from the radio locals, James Carey, the Philco union leader. From the electrical plants came the UE secretary-treasurer, Julius Emspak from the Schenectady GE plant. In September 1936 the UE, 15,000 strong, applied for a charter from the CIO and were admitted (Matles and Higgins 1995, 45–46).

The electrical industry organizing campaign was now two-pronged, with the UE organizing in electrical manufacturing and the industrial machinists in the IAM organizing the major machine shops. But when the AFL Metal Trades Department began picking apart the industrial-machinist locals for their own crafts, Matles led the locals out of the IAM and into the UE. They were greeted at the 1937 UE convention with the election of Matles to the new post of director of organizing and a name change to the United Electrical, Radio and Machine Workers of America. This unique history distinguished the UE, to become one of the largest CIO unions by 1945, from many other CIO unions. It was a coalition of independently organized locals, not a top-down organization created by the CIO Executive Council, and it had a fierce tradition of rank-and-file democracy. It also had a strong left-wing presence (Filippelli and McColloch 1995).

Organizing Auto

In 1930 and 1931, the Auto Workers Union–TUUL had unsuccessfully carried out strikes in auto, in addition to the work of their Unemployed Councils in marching on Ford's River Rouge plant in Dearborn. The IWW also tried organizing, as did various groups of skilled metalworkers. Finally, Briggs strikers attempted to create an organization, the American Industrial Association, under minister A. J. Muste (see "Experiences of the Early Depression" chapter). In 1933 AFL president William Green authorized one AFL staffer, William Collins, to organize the auto industry through directly affiliated Federal Locals; Williams reportedly signed up 100,000 auto workers in 1933. However, the machinists' union objected to these FLUs enrolling machinists from the auto plants, saying they belonged in IAM locals; the Metal Polishers International complained as well, and AFL president Green acquiesced (Bernstein 1969, 94). In addition, auto companies' spy networks did their job well enough to cause the firing of many workers who attended recruiting meetings; the 1933 auto drive was stalled. Instead of the AFL, a small organization of skilled tool-and-die makers, the Mechanics Educational Society of America (MESA), determined that they would face the auto companies. Invigorated by the NRA Section 7 (a), MESA tool-and-die makers struck GM and smaller parts companies in the Detroit-Pontiac-Flint area in September 1933. The auto companies responded with a general notice that all those who did not return to work by October 6 would be considered terminated. When MESA members did not go back, and their raiding parties picketed several other plants in Detroit, the Regional Labor Board of the NRA stepped in and negotiated a settlement of sorts with smaller companies, thus bringing to an end the long reign of the open shop. MESA had 21,000 members at the time. The majority of auto workers, however, remained unorganized. More important, this began a pattern of multiple unions in the auto industry (Bernstein 1969, 98).

The auto FLUs struggled against the adamant rejection of the NIRA by Henry Ford, the labor-spy systems in GM and Chrysler, and the company plans to inaugurate company unions in their plants. In the fall of 1933, the companies bragged that some 78 percent of GM workers, 86 percent of Chrysler workers, 90 percent of Dodge workers, and 91.9 percent of Hudson workers had voted for their own in-house employee representation plans. Of course each company had conducted its own election, under the watchful eye of supervisors (Fine 1963, 155–156). AFL organizers and members protested to the NRA that the company coercion in the balloting process made the election an unfair one. The new National Labor Board, now set up by regions, took up the task of interpreting Section 7 (a) for the automobile industry. As was becoming apparent in other industries, the NLB determined that majority rule would be the only workable way of determining one sole representative and that the NLB would have to be in charge of elections. Meanwhile, the Auto FLUs in outlying cities from Philadelphia to Cleveland to Toledo to Kenosha, Wisconsin, struck to bring employers to the bargaining table. President Roosevelt intervened and brokered a settlement in March 1934, which he appealed to auto unions to accept. "He asked us to trust him, and we will," said AFL representative Richard Byrd (Fine 1963, 226). But the settlement accepted company unions and left unresolved the question of proportional representation of labor organizations. Many unionists complained that it was a victory for the auto companies. The new Automobile Labor Board (ALB) would henceforth oversee labor relations in this volatile industry. The AFL, for its part, gave tepid support to the idea of organizing auto by agreeing to give the Auto FLUs their own charter, the International Union, United Automobile Workers (UAW) in October 1934.

When the NIRA was declared unconstitutional in May 1935, the ALB, which had little to show for itself in its year of existence, disappeared. In its stead rose the National Labor Relations Act, with a new emphasis on promoting and protecting workers' rights to choose their own collective-bargaining representatives, and for employers to bargain "in good faith." But little movement came from auto workers until the CIO was formed in November 1935, and then with the landslide victory of FDR in 1936, auto workers began to stir. "Union buttons began to sprout like dandelions everywhere" (Zieger 1995, 50). Strikes broke out

Sit-Down at Flint

The 44-day sit-down strike in two critical General Motors plants in Flint, Michigan—Chevrolet No. 1 and Fisher Body No. 2—was planned and carried out by local shop leaders. Wyndham Mortimer, former head of the Cleveland Auto Council and now a UAW vice president, was in Flint that day and advised local leader Bob Travis to use the restlessness of his members to provoke a strike, using the recently successful sit-down as a tactic. But not everything was that well planned—as strike committee chairman Bud Simons declared, the first few days were "the biggest nightmare I ever went through" (Fine 1969, 156). The strike committee made the decision to concentrate their numbers in the North Unit of Fisher Body No. 1, and to send the 300 women workers home rather than allow them to remain in the plant, thus simplifying organization (and forestalling rumors of immoral activities). The committee set up subcommittees for every imaginable task—food, recreation, information, education, postal services, sanitation, security patrol, and complaints. Great care was taken that the machinery and auto parts would remain undamaged during the strike. A strike kitchen, staffed by a volunteer Women's Auxiliary of strikers' wives and female relatives, was set up outside the plant to feed three meals a day to the 2,000 strikers inside. The Women's Auxiliary would soon evolve into the Emergency Brigade that was organized by Genora Johnson, wife of a strike leader in Chevrolet No. 4.

John L. Lewis, feeling that FDR owed his landslide election victory to the efforts of the CIO, appealed to FDR to convince the auto owners to recognize the UAW, and the president publicly refused. It should be noted that FDR and Secretary of Labor Frances Perkins were working behind the scenes to convince GM's chief Alfred P. Sloan to recognize the UAW. Lewis was left to remind the president publicly of the valuable role the CIO had played in his re-election in 1936, claiming a quid pro quo was in order. Roosevelt's failure to support the CIO publicly started the rift between Lewis and FDR that only widened by the end of the decade. The real support came from newly elected Michigan governor Frank Murphy, who refused to aid GM, which wanted to use the National Guard to oust the sit-downers from the plants; instead Murphy ordered them to keep peace around the plants. Murphy did consider the sit-down strike illegal, but was more concerned about preventing violence. He also felt that GM had brought the strike upon itself by ignoring the NLRA. Neither Governor Murphy's negotiating efforts nor those of Secretary of Labor Perkins moved GM president Alfred P. Sloan Jr., who still refused to talk until strikers had left all of the struck plants. The final union takeover by UAW members of Flint Chevrolet No. 4 on February 1 was a desperate attempt to bring GM to its knees. Here the UAW planned a decoy action, using Chevrolet No. 9 workers to feign a takeover to draw company police away from the more vital No. 4 plant. Even after GM won its injunction order against the UAW on February 2, the UAW workers refused to move and assembled thousands of UAW members from around the region to join the picketers and sit-downers in Flint. Murphy ordered his National Guard and the local police to wait for further

Sit-Down at Flint, Continued

court papers, and managed to persuade GM executives and UAW officials to meet in Detroit, conveying President Roosevelt's words that public welfare demanded that they reach agreement. On February 11, GM and the UAW signed an agreement that ended the strikes, with GM recognizing the UAW as the collective bargaining agents for their members (though limited to them only and not for all GM employees) and to begin negotiations on the demands of January 4. GM also promised to let all strikers return to work without discrimination or punishment. The Flint GM sit-down strike was over ("The Flint Sit-down Strike").

in Detroit and Cleveland auto plants. GM kept postponing a negotiating session with UAW leaders. As UAW strength grew in Fisher Body No. 1 and No. 2 plants in Flint, plans grew for a strategic, coordinated sit-down strike that would cripple GM's operations. A sit-down strike had advantages over a conventional strike. It could be carried out by a minority of workers in a company, and shielded

Members of the United Automobile Workers union stage a sit-down strike in the Fisher body plant factory in Flint, Michigan, in December 1936. (Library of Congress)

strikers from the violence of the picket line. No employer would dare risk violence in his own plant, putting the capital equipment at risk. On December 30, 1936, as rumors flew that GM was about to remove important dies from Fisher Body No. 1 in case of a strike, workers decided to act. Taking control of Fisher Body No. 1 and 2, workers threw out management personnel and locked themselves in the factory. The six-week struggle that gripped the nation had begun.

Women's Emergency Brigade

The Women's Emergency Brigade began by staffing strike kitchens to feed the men inside the plants. Their call to the picket line came on January 11, 1937, when GM forcibly tried to remove the strikers. First management cut off heat and power to the Fisher Body plant, and then police prepared to rush the plant. At this point, Genora Johnson, a striker's wife, accepted Victor Reuther's invitation to take the microphone, and proceeded to exhort the crowd gathered at the plant. As she recalled in a 1976 interview,

> I appealed to the women of Flint. I bypassed everyone else. . . . I said, "I beg of you to come down here and stand with your husband, your loved ones . . . your brothers, and even your sweethearts." And when I made that appeal, it was a strange thing. It was dark, too. . . . I could hear a hush over that crowd the minute a woman's voice went over. It was startling, you know. All night long, they didn't know there was even a woman down there. . . .
>
> I saw a woman struggling, and I noticed that she started to come down, and a cop grabbed her by the coat and she went right out of that coat. And this was in freezing weather. . . . And she just kept right on coming. And as soon as that happened, other women broke through, and again we had that situation where cops didn't want to fire into the backs of women. And once they did that, the men came, and that was the end of the battle (Weir and Hanlan 2004, 2:584–586).

In fact, the battle raged for hours, with strikers battling police, fighting off tear gas, clubs, and riot guns with car-door hinges and water from firehoses. The battle ended with strikers still in possession of the plant, and the clash became known as the "Battle of the Running Bulls" (Galenson 1960, 137–138). The Women's Emergency Brigade then became a formal organization, structured along semi-military lines with red armbands with white lettering and red berets. They bravely aided strikers when they seized Chevrolet No. 4 on February 1 by setting up a picket line around the plant to ward off police (Fine 1969, 201). The story is beautifully recounted in the documentary film *With Babies and Banners* (Gray and Goldfarb 1990).

"Sit Down!"

Maurice Sugar, attorney for the UAW during the GM sit-down strike, was busy at his piano after the settlement of that strike and while sit-down strikes were going on at other auto plants in Flint. Newspapers reported in March 1937 that picketers at the Hudson Motor Company were singing a new song written by Sugar:

When they tie the can
To a union man
Sit Down! Sit Down!
When they give him the sack,
They'll take him back.
Sit Down! Sit Down!
Chorus
Sit down, just take a seat.
Sit down, and rest your feet.
Sit down, you've got 'em beat.
Sit Down! Sit Down!
. . .
When the boss won't talk,
Don't take a walk.
Sit Down! Sit Down!
When the boss sees that
He'll want a little chat.
Sit Down! Sit Down!
(Johnson 1988, 212–213)

Sit-Down Strike Wave of 1937

In 1937, 477 of the 4,740 reported strikes in the United States were sit-downs that lasted at least one day, affecting at least 400,000 workers. The sit-down reached its peak in March when 170 such strikers were reported. Detroit continued to be the epicenter of the phenomenon, but sit-down strikes were everywhere. Every sort of workplace was involved—hospital kitchen and laundry workers in Brooklyn, Woolworth's store clerks, sailors, pencil makers, Western Union messengers, pie makers, garbage collectors. A *Detroit News* reporter remarked, "Sitting down has replaced baseball as a national pastime." Of the 477 sit-downs in 1937, 279 were called by CIO unions, while 100 were by AFL unions. As Sidney Fine's thorough study of the GM sit-down pointed out, the sit-down nationally was usually called by workers seeking *recognition* of their union, not over details of contract negotiations. He discovered that in 1937, "substantial gains" had been won with this tactic in 50.8 percent of the sit-downs and compromise victories in another 30.6 percent, compared to a 46.5 percent victory for all strikes in 1937. The sit-down was effective, not least in its dramatic allure. In the public's eye, however, the sit-down tactic went from general approval in January to increasing rejection in March. In the Gallup poll of that month, 67 percent of the respondents thought that legislation should be passed declaring the sit-down illegal (Fine 1969, 331–332).

A few days after the GM strike had been settled, the La Follette Committee on Civil Liberties began hearings on the tactic. In doing so, according to Jerald S. Auerbach, the committee allowed the UAW a public forum for its grievances and influenced its contract negotiations with GM. The hearings exposed GM's labor practices and espionage against workers, thus showing GM to have ignored the NLRA (Auerbach 1966, 112–115). Congressional sympathy was with the strikers, until the rash of sit-downs in March and concerns about "lawlessness" affected legislation then pending in Congress. As a compromise, a nonbinding resolution was passed that reiterated the rights of collective bargaining as defined in the NLRA, condemned those employers who denied those rights, and at the same time condemned the sit-down tactic as contrary to public policy.

Governor Murphy continued to defend his conduct in the GM sit-down strike, arguing that his restraint had "strengthened rather than weakened government and the law" (Fine 1969, 335) and that any use of force would have resulted in bloodshed and greater instability. He continued to publicly deplore the tactic, however. But the charge by Congressman Martin Dies's committee that he had aided the Communist role in the strike continued to follow Murphy in his reelection bid in fall 1938, and he was defeated (winning only 47 percent of the vote). While Murphy and some other party leaders initially suggested that the sit-down issue had been the cause of his defeat, a more sober assessment revealed that the recession of 1937–1938 was to blame (Fine 1969, 338).

The Sit-Down at the Five-and-Dime

On Saturday, February 27, 1937, at 11 a.m., the women who serviced the counters at the Woolworth's Five and Dime in downtown Detroit suddenly stepped away from their counters and folded their arms, refusing to serve customers or operate cash registers. The strikers, mostly members of Local 705 of the Waiters' and Waitresses' Union of Detroit (Hotel Employees and Restaurant Employees, HERE-AFL), declared a sit-down strike and presented management with a set of demands, including recognition of their union, a wage increase of 10 cents an hour, an eight-hour workday and time-and-a-half overtime pay after 48 hours a week, a seniority system, and a union hiring hall. By taking on Woolworth's, the retail giant of the 1930s, the salesgirls and waitresses were attempting to claim their power as workers in the growing service sector, something that had

Female employees of Woolworth's hold a sign indicating they are striking for a 40-hour workweek, 1937. (Library of Congress)

rarely been accomplished before. After locking the doors, the strikers settled in for a long wait while their organizing committee was upstairs talking to their manager. Some 200 customers were also inside the store. By noon, with the lunch counter full of food, the manager invited the strikers to dig in, "on the house." The festive mood was shattered when the district superintendent arrived and stated that no negotiations would proceed until the store had been emptied of strikers. Further, he threatened to shut down every one of the 39 other Woolworth's stores in the city if this strike was not ended immediately. The strikers said no. On the second day, the strikers set up their own internal committees to manage their sit-down: Food, Store Clean-up, Sales, Health, Cheer-up, Entertainment, Bed, and Scrapbook. They promoted their cause to the various reporters and newsreel cameras on the scene. They put up the sign, "All we want is a living wage," in the store window. When Woolworth management did not budge, the union carried its cause to a second Woolworth's store in the city, which promptly went on strike, and HERE threatened a strike of all Woolworth's stores across the country. Other Detroit labor leaders, such as President Homer Martin of the UAW, began arriving at the store to lend moral support to the young strikers, some of whom were 16 to 18 years old and still lived with their parents. Detroit labor leaders tried to bridge the growing tension between AFL and CIO unions on the national level by stating that they were all in support of these strikers, who were in AFL unions. On March 2, day four of the Woolworth strike, the waitresses and kitchen staff at Stouffer's Restaurant went on strike, joined by workers at Huyler's Cafeteria in the Fisher Building. Detroit employers of meat and grocery stores, as well as S. S. Kresge's Department Store, announced immediate wage increases.

On March 4, after U.S. Steel suddenly announced that it was signing a contract with the CIO's Steel Workers Organizing Committee (SWOC), Woolworth's management finally moved to grant a small wage increase in one of its Boston stores. A Woolworth's vice president appeared in Detroit to begin talks there. On Friday, March 5, the seventh day of the Detroit strike, an agreement was announced, in which Woolworth's consented to most demands and even agreed to pay the women 50 percent of their usual rate for the week they were on strike. In the aftermath of this victory, sales clerks in other Detroit stores and then in New York City went on strike, winning union representation and union contracts. Waves of sales clerks continued to organize throughout the rest of the year (Frank 2001).

Organizing Steel

Immediately after the NIRA was passed in 1933, the AFL encouraged the Amalgamated Association of Iron, Steel, and Tin Workers (AA) to undertake an organizing drive in steel. The AA represented fewer than 5,000 workers in 1933, mostly in small companies with highly skilled workers. There had been no union in basic steel since the AA had been defeated in the Homestead strike of 1894, and the fledgling industrial union of 1919 was dealt a crushing blow. Now, with labor insurgency all around, the U.S. Steel Company reinvigorated its Employee Representation Plan (ERP), a 1920s experiment that had been allowed to go dormant in the second half of the 1920s. As was true in the bituminous coal mines that U.S. Steel owned, U.S. Steel relied on this company-union formation to thwart independent unionism in the early 1930s.

The tactic proved successful in steel plants, up to a point. The ERPs attracted various skilled crafts and "tonnage-men" (those paid by the ton of output), native-born or of old-immigrant stock, who found that their grievances were fairly heard. But as the decade progressed, the ERPs evolved from company loyalists to militant representatives who "had developed a sophisticated shop-floor bargaining structure and grievance procedure" (Rose 2001, 102). Moreover, by 1936, the ERPs at various mills were communicating with each other and were attempting to build a central committee of all U.S. Steel ERPs to deal with the company on a united basis. At this point John L. Lewis announced a signed contract between SWOC and U.S. Steel in March 1937. In fact, the agreement merely recognized SWOC as a collective-bargaining agent for its own members alone. U.S. Steel president Myron Taylor refused to recognize SWOC as the *sole* union, and the contract even borrowed the ERP's grievance procedure. SWOC petitioned the NLRB to label the ERPs as company unions, which were forbidden under the NLRA, and to deny them a ballot line in forthcoming NLRB elections in various U.S. Steel mills.

In the meantime, the vast majority of steelworkers were semi-skilled operatives and unskilled laborers who were paid by the hour; their ethnic backgrounds were foreign stock (Eastern and Southern European immigrants and their sons) or African American. The ERP did not attract them, but the AA did. This old and nearly defunct AFL affiliate had revived itself in the heady NRA days, and built a covert organization within many mills. However, it found itself unable to rise to the historic occasion, and many AA members dropped out and became disillusioned with unionism as a result. In 1935 John L. Lewis convinced the AA officers to join the CIO's organization, the Steel Workers Organizing Committee (SWOC).

The steel organizing drive that began in June 1936 under the auspices of SWOC was financed by the UMW and led by UMW vice president Philip Murray. The AA had already integrated itself into SWOC. Now SWOC organizers, many from the UMW as well as veterans of AA, moved to convince all steelworkers, whether members of the company union or disappointed former members of the AA, that SWOC could successfully represent them. It was in this context that U.S. Steel chairman Myron Taylor decided to sign with SWOC in order to guarantee peaceful labor relations.

The one mill, Duquesne, that has been thoroughly analyzed reveals the dynamics of the SWOC campaign, as well as its difficulties. By early 1937, many ERP leaders at Duquesne were recruited as SWOC organizers and set about to convince former members of the AA that their disappointment with unionism would not be repeated. However, some ERP leaders remained loyal to the company and threatened to create an independent union. SWOC spent the remainder of the 1930s consolidating its organization and bargaining with the company, but it was not until 1942 that SWOC finally petitioned and won an NLRB election as sole bargaining agent at the Duquesne Works (Rose 2001).

SWOC Gets Involved in Local Politics

The pro- or antiunion stances of local and state officials could spell success or failure for labor organizing efforts, as many workers had learned over the decades. The 1930s was no exception, as detailed by the stories of strikes in this chapter. While the CIO attempted to affect national elections with the establishment of Labor's Non-Partisan League in 1936, union activists were working on a local level as well. The best example of union effects on local politics are the campaigns that SWOC carried out in 1936–1938 in the Monongahela Valley to overturn entrenched Republican city governments that were beholden to local steel mills. As detailed in SWOC activist George Powers's memoir, SWOC activists took over moribund Democratic Party organizations for the purpose of gaining a friendly face in City Hall (Powers 1972; Davin 2000). Indeed, it was the CIO that brought free speech and free assembly back to many of these steel towns. For example, Secretary of Labor Frances Perkins had been forbidden to speak in Homestead by the Republican burgess John J. Cavanaugh, and the governor's wife, Cornelia Pinchot, had similarly been forbidden to speak in Duquesne by Mayor James Crawford. Both Cavanaugh and Crawford were replaced by SWOC members in 1937 (Powers 1972; Davin 2000).

The Left in the CIO

The labor movement of the 1930s could not have been built without the dedicated efforts of leftists of all stripes, most prominently the Communist Party. Historians continue to debate the influence of Communist activity in the 1930s' political and social movements. The debate is strongest in the labor movement, given the post–World War II Cold War's effect on the CIO, which led it to purge itself of "left-leaning" unions. The first wave of historical scrutiny, such as Theodore Draper's 1957 book *The Roots of American Communism,* regarded American Communism as merely a reflection of the Soviet Union and its ideological evolution, and its 1930s activities as a masquerade (see "Popular Front" in the previous chapter). Bert Cochran made an attempt at balance in his 1977 book, *Labor and Communism,* though he emphasized Communist mistakes more than successes. As part of a re-examination of leftist history beginning in the 1970s and 1980s, the New Labor History of the 1970s and 1980s returned Communists to a respectful place in the fight to organize workers in the 1930s. (See, for example, Nelson, Barrett, and Ruck 1981; Healey and Isserman 1993; Nelson 1988a; Halpern 1997; Horowitz 1997.)

Ideological battles raged in the 1930s as well, as conservative commentators accused the rising industrial-union movement of being a Communist conspiracy. None was more visible than the wild accusations about John L. Lewis being a closet Communist because he employed known Communists as CIO organizers. His famous quip, after dismissing the charge, was "Who gets the bird, the bird-dog or the hunter?" In other words, he was using Communists as organizers because they were the best and most committed, yet the CIO itself would reap the benefits of their labors.

Beyond these tendencies in the historiography, there exists a vicious ideological "battle of the memoirs" in which sectarian interpretations of events sling accusations of "misleading the workers" at other rival leftist organizations. In addition, histories of the period produced by these organizations have similar flaws. Nonetheless, they are useful for the information they provide on the historical events they report, as well as for sampling the atmosphere of the times.

CIO Pioneers

Who were the CIO pioneers? Despite some variations depending on the industry and the geographic region, some generalities hold. Historian Ronald Schatz was the first to analyze local CIO leaders in the electrical industry of western Pennsylvania in the 1930s. He found that, of the thirty-five union pioneers he profiled, they were more likely than their workmates to be between the ages of 35 and 45, native-born or old-immigrant-stock, highly skilled workers who were not in the production work force but had considerable freedom to move about the plant (so-called autonomous workers), received high wages, and had some previous familiarity with unions and radical organizations. A significant minority belonged to a radical party, Communist or Socialist, or in the case of Philadelphia, the Industrial Workers of the World. "Male union pioneers, in other words, were members of an elite stratum of the industry's work force" (Schatz 1979, 598).

Female union activists, however, differed from their brethren: younger (21 to 30), unmarried (GE and Westinghouse banned married women from working), from new-ethnic stock, semi-skilled, and with shorter work histories. This profile was not unusual for women workers of this era, but in one important respect they were unlike their female co-workers, as they lived in nontraditional family settings or were members of committed union families. Thus, speculated Schatz, they lived outside the strict patriarchal authority of working-class families and were more able to act on their own behalf.

Union activists of this era had enough experiences in common with others to give them standing in the eyes of their fellow workmates, yet had sufficiently different perspectives to challenge employers over issues of economic justice. Similar patterns emerged in many other industries. A key question was which groups of workers would respond first and which would stick out the long haul toward recognition and final contract. Many workplaces were split by skill level and by ethnicity. Finally, an analysis of this type reveals that the CIO locals were in very precarious positions in many industries. The CIO lost members regularly throughout the late 1930s, especially in the "Roosevelt Recession" of 1937–1938.

Auto Worker Stalwarts

A meticulous study of the small (350-worker) Detroit Parts Company in Hamtramck, the Polish enclave in Detroit, reveals the internal dynamics of organizing in this crucial era. Rather than talking of "the workers," as if they were an undifferentiated mass, historian Peter Friedlander explored the ethnic and skill dynamics that permeated this one plant as it organized under the new UAW, achieved a first contract, and established its formal local structure. Friedlander primarily used the memories of a key founder of the local, Edmund Kord, who had been born in the United States, returned with his family to Poland where he grew up, and came back to Hamtramck as a young man in 1934. Kord quickly found a job as a grinder in the Detroit Parts Company. With his Socialist Party sensibilities and an awareness of the mindset of both first- and second-generation Polish immigrants, Kord was ready to take advantage of the widespread upsurge in hope within the ethnic working class after FDR's landslide victory in 1936. Buoyed by the GM sit-down strike in Flint, Kord and an Irish-American friend in the grinding department began talking in the plant about unionizing. Kord described the social characteristics of the various groups of workers. The heart of the union drive came from second-generation Polish welders who were older, married, and had the longest seniority; they became the union stalwarts. Second in importance were the press operators, newer hires who were part of a community subgroup of neighborhood gangs. The first wave of union memberships came en masse from these two groups. By playing up company fears of the atmosphere in Detroit, the union committee won a first, somewhat weak, contract, and the union forces decided to consolidate their gains. In 1938, new groups of workers were brought into the union: the large group of first-generation Slavic immigrants who had been too afraid to join initially and who now became the most loyal members; and the tool room, whose skilled workers had held aloof from the mostly foreign-stock workforce. The non-Slavic Protestants, including Appalachian whites and old-immigrant ethnics such as German and Scandinavians, were the most reluctant to join. A small group of second-generation Polish men who were devout Catholics and hostile to anything suggesting Communism formed a nucleus of the Association of Catholic Trade Unionists. These last two groups would become important factions in the 1940s. In a series of showdowns with management, first with a strike over the closed shop in 1938 and then by coordinated slowdowns of production in 1939 over paid vacations, the local won these important demands and consolidated its membership (Friedlander 1975).

The successful organization of the plant depended on the networks of affiliation in the neighborhood: the neighborhood gangs that the younger workers belonged to; the numerous ethnic lodges of sick and death benefit societies such as the Polish National Alliance, the Polish Roman Catholic Union, and the Polonia Society of the International Workers Order. Indeed, in late 1936 a Polish Trade Union Committee was established, made up of Polish workers from shops throughout the city. That was accomplished by the young UAW organizer Stanley Nowak, who also arranged to have the UAW purchase time on Waclaw Golanski's popular Polish radio show on station WEXL. The Polish-language newspapers also carried UAW news articles (Nowak 1989, 77–80). This process was also key to organizing the steel industry.

Ethnics and the CIO

Of crucial concern to labor organizers in the 1930s were the masses of recent immigrants and their children, called "foreign-stock" by the U.S. Census, who constituted a majority of the workers in mass-production industry. These first- and second-generation Americans were already connected in a web of ethnic community organizations, such as religious institutions and fraternal societies. Though historian Liz Cohen argued that it was the failure of these institutions to overcome the effects of the Great Depression that united these ethnics in a "culture of unity" around the Democratic Party and the New Deal, this was only partly true (Cohen 1990). First-generation ethnics remained attached to their Old World culture, even as their organizations underwent change. One specific change was the rise of the Communist-oriented International Workers' Order (IWO). (Also see the previous chapter.) The IWO played a key role in the SWOC organizing campaign begun in 1936. The vast majority of steelworkers in the United States were either foreign-born or the sons of the foreign-born, with a high concentration of Eastern Europeans. Over 38 percent of the IWO membership lived in the steel-producing states of Pennsylvania, Ohio, and Illinois. Polish immigrant Bill Gebert, whose birth name was Bronislaw Konstantine Gebert, became the point person for the IWO on the SWOC drive. After meeting with Gebert in June 1936, Phil Murray appointed Gebert to organize the fraternal societies in support of the SWOC initiative. Gebert arranged a series of conferences bringing together leaders from various fraternal societies. The largest gathering occurred on October 25 at Slovenian Hall in Pittsburgh. Delegates from 17 national fraternal organizations and 240 local lodges representing 593,085 members endorsed the SWOC drive. The participating organizations included the Croatian Fraternal Union, the National Slovak Society, the Slovak Evangelical Union, the Supreme Lodge of Lithuanians of America, the Workmen's Sick and Death Benefit Society, the Federation of Croatian Clubs, the Slovak League of America, the United Ukrainian Toilers, the Greek Workers Educational Federation, and the IWO. The conference set up a Fraternal Orders Committee to sponsor local conferences in their various cities. The IWO made a major contribution by bringing African American steelworkers into the committee. African American steelworkers were a sizable force in some sections of the industry, where they had been recruited as strikebreakers decades before. The AA's history of racism had made skeptics of these workers as far as unionism was concerned. Ben Careathers, a well-known and respected African American Communist in Pittsburgh whom Murray hired as a SWOC organizer, relied on the IWO to make connections with other African American fraternals (Keeran 1989, 389–395).

African Americans and the CIO—Packinghouse Workers

The CIO in general made a determined effort to overcome the workplace color line, to organize workers of all racial and ethnic backgrounds into the new industrial unions. In many industries, CIO unionists had to overcome the legacies of the AFL's racism. Of course, this was an imperative in order to build strong industrial unions. But in some industries, like meatpacking, it was the African American workforce that provided an important role in the 1930s campaign. Remarkably, the earlier effort to organize packinghouse workers in Chicago had fallen apart during the Chicago Race Riot of 1919. The CIO's creation of the Packinghouse Workers Organizing Committee (PWOC) in 1937 and its victories in Chicago rested on the activities of three crucial groups: first, Communists who had begun organizing in the early years of the Depression both on the job and in the neighborhoods; second, white ethnic workers who had been active in the World War I–era organizing drive of the Stockyards Labor Council and, though blacklisted from the big meatpacking plants, were still in smaller meat plants and the neighborhoods; third, African American workers hired in the 1920s and 1930s who decided to put aside the old distrust of the "white man's union" in order to build PWOC (Horowitz 1997, 60). Their success in building an interracial, democratic union allowed PWOC, which became the United Packinghouse Workers of America in 1943, to retain these qualities through the World War II and postwar periods (Halpern 1997).

Other CIO Unions—International Longshoremen's and Warehousemen's Union

The maritime unions after the San Francisco General Strike of 1934 combined into the Maritime Federation of the Pacific Coast, uniting the Sailors' Union of the Pacific (SUP), the Marine Firemen, Marine Engineers, and Marine Cooks and Stewards with the ILA. The Federation remained a volatile entity, split between the syndicalist tendencies of SUP, who had gained little from the 1934 strike settlement, and the longshoremen with their pro-Communist leadership. In 1936, the East Coast and Gulf Coast seamen struck, attempting to gain a measure of what had been won on the West Coast, and also trying to throw off the corrupt leadership of the International Seamen's Union. Harry Bridges supported this renegade movement, even taking a tour of East Coast docks to denounce the conservative ILA president Ryan. The more conservative West Coast Maritime Federation leaders condemned Bridges's statements. They were even more upset about Bridges's plan to "march inland" to extend the ILA's membership to warehousemen and others in the chain of transportation and distribution, in effect creating an industrial-style union. After the formation of the CIO, the West Coast ILA under Bridges left the ILA to become the International Longshoremen's

CIO organizers for the National Maritime Union use launches to campaign among harbor boatmen during a union election, 1937. (Library of Congress)

and Warehousemen's Union (ILWU) and joined the CIO in August 1937. The National Labor Relations Board certified the ILWU as the collective-bargaining agent for all longshoremen on the Pacific Coast. The Australia-born Bridges remained a defiant, outspoken radical throughout his years as leader of the ILWU (Nelson 1988a).

The National Dollar Stores Strike of 1937

The National Dollar Stores strike stands out as a milestone in the history of the San Francisco Chinatown. National Dollar Stores was not like other San Francisco Chinatown garment shops, as it was vertically integrated and controlled all aspects of the business from manufacturing to retailing. National Dollar Stores' 37 retail outlets on the West Coast sold its own women's light apparel. Its owner, Joe Shoong, was one of the wealthiest Chinese businessmen in the country. The International Ladies' Garment Workers Union (ILGWU) had been unable to crack the Chinatown garment industry, which undercut unionized garment shops in the rest of the city. Veteran ILG organizer Rose Pesotta was unable to make headway when she tried to organize in San Francisco Chinatown in 1934. But with the passage of the Wagner Act, another ILG organizer, Jennie Matyas, was successful in 1937. Matyas organized a majority of workers at the Dollar Stores factory and established ILGWU Local 341—Chinese Ladies' Garment Workers Union. When management retaliated by firing workers, reorganizing the production facility under separate ownership, and refusing to accept the results of the NLRB election, the majority of workers went on strike and picketed both the factory and the retail stores. In addition to recognition of the union and a pay raise, the union demanded a guarantee of 11 months of work a year. Community support was lacking, as many were fearful of standing up to Joe Shoong, who was a major contributor to community institutions. Nonetheless, the strikers were determined and carried out a strike that lasted 105 days. They were aided by the store clerks, who were members of the Retail Department Store Employees' Union, and who refused to cross the picket lines at the three retail stores that were being picketed. Leftist organizations like the Ping Sheh (Equality Society) and the Chinese Workers Mutual Aid Society also lent support (see previous chapter). The ILGWU finally reached an agreement with management that the workers reluctantly accepted. One year later, the factory closed. The union was able to find jobs for the laid-off Chinese workers in other factories outside of Chinatown, thus breaking down the anti-Chinese hiring patterns there. Debate still continues over the contract decision and the role of the ILGWU in San Francisco Chinatown. But it was a remarkable occurrence in an era where few unions penetrated such ethnic enclaves (Yung 1995, 209–222).

Workers Left Out of Federal Law

The NRA codes of 1933 and 1934 applied only to industries in or affecting interstate and foreign commerce, and they covered only half of all working women—mainly manufacturing, trade, communications, and some clerical (Wandersee 1981, 95). It never applied to professions. The NLRA also did not include agricultural workers, domestic servants, and public employees.

Agricultural Workers

Agricultural workers were not specifically left out of the NIRA in 1933, but field workers were excluded by the president's administrative decree three weeks later. But many farm workers thought that the federal government was supporting them under Section 7 (a) and thus had the courage to strike against determined employers. In 1933, there were 61 strikes involving 56,800 farm workers in 17 different states (Hahamovitch 1997, 139).

In California, the way had already been paved by the spontaneous activity of the 1930–32 years. Now under the leadership of the Cannery and Agricultural Workers–TUUL (CAWIU), 37 strikes involving some 50,000 workers took place in California from April through December 1933. Twenty-nine resulted in victories and increased wages (Weber 1994, 80). The strikes started in the Santa Clara fruit orchards and followed the path of migration through the berry, sugar beet, peach, lettuce, and grape harvests. The Mexican workers vowed to carry the strike wave through to the San Joaquin Valley cotton fields. When the strike reached the Tagus ranch at the beginning of the August peach harvest, some 700 Tagus workers went on strike, demanding an end to forced buying at the company store, as well as a pay increase, a 40-hour week, and union recognition. By mid-August, 4,000 workers were on strike, and the Agricultural Labor Bureau (ALB), an organization of growers, capitulated and raised wages. At the same time, growers began pressuring the state government to "repatriate" Mexican strikers (see "Experiences of the Early Depression" chapter). At this point the CAWIU organized to strike in cotton at the start of the September cotton harvest, where they had established 19 locals, with Tagus workers providing leadership. Cotton prices had risen with the implementation of the Agricultural Adjustment Act (AAA), and the ALB announced a slight increase in wages for the season. It was not enough, and 2,000 to 3,000 workers quickly walked out of the fields. The CAWIU declared a strike, and thousands more joined the walkout. As CAWIU's Caroline Decker recalled, the union "was in our heads and in our ideals but it . . . was when strikes began popping all over the state that the union began to take on an identity. . . . You had me and Pat Chambers and three or four people down here. A communist here. A radical worker there. No money. No knowledge of how to do these things. Just all good will and idealism" (Weber 1994, 83, 91).

The backbone of the union was the Mexicans, some of whom had experience in Mexican radical unions and had fought in the Mexican Revolution. A number of Anglo and Filipino workers also struck. Filipino immigrants had already established fraternal societies that provided the basis for labor unity. The largest walkouts occurred on farms of over 300 acres. Growers began evicting families from labor camps, which worked to the strikers' advantage as workers now were able to form their own "refugee" camps free from employer coercion. Family networks, community gathering places like pool halls and bars, and women's networks among the strikers, as well as food and other materials donated by local sympathizers, sustained the walkout. The CAWIU acted as an umbrella group to coordinate the strike.

The 1933 strikes revealed the economic and social tensions in California farming between big growers, processors, and financial institutions, and the small growers and local merchants who were beholden to these large-scale institutions that dictated the market. Big growers' reaction to the strike was swift and vicious, mostly in organizing armed vigilante gangs to intimidate strikers and small farmers who were sympathetic to the strikers' cause. The American Legion supplied many of the gangs (McWilliams 1939, 226). Violence erupted on October 10 as growers fired into a strikers' meeting in Pixley, and other groups of

Camp site of striking Mexican agricultural workers, Corcoran, California, October 1933. (Library of Congress)

growers attacked pickets at other fields. Two strikers, along with a Mexican consular representative, lay dead, with many more wounded, bringing the San Joaquin Valley strike to national attention. The Mexican government protested, demanding that Gov. James Rolph protect Mexican citizens and disarm growers. George Creel, director of the NRA Western District, eventually persuaded growers to agree to arbitration in return for federal subsidies from AAA and other programs. CAWIU represented strikers in hearings, calling for the inclusion of agricultural workers in NRA Section 7 (a), but with no success. The brokered agreement that ended the strike was the farthest that the federal government would go in defending farm workers' right to organize (Daniel 1981, 167–221). The CAWIU was broken by state government prosecution, what Carey McWilliams called an "anti-Red carnival" (McWilliams 1939, 228).

FERA transient-relief payments became an important factor in California farm-worker organizing because they were not subject to residency requirements, as were regular state and local relief funds. Even though relief payments were relatively low, $40 per month for a family of four, they provided a de facto minimum wage higher than the ALB rate, allowing farm workers a measure of extra bargaining power. Relief payments became a political issue in the 1934 gubernatorial campaign of Upton Sinclair and his End Poverty In California (EPIC) campaign (Weber 1994, 126–128). Agricultural interests' concerns played a large role in restructuring relief payments to place them in local hands. The farm-worker labor market changed considerably as refugees from the Dust Bowl poured into the state and were glad to accept any field job. But as Communist organizer Dorothy Healey remembered, the "Okies" were similarly inclined to support the union, to the dismay of growers. "I found it interesting to read the newspaper stories and editorials during the Kern County cotton strike in 1937. The same kind of propaganda that had been used against the Mexicans in the early 1930s—it was no use giving these people clean quarters, they liked to live like pigs, and so forth—was now being used to describe native-born Anglo-Saxon citizens" (Healey and Isserman 1993, 44).

Mexican workers who had already participated in the Confederación de Uniónes de Campesinos y Obreros Mexicanos (CUCOM) in the early 1930s reasserted themselves in 1936 under the leadership of Mexican anarchist William Velarde, became a major agricultural union in California, and began moving toward the progressive politics of the CIO. CUCOM was instrumental in forming the United Cannery, Agricultural, Packing, and Allied Workers of America (UCAPAWA) in 1938. Vicki Ruiz noted that Mexicans organized seven of the ten field-worker locals in the San Joaquin Valley by 1938 (Ruiz 1987, 52). Agricultural unions never had the mechanism of the NLRB to certify them as exclusive collective-bargaining agents, though it is unclear whether that would have made any difference. By 1938 and 1939, agricultural strikes were often lost as the economics of the industry changed, as the forced repatriation of Mexicans and their replacement by white Dust Bowl migrants changed the labor force, and as anti–New Deal sentiment pervaded the California legislature (Guerin-Gonzalez 1994).

On the East Coast, migrant farm workers were in similar straits, earning low wages and dealing with substandard housing. Strike patterns were similar to the NRA-induced West Coast agricultural strikes of 1933 and 1934. In 1934 300 African American and Italian American farm and cannery workers struck New Jersey's largest truck farm, Seabrook Farms. That strike had been advanced by the April 1934 strikes in Camden's soup, ship, and radio plants. Seabrook Farms had been caught unaware and quickly capitulated to the strikers, but prepared for the summer slack season by soon announcing a wage cut and layoffs, and organizing a vigilante group known as "A Committee to Combat Communism." Violence ensued.

Here, the federal government's role was crucial. The NRA, however, had drawn a line between the "area of production" where field workers were not included in the legislation's provisions, and processing workers, who were included. However, since Seabrook Farms had processing plants on farm property and an overlapping workforce between field and processing plant, both Seabrook and Florida citrus growers insisted that the NRA exclude all workers on their properties. The growers won that legal battle. The CAWIU then continued the strike, forcing Secretary of Labor Frances Perkins to send U.S. Conciliation Service staffer John Moffett to broker a settlement. One requirement of the settlement was the workers' renunciation of their Communist union. Once they did so, they

Carey McWilliams's Factories in the Fields

Carey McWilliams (1905–1980), a liberal lawyer who was active in supporting farm-worker unionization in California, was appointed in 1939 by new Democratic governor Culbert Olson to head the Division of Immigration and Housing, which regulated conditions in the farm labor camps. McWilliams's exposé of corporate agriculture, *Factories in the Field,* was published to immense public notice in 1939. It was perceived by many as the nonfiction complement to the very popular novel by John Steinbeck, *The Grapes of Wrath,* published that same year. McWilliams had published a series of muckraking articles in the mid-1930s. But the book outraged the Associated Farmers, the Farm Bureau, and other growers' lobbying groups who renewed their efforts to abolish the State Relief Administration and other assistance to farm workers. McWilliams emphasized the structural and racial dimensions of the plight of migrant farm workers in California. More important, he lobbied for inclusion of agricultural workers in state and federal labor legislation. "Agriculture, as an industry, in California, cannot be distinguished from any other highly organized American industry. California agriculture is monopolistic in character; it is highly organized; it utilizes familiar price-fixing schemes; it is corporately owned; management and ownership are sharply differentiated; it is enormously profitable to the large growers." In 1936, he noted the value of farm products from California was valued at $627 million (McWilliams 1939, 265–266).

became wards of the Conciliation Service, but as historian Cindy Hahamovitch has argued, the settlement created a model for federal migrant labor policies for the future (Hahamovitch 1997, 138–50). The farm workers, also abandoned by the 1935 National Labor Relations Act which did not include them, continued to receive federal government support through the Farm Security Administration (FSA), which ran the Migratory Camp Program for the rest of the decade.

Southern Tenant Farmers Union

The Southern Tenant Farmers Union (STFU) was organized in summer 1934 by eleven white and seven African American sharecroppers and tenant farmers in eastern Arkansas. An interracial organization, STFU was aided by local and national Socialist Party members. One local leader was H. L. Mitchell (1906–1989), a young, white sharecropper raised in Tennessee and converted to socialism in 1920 through reading the *Appeal to Reason* and the Haldeman-Julius Little Blue Books. Mitchell had become proprietor of a drycleaning place in Tyronza, Arkansas, and had attended the first meeting of sharecroppers to discuss how to get their fair share of the AAA payments that plantation owners were receiving

"Roll the Union On"

John Handcox, sharecropper, organizer, and troubadour of the STFU, wrote "Roll the Union On," which later became the third most popular labor song in the 20th-century United States.

We're gonna roll, we're gonna roll,
we're gonna roll the union on;
We're gonna roll, we're gonna roll,
we're gonna roll the union on.
If the boss is in the way,
we're gonna roll it over him,
we're gonna roll it over him;
We're gonna roll the union on.
(Mitchell 1987, 84)

from the federal government. Mitchell, along with his friend Clay East, whom he recruited into the Socialist Party, helped organize the Tenant Farmers Union, sending word to "all the socialists of the south" about its founding (Mitchell 1987, 24). The STFU filed a lawsuit to enforce the rights of sharecroppers under the AAA, brought a delegation to Washington to meet with Secretary of Agriculture Henry Wallace, and convinced Wallace to send an investigator to Arkansas; Wallace then suppressed the report. STFU continued organizing, finally striking in the summer of 1936. The governor of Arkansas called out the National Guard to break the strike, armed planters attacked the marchers, and the newsreel *March of Time* re-enacted the scenes in a film segment shown in 6,000 movie theaters across the country. Thereafter, STFU organizers had to operate from the safety of Memphis, rather than in the fields. The result of organizing activity, according to Mitchell, was the creation of the Farm Security Administration, which "was created to undo some of the evils of the New Deal in Agriculture" (Mitchell 1987, 45; Mitchell 1979). A final spectacular demonstration took place in January 1939 when 1,500 African American and white men, women, and children camped out on the public highways in Missouri after being evicted from nearby cotton plantations. After the Department of Agriculture finally ordered subsidy checks to be delivered directly to sharecroppers, Missouri planters gave sharecroppers a choice—either become wage-laborers or get off the land. After appealing directly to Eleanor Roosevelt, who wrote about their plight in her "My Day" column, the STFU proposed the development of cooperative farming communities with decent housing and land enough for subsistence food until the next cotton season. Five hundred and ninety-five houses were built, and families moved from the roadside into the government houses; individual homes in one community, the Delmo Farm Labor Homes, were eventually bought by the tenant families themselves for $800 each (Mitchell 1987, 48–51).

In 1937, when the CIO established the United Cannery, Agricultural, and Allied Workers of America (UCAWA), the STFU affiliated, but then ran afoul of the Communist Party–dominated leadership of UCAWA. Mitchell withdrew STFU from the UCAWA and continued lobbying for tenant farmer rights from an office in Washington, D.C. (Grubbs 1971).

Home Workers and Domestic Workers

In the 1930s, many industries still relied on outsourcing piecework to the home. The Women's Bureau in 1937 enumerated many jobs done at home: stringing toys; carding buttons, hooks and eyes, bobby pins, and safety pins; hooking rugs; addressing envelopes; shelling nuts; making garters; knitting; crocheting. The Bureau estimated that 80 percent of the women employed at home earned less than 20 cents an hour (Kessler-Harris 1982, 270). NRA codes in 1933 tried to regulate homework or abolish it completely in 86 percent of the codes it established. But even that was an uneven application, as 44 of those codes were for industries where there was no homework, and five homework industries lacked regulation at all. Moreover, the codes were confusing and contradictory in related industries. The Homework Committee of the NRA was established to sort out these problems. The Committee consisted of Department of Labor Women's Bureau and Children's Bureau veterans Clara Beyer and Mary Anderson, along with advisers from the NRA Consumers', Labor, and Industrial boards, and was expected to deal with the public outcry over extreme cases. The resulting President's Executive Order allowed handicapped persons or those caring for invalids at home to work at home if they were paid the factory rate. But while some male committee members had the sentimental impulse to argue that mothers should also be excluded from the ban, the women from the Labor Department argued that to do so would nullify the whole ban, since the majority of homeworkers were mothers who were forced to work at home so they could care for their children as well. As historian Eileen Boris has argued, the women's reform network opposed homework for a complex set of beliefs: "that mothers ought not to work and that homework most undermined motherhood because its low piece rates meant long hours, 'jeopardizing their health and family life'; but working women belonged in the factory in order to benefit from minimum wages and better working conditions, to have a real chance at economic independence" (Boris 1994, 214). It was this last point, that working outside the home guaranteed that this work could be regulated and tied to the social-welfare benefits of the New Deal, that made all the difference to these activists.

Domestic service was still the number one occupation of women in 1930, and even in 1940 one in every five women who earned wages worked as a domestic

African American maid with small children in Meridian Hill Park, Washington, D.C., ca. 1930. These working women were not covered by many New Deal programs, including the National Labor Relations Act and the Social Security Act. (National Archives)

in someone else's home. Half of these were African American or Latina. None of the labor legislation of the 1930s touched them at all. Most were poorly paid, even when room and board were factored in. The YWCA proposed $9.00 a week for live-in servants as a possible NRA code, while the Women's Bureau reported that $6.00 a week was typical for a Lynchburg, Virginia, domestic in 1937. Competition between white and African American servants in northern cities led many African American women to so-called slave markets, waiting on designated street corners for day-labor jobs, and negotiating pay on the spot (Kessler-Harris 1982, 271). In this occupation, the argument was made that the burden of New Deal regulation and payroll taxes was too much for the individual families who employed these workers.

In the final analysis, those workers left out of federal legislation like the NLRA, the Social Security Act, and the Fair Labor Standards Act were among the most vulnerable and lowest-income groups—African Americans, Latinos/as, women. This was not consciously racist or sexist legislation, but rather the consequence of economic patterns with deeper racist or sexist histories. The repercussions of this would be reflected in emerging patterns of poverty in the United States in later decades.

Women and Work

Women had been steadily increasing their participation in the paid workforce, reaching 24.3 percent of the labor force in 1930 (Kessler-Harris 1982, 258). While domestic service was still the number one women's occupation in 1930, the increase in women's workforce participation had come in the 1930s through an increase in the number of white-collar jobs. These jobs generally went to native-born young women. The labor force remained strictly sex-segregated, with jobs listed as "Male" and "Female," and employers unwilling to tinker with traditional gender lines. Foreign-born women were still clustered in the manufacturing and service sectors. The most dramatic change from the 1920s Census, in fact, was the increased number of married women who worked outside the home. As child labor ceased as a family-economy strategy, wives and mothers of school-age children were more likely to enter paid jobs. Ironically, the fact that women were clustered in a sex-segregated labor market meant that, as a group, women workers were less heavily affected by the Depression, which hit heavy manufacturing the hardest. This would have profound effects on gender roles in many working-class families, or at least that was what social workers were worried about (see "Private Lives" chapter).

The Paradox of the Sex-Segregated Labor Market

Sociologist Ruth Milkman first suggested that the rigidity of job segregation by sex had the paradoxical effect of protecting women from unemployment (Milkman 1976). Unemployment rates for clerical and service-sector jobs, where women were clustered, were generally lower than for manufacturing, except in the early years of the Depression. The clerical and service sectors recovered rapidly from the early years, and the expansion of social services and government jobs during the New Deal expanded the female job sector. Moreover, men were very reluctant to take "women's work," and employers hesitated to hire them for those jobs. It should be noted, however, that women in white-collar and professional jobs suffered more from antagonism toward women working, especially if they were married (Wandersee 1981, 84). The women who went to work in the 1930s often were married, slightly older, and more likely to be native-born than the working women of 1929. The social trend of lower birth rates and the Depression-era strategy of doubling up of households allowed for shared housework and child care and helped women work outside the home. Women increased their

Table 4.4. Leading 10 Occupations of Women Workers, 1930–1940 (ranked by numbers)

	1930	*1940*
1	Domestic servants	Domestic servants
2	School teachers	Stenographers, typists, and secretaries
3	Stenographers and typists	Teachers
4	Other office clerks	Clerical and kindred workers
5	Saleswomen	Saleswomen
6	Farm laborers	Operatives—apparel
7	Bookkeepers and cashiers	Bookkeepers, accountants, and cashiers
8	Laundresses (home)	Waitresses
9	Trained nurses	Housekeepers (private family)
10	Cooks	Trained nurses

Source: Adapted from Janet M. Hooks, *Women's Occupations through Seven Decades* (Washington, DC: GPO, 1947), 52.

workforce participation from 24.3 percent in 1930 to 25.1 percent in 1940 (Kessler-Harris 1982, 250–252, 258). Even so, women were expected to "take up the slack" of lowered family incomes by reversing any previous consumer dependence on packaged goods and services, and beginning once again to can food or to sew at home for the family's consumption (see "Private Lives" chapter).

Women and Unions

Further mechanization of production enabled women workers in many industries to gain jobs, as was apparent in cigar-making, textiles, and garment manufacturing. Women's lower wage rates, as well as their availability, allowed manufacturers to hire more women for these new "female"-labeled jobs. The NRA codes allowed this wage differential. This was clearly noticed by male AFL leaders, so that in spring of 1934 William Green announced a campaign to bring women into unions (Kessler-Harris 1982, 267–269). The CIO drives of 1936–1939 enrolled even more women workers in the mass-production industries.

White-collar women had their first opportunity to organize, though many of them considered themselves "middle class," as reporter Mary Heaton Vorse explained. Indeed, women office workers in the GM auto plant in Anderson, Indiana, quickly signed cards supporting the antiunion "Citizens' Committee." Vorse went on to explain which ones of the "salaried classes" seemed to respond to the calls for unionization: the insurance agents, the Newspaper Guild, small professional unions like those of social workers, nurses, librarians, research workers, pharmacists, and even the WPA professional workers. Of course, these groups included many occupations dominated by men. She expressed her fear that the lack of unionization among these groups would lead to conservative political alliances similar to those of Hitler's Germany (Vorse 1938, 182–189).

Of course, some labor leaders were antagonistic to women, as the history of the AFL had shown. But the problem was more systemic than that simple accusation. Historian Sharon Hartman Strom laid out her criticism of CIO unions in her 1983 article "Challenging 'Women's Place.'" She noted how male unionists reacted hostilely when their secretaries joined the CIO office union, the United Office and Professional Workers of American (UOPWA). Some CIO unions tried to exclude the office staff from their factory union-representation elections, and the NLRB usually agreed with them (Strom 1983). Of course, given the antiunion proclivities of this group, as described by Vorse above, these actions seem understandable. Women strikers were often portrayed unflatteringly. For example, the Woolworth's strikers of 1937 had been portrayed as silly girls more interested in manicures and dating than the politics of the times (Frank 2001, 73–76).

Modern feminism was still in its infancy, and many progressive activists gave little thought to questions of gender equity or even awareness. The results of this mindset have been debated in the historical literature. (See Kessler-Harris 1989 and a rejoinder by Margaret Hobbs 1993, as well as Faue 1991.)

Laws against Married Women's Work

One early response to the tremendous job loss of the early Depression was the passage of laws that discriminated against married women in the workplace. Of course, the early Depression caused the budget slashing of government budgets everywhere, and layoffs were usually decided by expendability of job function or by other social characteristics of the jobholder. Married women, whose workforce participation had increased tremendously during the previous decade, became a special target. Numerous state legislatures in 1930 and 1931 debated proposed laws dismissing wives from state government if their husbands earned a "living wage." Though these proposals did not pass, they created pressure on Congress to include the issue in its legislation. In the Federal Economy Act of 1932, designed to reorganize executive departments and to manage salary cuts, Section 213 prohibited "married persons" from working in federal government jobs if their spouse also had a government job. Though Hoover personally deplored that section, he nevertheless signed the bill. The National Women's Party (NWP) protested, noting that the "first impulse seems to be to 'wallop the ladies'" (Scharf 1980, 47). The NWP was joined by the Business and Professional Women's Clubs (BPW) as well as other women's organizations, but the law remained on the books pending the election season that was about to begin. By spring 1933, over 1,500 married persons had been discharged, mostly women from the post office, Treasury, War, Navy, and Veterans Administration departments.

The incoming Roosevelt administration was heavily lobbied by the NWP, the BPW, the League of Women Voters, the Women's Trade Union League, and the General Federation of Women's Clubs, as all recognized the attack on women's work aspirations. Eleanor Roosevelt even voiced her own opposition. Some women leaders began comparing this discriminatory legislation to the "back to the home" movements in Germany and Italy. Section 213 was finally repealed in July 1937, but this late date indicated how popular the idea was (Scharf 1980, 46–65). A 1936 Gallup poll found that 82 percent of Americans believed that employers should discriminate against married women (Oppenheimer 1976, 44; Milkman 1987, 28). Some single women felt the same, as married women's presence created additional competition for them. A new spate of similar state legislation engulfed the legislative year of 1939. The writer Norman Cousins famously offered this simplistic nostrum in 1939: "There are approximately 10,000,000 people out of work in the United States today. There are also 10,000,000 or more women, married and single, who are jobholders. Simply fire the women, who shouldn't be working anyway, and hire the men. Presto! No unemployment. No relief rolls. No depression" (Kessler-Harris 1982, 256).

The National Industrial Conference Board published a survey of their employer members in 1939, which reported that, though there was a preference for single women, three-fourths of the companies said they had no specific policy concerning their women factory employees who married, and 60 percent said they had no policy regarding their office employees. However, 84 percent of the insurance companies, 65 percent of the banks, and 63 percent of the public utilities had rules against married women working in their offices (Wandersee 1981, 100).

Women on Relief Jobs

The notion of one job per family became a powerful idea in the Depression era, though employers varied in their practices. But public relief jobs such as those on CWA, FERA, and WPA were restricted to those deemed "sole breadwinners." Here, even if women qualified as sole breadwinners, they received lower wages than men for similar work. Of the 372,000 women employed on the WPA, more than half worked on projects that emphasized simple domestic work. Garments and supplies made by these women, such as preserved and canned foodstuffs, were distributed to relief families and hospitals, schools, and other public institutions. Many were involved in the WPA's 1937 Household Service Demonstration Project, which provided training for women seeking domestic-service jobs (Wandersee 1981, 96). Professional and white-collar projects of the WPA, such as the various state Writers' Projects, aided many more unemployed women.

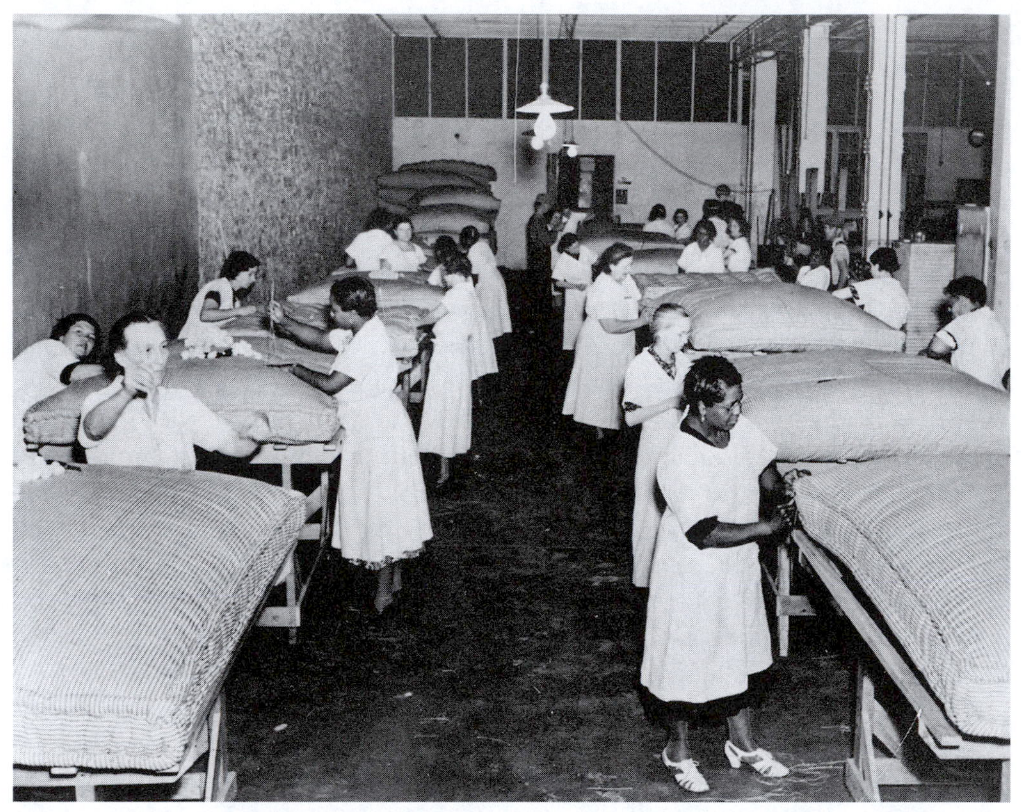

Works Progress Administration (WPA) mattress-making project, Topeka, Kansas, ca. 1936. (National Archives)

Labor's Place after 1937

Notwithstanding the dramatic events and successes of the sit-down year of 1937, there were intense areas of conflict and defeat. Some employers continued to resist the Wagner Act, confident that it would be overturned by the Supreme Court, as the NIRA had been in 1935.

Limits of the AFL: The Remington Rand Strike

The Remington Rand strike of the summer of 1936 was an early defeat for labor, though here it was the International Association of Machinists–AFL. It was also a forewarning of defeats to come in the following years. The IAM had contracts with the company at its plants in Middletown, Connecticut; Ilion, Tonawanda, and Syracuse, New York; Norwood, Ohio; and Cambridge, Massachusetts. In 1935, the IAM along with various other unions represented at these plants formed the Remington Rand Joint Protective Board of the District Council of Office Equipment Workers, under the auspices of the AFL Metal Trades Department. In the spring of 1936 the unions asked the company for increased wages, with no positive company response. When Syracuse workers staged a brief sit-down strike, they were fired. The union then announced a strike at all its plants for May 26, 1936. The company, based in Ilion, New York, responded by developing what became known as the Mohawk Valley Formula to rid itself of unions once and for all, a formula that would be used in future decades with great effect. The formula consisted of the following steps for management: form a "citizens' committee" in the community; label the union leaders as outside agitators; stir up violence or the fear of violence; have a "state of emergency" declared; organize a back-to-work movement; finally, have the back-to-work employees march into the plant protected by armed police (Bernstein 1969, 478–479). In the case of the Remington-Rand strike, the IAM continued to support a dwindling number of strikers until March 1937, when it reached a tentative agreement with the company to rehire the strikers if jobs were available; few union activists were actually re-employed. The IAM continued the struggle through the NLRB, arguing for the disestablishment of the company union that had replaced the IAM. The Mohawk Valley Formula depended on an antilabor local government and a small town that was largely dependent on the one company. Thus the union movement, and particularly the CIO, paid attention to local, state, and federal elections in a sustained way from 1936 on. "Little Steel" managers also drew lessons from this strike.

Limits of the CIO: 1937 Little Steel Strike

Even as U.S. Steel had made peace with SWOC in order to have uninterrupted production, "Little Steel," the mid-sized steel companies like Jones and Laughlin (J&L), Bethlehem, Republic, Youngstown Sheet and Tube, National, Inland, and American Rolling Mill (ARMCO) remained adamantly antiunion. In fact, it was the J&L case that decided the constitutionality of the Wagner Act in 1937. J&L had used its influence in Aliquippa, Pennsylvania, to get SWOC organizers beaten and run out of town, and SWOC members fired. SWOC Beaver Valley Lodge No. 200 had filed suit in January 1936 against J&L for violation of Section 8 of the Wagner Act. When the agreement with U.S. Steel was signed in March 1937, and the Supreme Court ruled against J&L in April, SWOC made its push at J&L, calling a two-day strike on May 12. J&L finally agreed to collective bargaining, allowed an NLRB election, which SWOC won handily, and signed a contract that was an improvement on the U.S. Steel contract in that SWOC was recognized as the exclusive bargaining agent for the entire bargaining unit.

However, the rest of Little Steel followed Republic's Tom Girdler in continued opposition to unionism, and elected Girdler president of the Iron and

Steel Institute, the business association that U.S. Steel had dominated up to then. Since Little Steel companies had already matched U.S. Steel's contract on wages and hours, the only thing still negotiable was recognition of a union and the signing of a contract between the union and the companies. Little Steel hoped to use the Mohawk Valley Formula to resist unionization of their plants, but Girdler also spent nearly $50,000 on munitions. To provoke a strike before SWOC was ready, he shut down his Canton and Massillon, Ohio, mills. SWOC then declared a strike against all Republic mills on May 26, along with mills at Sheet and Tube and Inland. The Youngstown strikes were very successful, the other Republic mills less so, while Chicago's strike was substantial, though it did not succeed in shutting the mill. The Bethlehem strike was delayed until June 11 (Bernstein 1969, 478–484).

Memorial Day Massacre

The 1937 "Memorial Day Massacre" stopped SWOC's Little Steel strike. The Chicago police had a reputation for aiding employers in breaking strikes. They had already broken up one gathering of Republic workers just before the strike, and continued to break up picket lines as the strike got underway. SWOC decided to protest restrictions on picketing, as well as boost the morale of Republic strikers by hosting a rally on Memorial Day near the Chicago Republic plant. After union speeches, the picnicking crowd, women and children included, decided to march to the main gate and set up a picket line. When stopped by the police two blocks from the plant, a marcher threw a tree branch toward the police line. A policeman responded with a pistol shot in the air, and then police fired point-blank into the crowd. According to witnesses, police then advanced into the crowd, shooting and swinging their billy clubs. When the smoke cleared, 10 marchers were dead, most shot in the back, and 30 more wounded by gunshot. Some 58 more were also beaten. The Chicago papers the next day reported the company's statements that Reds had fomented the violence. Newsreel footage of the incident was quietly quashed by the company. It was only weeks later that the La Follette Senate Committee on Civil Liberties obtained the Paramount News newsreel footage that clearly showed the police attacking the crowd indiscriminantly. The Committee report condemned the excessive force used by the police in an otherwise peaceful march (Auerbach 1966, 121–128).

Public opinion then turned against the steel company, but it was too late. The strike at Republic folded. The strikes at Bethlehem mills, which were just beginning, felt the full effects of the Mohawk Valley formula of Citizens Committees and Back-to-Work movements organized by the company, and SWOC was in disarray. The company officers refused mediation efforts by the NLRB. When President Roosevelt heard the news, he was quoted as saying, "A plague on both your houses." John L. Lewis was not amused, and the working relationship between the two men was now at an end. SWOC reported in fall 1937 that they had 439 collective-bargaining agreements in effect, but not with Bethlehem, Republic, Youngstown Sheet and Tube, National, and ARMCO. SWOC would have to await World War II to become firmly established in the steel industry (Bernstein 1969, 497).

Resurgence of the AFL

Historians of the labor movement had traditionally emphasized the decisive impact of the turn toward industrial unionism and the emergence of the CIO as the key determinant of the growth of organized labor in the 1930s. Christopher Tomlins, in a 1979 article, called that emphasis into question, noting that the AFL continued to organize large numbers of workers into its ranks after the CIO split. Indeed, by 1939 the AFL had nearly 3.88 million members to the CIO's 1.84 million. (see Table 4.1.) And even those CIO numbers reflected a fall-off from the 1938 reports, due to the decline in the manufacturing economy and the loss of members. This perspective reminds us that AFL unions had been adapting to the changes in the economy since the turn of the 20th century, and had altered their craft structure into "craft-industrial" unions as technological changes dictated. But AFL affiliates always relied on controlling jobs, rather than workplaces, and thus "relied on organizing strategic nuclei to maintain and extend their control of jobs in an industry" (Tomlins 1979, 1034). They were most effective in small-unit businesses with local or regional markets. Mass-production industries were not that kind of business. AFL unions were not concentrated in any one sector of the economy. In the 1930s, they grew in construction, the retail sector, and the service sector. In fact, the AFL chartered new unions after the split with the CIO. The Cement Workers, the Distillery Workers, the Pocketbook and Novelty Workers, the Spinners Union, and the State, County, and Municipal Employees Union were all new AFL affiliates. But it should be remembered that it was the federal government's control over the process of union certification and the definition of bargaining units that caused AFL unions to alter their structure. The NLRB favored industrial-style bargaining units, and employers seemed to prefer to deal with their employees in this sort of structure, if they had to deal with unions at all (Slichter 1941).

The CIO Stopped in Its Tracks

By contrast, the CIO was concentrated in manufacturing, with auto, electrical, and steel as key industries. The AFL challenged the CIO unions in NLRB elections in 24 percent of the NLRB cases filed between 1938 and 1940 (Tomlins 1979, 1040). As Walter Galenson noted, "The growth of organization in the traditional AFL trades, more imposing numerically, was less significant from a strategic point

Table 4.5. Largest CIO Unions, 1939

Union	*Membership*
United Mine Workers	478,500
Amalgamated Clothing Workers	239,700
Steelworkers	225,000
Textile Workers	83,300
United Electrical, Radio and Machine	47,800
Retail, Wholesale, Dept. Store	44,000
Rubber Workers	39,500
Packinghouse Workers	39,400
Marine and Shipbuilding	35,000
Maritime Workers	31,800
Mine, Mill and Smelter	30,100
Longshoremen	30,000
Total CIO	1,837,700

Source: Adapted from Leo Troy, *Trade Union Membership, 1897–1962* (New York: Columbia University Press, 1965), A20–A23.

Note: The CIO numbers are from annual dues reports; they do not reflect workers under contract with their employers, nor do they reflect the fluctuating monthly membership in some shops.

Table 4.6. Largest AFL Unions, 1939

Union	*Membership*
Teamsters	441,600
Carpenters	214,800
HERE	210,900
Hod Carriers	157,500
IBEW	125,100
Machinists	178,000
Musicians	127,300
Painters	102,500
Total AFL	3,878,000

Source: Adapted from Leo Troy, *Trade Union Membership, 1897–1962* (New York: Columbia University Press,1965), A1–A9.

Note: The International Ladies' Garment Workers Union (ILGWU) switched its affiliation from CIO to AFL in 1939 and is not included in either Table 4.5 or 4.6. The ILGWU membership fluctuated between 201,000 in 1938 and 212,500 in 1940.

of view than the CIO concentration in vital centers of American industrial might" (Galenson 1960, 592). More important, the CIO set the tone for political and social-ethnic ethos of the 1930s.

As historian David Brody noted in his 1964 essay, "The Emergence of Mass-Production Unionism," the CIO' s situation was still precarious in 1939 (Brody 1964/1993, 82–119). The Wagner Act did not compel employers to do more than bargain "in good faith," and that phrase was open to various interpretations before it was given substance by NLRB and court rulings in the next few years. It did not mean that a contract had to be signed between employer and certified union. Indeed, the "bitter-enders" among employers included some major firms, such as Westinghouse, Goodyear, Ford,

Debate on Labor and the New Deal

The history of labor in the 1930s seemed to be a settled affair until the 1970s and the rise of the New Labor History. Before the 1970s, depending which side someone was on, the labor movement was engaged in a valiant struggle for economic and social justice, or the labor movement was a facade for the Communist menace. Liberal historians of the Old Labor History, such as Irving Bernstein and Walter Galenson, wrote institutional histories of the AFL and CIO that concentrated on the debate between craft and industrial unionism. Their focus was on the institutional stability, or lack thereof, that defined success for the AFL or CIO. More recently, David Brody's writings represent a liberal approach that goes beyond a broad institutional focus and delves into the fit between the CIO and a modern American capitalism. He anticipated New Labor History emphasis on incorporation of unions into the structure of American monopoly capitalism in the late 20th century.

One approach of the New Labor History, dominated by adherents of the New Left, took its cue from Staughton Lynd's 1972 article on the steel industry, arguing that a radical rank-and-file movement in the early 1930s was suppressed by a CIO that was becoming bureaucratic in its efforts to achieve victory with the help of New Deal agencies. A stable collective-bargaining system was not a worthy goal for Lynd or other critics from the left. This argument got fuller treatment in the 1989 collection of essays, *The Rise and Fall of the New Deal Order* (Fraser and Gerstle 1989), particularly Steve Fraser's article, "The 'Labor Question.'" The New Deal collective-bargaining system, in Fraser's analysis, was responsible for "the legalization and federalization of industrial unionism and its subordination to the rule of administrative law under the Wagner Act" (Fraser 1989, 56). Repeated by others in various forms, this analysis reflected the 1980s' disillusionment with the state of the labor movement. The reasoning went that the Wagner Act and its later amendments had so hemmed labor in with court rulings that when the federal government and some employers turned hostile to labor, the labor movement had no weapons with which to fight back. In others words, labor had made a deal that crippled its basic ability to organize a social movement for economic justice in return for an increasingly narrow legal framework that guaranteed stable collective bargaining. That debate continues, as evinced by Lynd's recent 1996 anthology *"We are all leaders": The Alternative Unionism of the Early 1930s,* in which case studies explore the many examples from the 1930s in which rank-and-file militancy was thwarted by the AFL or CIO.

On another track, historian Melvyn Dubofsky broke through this New Left debate with his 1979 essay "Not So 'Turbulent Years,'" proclaiming that American workers were not radical at all in the 1930s (Dubofsky 2000). Daniel Nelson also pointed out the disunity of industrial workers, and their relative indifference to the leftists among them, in his study of rubber unionism (Nelson 1988b). John Bodnar added to this argument in a 1980 essay, where he described the average foreign-stock industrial worker as motivated by a worldview he called "working-class

Continued on next page

Debate on Labor and the New Deal, Continued

realism," in other words arguing that workers in the 1930s were actually rather conservative in that they fought these battles in order to preserve their traditional way of family life (Bodnar 1980).

These arguments need to be taken into account in any analysis of the labor movement of this era, just as social movements of the right and left in the 1930s need to take their place on a map of the social history of the 1930s.

and Republic Steel. But as Brody noted, they were in the minority, and many firms saw the utility in negotiations and peaceful labor relations. For workers in these latter firms, modest gains in wages, hours, and benefits did occur. Then the economy soured; in 1938 industrial unions had to resist wage cuts, unsuccessfully in some cases. There were layoffs, reducing union members. From 1938 to 1940, after which the economy picked up again due to military production, the CIO made very few gains.

Finally, in spite of rulings by the NLRB in 1937 and 1938 that ordered company unions dissolved, a study done in 1939 revealed that 60 "independent" unions had been re-formed after the dissolution of company unions and had many of the same leaders. Most had been formed during an outside union drive or during a strike as a back-to-work movement; few actually obtained formal agreements with their employers after the event (Wilcock 1957, 297).

Biographies

Len De Caux, 1899–1991

Labor Journalist

Len De Caux became the national publicity director for the Committee for Industrial Organization when it was organized in 1935 and editor of the CIO News from 1937 to 1947, when he was forced to resign both positions because of his Communist affiliations. De Caux, a New Zealander, had entered the United States in 1921, and became associated with the labor movement through his reporting and editing for labor papers, from the IWW's *Industrial Solidarity* to the *Locomotive Engineers Journal*. In the 1930s, he became the Washington correspondent for the Federated Press, a news outlet with strong ties to industrial unionists and the emerging CIO (De Caux 1970).

Genora Johnson Dollinger, 1913–1995

Women's Emergency Brigade Founder

The wife of a striker, Genora Johnson organized the Women's Auxiliary during the Flint sit-down strike of 1936–37, out of which emerged the paramilitary Women's Emergency Brigade to defend strikers against police attack. Her first husband, Kermit Johnson, worked at GM Plant No. 4 and proposed it as the focus of the eventual strike, which was decided upon due to Genora's insistence. In 1938–1989, Genora Johnson organized the first unemployed union to be affiliated with the UAW, serving as its secretary. She joined the Socialist Workers Party in 1938 (Buhle, Buhle, and Georgakas 1998, 407).

Genora Johnson Dollinger, leader of the Women's Emergency Brigade during the Flint sit-down strike of 1936–1937. (Walter P. Reuther Library)

James J. Matles, 1909–1975

Union Leader

Born Eichel Matlis Fridman in Romania, he immigrated to the United States in 1929. Matles worked as a machinist and quickly joined the IAM. He then became a leader of the TUUL Metal Workers Industrial Union (1930–1934), was secretary of the Federation of Metal and Allied Unions (1934–1935), and took his federation into the IAM in 1937, where he became a grand lodge representative. In the wake of the CIO's organization in 1936, he joined his machinist locals to the fledgling United Electrical and Radio Workers of American (UE) in 1937, which changed its name to United Electrical, Radio, and Machine Workers of America. He was elected director of organization at that time, a post he held in the union until 1962, at which time he was elected secretary-treasurer. He retired in 1975. He regularly faced accusations of being a member of the Communist Party.

Wyndham Mortimer, 1884–1966

Labor Activist

A key organizer in the auto industry, first with the AFL's Federal Local 18463 at Cleveland's White Motor Company, Wyndham Mortimer became president of the Cleveland Auto Council in 1934, and led the organizing efforts in Flint, Michigan, before the sit-down strike at the Fisher Body Company in 1936. He was a leader of the left-wing Unity Caucus in the UAW, helped lead the budding UAW into the CIO, and led the opposition to UAW president Homer Martin in 1937–1938.

Maurice Sugar, 1891–1974

Labor Lawyer

Born to immigrant Russian Jewish parents in Michigan, Maurice Sugar was an influential labor lawyer in Detroit, serving variously as lawyer for the Detroit Federation of Labor, the International Labor Defense, auto unionists arrested after the Ford Hunger March of 1932, the Auto Workers' Union after the Briggs strike of 1933, and the Mechanics Educational Society in 1934. He became the main lawyer for the new UAW in 1937 and handled the communications with Gov. Frank Murphy during the Flint sit-down strike; he wrote the song "Sit Down." A founder and charter member of the National Lawyers Guild, he was the lawyer for the Unity Caucus in its fight against Homer Martin in 1937–1938. He became UAW general counsel in 1939 and was an adviser to George Addes and R. J. Thomas of the Unity Caucus until Walter Reuther's victory over the Unity Caucus in 1947 (Johnson 1988).

References and Further Readings

Auerbach, J. S. 1966. *Labor and Liberty: The La Follette Committee and the New Deal.* Indianapolis: Bobbs-Merrill.

Bernstein, I. 1969. *The Turbulent Years: A History of the American Worker, 1933–1941.* Boston: Houghton Mifflin.

Bodnar, J. 1980. "Immigration, Kinship, and the Rise of Working-Class Realism in Industrial America," *Journal of Social History* 14 (Fall): 45–59.

Bodnar, J. 1983. *Anthracite People: Families, Unions and Work, 1900–1940.* Harrisburg: Pennsylvania Historical and Museum Commission.

Boris, E. 1994. *Home to Work: Motherhood and the Politics of Industrial Homework in the United States.* New York: Cambridge University Press.

Brody, D. 1964/1993. "The Emergence of Mass-Production Unionism." In Brody, *Workers in Industrial America: Essays on the Twentieth-Century Struggle,* 82–119. New York: Oxford University Press.

Bucki, C. 2001. *Bridgeport's Socialist New Deal, 1915–1936.* Urbana: University of Illinois Press.

Buhle, M. J., P. Buhle, and D. Georgakas, eds. 1998. *Encyclopedia of the American Left*. New York: Oxford University Press.

Cochran, B. 1977. *Labor and Communism*. Princeton, NJ: Princeton University Press.

Cohen, L. 1990. *Making a New Deal: Industrial Workers in Chicago, 1919–1939*. New York: Cambridge University Press.

Daniel, C. E. 1981. *Bitter Harvest: A History of California Farmworkers, 1870–1941*. Ithaca, NY: Cornell University Press.

Davin, E. L. 2000. "Blue Collar Democracy: Class War and Political Revolution in Western Pennsylvania, 1932–1937," *Pennsylvania History* 67 (2): 240–97.

De Caux, L. 1970. *Labor Radical: From the Wobblies to CIO, a Personal History*. Boston: Beacon Press.

Draper, T. 1957. *The Roots of American Communism*. New York: Viking Press.

Dublin, T., and W. Licht. 2005. *The Face of Decline: The Pennsylvania Anthracite Region in the Twentieth Century*. Ithaca, NY: Cornell University Press.

Dubofsky, M. 2000. *Hard Work: The Making of Labor History*. Urbana: University of Illinois Press.

Dubofsky, M., and W. Van Tine. 1986. *John L. Lewis: A Biography*. Urbana: University of Illinois Press.

Faue, E. 1991. *Community of Suffering and Struggle: Women, Men, and the Labor Movement in Minneapolis, 1915–1945*. Chapel Hill: University of North Carolina Press.

Feurer, R. 1996. "The Nutpickers' Union, 1933–34: Crossing the Boundaries of Community and Workplace." In *"We Are All Leaders": The Alternative Unionism of the Early 1930s*, ed. S. Lynd, 27–50. Urbana: University of Illinois Press.

Filippelli, R. L., and M. D. McColloch. 1995. *Cold War in the Working Class: The Rise and Decline of the United Electrical Workers*. Albany: State University of New York Press.

Fine, S. 1963. *The Automobile under the Blue Eagle*. Ann Arbor: University of Michigan Press.

Fine, S. 1969. *Sit-Down: The General Motors Strike of 1936–1937*. Ann Arbor: University of Michigan Press.

"The Flint Sit-Down Strike." N.d. HistoricalVoices Web site, http://www.historicalvoices.org/flint/.

Frank, D. 2001. "Girl Strikers Occupy Chain Store, Win Big: The Detroit Woolworth's Strike of 1937." In F. Zinn, D. Frank, and R. D. G. Kelley, *Three Strikes: Miners, Musicians, Salesgirls, and the Fighting Spirit of Labor's Last Century*, 59–118. Boston: Beacon Press.

Fraser, S. 1989. "The 'Labor Question.'" In *The Rise and Fall of the New Deal Order, 1930–1980,* ed. S. Fraser and G. Gerstle, 55–84. Princeton, NJ: Princeton University Press.

Fraser, S. 1991. *Labor Will Rule: Sidney Hillman and the Rise of American Labor.* New York: Free Press.

Fraser, S., and G. Gerstle, eds. 1989. *The Rise and Fall of the New Deal Order, 1930–1980.* Princeton, NJ: Princeton University Press.

Friedlander, P. 1975. *The Emergence of a UAW Local, 1936–1939: A Study in Class and Culture.* Pittsburgh: University of Pittsburgh Press.

Galenson, W. 1960. *The CIO Challenge to the AFL: A History of the American Labor Movement, 1935–1941.* Cambridge, MA: Harvard University Press.

Gray, L., and L. Goldfarb, dir. 1990. *With Babies and Banners: Story of the Women's Emergency Brigade.* Women's Labor History Film Project. New York: New Day Films.

Grubbs, D. H. 1971. *Cry from the Cotton: The Southern Tenant Farmers' Union and the New Deal.* Chapel Hill: University of North Carolina Press.

Guerin-Gonzalez, C. 1994. *Mexican Workers and American Dreams: Immigration, Repatriation, and California Farm Labor, 1900–1939.* New Brunswick, NJ: Rutgers University Press.

Hahamovitch, C. 1997. *The Fruits of Their Labor: Atlantic Coast Farmworkers and the Making of Migrant Poverty, 1870–1945.* Chapel Hill: University of North Carolina Press.

Halpern, R. 1997. *Down on the Killing Floor: Black and White Workers in Chicago's Packinghouses, 1904–54.* Urbana: University of Illinois Press.

Healey, D. R., and M. Isserman. 1993. *California Red: A Life in the American Communist Party.* Urbana: University of Illinois Press.

Hobbs, M. 1993. "Rethinking Antifeminism in the 1930s: Gender Crisis or Workplace Justice? A Response to Alice Kessler-Harris," *Gender and History* 5 (1): 4–15.

Horowitz, R. 1997. *"Negro and White, Unite and Fight!": A Social History of Industrial Unionism in Meatpacking, 1930–90.* Urbana: University of Illinois Press.

Irons, J. C. 2000. *Testing the New Deal: The General Textile Strike of 1934 in the American South.* Urbana: University of Illinois Press.

Johnson, C. H. 1988. *Maurice Sugar: Law, Labor, and the Left in Detroit, 1912–1950.* Detroit: Wayne State University Press.

Keeran, R. 1980. *The Communist Party and the Auto Workers Unions.* Bloomington: Indiana University Press.

Keeran, R. 1989. "The International Workers Order and the Origins of the CIO," *Labor History* 30 (Summer): 385–408.

Kessler-Harris, A. 1982. *Out to Work: A History of Wage-Earning Women in the United States.* New York: Oxford University Press.

Kessler-Harris, A. 1989. "Gender Ideology in Historical Reconstruction: A Case Study from the 1930s," *Gender and History* 1 (1): 31–49.

Kozura, M. 1996. "'We Stood Our Ground': Anthracite Miners and the Expropriation of Corporate Property, 1930–41." In *"We Are All Leaders": The Alternative Unionism of the Early 1930s,* ed. S. Lynd, 199–237. Urbana: University of Illinois Press.

Kraus, H. 1985. *The Many and the Few: A Chronicle of the Dynamic Auto Workers.* Urbana: University of Illinois Press.

Levinson, E. 1938. *Labor on the March.* New York: Harper.

Library of Congress, Archive of Folk Culture. 1965. *Songs and Ballads of the Bituminous Miners.* LP Record L60.

Lynd, S., ed. 1996. *"We Are All Leaders": The Alternative Unionism of the Early 1930s.* Urbana: University of Illinois Press.

McWilliams, C. 1939. *Factories in the Field.* Boston: Little, Brown.

Matles, J. J., and J. Higgins. 1995. *Them and Us: Struggles of a Rank-and-File Union.* Englewood Cliffs, NJ: Prentice-Hall.

Milkman, R. 1976. "Women's Work and Economic Crisis: Some Lessons of the Great Depression," *Review of Radical Political Economics* 8 (Spring): 73–97.

Milkman, R. 1987. *Gender at Work: The Dynamics of Job Segregation by Sex during World War II.* Urbana: University of Illinois Press.

Millikan, W. 2001. *A Union against Unions: The Minneapolis Citizens Alliance and Its Fight against Organized Labor, 1903–1947.* St. Paul: Minnesota Historical Society Press.

Mitchell, H. L. 1979. *Mean Things Happening in This Land: The Life and Times of H. L. Mitchell, Cofounder of the Southern Tenant Farmers' Union.* Montclair, NJ: Allanheld, Osmun.

Mitchell, H. L. 1987. *Roll the Union On: A Pictorial History of the Southern Tenant Farmers' Union.* Chicago: C. H. Kerr Pub.

Nelson, B. 1988a. *Workers on the Waterfront: Seamen, Longshoremen, and Unionism in the 1930s.* Urbana: University of Illinois Press.

Nelson, D. 1988b. *American Rubber Workers and Organized Labor, 1900–1941.* Princeton, NJ: Princeton University Press.

Nelson, S., J. R. Barrett, and R. Ruck. 1981. *Steve Nelson, American Radical.* Pittsburgh: University of Pittsburgh Press.

Nowak, M. C. 1989. *Two Who Were There: A Biography of Stanley Nowak.* Detroit: Wayne State University Press.

Oppenheimer, V. K. 1976. *The Female Labor Force in the United States: Demographic and Economic Factors Governing Its Growth and Changing Composition.* Westport, CT: Greenwood Press.

Ottanelli, F. M. 1991. *The Communist Party of the United States: From the Depression to World War II.* New Brunswick, NJ: Rutgers University Press.

Powers, G. 1972. *Cradle of Steel Unionism: Monongahela Valley, Pa.* East Chicago, IN: Figueroa Printers, Inc.

Preis, A. 1972. *Labor's Giant Step: Twenty Years of the CIO.* New York: Pathfinder Press.

Rose, J. D. 2001. *Duquesne and the Rise of Steel Unionism.* Urbana: University of Illinois Press.

Ruiz, V. L. 1987. *Cannery Women, Cannery Lives: Mexican Women, Unionization, and the California Food Processing Industry, 1930–1950.* Albuquerque: University of New Mexico Press.

Salmond, J. A. 2002. *The General Textile Strike of 1934: From Maine to Alabama.* Columbia: University of Missouri Press.

Scharf, L. 1980. *To Work and to Wed: Female Employment, Feminism, and the Great Depression.* Westport, CT: Greenwood Press.

Schatz, R. 1979. "Union Pioneers: The Founders of Local Unions at General Electric and Westinghouse, 1933–1937," *Journal of American History* 66 (3): 586–602.

Slichter, S. H. 1941. *Union Policies and Industrial Management.* Washington, DC: The Brookings Institution.

Strom, S. H. 1983. "Challenging 'Woman's Place': Feminism, the Left and Industrial Unionism in the 1930s," *Feminist Studies* 9 (2): 359–86.

Tomlins, C. L. 1979. "AFL Unions in the 1930s: Their Performance in Historical Perspective," *Journal of American History* 65 (March): 1021–42.

Vorse, M. H. 1938. *Labor's New Millions.* New York: Modern Age Books.

Wandersee, W. D. 1981. *Women's Work and Family Values, 1920–1940.* Cambridge, MA: Harvard University Press.

Weber, D. 1994. *Dark Sweat, White Gold: California Farm Workers, Cotton, and the New Deal.* Berkeley: University of California Press.

Weir, R. E., and J. P. Hanlan, eds. 2004. *Historical Encyclopedia of American Labor.* Vol. 2. Westport, CT: Greenwood Press.

Wilcock, R. C. 1957. "Industrial Management's Policies toward Unionism." In *Labor and the New Deal,* ed. M. Derber and E. Young, 193–237. Madison: University of Wisconsin Press.

Yung, J. 1995. *Unbound Feet: A Social History of Chinese Women in San Francisco.* Berkeley: University of California Press.

Zieger, R. H. 1995. *The CIO, 1935–1955.* Chapel Hill: University of North Carolina Press.

Rural Life

By Catherine McNicol Stock

Overview

Most rural Americans in the 1930s would have agreed with North Dakota teenager Ann Marie Low when she reflected that her state was "way ahead" of the eastern states when it came to the hard times brought about by the stock-market crash. "The hailstorm in July of 1928 and bank failures that fall wiped out a lot of people locally. As far as that goes, most of North Dakota was hard hit last year" (Low 1984, 3). As discussed in the first chapter, the agricultural economy never shared in the boom times enjoyed by other sectors in the 1920s. In fact, the prices paid for corn, wheat, and cotton during World War I had already fallen sharply by 1925. Meanwhile, farmers' costs (what they paid for seed, feed, farm implements, mortgage payments, taxes, and so on) stayed the same or rose. For the first time in American history, rural Americans earned less on average than urban Americans did, only 70 percent as much by 1928. To make matters worse, their access to popular culture, including magazines, films, and radio, made rural Americans increasingly aware of the gap between urban and rural standards of living. In 1930, 45 million rural Americans still did not have indoor plumbing; millions more did not have electricity. Yet cold outhouses and darkened evenings were hardly what they saw on the rare occasion when they went into town for a movie. The imbalance between the rural and urban economy, according to policymakers, was "the central problem of the economy" in the 1920s (Kennedy 1999, 20). For rural Americans it was the central problem of their everyday lives.

As difficult as the 1920s were for rural Americans, nothing in their experience prepared them for the Great Depression. On the Great Plains, a collapsing market for agricultural goods combined with the ecological disaster of the Dust Bowl to push many families toward utter deprivation. By the end of the 1930s in Ann Marie Low's home state, one-third of farmers lost their farms, tenancy had risen to nearly 50 percent, and 150,000 people had simply packed up and headed west. In 1933 journalist and New Deal administrator Lorena Hickok wrote to Harry Hopkins from the capital of South Dakota: "This is the 'Siberia' of the United States," she said. "A more hopeless place I never saw" (Lowitt and Beasley 1981, 82). Meanwhile, in the Southeast, home to more than a third of all rural Americans, men and women were trapped in the "virtual peonage" of sharecropping and, if they were African American, legalized racism. Writer Erskine Caldwell visited a Georgia sharecropper's home and discovered three families living in two rooms. While one young boy licked the garbage, two infants lay by the fire trying to nurse from the nipples of an old dog (Kennedy 1999, 208). To many observers, the poverty of rural Americans in the Great Depression equaled that of poor people anywhere else in the world.

New Deal programs provided aid to many of the rural poor, even those like Ann Marie Low who dreaded accepting outside "help." It brought farm subsidies, improved roads, municipal facilities, electricity, soil conservation practices, and agricultural planning to areas where such things had never existed. But critics of the New Deal's agricultural programs abounded. They ranged from people who felt the relief programs made Americans lazy to those who felt the programs privileged the already-powerful, commercialized farmers in their communities. Most ardent were those who accused the New Deal of complicity with white racists in the South and with the destruction of the grasslands in the West. In response, a few New Deal administrators experimented with programs to rehabilitate the soil, promote subsistence farming, build model rural communities, and help sharecroppers and other tenant farmers move to better land. Their ideas, however, were often dismissed as being too radical, and possibly even influenced by the ideals of communism. Nevertheless they benefited millions of people living in rural poverty across the country.

In short, most rural Americans faced a harsh choice in the 1930s: hit the road to another part of the country—California, the Pacific Northwest, or the urban areas of the industrial North—or stay put and struggle to survive. In some regions, rural Americans returned to subsistence farming for a time, while in others they leaned for support on traditional religious and ethnic ties. Several different groups of rural Americans experienced increased racial discrimination and violence. As the decade wore on, most men and women in the countryside became somewhat accustomed to the new power of the federal government. As a new war loomed in Europe, however, they also feared that the Roosevelt administration would lead them into battle before the economic troubles at home had been solved.

Understanding the experiences of rural people in the 1930s helps to explain an important yet poorly understood political shift that followed hard times. Throughout the early 20th century, rural people had participated in leftist political movements ranging from communism and socialism to the Non-Partisan League, the Farm-Labor Party, and the Farmers' Holiday Association. Like the Populist movement in the 1880s, these organizations suggested that rural people still preferred cooperation, local control, and small producerism over centralization and modernization. However, after World War II and increasingly in the 1970s and 1980s, rural people were attracted to the right-wing language of anticommunism, antifederalism, and social and religious conservatism. Rural Americans seemed to have drifted from the left to the right in American politics.

Such an apparent conundrum is not nearly so difficult to understand when put in the context of rural Americans' experiences in the 1930s. Desperately poor, they were willing to "try anything" to survive. Yet they still did not always welcome the federalism that accompanied relief. In many states, support in rural counties for Roosevelt began to slip as early as 1938. By the late 1930s and early 1940s, anticommunism was a familiar part of political rhetoric. In their own descriptions of the threat of communism and fascism, rural people reflected their interactions with a large bureaucracy in which intellectuals and other "men in suits" told common folks what to do. In the years after the Great Depression, such calls for individual freedom and anti-government sentiments began to sound much more "right" than "left." By the 1980s, extremist groups in the countryside would express their hatred for the state and its representatives through the muzzle of a gun or a fertilizer bomb. Mainstream men and women simply made their stand at the ballot box every November, until by the first decade of the 21st century, the conservative revolution in the countryside seemed virtually complete.

Timeline

1932 Farm prices fall to 53 percent below prices of 1929.

FDR is elected, winning electoral votes from several previously Republican rural states.

Milo Reno establishes the Farmers Holiday Association in Iowa.

1933 Lorena Hickok begins her travels for Harry Hopkins around the United States.

AAA institutes subsidies for growers of seven basic commodities. In late summer the agency orders the slaughter of 6 million pigs to control prices.

	Congress passes Tennessee Valley Authority project over objections of many conservative congressmen.
	Congress creates the Civilian Conservation Corps. First 250,000 young men are sent to work in 1,468 camps in mostly rural areas.
1934	Congress passes the Farm Mortgage Refinancing Act.
	May 9—"Black Sunday"—dust storm travels from plains to Atlantic Ocean where it drops dust from the Great Plains onto ships at sea.
1935	FDR establishes the Resettlement Administration.
	FDR establishes the Rural Electrification Administration so that local cooperatives can bring electricity to rural people's homes and businesses.
1936	*The Future of the Great Plains: The Report of the Great Plains Committee* is published.
	Butler v. United States declares the AAA unconstitutional.
	Dorothea Lange visits a pea-pickers' camp in the San Joaquin Valley in California, where she takes the "Migrant Mother" series of photographs.
	Pare Lorentz completes *The Plow That Broke the Plains,* but the film is banned from distribution in South Dakota.
	FDR wins re-election and carries every state except Maine and Vermont, including his opponent Alfred Landon's home state of Kansas.
1937	Greenbelt, Maryland, opens for settlement.
1939	Thousands of rural Americans write their congressmen to protest the Lend-Lease Act.

Dust Bowl

Only a few times in world history has an ecological disaster devastated as large an area of a continent as the drought of the 1930s that devastated the Great Plains. The first dry year was 1930, and there were not two consecutive years with above average rainfall until the decade was over. As one rancher remem-

As a result of poor land management and severe drought, spring winds carried off the topsoil of a large area in the southern Great Plains during the Great Depression. This 1936 photo shows the destitution of farm families threatened by the clouds of dust. The Great Plains Drought Area Committee was created to investigate the conditions that brought on the Dust Bowl. (Library of Congress)

bered it, "The depression came out and every year it got worse. It started to get dry [in 1930] and '31 was drier than that and '32 was drier than that and '33 was drier than that" (Stock 1992, 20). Many counties in Oklahoma, Kansas, and the Dakotas did not even receive half the moisture they expected in an average year. The entire state of Oklahoma, for example, was rated moderate, severe, or very severe in drought intensity. If rain came, it poured, hailed, or stormed briefly and violently, doing no long-term good. Soon entire fields turned brown, whole crops failed, and annual incomes were decimated.

Accompanying the drought in the 1930s were searing heat and clouds of grasshoppers. Records for high temperatures across the region were broken, reset, and broken again. Many of them stand to this day. Long before air-conditioning in any region, extreme heat was deadly, especially for the elderly and newborn.

Lois Phillips Hudson, a young farm girl, remembered that each hot night she spent trying to fall asleep was "like the worst two days of the measles" (Stock 1992, 24). Due to the heat and dry conditions, huge clouds of grasshoppers arrived to finish off anything left behind. Often men and women would see a black cloud in the sky and hope it was the portent of a rainstorm. Instead, within a few minutes thousands of grasshoppers descended on their homes, eating crops under the ground, wood from pitchforks, siding from homes, and even clothing from the line. In Killdeer, North Dakota, after one such storm grasshoppers lay in swarming masses four inches deep. For many rural people, whose faith was central to their worldviews, these "plagues" seemed like the acts of an angry God, and they feared deeply for their futures.

Dust Storms

Even with all the heat, drought, and 'hoppers, what farmers and ranchers remembered best about the "dirty thirties" were the dust storms, huge gales of blowing soil in which their land literally blew away. Over and over, hot winds early in the day brought "black blizzards" of dust and dirt by afternoon. The storms often did not end until after sundown and, when they passed, everything inside and out was covered with dust. Even with windows shut tightly, dust covered dishes, cupboards, counters, beds, clothing, food, and utensils. In the summers of 1934 and 1936, the storms were especially relentless. On one evening in early July, Ann Marie Low sat in 110-degree heat and wrote in her diary: "I'm writing this on the living room floor, dripping sweat, and watching the dirt drift in the windows and across the floor. I've dusted this whole house twice today and won't do it again" (Low 1984, 36).

More than just taxing, the storms were dangerous. Many animals suffocated unless farmers had placed muslin bags over their snouts. Cattle drifted away unable to see, with hides coated in dirt and stomachs filled with mud. Caught on a road during a storm, drivers lost control of their cars, the motors destroyed. Children got lost in dust storms as easily as they did in blizzards. On March 15, 1935, an early spring dust storm caught the people of Smith Center, Kansas, unprepared. A seven-year-old boy lost his way and suffocated in a drift. Another lived to tell the tale, having been caught on a barbed-wire fence. A reporter remarked that "an uncorked jug placed on sidewalk two hours, [was] found to be half filled with dust. Picture wires [gave] way due to excessive weight of dust on frames. . . . Lady Godiva could ride thru streets without even the horse seeing her" (Worster 1982, 17).

The dust storms were so intense that their impact was sometimes felt hundreds of miles away. On "Black Sunday"—May 9, 1934—350 tons of Great Plains land blew eastward toward the more populous regions of urban America. Chicagoans saw 12-million tons settle on their city that day; Bostonians were sprinkled with

Cimarron County, Oklahoma

Among the most devastated counties in the country in the 1930s was Cimarron County, Oklahoma, the location of Arthur Rothstein's famous photographs of dust storms and rural poverty. Flat topography with sandy soils and subsoils made Cimarron a prime target for soil and wind erosion. In 1936 the federal government declared that the entire county had been "very severely" impacted by the drought. By 1940 many farmers and ranchers had sold or lost up to 80 percent of their stock. But in 1933, Texas journalist Albert Law could already see the ways in which the land and its inhabitants were being "blown out." He wrote:

"Not a blade of wheat in Cimarron County, Oklahoma; cattle dying there on the range; a few bushels . . . against an average yield of from four to six million bushels; with all the stored surplus not more than fifty per cent of the seeding needs will be met—ninety percent of the poultry dead because of the sand storms; sixty cattle dying Friday afternoon between Guymon and Liberal from some disease induced by dust—humans suffering from dust fever—milk cows going dry, turned into pasture to starve, hogs in such pitiable shape that buyers will not have them; cattle being moved from Dallam and other counties to grass; no wheat in Hartley County; new crops a remote possibility, cattle facing starvation; Potter, Seward, and other Panhandle counties with one-third of their population on charity or relief work; ninety percent of the farmers in most counties have had to have crop loans, and continued drought forcing many of them to use the money for food, clothes, medicine, shelter" (Worster 1982, 31).

disaster two days later. To their amazement, sailors on boats 300 miles off the Atlantic coast reported dust on their decks by the end of the week. Another "Black Sunday" came the next year, on April 14, 1935. So intense was the dust that day that people feared for their lives and for months afterwards they suffered epidemics of respiratory infections. In the four tiny hospitals in Meade County, Kansas, 33 patients died of respiratory distress in the month of April. The Red Cross set up six emergency hospitals in Kansas, Colorado, and Texas. One study showed that during five storms that year, 4.7 tons of dirt per acre fell on the southern plains. That dirt was the source of every plainsman and -woman's livelihoods; it was nothing less than the land itself. Without it they knew they could not survive.

Causes of the Dust Bowl

One critical thing differentiated the Dust Bowl of the 1930s from other droughts that had destroyed land and lives in past centuries. The ecological disaster of the Dust Bowl was not a "natural phenomenon" or an "act of God." Instead it was a predictable outcome of the actions of the people who lived there, the

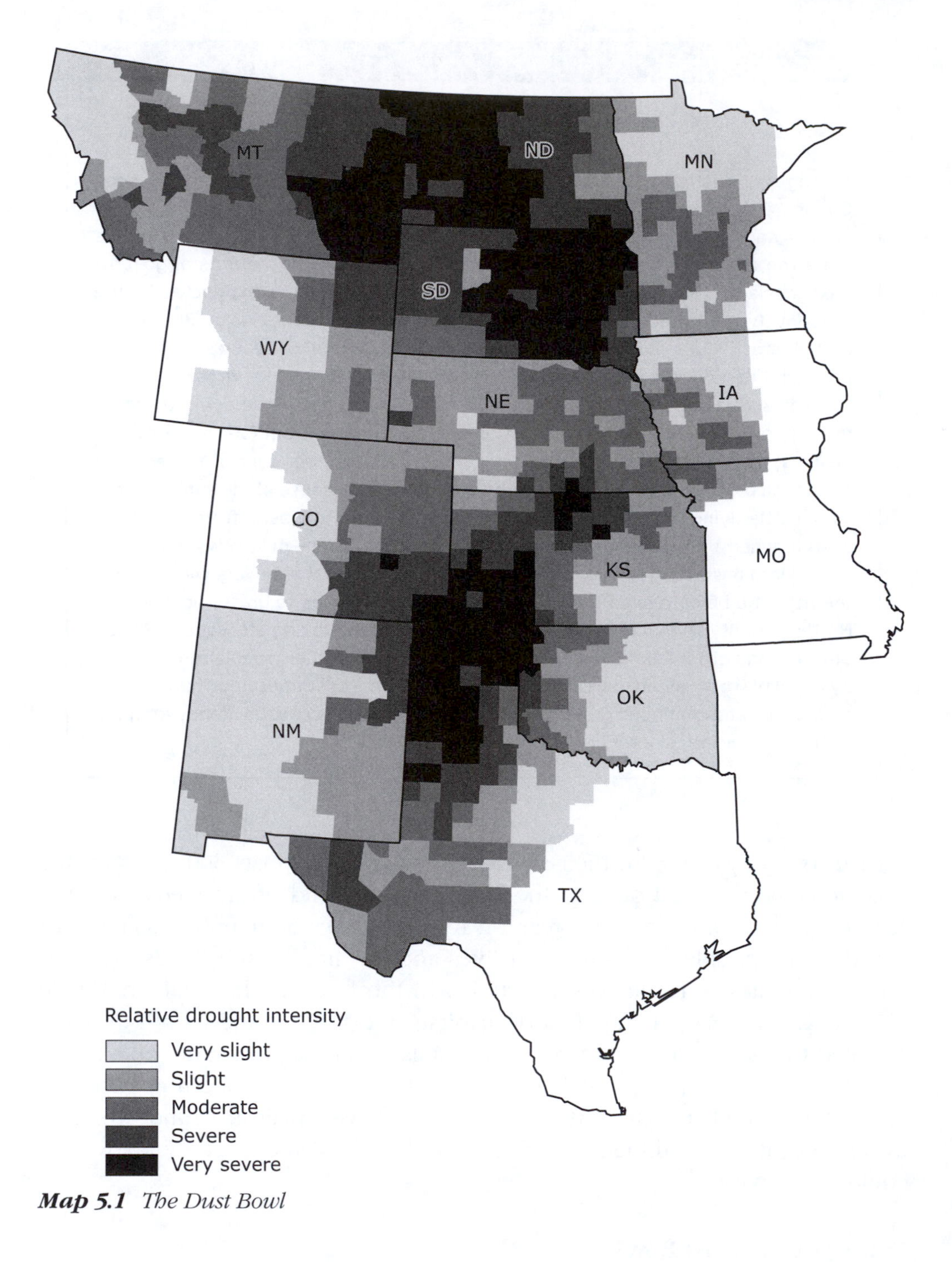

Map 5.1 *The Dust Bowl*

policies of their government, and the ideals of capitalist, commercialized agriculture. The Great Plains was one of the last parts of the United States to be "put to the plow." Previous visitors, like Capt. Steven Long who explored the area in the 1820s, had considered the area a "Great American Desert," utterly unfit for cultivation. Half a century later, John Wesley Powell, director of the U.S. Geological Survey, recommended in his *Report on the Lands of the Arid Region of the United States* (1878) that the lands be used only for ranching, not agriculture, and that homesteads be limited to a minimum of 2,500 acres rather than the 160 acres allowed in the Homestead Act of 1862. In the years before and after World War I, however, lust for land and profits and a fundamental belief in the moral goodness of the agrarian way of life combined with temporarily high prices and rainfall amounts to encourage people onto this last "frontier" of farming. Armed with tractors and deep plows, they turned over the deeply rooted grasses that literally held the soil in place.

In this same era, before hard times set in, dry-farming techniques and the mechanization of agriculture both encouraged capitalist agricultural practices and worsened their impact on the arid ecosystem. Proponents of "dry-farming" like Hardy Campbell did not believe, as some 19th-century expansionists did, that "rain would follow the plow." Instead he believed that, by deep plowing in

Power farming displaces tenants from the land in the western dry cotton area. Childress County, Texas Panhandle, June 1938. Photograph by Dorothea Lange. (Library of Congress)

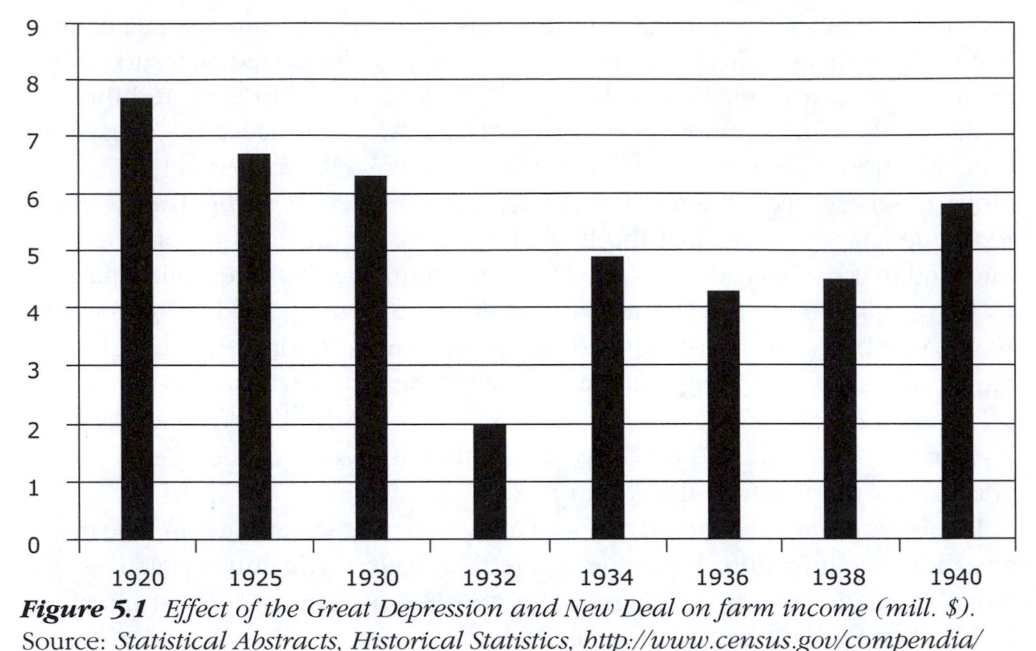

Figure 5.1 *Effect of the Great Depression and New Deal on farm income (mill. $).* Source: *Statistical Abstracts, Historical Statistics, http://www.census.gov/compendia/statab/hist_stats.html.*

the fall and leaving some fields fallow in the summer, Americans could access the greatest possible amount of moisture in the soil. He also encouraged farmers to switch to new grains, including winter wheat and sorghums that seemed to resist drought. At the same time, farmers exchanged their horses and plows for motorized tractors and combines. As war was breaking out in Europe and demand for food surged, farmers had the means to plow more and more land and plant more and more wheat. Meanwhile, the Wilson administration cheered them on, equating expansionism with patriotism. Finally, when the Food Control Act of 1917 guaranteed wheat prices of over two dollars a bushel, farmers bought land on credit and put it to the plow as quickly as they humanly could. In Finney County, Kansas, alone, acreage under cultivation in field crops increased from 76,000 in 1914 to 122,000 in 1919 (Worster 1982, 89).

Table 5.1. Decline in Rural and Farm Population, 1900–1970

	1900	*1930*	*1945*	*1970*
Number of farms (millions)	5.7	6.3	5.9	2.9
Farmers as percentage of U.S. population	39	25	17	5
Rural people as percentage of U.S. population	60	44	36	26

Source: Economic Research Service, U.S. Department of Agriculture, www.ers.usda.gov/briefing/rural.

Table 5.2. Resident Population Percent Change by State, 1910–1950

	1910–1920	*1920–1930*	*1930–1940*	*1940–1950*
Great Plains				
North Dakota	12.1	5.3	−5.7	−3.5
South Dakota	9.0	8.8	−7.2	1.5
Nebraska	8.7	6.3	−4.5	0.7
Kansas	4.6	6.3	−4.3	5.8
Oklahoma	22.4	18.1	−2.5	−4.4
Far West				
Washington	18.8	15.2	11.1	37.0
Oregon	16.4	21.8	14.2	39.6
California	44.0	65.7	21.7	53.3

Source: Statistical Abstracts, Historical Statistics: Resident Population by State at http://www.census.gov/compendia/statab/hist_stats.html.

Coping with the Crisis

Rural people did the best they could to cope in the Dust Bowl, scrimping and saving even more than they had before. When there was no more feed, they gave their stock Russian thistle, a weed that resembled barbed wire and likely nourished cattle almost as well. They also learned when an animal was beyond saving, beyond the expense of the local veterinarian or a family member's care. Ann Marie Low's younger brother, Bud, faced such a realization when a prize-winning heifer he had raised since birth suffered from a heat-related illness. "There were no words or tears," Low wrote. "Bud just went into the house and got his gun. Somehow to me, the look on his face when he shot Isabelle stood for this whole tragedy of a land laid waste, a way of life destroyed, and a boy's long struggle ending in despair" (Low 1984, 52).

Farm women in the 1930s learned to "make do" or "do without" year after year. They made "Pillsbury's Best" flour sacks into underwear, men's suits into boys' pants and coats, worn-out shoes into wearable shoes, corn cobs and Russian thistle into fuel, and ashes into cleanser. While women's production had always been critical to the success of a farm household, in the 1930s it sometimes made all the difference. In the 1930s in the Dakotas, for example, women produced half or more of the family's income during the drought by increasing both the size of their gardens and poultry flocks and the amount of eggs, butter, and cream that they manufactured for sale. With little or no money for doctors' visits, they practiced traditional home remedies and helped each other through pregnancy and childbirth. But women in the Dust Bowl regions were also well aware that other families in the United States did not live the way they did. In frustration, one woman wrote to her local farming magazine and explained that no matter how hard she tried, it just wasn't possible for her to have a "modern home."

> When one has no modern conveniences, one can't keep the house bright; especially when one has no rugs, no paint on the floor, nor anything else of that sort to make things look nice. . . . It is very different in beautiful houses where everything runs with power and everything is up-to-date. . . . How nice it would be for hard-working women to enjoy pushing a dust mop along waxed floors, instead of scrubbing slivery unpainted floors. I would gladly trade (Stock 1992, 154).

Many rural families felt ashamed of their poverty in the Great Depression and did the best they could to hide it. Women in Sublette, Kansas, for example, kept up their social club activities even in the hardest years. But in her travels, Lorena Hickok discovered that, as hard as families tried, they could not hide their troubles forever. Between 1932 and 1937 per capita income in every state on the Great Plains was a mere fraction of the average in the United States. In 1933 a typical family in Nebraska, for example, had only $145 to spend. They rationed food, clothes, bed sheets, blankets, coffee, until in the end they all gave out. In Bottineau County in the winter of 1933 it was 20 degrees below zero. Hickok visited houses patched together with tin and families sleeping in one bed. She estimated that families in one isolated rural county alone needed 5,000 suits of underwear, 5,000 pairs of shoes and socks, 20,000 yards of dress material, 1,500 heavy quilts, and 1,000 blankets "right away!" (Lowitt and Beasley 1981, 62).

Finding Solace in the Church

The hard times of the Great Depression made it more difficult even for families to turn to their traditional refuge and place of solace: the church. On the Great Plains, most farm families were Protestant, but large Catholic parishes had also thrived in ethnic German or Czech communities. No matter their specific denomination, however, ministers feared for their own as much as they did for their parishioners' well-being. Many communities could no longer afford to pay ministers, pay for upkeep on their buildings, or even heat the sanctuaries. In some places, the ministers were among the poorest people in their communities. They also feared growing "immorality" among people who knew such deprivation and hopelessness. To make matters worse, New Deal programs made no attempt to distinguish between the "worthy" or "unworthy" poor. To them and many others, the Dust Bowl was a crisis of the soul as well as the pocketbook.

The loss of their farms and homes was the central concern of every farm family in the 1930s. The poorest were the first to go. Tenants found themselves unable to pay rent. Likewise sharecroppers could no longer survive on what little crop remained after they had given over a share to the landlord. Rather than "moving up the agricultural ladder" to ownership, they were caught in an endless cycle of work, deprivation, and migration. Tenants on the northern and southern plains packed up what few possessions they had and left the region for the farm fields of California or the orchards of Washington and Oregon. Others,

"Penny Auctions"

In the 1930s family farmers who owed money to local banks and other creditors were often no more secure than tenant farmers and sharecroppers were. Encouraged by high prices and government calls to expand in the years around World War I, many farmers had no way to pay off their debts. Bank foreclosures and farm auctions became common. In some regions local people and politicians developed ways to fight back, including the "penny auction" or "Sears and Roebuck" sale. At these events, huge numbers of farmers gathered at the site of an auction to intimidate serious bidders and to bid extremely low prices themselves. At one penny sale in Milbank, South Dakota, for example, the entire property and all its goods netted the auctioneer only $6.30, which the original owner of the property promptly paid. Sometimes intimidation took physical form, as local men blocked roadways to keep sheriffs and out-of-town bidders away. In Steele County, North Dakota, a local Farmers Holiday Association leader told a banker who wanted to foreclose on the property of a woman whose husband had recently committed suicide, "If you foreclose on that woman, we'll hang you" (Stock 1992, 139). North Dakotans found support from their outspoken and controversial governor, William Langer. Before ordering a moratorium on foreclosures in the state, he was known to have telegrammed local officials directly to end an eviction or sale. The Iowa legislature also ordered a moratorium on foreclosure sales when more than 70 penny auctions took place in 1933 alone.

including African Americans from the Southeast and whites from Appalachia, headed north to the industrial cities of the Midwest and Northeast. They were soon joined by families from all regions who had owned their farms but lost them to bank foreclosure and auction. By the early 1940s, the migration of dispossessed rural Americans to the cities of the North and West became one of the most transformative migrations in American history.

Okie Migration

Despite their best efforts, many families were "blown out" in the 1930s, learning the hard way that there was no future for them on the Great Plains. Hundreds of thousands left the northern plains for Washington and Oregon. Even more left the southern plains, most of them heading for California. Traveling along Route 66 in old cars and trucks loaded with all of their possessions, these migrants soon became referred to as "Okies," because so many of them had come from Oklahoma. In fact, 15 percent of the population of Oklahoma left home for California. Their experiences became widely known as a result of John Steinbeck's Pulitzer prize–winning novel, *The Grapes of Wrath*.

Sharecropping

The words *sharecropper* and *tenant farmer* are sometimes used interchangeably, but they actually describe two different relationships between landlords and the farmers who farmed their lands, especially in the 1930s. Neither sharecroppers nor tenants owned land; thus both had to pay in some way for its use. The difference lay in the way they paid. Tenant farmers often paid in cash, sometimes in combination with labor. Sharecroppers on the other hand paid with a "share"—usually a third but often as much as a half—of what they grew.

Most sharecroppers lived in the Southeast. It is estimated that 80 percent of African American and 40 percent of white farmers were sharecroppers at the beginning of the 1930s. The vast majority had no land or farming equipment of their own and took up sharecropping relationships with white landowners, some of whom still lived on the land their families had farmed with slave labor. The sharecroppers were also required to buy all their "furnishings"—seed, cloth, food, and so on—from the local store, and they were expected to pay off their debt for the furnishings when their crop came in the following year. Because storeowners inflated their prices and charged exorbitant interest, however, most sharecroppers only went further and further into debt. To make matters worse, with the exception of some women, the majority of sharecroppers were semi-literate and thus could not fully participate in the negotiations at year's end.

Sharecropping took a toll on poor farmers themselves and on the land and culture of the South over many generations leading to the Great Depression. As historian Robin D. G. Kelley tells us, "Living day-to-day on a diet of 'fat back,' beans, molasses, and cornbread, most Southern tenants suffered from nutritional deficiencies—pellagra and rickets were particularly common diseases in the black belt" (Kelley 1990, 35). Moreover, because they had to grow a cash crop, they returned to cotton cultivation year after year, leaving only a small garden for subsistence. As in the Midwest, increased production and monocropping contributed to the decline in prices in the late 1920s and 1930s and in some areas the exhaustion of the soil. In sum, sharecropping was physically, environmentally, and socially debilitating. And yet many farmers could not escape the cycle of debt and had to stay on the land year after year. These arrangements, together with the constant fear of violence and the denial of suffrage rights, returned African Americans to a condition of virtual slavery.

Okies and their compatriots from other states (those from Arkansas were called "Arkies") encountered harsh working and living conditions in California during the Great Depression. California agriculture had never been organized in traditional family farm units but had instead long depended on large agricultural units, or corporate farms, and the migrant labor of Mexican, Native American, African American, Chinese, Japanese, and Filipino men, women, and children. Low wages, substandard housing (when there was any), little or no

A sharecropper and his family on the Pettway Plantation in Gee's Bend, Alabama, in 1939. (Library of Congress)

health care, and long hours in terrible conditions were the norm. Because of their poverty, geographic isolation, and racial and ethnic differences, California farm workers had difficulty organizing unions and were met with violent reprisals when they did. Social critic and political activist Carey McWilliams named these farms "factories in the field" and worked toward the organization of all farm workers in California (McWilliams 1939/2000). The Communist Party also worked to organize workers and help them see their common cause, as was portrayed in John Steinbeck's *In Dubious Battle.*

Okies also experienced significant social prejudice in the 1930s. They were considered ignorant, disease-infested, and prone to criminal activities. Their evangelical-Christian religious beliefs and practices were seen as fanatical and cult-like. To be successful, the migrants had to hide their accents and learn not to use expressions common at home. Nevertheless, officials worried that they were overburdening the public schools, relief programs, and local hospitals. In 1937 California passed a law making it a crime to assist in "bringing into the State any indigent person who is not a resident of the State." This was referred to as the "anti-Okie law." The law was overturned in 1941, but the prejudice of Californians toward white migrants did not die for more than a generation. Neither did the alienation from California culture that many Okies felt. Families who

Historians' Debate: What FSA Documentary Photographs Tell Us

Some of the best and most accessible documents about rural life in the 1930s come from the Farm Security Administration's documentary photography project. Indeed Dorothea Lange's "Migrant Mother" and Arthur Rothstein's "Dust Storm" are among the most famous American photographs ever taken. But historians debate the degree to which they can help us understand fully the experience of the 1930s. Many historians, including Donald Worster (1982) and Robert McElvaine (1984), use the FSA photographs to illustrate their works as if they "tell the truth" about what people's lives were like in that era. Other historians, however, suggest that the photographs tell us more about the goals, ambitions, and ideals of the photographers than they do about their subjects. According to John Curtis in *Mind's Eye, Mind's Truth,* for example, Lange was careful not to show her "migrant mother" actually breast-feeding her child so as not to offend the sensibilities of middle-class viewers whose sympathies she was seeking. Neither did she explain that the woman was traveling with a male companion (not her husband), nor that she had four other children. Likewise, Curtis explains that Arthur Rothstein's famous South Dakota image, "The Skull," was created by moving the skull from its original location to a more searing one (Curtis 1989). This outraged local people who felt that the photographers were exaggerating the difficulties in their communities. In *Main Street in Crisis,* Catherine McNicol Stock, on the other hand, contrasts the work of New Deal photographers with that of local artists. In South Dakota, for example, she found that local photographers recorded images of pleasure and relative prosperity rather than bleakness and suffering. Neither set of photographs is any more "true" than the others; instead they provide a window onto the ways different people in different circumstances wanted to record and represent the Great Depression.

claimed their roots on the southern plains and had never fully assimilated into the liberal, secular world of postwar California made up a large part of the new conservative Reagan coalition in California which came to power in the 1960s and 1970s (Morgan 1992, 467–70).

The New Deal Response and Its Impact on Rural People

Rural people themselves knew that something was wrong—terribly wrong—by the fall of 1932. They only hoped that a new administration might have new ideas for how to help. Fortunately, the architects of the New Deal recognized the importance of the agricultural sector to the American economy. Franklin Roosevelt lived on a large, rural estate in Hyde Park, New York, and considered himself a farmer, however gentlemanly. Similarly, nearly all of the administrators in the New Deal's Department of Agriculture had come from farming backgrounds. They believed that improving the agricultural economy was the key to ending the Great Depression. But they also saw in the Depression an opportunity to improve the workings of the agricultural sector for the long haul: by using centralized planning and local administration, they believed they could halt the destructive cycle of boom and bust, overproduction and low prices that had made farming in the United States difficult for many years already. Moreover, they sought to improve the infrastructure of rural America through public works projects and electrification. Finally, the more radical among them saw an opportunity to change the fundamental nature of farming on the Great Plains and to empower sharecroppers and tenant farmers throughout the country.

As rural people themselves would recognize as the decade wore on, some of the ideas of the New Deal farm programs were contradictory and some of the New Deal administrators were at odds with one another. Neither fact bothered Roosevelt in the slightest. His idea was to try anything and everything until something worked. What he may not have realized at the time was that once the government got "into the farming business," it would never get out again. By 1938 one-third of farm income in the United States came in the form of government payments (Danbom 1995, 121). Many of these programs remain in place today. Moreover, much of the money that poured into the countryside reinforced the status quo by helping those who needed it least—the larger commercial growers and property holders. When war arrived in the 1940s, bringing with it high prices once again, the most powerful people in rural America were still those farmers—nearly all of them white—who were willing to grow crops anywhere they might turn a profit.

The AAA and the Introduction of Domestic Allotment

In 1932 Americans were starving in cities and towns all over the country. Rural men and women wrote hundreds of thousands of letters to the new president telling him exactly that and begging him for help. Nevertheless, Roosevelt and his advisers believed that the key to improving the agricultural economy was to cut back on the production of crops by asking farmers to reduce voluntarily the amount that they grew until prices rose. While the New Dealers embraced such notions, many farmers rejected them outright. After all, only a decade earlier they had been encouraged to grow as much as they could. But agricultural economist M. L. Wilson of Montana State Agricultural College, Rexford Tugwell of Columbia University, and Secretary of Agriculture Henry Wallace believed that, along with providing better security for farm property, reducing production was

How Were Farm Subsidies Determined?

In trying to measure farm income, determine how much relief farmers might need, and then to assess the new farm programs, New Deal administrators used a new statistical concept they called *parity,* a concept still widely in use today. Parity was defined as equality between farmers' incomes or earning power and their costs or purchasing power. Because crop prices declined steeply in the Great Depression, but other costs stayed the same, farmers' purchasing power also plummeted. In fact, because crop prices had begun to decline in the 1920s, New Dealers believed that the last time farmers had achieved true parity was in the years between 1910 and 1914. As a result, they indexed subsidies with the hope of achieving a ratio of income to purchasing power similar to the one in place in that period. Unfortunately they never fully reached that goal in the 1930s. They averaged around 80 percent of parity between 1933 and 1940; the closest they came was 89.9 percent in 1936. In the years since the Great Depression costs for farmers, particularly in the technology sector, have continued to rise. In 2001 the price for a tractor was 3,611 percent of parity. Some critics feel that the concept of parity is now outdated, but it still serves as an important index for federal agricultural programs (Ganzel 2003b).

the countryside's most important task. Thus after designing the Farm Credit Administration, which purchased mortgages and refinanced them over longer terms with lower rates, they turned their attention to domestic allotment—and to convincing skeptical farmers to participate.

As discussed in the "New Deal and American Society" chapter, the Agricultural Adjustment Act (AAA), passed in May 1933, was essentially a program in which farmers agreed to take a certain percentage of their acreage out of production and the government paid them "rent" for doing so. At first the program was limited to the seven basic commodities: corn, cotton, hogs, milk, rice, tobacco, and wheat. Then it was extended to barley, beet and cane sugars, cattle, flax, peanuts, potatoes, rye, and sorghum. In all cases farmers provided local county agents with their acreage and production figures from the past five years. Based on those numbers the agents determined the acreage each farmer would put into production and the acreage he or she would leave fallow. The program, planners hoped, would raise farm incomes in two ways: by immediately providing cash subsidies to "cooperators" in the program and by eventually raising farm prices through decreased supply.

Even though farmers were skeptical about some of its basic philosophy, the AAA was somewhat successful in accomplishing these aims. Still it was not as successful as either the farmers or its planners had hoped. The devastating

Historians' Debate: New Deal Agricultural Programs and Charges of Communism

Farmers in rural America—even the African American sharecroppers who would eventually join the Communist Party—were initially skeptical of "outside" ideas and influences. For example, many were suspicious that the ideas of the New Deal were also influenced by "un-American" politicians. Then, in the McCarthy era, many former New Dealers were accused of having Communist ties, including former administrators at the USDA. Since that time, liberal historians like David Kennedy (1999) and Barton Bernstein (1968) have contended that New Deal reforms were intended to "save capitalism" from communist and socialist threats, not to turn American capitalist free enterprise fundamentally to the left. Indeed Bernstein and others have suggested that New Deal programs were hardly radical at all, but rather quite conservative in their consequences. A younger group of agricultural historians, while they do not accuse USDA officials of being Stalinist sympathizers or the New Deal of having been radical, have recently reopened the question of how much the planners in the USDA were influenced by collectivization and other programs in the USSR. In her 2001 essay, "Accounting for Change: Farmers and the Modernizing State," Deborah Fitzgerald discussed the important trip taken by M. L. Wilson to the Soviet Union (USSR) to visit collective farms. Henry Wallace, also, was intrigued by the model of centralized planning provided in Russia in the 1920s and 1930s. Fitzgerald concluded that "high modernism" was a global intellectual force in these years and that historians should recognize that New Dealers were at once interested in the ideas of collectivism and repulsed by the political structures of fascism and totalitarianism (Fitzgerald 2001).

drought on the Great Plains decreased production and thus raised prices somewhat. But overall production actually did not decline as much as planners had thought it would. Several things caused this disjuncture: First, some farmers did not participate in the program and, instead of curtailing production, actually increased it in the hope that prices would rise. Second, even those who participated in the AAA did not always do so according to the spirit of the program. For example, because farmers voluntarily reported previous acreages, sometimes they minimized what they had produced in the past. Moreover, sometimes they agreed to take out of production less productive acreage, or acreage that they had been planning on leaving fallow anyway. Ironically, the program also encouraged production of the same commodities it sought to limit, since farmers could only participate if they grew those commodities. Finally, new hybrids developed by the U.S. Department of Agriculture (USDA) in that decade also allowed for increased production per acre.

Critics of the AAA

Rural people who were skeptical of the New Deal were hardly alone. Critics of the AAA spoke out everywhere in America and from all political perspectives. Beginning in the late 1920s, for example, farmers and farm organizations had called for programs based on the "cost of production" rather than domestic allotment. These programs would have allowed farmers to grow as much as possible and have the government set a minimum price for what they sold. John Simpson of the Farmers' Union continued to speak out against the basic concept behind the AAA as late as the spring of 1933. Distaste for the AAA grew even more pronounced when, due to the late passage of the bill, farmers were asked to destroy crops they had already planted and young pigs that had already been borne. Although only the cotton and hog sectors were directly affected, farmers across the United States were shocked by such apparent wastefulness.

Even as they signed up to "cooperate" with the AAA, some farmers remained opposed to its ideology and structure. They had never liked the county extension agents very much and they worried that the AAA would mean an "army of bureaucrats" looking into their accounts and telling them what to do. What did the "brain trust" group of "professors" in Washington know about the day-to-day work of farming? Wasn't this just their government giving them a "Russian Five Year plan" like Stalin had given his people? Quickly agents realized that, far from "cooperating," many farmers had signed up for the plan but were continuing to resist it. As one agent in Renville County, North Dakota, put it, his clients did not have faith in the AAA. They were simply in "absolute despair" and "willing to try anything" (Stock 1992, 144, 145). Nearly every farmer participated and benefited from the AAA. But, as historian David Danbom put it, "farmers in 1936 willing to say they really liked the agricultural programs of the New Deal were few and far between" (Danbom 1995, 215).

Other critics came from urban America, Congress, and the courts. Consumers were quick to realize that, since the AAA's subsidy payments came from a tax on commodities processors, these costs were passed on to them in the form of higher prices for groceries. They wondered why, when they could not afford basic foodstuffs already, they were being asked to pay more for them. Republicans also objected to the use of the federal government to control market production and private enterprise. The Republican-dominated Supreme Court concurred in *United States v. Butler* (1936) when it ruled that the AAA was unconstitutional. The justices said that Congress had neither the right to regulate agricultural production nor the right to tax processors. The Roosevelt administration quickly responded by replacing the AAA with the Soil Conservation and Domestic Allotment Act, which emphasized soil conservation and paid farmers from general funds. The Court believed that soil erosion was an interstate problem and thus fell under federal jurisdiction. A "second" AAA, which included federal crop insurance, passed in 1938.

Evicted sharecroppers along Highway 60, New Madrid County, Missouri, 1939. Photograph by Arthur Rothstein. (Library of Congress)

Radical Voices within the USDA

The ongoing poverty of rural Americans, and of African Americans in the South in particular, spoke volumes to the inability of the New Deal to make real change. As a result, some of the most prominent critics of the AAA were New Deal administrators themselves. As David Danbom puts it, "the problem was that commodity-based programs were not very effective means of addressing such human problems as low income, rural poverty, and the demise of the family farm" (Danbom 1995, 213). Because New Deal programs favored commodity producers, the larger the better, subsistence farmers in many regions, including Appalachia and northern New England, received little or no help. Most glaringly, in the Cotton South the programs actually did the opposite of helping the poor—they allowed them to be dislocated entirely. The problem was that the payments from the AAA went directly to the landlords, and while language in the contracts stipulated that landlords divide the payments with sharecroppers, they very frequently did not do so, particularly if the croppers were African American. Moreover, rather than having each of their sharecroppers take some of his or her land out of production, landlords often took all of one or two croppers' lands out of production, thus forcing these families off the land. Moreover, landlords saw the existence of other relief programs, like the Works Progress Administration (WPA), the Public Works Administration (PWA), and the Civilian Works Administration (CWA), as a secondary means of support for sharecroppers that effectively relieved them of further responsibility. They also knew that the threat of violence, enforced through clandestine groups like the KKK and public ones like all-white juries, would keep many African Americans from voicing their frustrations.

Most New Dealers, including Franklin Roosevelt himself, felt that the problems in southern culture were too deeply entrenched to be changed through the AAA. Moreover, they chose not to alienate southern whites whose support was critical to the success of the national Democratic Party. Others disagreed vehemently. In 1935, a group of young lawyers within the AAA worked determinedly to help sharecroppers—so much so in fact that they were eventually "purged" from the USDA. Meanwhile, the Southern Tenant Farmers Union worked directly with displaced sharecroppers in Arkansas to help them to stand up for their rights (see "The Labor Movement" chapter). In Alabama the Communist Party USA organized African Americans and poor whites. For most sharecroppers, however, the decade changed little or nothing about their lives. Illiteracy, little or no health care, poor nutrition, dire poverty, and outright fear marked the outlines of their experience.

Farm Security Administration

Fortunately for those men and women who benefited from them, a few more inclusive programs were introduced to help the poorest farmers, both in the South and on the Great Plains. Founded after the "purge" of the AAA, the Resettlement Administration (RA), for example, aimed to move farmers on "submarginal land" to better locations and to give them technical support and advice. Roosevelt put activist Rexford Tugwell at its head but only allocated a small amount of money for its administration. According to historian Robert McElvaine, in the end the RA was able to help less than 1 percent of the 500,000 families it had intended to help (McElvaine 1984, 301). In 1937, the RA was renamed the Farm Security Administration (FSA) under the provisions of the Bankhead-Jones Farm Tenancy Act. The FSA had better funding than the RA; indeed, it spent over a billion dollars between 1937 and 1941. In some parts of the southern plains as many as 20 percent of farm families received assistance from the FSA through the programs of Rural Rehabilitation. Often, a family would be given a loan to lease new acreage, provided that they put that land into pasturage rather than commercial crops. Although some clients felt it was an embarrassment to receive Rural Rehabilitation funds (only the poorest families qualified, as opposed to all farmers who qualified for the AAA), others saw it simply as a means to end the cycle of tenancy.

Even a billion dollars could make only the smallest dent in the profound problem of rural poverty. Letters continued to pour into the president from rural Americans who hoped his family could send them money, food, and even their used clothing (McElvaine 1983, 155–170). However, some programs of the RA and FSA had significant long-term benefits. The RA built camps for migratory workers in California and other areas of the South and West, so that Okie families and others no longer lived in their cars and under bridges. It also established over 200 subsistence homesteads, where groups of farmers grew all or most of the food needed for the community. Most memorably, under the auspices of its Information Office, the FSA funded its world-renowned documentary photography project, headed by Tugwell's friend Roy Stryker. Stryker hired some of America's most important photographers—including Dorothea Lange, Arthur Rothstein, Ben Shahn, Walker Evans, Marion Post Wolcott, Russell Lee, and John Vachon—to capture the suffering of rural people whom the New Deal desired to help. Together they left a priceless documentary legacy of the Great Depression. As Robert McElvaine put it, "even if the RA/FSA had done nothing else, this effort would easily secure its place as an important contribution of the New Deal" (McElvaine 1984, 302).

Organizing Sharecroppers

Largely forgotten in the histories written in the middle of the 20th century is the powerful story of sharecroppers who organized unions and even went on strike for better working and living conditions. A variety of groups worked with sharecroppers, but in Alabama and other parts of the Cotton South the most successful were affiliated with the Communist Party and the Socialist Party. These were ardently antiracist and advocated biracial organizations. Racial integration was particularly nearly impossible to accomplish in the South, as both radical African Americans and antiracist whites met violence, murder, and ostracism. Nevertheless, the two most successful of the groups, the Sharecroppers Union and the Southern Tenant Farmers Union, boasted 8,000 and 25,000 members respectively (Harris 1995).

In the early 1930s sharecropping, which had always been the most exploitative of labor systems, grew worse. A boll-weevil epidemic destroyed crops, and with soaring unemployment and plunging prices for cotton, African Americans and poor whites who had been on the margins of survival quickly became desperate. Many took note when the Communist Party, under the auspices of the International Labor Defense (ILD), took the lead in the defense of the Scottsboro Boys, nine African American men accused and convicted of raping two white women. The ILD won its first two appeals of the case in front of the U.S. Supreme Court. In this work, the ILD linked judicial and civil rights with antilynching, unemployment, and the Jim Crow system as a whole.

In the spring of 1931 in Tallapoosa County, Alabama, a small group of sharecroppers banded together with help from the Communist Party. Soon they had formed the Croppers and Farm Workers Union and had gathered a membership estimated at 800. The group was attacked by white authorities almost from the beginning, including a shoot-out at Camp Hill, Alabama, in July 1931, and an incident near Reeltown, Alabama, in December 1932 in which three union members were killed. Many others were shot or badly beaten; even a blind woman reported to be 100 years old was pistol-whipped (Kelley 1990, 50). Later an all-white jury convicted five union members of assault with a deadly weapon. Ned

Let Us Now Praise Famous Men

In July and August of 1936, writer James Agee and photographer Walker Evans traveled to Greensboro, Alabama, to research a story on sharecropping for *Fortune* magazine. They were to "produce a photographic and verbal record of the daily living and working environment of an average white family of tenant farmers." What they returned with, however, was so heart-wrenching and politically provocative that the magazine did not publish it. Instead it became one of the most important literary works of the era (Evans and Agee 1939/1988). Evans photographed and Agee wrote about three families they encountered: the Gudgers, Woods, and Ricketts (pseudonyms for the Burroughs, Tengles, and Fields). Like most sharecroppers in the South—African American as well as white—they were desperately poor. They lived in run-down one- and two-room shacks, were thin and gaunt, and had poor health. Evans's pictures bore witness to children without pants, parents without teeth, wounds without dressings, and homes without barest essentials. And yet both author and photographer aimed to respect their subjects and to show what Agee called their ultimate "divinity." The book itself was unusual and experimental in its format. The photographs came first rather than interspersed with the narrative. Moreover, Agee spoke for himself, nearly as a separate character in the book, about his own "worthiness" in writing about the families and his own ability to represent the families' reality. In a sense, then, the book served as a critique of works that merely "pitied" the poor or portrayed them as victims, and that exploited them for profit and personal gain. From a political perspective, however, the book also critiqued the New Deal's inability to reach those who needed help the most.

Cobb, who had sharecropped land by himself since he was 15 years old, was sentenced to 12 to 15 years.

Implicit racism in the New Deal relief programs amplified African Americans' need for action. When they realized that New Deal funds would not be fairly distributed and that some landlords were dispossessing long-time tenants, even more African Americans came to the Share Croppers Union (SCU) for help. (In Arkansas and Texas, they joined the Socialist Party–led Southern Tenant Farmers Union; see "The Labor Movement" chapter). In the summer of 1934 the SCU led a series of cotton pickers' strikes in Tallapoosa, Montgomery, and Lee counties. They aimed, first and foremost, to increase pickers' wages to one dollar per 100 pounds. (In these counties many pickers only earned 40 cents per 100 pounds.) But they also demanded a 10-hour day, two meals or free transportation to the fields, and equal wages by sex, age, and race. In Tallapoosa County they achieved their initial goal, despite facing terrible violence and repression. But in other counties strikers made few gains and could only mourn their dead through

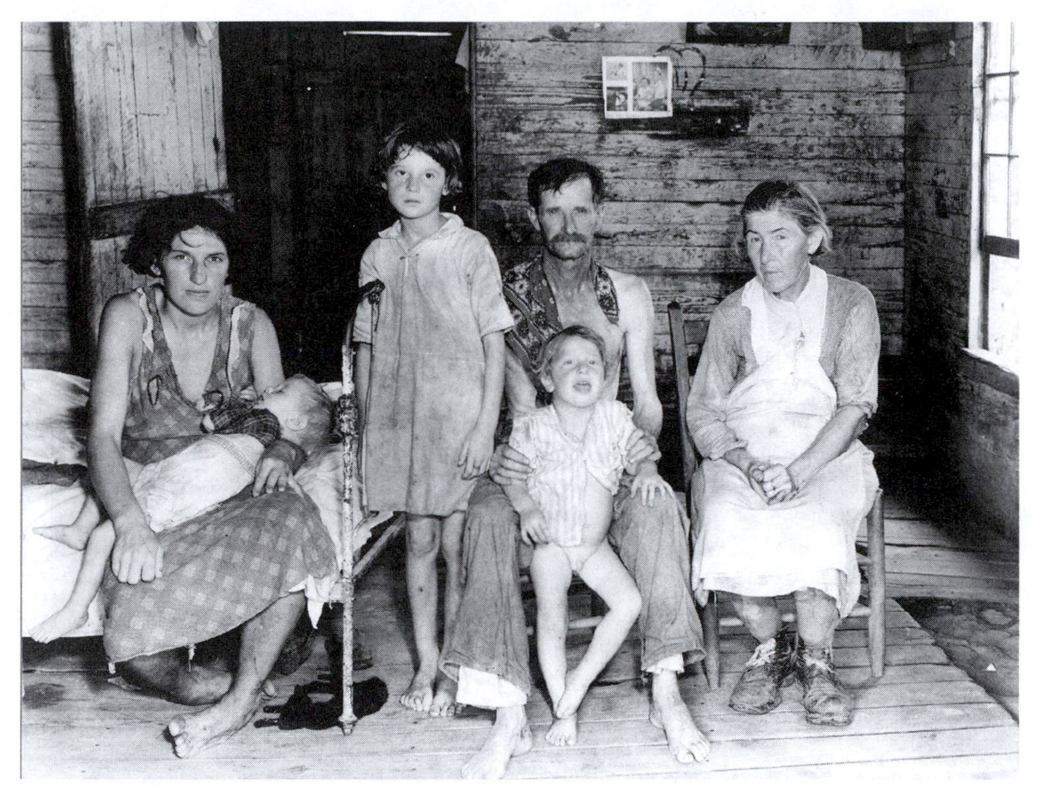

Sharecropper Bud Fields and his family, ca. 1935. Image by documentary photographer Walker Evans. (Library of Congress)

angry poems and songs like the one written by SCU leader Clyde Johnson, "Look yonder, you who still believe / The rotten lies the Landlords tell / Look at the blood drenched cotton fields / Where your brothers fought and fell" (Kelley 1990, 167).

Soil Conservation Programs

Farmers on the Great Plains were recipients of funds set aside for soil conservation—and this, too, led to controversy. The Soil Conservation Service (SCS), like the AAA, sought to help farmers remain on the land and did not question their fundamental economic or cultural beliefs. The SCS was headed by a strong advocate for the study of conservation agronomy, Hugh Hammond Bennett. Contending that there was nothing ethically or ecologically wrong with farming the Great Plains, Bennett believed that farmers needed to learn how to do it better. He argued that with the proper methods and techniques farmers could "make the land pay off." Moreover, he did not believe that the plains specifically or the American economy as a whole had reached its "food production

The Report of the Great Plains Committee (1936)

The Future of the Great Plains: The Report of the Great Plains Committee was a 194-page report submitted to President Roosevelt in December of 1936. It was written by representatives of two committees who had traveled the northern and southern plains, from Texas to South Dakota, in the summer and fall of 1936, visiting drought areas and talking with farmers in towns and villages. Rexford Tugwell, Morris Cooke (head of the Rural Electrification Administration), and Lewis Gray were members of one or both committees. The committees' goals were to create a model for land-use planning and to find workable plans for restoring environmental stability. The report, however, reflected the contradictions within the conservation policies of the New Deal. For example, it listed 12 "attitudes of mind" that created the conditions in which the Dust Bowl occurred. These included a "domination of nature ethic" and a dedication to expansionism. In short it described—and ascribed blame to—the fundamental cultural beliefs of capitalist agriculture. But the writers were unwilling to conclude that solving the agricultural crisis required repudiating these same beliefs. The report did, however, say that the Dust Bowl could be blamed on institutions and practices "brought from the humid part of the country." Thus the report was the first official government document to attest that the Dust Bowl was not caused by nature but by human cultural practices.

limits." "As a nation we need to renew our acquaintance with the land," he wrote, "and reaffirm our faith in its continuity of productiveness—when properly treated. If we are bold in our thinking, courageous in accepting new ideas, and willing to work with instead of against our land, we shall find in conservation farming an avenue to the greatest food production the world has every known" (Worster 1982, 212, 214).

This attitude pleased commercial farmers and large landholders in particular, but was directly at odds with the thinking of some top figures in the New Deal, including Rexford Tugwell, head of the Resettlement Administration (RA). Together with Lewis Gray, Tugwell had come to believe that the ethos and practices of capitalist agriculture had spelled ecological disaster on the plains. They believed that, rather than a freakish anomaly, the Dust Bowl had been created by American "attitudes of mind"—and that they had to be changed. If Tugwell and Gray could have had their way, they would have moved all farmers off "sub-marginal lands" and refused access to farm programs for those who stayed behind. They also leaned toward a "pasturage" ideal reminiscent of John Wesley Powell's *Report on the Arid Lands* and hoped for the day when local farm committees would limit expansion and control resources themselves. Support for grassroots collective planning and powerful government constraints were part of what earned Tugwell the nickname "Rexford the Red." As the decade ended and war approached, few in Congress wanted to hear that the American way of life was in any way fundamentally flawed.

The Plow That Broke the Plains

The contradictory political views at the heart of the New Deal's agriculture programs was also captured in the 1936 film, *The Plow That Broke the Plains,* directed by Pare Lorentz for the Farm Security Administration. The film sought to answer the question of what caused farmers to come to the plains and proudly "break the land." To Lorentz, the answer was the rapacity of technology. He created montages of great lines of tractors tearing through the soil, juxtaposed with images of tanks in European killing fields. In the background sounded Virgil Thomson's beautiful and haunting score, filled with American folk tunes and implicit calls to national action. Like the "Report of the Great Plains Committee," Lorentz did not blame the farmers as individuals. He hoped that under the New Deal, agricultural practices could be reformed and the land saved. His cameramen, on the other hand, "wanted it to be all about human greed, and how lousy our social system was. And I couldn't see what this had to do with dust storms" (Worster 1982, 96).

Even though Lorentz felt he had not blamed farmers for the Dust Bowl, many of them felt personally attacked by the film. Just as they questioned the photographs produced by the Farm Security Administration, they objected to the distribution of *The Plow That Broke the Plains.* Many small-town movie theaters refused to show the film; the South Dakota legislature banned it outright. In their local celebrations, pageants, and parades, rural people documented the past on their own terms and provided their own explanations for their troubles. They believed that the courage and faith of the pioneers had seen them through hard times, and that the same virtues would guide them through their struggles as well. Rather than making them question themselves or their culture, the problems of the Great Depression thus served to bind rural people to their forefathers who believed, as Karal Marling put it, "in the mighty dream that always came true" (Stock 1992, 197).

MODERNIZING RURAL AMERICA

Since the early 20th century modernization of the countryside had been an important goal of federal programs for rural America. Extension agents of the state agricultural colleges brought home economics, school consolidation, modern accounting practices, and soil conservation systems to farmers and their families. As we have seen, these goals were significantly extended through several programs of the New Deal. Although many rural American still did not trust "a man in a suit" to tell them how to run their farms or communities, many came to accept and benefit from the improvements to their infrastructures that came about in the Great Depression. On the eve of World War II, life on the farm did not seem as utterly different from life in urban America as it had in 1928.

Public Works Projects

As discussed previously in "The New Deal and American Society," many New Deal relief programs were informed by the concept that people should not simply receive handouts, but should work for the aid they received. Roosevelt and his advisers imagined that billions of dollars in improvements to community infrastructure would uplift the "spirits of men" and their communities at the same time. The Civilian Works Administration (CWA), Works Progress Administration (WPA), and Public Works Administration (PWA) built roads, dams, courthouses, post offices, and recreational facilities in rural communities as well as urban ones—$35 million worth in South Dakota alone. The rural poor, including African Americans who were placed in segregated programs, earned $40 per month, working on government projects. In small communities, however, the stigma associated with being "on the dole" could be intense. Lois Phillips Hudson preferred to go hungry at lunchtime rather than eat the apples and other food provided by the government. Class and racial tensions were exacerbated by the fact that local people determined who qualified for relief and who did not. "Taking a check from a guy who sat behind you in fifth grade" was more than one farmer could take. He preferred to do without (Stock 1992, 1, 93).

The Civilian Conservation Corps (CCC) brought large-scale and long-term environmental improvements to rural areas across the country. The CCC aided unemployed, unmarried men between the ages of 18 and 25 who were still dependent on their parents' often meager incomes and ripe, it was feared, for delinquency or political agitation. The young men came from both urban and rural America; they were often sent to remote locations to build dams, plant trees, clear beaches, construct wildlife shelters, kill rodents and other pests, and put up firebreaks, lookouts, campgrounds, and trails in national forests and parks. By 1942 three million men had worked at a wage of $30 a month, $25 of which they were required to send home. While local people like Ann Marie Low's family resented the intrusion of government agents and the purchase of lands for federal projects, most rural and urban Americans believed the CCC programs were money well spent. For many recruits the CCC camp was the first place where they had ever eaten three square meals a day and had two sets of clothes.

There was no doubt, however, that the camps had militaristic overtones and functions—and these did not escape the eyes of many rural families who increasingly feared the involvement of the United States in a new European war.

Members of a Civilian Conservation Corps crew work on a reforestation project during the Great Depression. (Franklin D. Roosevelt Presidential Library)

The assistant secretary of war did not help assuage concerns when he suggested that the Army take over the CCC and make the boys "economic storm troops." Three thousand reserve Army officers ran the camps. The boys wore uniforms and followed a highly regimented schedule. Rather than turning large numbers of young men into soldiers during peacetime, however, the CCC camps actually prepared the Army to handle large numbers of young men during wartime. In the 1940s millions of young men just like the CCC boys—malnourished, poorly clad, and barely educated—would become part of a real Army that needed them for battle immediately. Beginning in 1942, some CCC camps were used for military training; others for Japanese internment. Aspen, Colorado, for example, where only 750 people had lived in 1925 became home to a CCC camp in the 1930s, the training site for the 10th Mountain Division of the U.S. Army in the 1940s, and a world-famous ski resort in the 1950s and 1960s. Federalization of the countryside in the 1930s and 1940s thus led some very remote areas to full integration into the global economy in the postwar era.

Tennessee Valley Authority

Many major political figures of the 20th century, including Lyndon Johnson, Orval Faubus, and George McGovern, remembered homes where reading was nearly impossible at night and hand-scrubbing everything—clothes, floors, dishes, walls—often with water carried in from a well, was the order of the day. Thus among President Roosevelt's highest priorities for improving the infrastructure of rural America was providing electricity. As governor of New York in the 1920s, he had worked aggressively to promote electrification because he believed that it provided both improved quality of life and long-term economic benefits. As president he carried on these initiatives. Although electricity had been commonplace in urban areas for decades, rural America lagged behind, in large part because of the expense of running wires down miles and miles of county roads. Many modern conveniences—labor-saving devices for the home and the farm—were impossible for rural Americans to use. This decreased their productivity and exacerbated their sense that the countryside was a different world altogether from the rest of America.

For many years, progressives like Sen. George Norris of Nebraska had pointed to the Wilson Dam on the Tennessee River at Muscle Shoals, Alabama, as a prime opportunity for the federalization of public power. The dam had been built during World War I to help with the manufacture of explosives, but had sat unused in one of the poorest regions of the country ever since, while Progressives in the Senate and private utility companies fought over its future. After visiting the dam in January of 1933, Roosevelt surprised Norris by proposing not simply the federalization of the Wilson Dam in Alabama, but the federalization of the entire Tennessee Valley. Roosevelt said the impoverished region was "an opportunity of seeing an example of planning, planning not just for ourselves but planning for the generations to come, tying in industry and agriculture and forestry and flood prevention" (McElvaine 1984, 155). He envisioned a project that would bring workers from urban areas and that would improve the economic infrastructure of an entire seven-state region. The TVA was passed in May 1933, among the first of the New Deal's major pieces of legislation. When asked to characterize its political philosophy, Roosevelt was characteristically practical, saying, "I'll tell them it's neither fish nor fowl, but whatever it is, it will taste awfully good to the people of the Tennessee Valley" (Kennedy 1999, 148).

As with all other major pieces of New Deal legislation, critics of the TVA abounded—including some local people. Roosevelt's project did not just expand the power of the federal government for distributing power; it also allowed the federal government to appropriate land for the creation of new dams and the construction of a 650-mile navigable waterway. Republicans were horrified at the precedent set by the TVA, and worked long hours to ensure that it did not become a model for other regions. Some local people also did not like being told what to do—especially when it came to losing land or being told what to do by "men in suits." But the project delighted both Progressives in the North and conservative Democrats in the South—two groups that Roosevelt had to retain if his new political coalition was to survive. Meanwhile, members of his administration nearly crowed with delight when they saw what their political muscle

What Electrification Meant to One Kentucky Home

Beginning in 1935, rural electrification literally changed the lives of many farm families. While urban families purchased appliances to save labor around their homes and to make reading and working at night safer and easier, rural families remained in the dark. One Shelby County woman, Rose Dudley Scearce, described in her local cooperative's newsletter "what REA service means to our farm home." Her first purchases were lamps, which were "so much easier on the eyes" than her old oil lamps had been. She also told of the benefits of the electric radio, electric range, and electric refrigerator. Interestingly, though, it was her vacuum cleaner that she cherished most, because she knew the new standard of cleanliness that women were meant to maintain in the modern era. She wrote, "I do not know what kind of a person you are, but I expect that you are a nice, neat person and that when it rains you put on your overshoes on the porch before you go out and take the muddy overshoes off on the porch before you come into the house. We don't do it that way at our house. We rush out when it rains without overshoes, and when we come in we wipe half the mud on the mat at the door and the other half we wipe on my living-room carpet. I have an old-fashioned Brussels carpet on my living-room floor, and when I swept it I raised as much dust as if I had been sweeping the dusty pike. When I finished I was choking with the dust, the carpet was not clean, and I was in a bad humor. Now with the vacuum cleaner, I can even dust the furniture before I clean the carpet, the carpet gets clean, and I stay in a good humor" (Scearce 1939).

had wrought. Visiting the site of the construction of the new Norris Dam, Lorena Hickok wrote Harry Hopkins: "Ten thousand men are at work, building with timber and steel and concrete the New Deal's most magnificent project, creating an empire with potentialities so tremendous and so dazzling that they make one gasp. I knew very little about the Tennessee Valley Authority when I came down here last week. I spent part of my first day, in Knoxville, reading up on it. I was almost as excited as I used to get over adventure stories when I was a child. This IS an adventure!" (Hickok 1934).

Rural Electrification Administration

Rural electrification was promoted outside the Tennessee Valley when in 1935 Roosevelt created the Rural Electrification Administration (REA) and appointed Morris Cooke, former member of the New York Power Authority during his first term as governor, to its head. Rather than federalizing the manufacture and distribution of power, as the TVA had, however, the REA acted mainly as a financing organization, providing low-cost loans to any group, private or public, who wanted to bring electricity to an area. Cooke and others who had hoped to use the TVA as a model for the distribution of power were sorely disappointed. Even though complete federalization proved unworkable, they did succeed in promoting a cooperative model, whereby neighbors could join together in a nonprofit venture to distribute electricity. In many areas the cooperative model was used; in others private companies that had been reluctant to invest now did so with confidence. In only the first two years, 350 projects brought electricity to 1.5 million farms. By the end of the decade 25 percent of all farms had electricity; by the mid-1950s nearly all farms in America did. Moreover, the default rate on the loans was less than 1 percent. Not surprisingly, when farm prices rebounded during World War II, the demand for electrical appliances for the home and farm surged. According to many rural women, rural electrification was the answer to their prayers.

Special Concerns in Other Rural Regions

While the Great Plains and the Cotton South garnered the most attention from the media in the 1930s (and the most attention from historians since), country people in other regions faced numerous challenges of their own. In New England and the mid-Atlantic, subsistence farming regained popularity and the back-to-the land movement brought new people and new communities. In the Far West and Southwest, members of rural ethnic communities tightened their bonds, turning to traditional support services and household economies to survive. Despite these social structures, some rural people experienced a distinct increase in discrimination in this period. Many Mexicans, Mexican Americans, and Filipinos, for example, were forced to return to their native countries. As the decade ended, whites in the countryside had grown somewhat accustomed to federal power, and yet were increasingly fearful of American involvement in another foreign war. Their relationship with the federal government had changed forever, but they were far from convinced that it was a change for the better.

The Old Order Amish in Lancaster County, PA

The Old Order Amish, whose founding members settled in Lancaster County, Pennsylvania, practiced subsistence farming throughout the early 20th century, relying on family labor and forgoing technological advancement, including electrification, in accordance with their religious beliefs. This made them different from nearly all other farming groups in the United States. Not surprisingly, then, when the Amish weathered the Great Depression better than most farm families, they aroused the curiosity of New Deal administrators. Several important studies, including Carl Taylor's work on six diverse rural communities, examined "habits of mind," farming, and home production practices that had helped these families and communities maintain relative economic stability. In fact, some New Deal researchers concluded that the Amish people's rejection of modernization was admirable. Walter Kollmorgan of the Bureau of Agricultural Economics even tried to make his family adopt Amish ways, much to the consternation of his teenage daughter.

A great deal of the success of Amish families—and of other families from similar religious sects—was due to the productive work of women. These women were interested neither in social clubs nor in popular culture. They kept large farm gardens and flocks of poultry so their families did not have to depend on store-bought goods. One Mennonite woman remembered that the 1930s "did us a lot of good. We learnt to save. We learnt to make do" (Worster 1982, 175). In Lancaster Country the home production of Amish women far outpaced that of non-Amish women—even though, as we have seen, farm women's work in all regions of rural America increased in the Great Depression. On average Amish women canned 30 more quarts of fruits and vegetables per year than non-Amish women did, which, together with other home products, was worth $63 (Stock and Johnston 2001, 250). Amish women also reported far more satisfaction with their work and their participation in the farm economy than women from non-Amish families did. New Deal researchers suggested that while both Amish and non-Amish women lived under patriarchy, the Amish women's labor was more fully valued and had an even more appreciable impact on their families' economic stability.

Japanese and Japanese Americans in the Far West

Despite state laws making it difficult or impossible for them to own land, thousands of Japanese (*Issei*) and Japanese Americans (*Nisei*) lived and worked on farms and orchards in rural areas of Washington, Oregon, and California in the 1920s and 1930s. For the most part they concentrated on fruit and vegetables or "truck crops"—produce that could be trucked into market at nearby cities. For example, as early as 1910 Japanese produced 70 percent of California's strawberries. By 1940 they grew 95 percent of the state's fresh snap beans and more than half of all fresh tomatoes, celery, onions, and peas. In 1920 Japanese farmers worked nearly half a million acres of land in California (Takaki 1989, 190). In that same year 46 percent of all Japanese in the United States were employed in agriculture. They imported their knowledge of intensive farming and of irrigation and drainage to create fertile acreage in difficult soils of the San Joaquin, Sacramento, and Imperial valleys. For example, Japanese cultivators were the first group to grow rice successfully in the arid West.

Japanese American farmer harvests cauliflower on a ranch near Centerville, California. Photograph by Dorothea Lange. (Library of Congress)

By scrimping, saving, and depending on family labor, many Japanese held on to their land during the Great Depression. For those who had entered into agreements that violated the various Alien Land laws, however, hard times increased their fear that they would be discovered by authorities. In general, Japanese American families drew the cords of community closer, helping out all Japanese in their time of trouble. Kiko Konagamitsu grew up on a farm in southern California where Okies sometime performed migrant labor for his family. His father was careful to watch over other Japanese who were not coping with hard times as well as he was. Kio remembers, "My father had many old-type Oriental feelings about things. If one of his friends had trouble and couldn't afford to have anyone working for him, my father would ask me to go over. I remember once feeling badly. I had worked all day for this man, cleaning lettuce, stacking vegetables. He didn't pay me. My father gave me a real tongue-lashing: 'You're not expected to get paid. He didn't ask you to. *I* asked you to go'" (Terkel 1970, 69).

The generation of Japanese Americans who came of age in the 1930s struggled against the heritage of discrimination and exclusion. In 1929 the Japanese

American Citizens League (JACL) was founded in California, where more than 100 statutes limited the economic and civil rights of the Japanese. The JACL worked to secure civil rights, to end violence against Japanese, and to win the right to naturalized citizenship for their parents, the Issei. For the Nisei, because they had been born in the United States and thus were already citizens, the JACL promoted cultural assimilation, urging Japanese Americans to speak English, to participate in the electoral process, and to affirm their loyalty to the United States. They even urged cooperation with the internment orders that came in 1942 and provided aid and materials to Japanese Americans in the camps. Even so, nearly all the property owned by Japanese in the 1920s and 1930s was lost during their internment.

Mexican Americans in the Southwest

Like the Japanese, Mexicans in the United States had struggled against discrimination for many years before the Great Depression. A fundamental difference in their experience, however, was the proximity of their homeland. Thousands of people of Hispanic heritage lived in the American Southwest when the territory was annexed to the United States in 1848. In the 1910s and 1920s these *tejanos* and *californios* were joined by others brought to the United States as migrant workers. By the 1920s, at least three-quarters of California's 200,000 farm workers were Mexican or Mexican American. Whether old or new members of the Chicano/a community, however, they all experienced legalized discrimination in housing, marriage, judicial matters, and many other aspects of American life. Moreover, vigilante groups like the Texas Rangers, much like the KKK in the South, used physical intimidation to control the Mexican American population.

With the deterioration of the agricultural economy came the deterioration of conditions for Mexican Americans. In Texas, Mexican American sharecroppers met the same fate that African Americans in the Cotton South did; either AAA payments were never shared with them or allotment meant that they suddenly had no more land to farm. Similarly, with hundreds of thousands of whites migrating from the Dust Bowl regions, Mexicans soon found themselves without work in the "factories in the fields." Beginning in the early 1930s and continuing throughout the decade, many whites were calling for the deportation of Mexicans. In the end, deportation orders were passed by both the Texas and California legislatures. More than half a million Mexicans and their American-born children were deported to Mexico in boxcars, cars, and trucks under armed guard. Filipino laborers suffered the same fate when, in 1934, the Tydings-McDuffie Act made the Philippines an independent Asian commonwealth and thus overnight her people became aliens ineligible for immigration to or citizenship in the United States.

Factories in the Fields

Although there were some family farms in California, by the 1930s larger corporate agribusinesses dominated the industry. Located in the valleys near Bakersfield, Salinas, and other inland communities, these huge farms produced immense crops of fruits and vegetables, including many "stoop crops" like asparagus that required difficult cutting and packing in the fields. Having immigrated from Mexico or Asia and encountered discrimination in other sectors of the economy, men, women, and children worked for pennies, long hours in terrific heat. Moreover, owners often set different ethnic groups against each other, particularly as the economy worsened. Mexicans, for example, were asked to work as strikebreakers when Filipinos or Chinese refused to work. The desperation of these times was recorded in two of the United States' most important works of ethnic literature, Ernesto Galarza's *Barrio Boy* (1971) and Carlos Bulosan's *America Is in the Heart* (1946/1974).

An important political exposé of the conditions of work in California was Carey McWilliams's *Factories in the Field,* published in 1939. Because this fact-based work was published in the same year as Steinbeck's *Grapes of Wrath,* it helped to substantiate much of what the novel portrayed. McWilliams took an administrative position in the California state government through which he hoped to push significant reforms, including protections for migratory workers who wished to unionize. Frustrated in his aims, McWilliams ultimately resigned his post, having effectively been fired by Gov. Earl Warren. The issue of working conditions, pay, and unionization for migrant workers has not been resolved to this day. In the 1950s, '60s, and '70s, Cesar Chavez worked for unionization and founded the National Farm Workers Association (NFWA) in 1962. Nevertheless, throughout rural America hundreds of thousands of migrant workers still labor long hours for little pay in searing heat with their children by their sides.

Back to the Land Movement

At the same time that many rural Americans were struggling to survive, many urban Americans decided that a self-sufficient rural life was preferable to the urban, industrial world. The expression of this ideology took different forms in different regions of the United States. In New England, city people moved to Vermont and New Hampshire and tried to live off the land for the first time. Elsewhere university professors and New Deal urban planners led the movement. While the proponents of agrarianism or the back-to-the-land movement did not always see eye to eye, they shared a common nostalgia for a simpler time. Occasionally it was based on simple ignorance of the suffering in rural America. Northeastern back-to-the-land leader Ralph Borsodi wrote, for example, "if you go through the smaller communities of New York and Connecticut you

Filipinos cut lettuce, Salinas, California, 1935. (Library of Congress)

will find no starvation, no evictions, few people who have not got an overcoat or a pair of shoes. And if you go into the farming areas you will not find people starving on the farms. On the contrary. There is suffering, there is deprivation; but in the smaller communities and on the farms, there is not the same kind of being up against it, of not knowing where you are going to sleep tonight or where you are going to get the next meal that you find in cities" (Borsodi 1934)

In the South, these ideals were best expressed through the written works of the "Southern Agrarians," twelve writers and poets associated with Vanderbilt University. They joined together in 1930 to compile their "agrarian manifesto," *I'll Take My Stand*. They wrote, "All the articles bear in the same sense upon the book's title-subject: all tend to support a Southern way of life against what may be called the American or prevailing way; and all as much as agree that the best terms in which to represent the distinction are contained in the phrase, Agrarian *versus* Industrial" (Twelve Southerners 2006, 1). The Southern Agrarians were clearly calling for a return to the culture and traditions of the "Old South." Yet they also critiqued industrialization as a whole, particularly the accompanying hectic pace, emphasis on consumption, and impoverishment of high culture. The theory of agrarianism, on the other hand, "is that the culture of the soil is the best and most sensitive of vocations, and that therefore it should have the economic preference and enlist the maximum number of workers." These writers, among them Robert Penn Warren and John Crowe Ransom, continued their calls for a return to a more pastoral society well into the 1940s.

Greenbelt Communities

Within the New Deal some men and women also admired a self-sufficient, traditional rural life and sought to promote it. Rexford Tugwell, with the active participation of Eleanor Roosevelt, initiated plans for six "green" communities: planned, self-sufficient, rural towns just outside major urban areas where workers could experience a healthier, more nurturing environment. Three of these towns were built: Greenbelt, Maryland; Greendale, Wisconsin; and Greenhills, Ohio. Each was designed to encourage residents to associate with one another and participate in civic life. Thus the towns had interconnected walkways, schools and businesses within walking distances of neighborhoods, and community-based recreational facilities. Downtown areas included daycare centers, grocery stores, and cooperative credit unions. The towns were also meant to promote class and ethnic diversity. In Greenbelt, Maryland, for example, planners set quotas for the number of Protestants, Catholics, and Jews permitted to reside there. More than simply rural towns, then, the Greenbelt communities were planned social experiments, utopias of the mind for New Deal intellectuals.

Like so many New Deal programs, the promise of the Greenbelt communities was hijacked by the planners' ultimate capitulation to local biases and "habits of mind." In Greenbelt, Maryland, few Jewish families were ever admitted. Likewise, in none of the towns were African American families welcomed; families whose mothers worked outside the home were also not permitted to apply. Finally, because cost overruns were so high, the minimum income level of applicants had to be raised, so few if any low-income families benefited from the projects.

The Rural Political Legacy of the 1930s

For rural Americans, the 1930s stood as the hardest times they had ever known. Plummeting crop prices, combined with dust storms, foreclosure sales, and desperate migrations across the continent became the stuff of enduring novels, photographs, and films. In the 1930s, however, they were the daily realities of individual families' lives. While the New Deal's various relief programs aided many farmers and their communities, for others it was simply too little too late. Not surprisingly, farmers who had the opportunity to "cooperate" with the New Deal did so, but often with serious reservations. Along with the New Deal, they carefully considered alternative political groups and parties, including the Farmers Holiday Association, the Southern Tenant Farmers Union, the Communist Party of America, the Save Our Wealth movement, the Non-Partisan League, and many others (see "Social Movements" chapter). A few considered the fascist appeals of openly anti-Semitic, anti-Roosevelt leaders like William Dudley Pelley and Gerald Winrod. When the threat of war added to their fears, rural Americans were quick to form new groups, like the America First Committee, to ensure peace at home.

Thus rural America in the 1930s at times represented one of the weakest pieces of the Roosevelt coalition. Indeed it was not long before some rural counties turned back to Republican candidates on local, state, and national ballots. In South Dakota, for example, the congressional election of 1938 saw the triumph of social and political conservatism over New Deal liberalism. Moreover, for the first time in the state, explicitly anti-Communist language was used to attack the Democratic candidate. By the 1940s, anticommunism would attract the support of many rural whites from the Midwest and Great Plains to the South and California. South Dakota senator Karl Mundt, for example, served as Wisconsin senator Joseph McCarthy's right-hand man during the McCarthy hearings, and remained nearly unassailable in the polls in his home state. When many rural areas of the West and South became the beneficiaries of defense spending in the 1950s and 1960s, anticommunism grew deep economic roots as well.

Rural Americans' turn to the right after the Great Depression is not such a great surprise, however, given the misgivings they had felt about the New Deal from its beginning. Most farmers in the Midwest and on the Great Plains had preferred cost of production to domestic allotment; and even the poorest men and women in the Tennessee Valley had resented "men in suits" telling them how to live. Many did not like or trust the eastern intellectual elite. What they feared about communism was the same thing: a large, powerful centralized government that gave ordinary people no say in their own lives, and no way to survive without it. For an essay contest defining "Americanism," one farmer said that it was "something that grants every individual and every family the right to put himself on his own feet, independent, and self-directing." Another claimed that "Americanism admits of no superior, overlord, king, or dictator" (Stock 1992, 214). Well before the "Reagan Revolution" of 1980 rural people, and rural white men in particular, feared the power of a government grown out of control—whether that was at home or abroad. After the farm crisis of the late 20th century, some would claim retribution through militia organizations, the Posse Comitatus, and individual attacks on federal officials. Others would simply throw their support each November to an emerging coalition of conservative states. While this shift may have compelled some commentators to wonder "what's the matter with Kansas," to the people of Kansas and other rural states, armed with the collective memories of the Great Depression and New Deal years, as well as the continuing impoverishment of the rural economy in postwar America, nothing was "the matter" at all (Frank 2004, passim).

As the Great Depression wore on and the possibility of another war in Europe emerged, many rural Americans, particularly in the Middle West, became vehemently opposed to intervention and they vowed "never again to see the world drenched in blood" (Stock 1992, 212). With the memory of the physical and economic toll of the last world war still fresh in their minds, several peace groups insisted on an investigation into the alleged role played by munitions manufacturers in the Wilson administration's decision to enter the war. Sen. Gerald Nye of North Dakota led the investigation from 1934 until 1936. Like many of his constituents, Nye suspected that "American boys" had been sent to the war not as much for honor as for profit (and Eastern profit at that). He concluded that "giant fortunes [were] carved by men and corporations out of war while millions died" (Stock, 212). Although the committee could never prove wrongdoing by the "merchants of death," Nye left no doubt that he believed that the Wilson administration had been duped. The only winners of that war had been rich financiers and businessmen. He only hoped that such a calamity could never happen again.

Later in the decade, Minnesota-born aviator Charles Lindbergh, a national hero in the 1920s, became the primary spokesman for the America First Committee, a fiercely isolationist organization committed to keeping America out of war. At one point it was said to have 800,000 members, most in Illinois, Iowa, and Minnesota. Members believed that the problems of the Depression had to be solved "first." They also believed that the great oceans that had protected the United States from previous wars would continue to do so. "An Ocean is a formidable barrier, even for modern aircraft," argued Lindbergh (Kennedy 1999, 433). In 1939 when Roosevelt moved to amend the Lend-Lease Agreement, outraged citizens sent more than a million telegrams, letters, and postcards to Washington. After Pearl Harbor, rural Americans were quick to join the Armed Forces and contribute money and materials to the war effort. For many, though, their distrust of the military and its motives would continue well into the cold war. Even more broadly, their distrust of a powerful, centralized government would mark their political and cultural views for the next 60 years.

Biographies

Ned Cobb, 1885–1973

Sharecropper, Organizer

Born in Tallapoosa County, Alabama, in 1885, Ned Cobb, also known as Nate Shaw, lived in the shadow of African American slavery. Cobb's father, a former slave, was often violent and cruel, unable to overcome the legacy of the past. Ned, however, was a fairly successful farmer, due to his extensive understanding of animals and crops, and he became a tenant farmer at a young age. In 1931, the Communist Party came to Alabama to defend African Americans and tenant farmers accused of false crimes. Impressed by the party's similarities to the abolitionists, Cobb joined the Communist Union, which was later called the Share Croppers Union. Cobb continued his life as a sharecropper and lived his life dedicated to the Union. In 1952 the local law enforcement tried to foreclose a house of a friend of Cobb's. The dispute ended with Cobb wounded from a shootout and under arrest. When given the choice between two sentences, one lighter if Cobb would cooperate and give out names of various Union members, the other a heavier jail sentence, Cobb chose the latter. He served thirteen years in prison for being unable to compromise his beliefs. In 1969 Cobb told the story of his life to Theodore Rosengarten, a Harvard scholar. Rosengarten's book, *All God's Dangers: The Life of Nate Shaw,* detailed many of Cobb's life experiences under the pseudonym Nate Shaw.

Morris Llewellyn Cooke, 1872–1960

New Deal Administrator

Cooke was the head of one the New Deal's most successful agencies: The Rural Electrification Administration. Long a political adviser to Roosevelt, he served under FDR on the board of the Power Authority of the State of New York, where he first began the work of bringing electricity to remote rural areas and thus better integrating them into the national economy. Roosevelt appointed Cooke to head the REA in March of 1935. Unlike the Tennessee Valley Authority, which Cooke greatly admired, the REA would not federalize the creation and distribution of power, but would serve as a lender to private groups. He strongly supported the creation of local cooperatives to purchase and distribute power. Cooke also served as chair of both the first and second Great Plains committees and, together with Lewis Gray of the Resettlement Administration, was responsible for much of the content of the final report, *The Future of the Great Plains.*

Morris Llewellyn Cooke, New Deal administrator (1872–1960). (Library of Congress)

William Langer, 1886–1959

North Dakota Governor, U.S. Senator

"Wild Bill Langer" was a highly controversial but enormously popular and successful North Dakota politician, who served as governor of the state from 1933 to 1934 and from 1937 to 1939. Langer went on to serve in the U.S. Senate from 1940 to 1959. He attended the University of North Dakota and Columbia University Law School. He always had the intention of returning to North Dakota to enter politics. He was a member of the Nonpartisan League, a radical branch of the Republican Party that looked out for the interests of farmers and small businessmen in the tradition of the Populist Party of the late 19th century. Thus when hard times hit in the 1930s he aggressively sought to protect the property and the incomes of the common people of his state. He passed an embargo on the sale of wheat until the price reached what activists called the "cost of production." Similarly he ordered an end to all farm foreclosures in the state. As for bankers, he famously said, "Treat the banker like a chicken thief. Shoot him on sight." As popular as he was with rural people, Langer had his share of enemies both among the upper class in the state and in Franklin Roosevelt's administration. In 1934 he was found guilty of fraud for allegedly forcing state employees to buy subscriptions to the *Nonpartisan Leader,* a political publication. He was acquitted of these charges in 1935. In the late 1930s, as a U.S. senator, Langer spoke out fervently against involvement in the European war. In 1945 he voted against the United Nations charter. Langer died in office in 1959. Many North Dakotans cast write-in votes for him long after his death.

Pare Lorentz, 1905–1992

Filmmaker, Social Critic

Lorentz was a critically acclaimed but often controversial documentary filmmaker whose films from the 1930s focused on the environmental impact of the drought on the Great Plains. The best-known of these are *The Plow That Broke the Plains* (1936) and *The River* (1938). In *The Plow That Broke the Plains* he documented the damage to the high plains environment done by plowing and dry farming in the years around World War I. Its score was written by composer Virgil Thomson and uses folk melodies and powerful orchestral accompaniment to signal the seriousness of the problem as well as its connection to the fundamental tenets of American culture. Lorentz spent more than three times what the government had budgeted for the film, sometimes paying expenses himself. The film itself was banned in some western states because local officials understood its meaning to be harshly critical of the men and women who had settled and continued to farm its lands.

Ann Marie Low, 1912–

North Dakota Farm Girl, Teacher

Ann Marie Low was a 16-year-old girl living in the Stony Brook country of central North Dakota at the time of the stock-market crash. She began keeping a diary of her experiences during the Great Depression and kept it for nearly 10 years. In the diary she recorded the work of running a family farm, particularly during an economic and ecological crisis. She also provided an inside view of the kinds of work that women did to help their families in this time. As a teenager, Low worked long hours in the family kitchen, cooking, cleaning, and canning fruits and vegetables from their garden. But she was also an accomplished horsewoman and helped her father and brother Bud in the fields. When she grew older, Low taught school and, by watching each penny, sent as much of her income home as she could. In Stony Brook her family coped with the intrusions and conflicts brought about by the construction of a wildlife refuge by the Civilian Conservation Corps on adjacent property. The family resented these intrusions and laughed at the "city boys'" inability to adjust to the harsh climate. But they also believed that the New Deal workers considered them to be a bunch of "yokels" and their land to have no value. Eventually Low would marry one of these managers, a Massachusetts man who, when he had learned of his assignment, had picked up a map to find out where North Dakota was.

John Steinbeck, 1902–1968

Novelist, Social Critic

Steinbeck was the author of several novels about rural life in the Great Depression, including *In Dubious Battle* (1936), *Of Mice and Men* (1937), and *The Grapes of Wrath* (1939). He portrayed the courage of ordinary people confronted with events larger than themselves. In the novel *In Dubious Battle,* he portrayed the involvement of the Communist Party (which he identified only as "the Party") in the California workers' strikes. In this way he demonstrated his advocacy for the working class in their struggles against the wealthy owners of agribusiness corporations. He also changed the style of much proletarian fiction by including profanity and other coarse language, saying he was tired of working people being portrayed "as some kind of junior college professor." His portrait of the Joad family in *The Grapes of Wrath* became one of the best-known images of the Okie migration to California in the Dust Bowl years. He was awarded the Pulitzer Prize in 1939 for the work. *The Grapes of Wrath,* whose title came from a line in the song "The Battle Hymn of the Republic," was made into an Academy Award–winning film, directed by John Ford and starring Henry Fonda as Tom Joad. Unlike traditional "westerns," Steinbeck's novels portrayed California society as socially and economically stratified. He remains one of the most widely read American authors of the early and mid-20th century.

The photograph that has become known as "Migrant Mother" is one of a series of photographs that Dorothea Lange made in February or March of 1936 in Nipomo, California. Lange was concluding a month's trip photographing migratory farm labor around the state for what was then the Resettlement Administration. The woman, Florence Thompson, was 32 years old and the mother of seven children. (Library of Congress)

Florence Owens Thompson, 1903–1983

Migrant Worker, Mother

Thompson is known as the "Migrant Mother" in Dorothea Lange's famous 1936 photograph of that name, one of the most important and best-known images from the Farm Security Administration's documentary photography project. Thompson was a Cherokee from Oklahoma. She and her husband, Cleo Owens, moved to California in 1924, where she gave birth to seven children. After his death from a high fever in 1932, she moved back to Oklahoma, where she left her newborn son with his grandparents to raise, and then headed back to California to travel with transient families looking for work. In 1936 Thompson and her male companion were traveling down U.S. Highway 101 when the car broke down. It was then that Dorothea Lange happened upon Thompson and her children. She snapped six images and spoke with her briefly about her circumstances. Later, one of Thomson's children would claim that Lange had reported some of the details of their lives incorrectly, having perhaps gotten them mixed up with another poor family. Thompson died in 1983, but was remembered as the "migrant mother" on her tombstone.

M. L. Wilson, 1885–1969

Agricultural Economist, New Deal Administrator

Together with Henry Wallace and Raymond Motley, Wilson was one of the architects of the New Deal's domestic allotment program, as articulated in the Agricultural Adjustment Act. Wilson, an agricultural economist at Montana State University, was interested in the centralization of the agricultural economy beginning in the 1920s. He was also convinced that overproduction was the key problem which kept farmers from reaching economic parity in income level with urban Americans. He first came to Washington in the winter of 1932, during the "lame duck" period between Hoover's and Roosevelt's administrations. Unable to get cooperation from Congress at that time, he left in disgust, only to return when the AAA got underway. Wilson, like many others in the AAA, was influenced by the strategies of collectivization being developed in the USSR. He visited a collectivist farm in the 1930s. Like others in the Department of Agriculture he would have considered himself an agrarian fundamentalist, believing strongly in both the economic and cultural importance of having a strong, family-farm-based agricultural sector. Nevertheless he believed that modernization and centralization were the keys to a healthy economic future.

References and Further Readings

Adams, J. 1994. *The Transformation of Rural Life: Southern Illinois, 1890–1990.* Chapel Hill: University of North Carolina Press.

Bernstein, B. 1968. *Toward a New Past: Dissenting Essays in American History.* New York: Random House.

Bonnefield, P. 1979. *The Dust Bowl: Men, Dirt, and Depression.* Albuquerque: University of New Mexico Press.

Borsodi, R. 1934. "Subsistence Homesteads," *Survey Graphic* 23 (June): 11.

Bulosan, C. 1946/1974. *America Is in the Heart: A Personal History.* Seattle: University of Washington Press.

Cannon, B. 2004. *Remaking the Agrarian Dream: The New Deal's Rural Resettlement Program in the Mountain West.* Albuquerque: University of New Mexico Press.

Conrad, D. 1965. *The Forgotten Farmers: The Story of Sharecroppers in the New Deal.* Urbana: University of Illinois Press.

Cunfer, G. 2005. *On the Great Plains: Agriculture and Environment.* College Station: Texas A&M University Press.

Curtis, J. 1989. *Mind's Eye, Mind's Truth: FSA Photography Reconsidered.* Philadelphia: Temple University Press.

Danbom, D. 1995. *Born in the Country: A History of Rural America.* Baltimore: Johns Hopkins University Press.

Davis, K. 1986. *FDR: The New Deal Years, 1933–1937.* New York: Random House.

Evans, W., and J. Agee. 1939/1988. *Let Us Now Praise Famous Men.* Boston: Houghton Mifflin.

Fink, D. 1992. *Agrarian Women: Wives and Mothers in Rural Nebraska, 1880–1940.* Chapel Hill: University of North Carolina Press.

Fitzgerald, D. 2001. "Accounting for Change: Farmers and the Modernizing State." In *The Countryside in the Age of the Modern State: Political Histories of Modern America,* ed. C. Stock and R. Johnston, 189–212. Ithaca, NY: Cornell University Press.

Frank, T. 2004. *What's the Matter with Kansas: How Conservatives Won the Heart of America.* New York: Metropolitan Books.

The Future of the Great Plains: Report of the Great Plains Committee. 1936. Washington, DC: Government Printing Office.

Ganzel, B. 1984. *Dust Bowl Descent.* Lincoln: University of Nebraska Press.

Ganzel, B. 2003a. "Farming in the 1930s." Wessel's Living History Farm, http://www.livinghistoryfarm.org/farminginthe30s/farminginthe1930s.html.

Ganzel, B. 2003b. "Parity." Wessel's Living History Farm, http://www.livinghistoryfarm.org/farminginthe30s/farminginthe1930s.html.

Galarza, E. 1971. *Barrio Boy.* South Bend, IL: University of Notre Dame Press.

Gregory, J. 1989. *American Exodus: The Dust Bowl Migration and Okie Culture in California.* New York: Oxford University Press.

"Growing a Nation: The History of American Agriculture." Agriculture in the Classroom Web site. http://www.agclassroom.org/gan/index.html.

Harris, T. 1995. "Sharecropping." In *The Oxford Companion to Women's Writing in the United States,* ed. Cathy N. Davidson and Linda Wagner-Martin. New York: Oxford University Press. Online at www.english.uiuc.edu/maps/poets/a_f/brown/sharecropping.html.

Hickok, L. 1934. "Letters from the Field: Lorena Hickok Reports on the State of the Nation." New Deal Network.2003, http://newdeal.feri.org.

Hurt, R. D.. 1981. *The Dust Bowl: An Agricultural and Social History.* Chicago: Nelson-Hall.

Jellison, K. 2001. "An 'Enviable Tradition' of Patriarchy: New Deal Investigations of Women's Work in the Amish Farm Family." In *The Countryside in the Age of the Modern State: Political Histories of Modern America,* ed. C. and R. Johnston, 240–257. Ithaca, NY: Cornell University Press.

Kelley, R. 1990. *Hammer and Hoe: Alabama Communists during the Great Depression.* Chapel Hill: University of North Carolina Press.

Kennedy, D. 1999. *Freedom from Fear: The American People in Depression and War.* The Oxford History of the United States. New York: Oxford University Press.

Lookingbill, B. 2001. *Dust Bowl USA: Depression America and the Ecological Imagination, 1929–1941.* Athens: Ohio University Press.

Lorentz, P. 1936. *The Plow That Broke the Plains.* Washington, DC: Resettlement Administration.

Low, A. 1984. *Dust Bowl Diary.* Lincoln: University of Nebraska Press.

Lowitt, R. 1984. *The New Deal and the West.* Bloomington: Indiana University Press.

Lowitt, R., and M. Beasley, eds. 1981. *One-Third of a Nation: Lorena Hickok Reports on the Great Depression.* Urbana: University of Illinois Press.

McElvaine, R. 1984. *The Great Depression: America 1929–1941.* New York: Random House.

McElvaine, R., ed. 1983. *Down and Out in the Great Depression: Letters from the Forgotten Man.* Chapel Hill: University of North Carolina Press.

McWilliams, C. 1939/2000. *Factories in the Field: The Story of Migratory Farm Labor in California.* Berkeley: University of California Press.

Morgan, D. 1992. *Rising in the West: The True Story of an "Okie" Family from the Great Depression through the Reagan Years.* New York: Knopf.

Morlan, R. 1985. *Political Prairie Fire: A History of the Nonpartisan League, 1915–1922.* Reprint. St. Paul: Minnesota Historical Society Press.

Olsen, T. 1974/2000. *Yonnondio: From the Thirties.* Lincoln: University of Nebraska Press.

Ortiz, R. 1997. *Red Dirt: Growing Up Okie.* New York: Verso.

Saloutos, T. 1982. *The American Farmer and the New Deal.* Ames: Iowa State University Press.

Scearce, R. 1939. "What REA Service Means to Our Farm Home." *Rural Electrification News* (March). Online at http://newdeal.feri.org/tva/tva23.html.

Schlesinger, A. 1960. *The Politics of Upheaval.* Boston: Houghton Mifflin.

Stock, C. 1992. *Main Street in Crisis: The Great Depression and the Old Middle Class on the Northern Plains.* Chapel Hill: University of North Carolina Press.

Stock, C. 1997. *Rural Radicals: From Bacon's Rebellion to the Oklahoma City Bombing.* New York: Penguin.

Stock, C., and R. Johnston, eds. 2001. *The Countryside in the Age of the Modern State: Political Histories of Rural America.* Ithaca, NY: Cornell University Press.

Takaki, R. 1989. *Strangers from a Different Shore: A History of Asian Americans.* New York: Penguin.

Terkel, S. 1970. *Hard Times: An Oral History of the Great Depression.* New York: Avon Books.

Twelve Southerners. 1930/2006. *I'll Take My Stand: An Agrarian Manifesto*. Baton Rouge: Louisiana State University Press.

Wormser, R. "Biography of Ned Cobb." *Chicken Bones: A Journal for Literary and Artistic African-American Themes,* http://www.nathanielturner.com/allgodsdangersnateshaw3.html.

Worster, D. 1982. *Dust Bowl: The Southern Plains in the 1930s*. New York: Oxford University Press.

Culture of the 1930s

By Kathy M. Newman

Overview

The 1930s was the era when the very idea of "culture" began to become redefined. Anthropologists like Ruth Benedict and Franz Boaz, who had been taught that "culture" meant "high culture"—esteemed forms, like opera, classical music, and great literature—began to define *culture* as the entire way of life of a people: their institutions, stories, songs, habits, rituals, beliefs, and ideas about themselves. This chapter uses the era's own, anthropological definition of culture, treating the culture of the 1930s as a concoction of all the cartoons, games, fads, songs, trends, films, plays, paintings, poems, novels, and manifestos that were produced by or enjoyed by Americans during the Great Depression.

The culture of the 1930s had to manage the deep tensions of the era produced by the economic crisis that shaped the lives of so many ordinary people. On the one hand, out-of-work Americans had more "leisure" time than ever before. However, if they used that "leisure" unproductively, they risked falling deeper into debt or, worse still, into a life of crime. In another ironic twist, mass culture and mass advertising reached new heights during the 1930s, especially via radio, even though Americans had less to spend than ever before. The contrast between what Americans could buy and what they could afford was painful for many families.

Throughout the 1930s many forms of popular culture were influenced by a new spirit of left politics—a phenomenon that historian Michael Denning has called the "Cultural Front." First- and second-generation immigrants from Southern and Eastern Europe, Latin America, and Asia—as well as African American migrants from the South to the northern cities—formed a new generation of politically left artists, writers, musicians, playwrights, actors, filmmakers, and photographers who were committed to the rebirth of a more democratic American society; they were committed to antiracism, union rights for workers, women's rights, antifascism, and, in many cases, the Communist Party at home and abroad.

At the same time, the 1930s saw the rise of a new corporate culture. Advertisers cluttered the airwaves with radio ads for Listerine, Pepsodent, ginger ale, Nervine (a sleeping pill), laxatives, soap, Fleishmann's yeast, Gillette razors, and products that were brand-new in the 1930s, like Twinkies, Sugar Daddy suckers and the candy bar Pay Day. Conservative radio commentators were also very popular, including the anti-Semitic radio priest Father Coughlin and the British-born antilabor demagogue Boake Carter.

Youth culture, which had its roots in the jazz craze of the Roaring Twenties, also dominated in the 1930s. White and African American youths alike danced the "Lindy hop" (a dance that took its name from the flying stylings of pilot Charles Lindbergh) to the big band sounds of white bands like the one led by Benny Goodman and African American bands like the ones led by Duke Ellington and Count Basie. Young adults also tried to earn extra cash by competing in multiday bike races, roller derbies, and dance marathons. The dance marathon record was set in 1934 by actress June Havoc and Elmer Dupree; they danced for 3,600 hours, or 21 weeks, taking only one 15-minute break after every hour of dancing. They shared the cash prize of $40.00. More students attended college in the 1930s than at any previous time in American history, and bizarre fads swept college campuses, like the fad of goldfish swallowing. It started as a bet between a couple of Harvard freshmen in 1939; Lothrop Withington swallowed one goldfish, and soon college men across the country were trying to better his record. It became so controversial that the Massachusetts state legislature tried to outlaw it, and the U.S. Public Health service warned of the risk of contracting tapeworms.

Though it was a decade of great hardship for many, women and minorities gained new respect for their unique accomplishments. Amelia Earhart, the first woman to make a solo airplane flight across the Atlantic, became one of the heroes of the decade; her celebrity turned to tragedy, however, when near the end of a trip, her plane disappeared over the Pacific Ocean and she was never seen or heard from again. "Women must try to do things as men have tried. When they fail their failure must be a challenge to others," she wrote in a letter to her husband, George Putnam, before that fatal flight (Earhart 1937). Another notable woman from the 1930s, Babe Didrikson, excelled in basketball, track and field, and golf. While she did not achieve her ambition to become the "greatest athlete who ever lived," the Associated Press voted her the "Greatest Female Athlete of the first half of the 20th century."

For African Americans it was also a decade of outstanding achievement. Americans, African American and white, rooted for African American track-and-field star Jesse Owens when he beat his white competitors at the 1936 Olympics, which were held in Nazi Germany. Owens won the gold in the 100-meter dash, the 200-meter dash, and the broad jump. Joe Louis also embodied the achievement and the pride of the African American community when, in 1935, he knocked out the former world heavyweight champion, Primo Carnera, and two other fighters, Max Baer and Paolino Uzcudun, neither of whom had been knocked out before. Louis lost a fight in 1936 to the German fighter Max Schmeling, who had been linked to the Nazi Party, even though he helped Jewish friends escape the death camps in Nazi Germany. At their rematch in 1938 Louis knocked out Schmeling in the first round. In the performing arts, African American singers like Billie Holiday and Ella Fitzgerald became renowned jazz performers, and the performers Lena Horne and Ethel Waters started their film careers with films like *The Gift of Gab* (1934) and *The Duke Is Tops* (1938).

Timeline

1930 The practice of apple peddling in urban areas begins to spread.

1931 African American newspaper, the *Pittsburgh Courier,* organizes boycott of the "blackface" radio comedy *Amos 'n' Andy.*

Openly gay British director James Whale makes the monster film *Frankenstein.*

The Empire State Building is completed.

Chinese actress Anna Mae Wong stars in *Daughter of the Dragon.*

1932 FDR uses popular song "Happy Days Are Here Again" in his 1932 presidential campaign.

British-born populist radio commentator Boake Carter attracts notoriety when he broadcasts round-the-clock updates on the kidnapping of Charles Lindbergh's baby from the Stacy Trent Hotel in New Jersey.

Gangster film *Scarface: The Shame of a Nation* debuts.

Duke Ellington records "It Don't Mean a Thing if It Ain't Got That Swing."

1933 Prohibition is repealed, making beer, wine, and hard liquor legal again.

The Continental Baking Company in Indianapolis introduces the Hostess "Twinkie."

Arthur Kallet's best-selling consumer activist tract, *100,000,000 Guinea Pigs: Dangers in Everyday Foods, Drugs and Cosmetics,* is published.

Frank Capra makes a movie about an elderly apple peddler, "Apple Annie," called *Lady for a Day.*

What would become the first long-running soap opera, *The Romance of Helen Trent,* debuts.

President Roosevelt broadcasts the first of his "fireside chats."

King Kong, a special-effects movie masterpiece, is released.

1934 June Havoc and Elmer Dupree set dance marathon record of 3,600 hours.

Patterns of Culture by anthropologist Ruth Benedict is published.

African American singer/movie star Ethel Waters has her first starring role in *The Gift of Gab.*

Chicago Tribune debuts the cartoon *Apple Mary* by Martha Orr.

Under the leadership of Joseph Breen, the federal government begins to enforce the Production Code, a set of censorship guidelines for motion pictures.

Nelson Rockefeller destroys the Diego Rivera mural he had commissioned, *Man at the Crossroads,* after Rivera refuses to remove the mural's portrait of Lenin.

1935 Young dancer Frankie Manning creates the aerial swing dance style that becomes known as the "Lindy hop" (after pilot Charles Lindbergh) at the Savoy Ballroom in Harlem.

Parker Brothers buys rights to produce the board game Monopoly, making copyright holder Charles Darrow the first board-game millionaire.

Establishment of the Works Project Administration which in turn creates the Federal Theater Project, the Federal Writers Project, and other Federal Arts initiatives.

The radio talent contest *Major Bowes Amateur Hour* begins.

The Chicago Cubs become the first major-league baseball team to broadcast their games via the radio.

1936	African American track and field phenomenon Jesse Owens challenges white supremacist ideology, winning four gold medals at the Olympics held in Nazi Germany.
	Charlie Chaplin's film classic, *Modern Times,* debuts.
	Formation of the Indian Actors' Association, a group dedicated to improving the representation of the Hollywood Native American Indian.
	Carl Sandburg publishes his epic poem, *The People, Yes.*
	Life magazine publishes its first issue, selling for 10 cents an issue.
	The Negro Unit of the Federal Theater Project presents a melodrama set in a Florida swamp, *Turpentine.*
1937	Radio reporter Herbert Morrison broadcasts the phrase, "Oh the humanity," upon watching the explosion of the *Hindenburg*.
	Consumer activist Ruth Brindze's hard-hitting critique of commercial radio, *Not to Be Broadcast,* is published.
	You Have Seen Their Faces, a photo collection of southern subjects by Margaret Bourke-White (photos) and Erskine Caldwell (text), is published.
1938	Swing music festival at Randall's Island Park in Manhattan includes interracial couples.
	African American boxer Joe Louis knocks out German champion Max Schmeling.
	African American singer/movie star Lena Horne gets her first screen role in *The Duke Is Tops.*
	Orson Welles conducts a radio broadcast of H. G. Wells's *The War of the Worlds,* causing a nationwide panic.
	The performance of Federal Theater Project's musical, *The Cradle Will Rock,* is shut down. While the government cites financial difficulties, FTP participants suspect that conservative politics are at work and stage an impromptu production of the musical.
	Cuban-born artist Carlos Lopez paints *Plymouth Trail,* a mural for the Plymouth, Michigan, post office.
1939	Harvard freshman Lothrop Withington swallows a goldfish and starts a national trend in goldfish swallowing that sweeps college campuses.

Pepsi unveils first "stand-alone" radio jingle.

Filmmaker Frank Capra debuts Jimmy Stewart classic, *Mr. Smith Goes to Washington*.

Popular Culture and the Great Depression

The End of Prohibition and the New Deal Cocktail

The repeal of Prohibition marked the end of the ousted Hoover administration and the beginning of Franklin Delano Roosevelt's. On March 22, 1933, President Roosevelt signed the Twenty-first Amendment, thus making wine, beer, and hard liquor legal again; nine months later, on December 5, 1933, after Utah ratified the amendment, Americans in most states were free to drink alcohol legally for the first time in 14 years. According to some accounts, Americans toasted each other with a "New Deal Cocktail," a bracing combination of Bourbon whiskey, Amer Picon (a bitter cordial), a dash of sugar, and orange peel over ice ("'Lynching' in Broadway" 1933).

According to historian Lewis Erenberg, the repeal of Prohibition lifted the urban entertainment industry out of the early Depression-era doldrums it had been suffering. In New York, according to *Variety,* there were "more niteries, pubs, taverns, roadside inns, large and small cafes, hotels and nite spots offering entertainment than there were speakeasies" during Prohibition. Even in smaller cities like Cleveland, Boston, Pittsburgh, St. Louis, and Denver, repeal produced a "renaissance of nite life." According to Erenberg, nightclub culture spread to cities as diverse as Seattle, Salt Lake City, Omaha, Akron, Albany, and Buffalo. Even small Pennsylvania towns like Allentown and Easton began to open nightclubs that put on regular floor shows for eager middle-class patrons (Erenberg 1986, 765).

Ironically, with the new spread of nightclub culture, going out on the town became a respectable, middle-class activity. In the post-Prohibition song "Cocktails for Two," drinking was represented as a civilized ritual, rather than an illicit, underground activity:

In some secluded rendezvous
That overlooks the avenue
With someone sharing a delightful chat
Of this and that and cocktails for two.

The repeal of Prohibition also marked a new, if temporary optimism about the state of American culture. The song composed by Milton Ager and Jack Yellen in 1929, "Happy Days Are Here Again," surged in popularity after Roosevelt used it in his 1932 campaign. "Happy Days Are Here Again" captured the spirit of dogged optimism embraced by some—even as they were facing the worst economic crisis in American history.

Representing the Depression

One of the most iconic images from the Great Depression was the image of a man selling apples out of a cart on the street corner. The photographs usually depicted a man, looking somewhat shabby, wearing a coat and hat, and standing abjectly next to a cart of apples. There was usually a sign that read "Apples, 5 cents."

Apple peddling was a relatively short-lived phenomenon at the start of the 1930s, but the image of the apple peddler grew into one of the most remembered images of the period. The trend started in the early years of the Depression, in 1929 and 1930, when apple growers in Washington State and Oregon produced more apples than they could sell. In the fall of 1930, during "National Apple Week," Joseph Sicker of the International Apple Shippers Association decided to turn the apple surplus into a relief system for the growing armies of unemployed. Starting in the fall of 1930 a hard-luck man or woman could buy a crate of 100 apples for $2.00 (often on credit), and sell the apples for 5 cents apiece, for a possible profit of $3.00. In the fall of 1931 there were more than 4,000 apple peddlers on the streets of New York City alone ("Denies Apple Men Profit on Jobless" 1930, 4, and "Police to Bar Apple Vendors from Midtown" 1931, 26).

A man sells apples on the street in Washington, D.C., during the Great Depression. (Library of Congress)

By 1932 the practice of apple peddling had all but died out. But the image began to take on a life of its own in popular culture. In 1933 the movie director Frank Capra transformed the corner apple seller from a "forgotten man" to a courageous older woman named "Apple Annie." His film, *Lady for Day,* tells the story of an apple peddler who tells her daughter living in Spain that she is a lady of great wealth. When the daughter plans a trip to see her mother in America, Apple Annie enlists the help of her mob buddy, "Dave the Dude," to trick her daughter into thinking she is truly wealthy. Dave the Dude sets her up with fancy clothes in a ritzy hotel, Cinderella style, for one night. The scheme goes awry, but mother and daughter reconcile in a happy ending. After all, this is the same Frank Capra who made the Christmas Eve classic *It's a Wonderful Life*.

In 1934 Martha Orr, the niece of an editorial cartoonist for the *Chicago Tribune,* created the comic strip *Apple Mary*. Probably based on Capra's Apple Annie, Apple Mary was an frumpy old lady who sold apples from a pushcart for 5 cents apiece; she wore a black, crushed velvet hat and a checkered overcoat, and she carried a neat, brown pocketbook with a short handle over the crook in her arm. Apple Mary also had a crippled grandson, Dennie, with whom she schemed to solve crimes and bring joy into the lives of those brought down by economic hardship.

The popular culture of the 1930s was inextricably linked to the economic hardship that faced so many during the Great Depression. In this first example, the destitute man or woman on the street corner, selling apples for a nickel, became transformed into the plucky Apple Annie and the sentimental, good-hearted Apple Mary. But popular culture did not merely "reflect" the economic conditions of the time—popular culture also helped to shape the reality of the 1930s. Jobless apple sellers, who probably did not make a very good living from their apple peddling, became icons of self-reliance when they were transformed into photographic images, movie characters, and comic-strip heroines. When the creators of popular culture in the 1930s transformed the economic hardship around them into stories, songs, comic strips, films, athletic competitions, plays, photographs, and radio programs, they changed the way Americans thought about themselves. They also changed the way we look back on the period.

Unemployment and the "Problem" of Leisure

If the 1920s was marked by a revolution in prosperity, participation in mass leisure and mass consumption, especially for middle-class Americans, in the 1930s leisure became a "problem." Americans had more time on their hands, not because they had more disposable income, but because more and more of them—especially working-class men—were out of work. The icon of the apple peddler was replaced with a new image, documented in photographs and cartoons, of ragged men and women standing in breadlines, or displaced midwestern farmers taking their families in broken-down jalopies to California to look for migrant farm work. The anxiety about the "leisure" of the newly unemployed peaked in the summer of 1932, when unemployed veterans still waiting for a veteran's bonus promised by the Hoover administration began trekking across the country to camp out in Washington, D.C. These "bonus marchers" drew visible, if uncomfortable attention to the twin problems of leisure and unemployment (see "Experiences of the Early Depression" chapter).

With Franklin Delano Roosevelt at the helm, the federal government began to see the problem of idle hands as a national concern, and the provisions of the New Deal included plans for organized leisure and recreation. The Works Project Administration (WPA) and other programs of the New Deal created community theater groups, sports leagues, after-school programs for kids, summer camps, and recreation centers for workers. According to historian Susan Currell, by 1938, "employment on recreation projects averaged thirty-eight thousand people . . . in every state apart from Maine and in more than half of the three thousand counties of the country" (Currell 2006, 51).

New magazines, like *Hobby, Leisure,* and *Recreation,* helped to promote this new national culture of "productive" leisure. Cheap, stay-at-home forms of recreation, like board games, bridge, and bingo, also became popular. Government officials preferred folk dancing and home crafts, hobbies and softball leagues, to the more "suspect" forms of leisure like movie-going and dance halls. Nonetheless, movie-going was ranked the third most popular form of leisure during the Depression, following only newspaper reading and radio listening. In the mid-1930s it was estimated that 77 million Americans attended at least one movie per week, and 36 percent of those in attendance were children (Currell 2006, 126). Officials also worried about the corruptive potential of roadhouse dancing and "taxi dance halls," where professional dancers, usually women, were paid 10 cents a dance to "teach" their male partners how to swing.

Monopoly and Other Fads

As Parker Brothers lore would have it, an unemployed salesman from Germantown, Pennsylvania, Charles Darrow, asked the game company to consider mass-marketing his homemade board game, Monopoly. Parker Brothers began marketing the game in 1935, and by 1936 Parker Brothers was making 20,000 sets of the game per week. Charles Darrow soon became a millionaire—the first game designer ever to earn this much money.

Of course, the real story of Monopoly is nearly as intriguing and political as the game itself. In 1904 a young Quaker woman, Lizzie Magie, was granted a patent for a board game she called "The Landlord's Game." At the time she invented her game, Magie was a new member of a growing antirent movement pioneered by the charismatic Henry George, who believed that land was a "gift of nature" and should not be owned by a few and rented by many. He also believed that all taxes except for property taxes should be abolished. Magie's game reflected George's critique of the system of "rentier capitalism"—a system in which property ownership leads to the increasing concentration of capital in the hands of an elite few. By 1924 Magie had moved to Chicago and secured a

Yo-yo competition, 1932. (Hulton-Deutsch Collection/Corbis)

second patent for her game. More interested in education than in profit, she did not enforce her patent, and thus an underground group of game fanatics, made up especially of college students, passed homemade copies of Magie's game from player to player (Kennedy 2004, 8–12).

Through a network of college roommates, Quakers, and neighbors, Charles Darrow was introduced to "The Landlord's Game," which had come to be called "Monopoly," in 1931. He showed a keen interest in the game, and he made copies of the rules as well as his own version of the board. Excited about the commercial possibilities, Darrow approached Milton Bradley and Parker Brothers. When both companies refused to mass-produce the game in 1934, Darrow struck out on his own, producing 5,000 copies with the help of a friend. The first copies were sold at such toy store chains as F. A. O. Schwartz. Eventually, after the independent success of the game, Parker Brothers bought the game from Darrow and offered him a royalty as well.

The game of Monopoly represented the many contradictions that characterized the popular culture of the 1930s. On the one hand the game had its origins in the antimonopolistic culture of the Gilded Age; the game offered a harsh critique of the kind of monopoly capitalism that had played a role in the stock-market crash of 1929. On the other hand, as the game evolved, players learned that monopoly was the winning strategy: the goal of the game was to collect as much rent as one could, even if it meant bankrupting other players.

Another toy sensation of the 1930s was the yo-yo, popularized by a Filipino immigrant, Pedro Flores. The word for yo-yo comes from a word in the Tagalog language meaning "come back." According to historians William Young and Nancy Young, Filipino yo-yo experts were hired to "hang out" in school yards demonstrating their yo-yo virtuosity in order to tempt prospective buyers. Other fads of the decade included stamp collecting, miniature golf (especially popular among Hollywood celebrities in the kitschy landscape of the sprawling city of Los Angeles), the zipper (a low-cost alternative to buttons), and drive-in movie theaters (Young and Young 2002, 129).

Consumer Culture and the Culture of the Airwaves

In the 1930s radio emerged to become the dominant medium in American life. By the end of the decade more Americans were likely to own a radio than they were to own a phonograph, a telephone, a newspaper subscription, or a magazine subscription. Radio even trumped the movies: when Americans were asked, "Which would it be more difficult for you to give up, your radio, or going to the movies?" most Americans said they would rather give up going to the movies than part with their beloved radios. During the Depression Americans had a fierce appreciation for entertainment that didn't cost them very much; radio manufacturers like Philco made small, table-top radio receivers that were cheap enough that even the lowest-paid workers could buy one for their families (between $20 and $30), thus making the radio one of the most ubiquitous appliances of the decade.

Popular radio programming reflected the medium's broad appeal. On the working class end of the scale, popular programs included *National Barn Dance,* a hillbilly variety show that was broadcast out of Chicago, *Major Bowes Amateur Hour,* an amateur performance competition (in which the listeners voted for their favorites via postcard), and the newscasts of Boake Carter, a British-born commentator with a large working-class following (even though his political perspective was decidedly antiunion). Middle-class and elite listeners preferred shows like *The Philadelphia Orchestra* and the *General Motor Symphony.* Shows that appealed to all income groups included *Amos 'n' Andy,* a comedy about African American migrants to the big city written and voiced by the white performers Freeman Gosden and Charles Correll; stand-up comedy performers, like Jack Benny and Fred Allen; and soap operas like *Ma Perkins* (the story of an American mother who owned and operated a lumber yard), *The Romance of Helen Trent* (about a woman "over the age of 35" who could still find romance), and *Stella Dallas* (the trials of an impoverished woman who renounced her daughter so that her daughter could marry a rich man). The "soap" in the nickname "soap opera" came from the fact that most daytime programming was sponsored by Procter and Gamble—a company best known for its many soap products. Radio soaps were also called "washboard weepers" since housewives were known to "weep" over their daytime dramas while doing the laundry (Newman 2004, 112–123).

The fact that we know which income groups preferred which shows reflects the fact that modern audience research came of age in the 1930s. The newly formed radio networks, NBC and CBS, collaborated with university professors to produce studies on the "psychology of radio," so that advertisers could learn how to sell specific products to specific demographic groups. Researchers divided the audience into four income categories, but also into groups defined by gender, age, religion, and region. Researchers learned that radio was a more intimate medium for audiences than print or film, giving listeners an emotional connection, what the novelist John Dos Passos called the "youandyouandyou." President Roosevelt capitalized on the intimacy of the medium when he started his fireside chats in 1933, a series of radio addresses designed to calm—and inspire—Americans, giving them a greater feeling of togetherness and responsibility. Studies from the period also showed that radio had an awesome power to create a sense of group identity. Ratings for particular programs were established by several competing companies including C. E. Hooper (who used telephone surveys to determine program popularity), and the ultimately triumphant Nielsen company, which used personal interviews, listener diaries, and grocery-store surveys (Newman 2004, 17–51).

Radio quickly became the medium that Americans turned to for news and sports; radio's powerful "nowness" made it well suited to time-sensitive events. In 1935 the Chicago Cubs began to broadcast all of their games over the radio; other big-market teams like the New York Giants, the Brooklyn Dodgers, and the New York Yankees followed suit in 1938. Radio broadcasting also played an increasing role in determining how national and international crises would be covered; when the famous aviator Charles Lindbergh's infant son was kidnapped in March of 1932, broadcasters like Boake Carter camped out at the Stacy Trent Hotel in Trenton, New Jersey (near the Lindbergh home), and broadcast updates about the kidnapping around the clock. In another famous broadcast, radio reporter Herbert Morrison narrated the explosion of the *Hindenburg,* a hydrogen-filled zeppelin, as he witnessed it blow up during a landing in New Jersey on May 6, 1937. The explosion killed 36 of the 97 crew members and passengers aboard. Morrison was making a report that would not air until the next day on Chicago radio station WLS. His report, laden with emotion, became one of the most famous recordings in 20th-century history: "it burst into flames . . . oh my, get out of the way please . . . this is one of the worst catastrophes in the world. . . . oh the humanity!"

Radio increasingly brought the world, and especially the specter of war in Europe, closer to home. Newscasters like H. V. Kaltenborn and Edward R. Murrow offered Americans up-to-the minute coverage of the German invasions of Czechoslovakia and Austria in 1938. Kaltenborn's commentary was so full of anti-Nazi commentary that German-American and Catholic listeners wrote to Kaltenborn's sponsor, General Mills, with the complaint that the "Gold Medal Flour" that sponsored Kaltenborn's news broadcasts was "tainted" with anti-German and anti-Catholic sentiment. General Mills actually fired Kaltenborn over the controversy—despite the fact that he was one of the most popular radio newsmen in the country. Pure Oil soon picked up Kaltenborn's contract, and he was restored to the airwaves. Even more famous than Kaltenborn, CBS radio reporter Edward R. Murrow became associated with the opening line of his newscast when he began broadcasting from the European front: "*This* is London."

The gravity of broadcasters like Murrow and Kaltenborn became subject to parody later in 1938 when the young prankster/radio genius Orson Welles orchestrated one of the most infamous media hoaxes of all time. On the eve of Halloween, October 30, 1938, Orson Welles's *Mercury Theatre on the Air* began its weekly program with sounds of an orchestra playing a tango. Twelve minutes into the program, when Welles knew that listeners would be turning the dial from the usually dull opera portion of the popular *Edward Bergen Show,* the orchestra music was interrupted by a seemingly real radio reporter in Grover's Mill, New Jersey, who claimed that strange alien canisters had fallen to earth and were beginning to arise and terrorize the citizens of the eastern seaboard. The radio actors who performed the play, including Welles himself, used the serious tone of reporters like Kaltenborn and Murrow, and the emotionally charged style of *Hindenburg* witness Morrison, to create the sense that the alien invasion was being witnessed firsthand. The radio play of the phony invasion, adapted by writer Howard Koch from H. G. Wells's novel *The War of the Worlds,* fooled thousands, and possibly millions of listeners into thinking that America was being attacked by giant, vicious invaders. And, because of the specter of Nazi aggression in Europe, many listeners assumed that America was being attacked by Germans, not by Martians. The radio version of *The War of the Worlds* offered an unsettling echo of the actual world war that was threatening across the Atlantic. And it also raised the question: was radio becoming too powerful?

Controversy over *Amos 'n' Andy*

On March 19, 1928, two former vaudevillians, the white comedians Freeman Gosden and Charles Correll, broadcast the first episode of their "blackface" radio comedy, *Amos 'n' Andy,* over Chicago radio station WMAQ. In 1929 the series was picked up by the NBC network, with the sponsor Pepsodent toothpaste, and, according to historian Melvin Patrick Ely, sales of radio sets "soared during the months of *Amos 'n' Andy*'s debut." By 1930 *Amos 'n' Andy* was the most popular program on the radio. The show soon spawned several comic books, a movie (starring Gosden and Correll in blackface), a candy bar, toys, games, and dozens of other marketing tie-ins. Store merchants, restaurants, and even movie theaters broadcast a new episode of the show six nights a week at 7:00 p.m. so as not to lose customers, who were likely to rush home to hear the show. *Amos 'n' Andy* continued to air for more than 30 years. Though in its later years *Amos 'n' Andy* was broadcast once a week, during radio's "Golden Age" new 15-minute episodes of *Amos 'n' Andy* were broadcast every day.

Freeman Gosden and Charles Correll, the radio team of Amos 'n' Andy in "blackface." *(Bettmann/Corbis)*

Amos 'n' Andy was the story of two hapless African Americans who had migrated to Chicago from Atlanta, Georgia, and who had trouble adjusting to the big city. Amos was the more upstanding of the two; Andy, fitting the 19th-century "coon" stereotype, was more conniving, low-down, lustful, and shifty. Together they ran a small business, the Fresh Air Taxi Cab Company. Their speech was full of comic malapropisms, like "I'se regusted" (I'm disgusted) and "mulsify" (multiply). At the height of the show's popularity, from 1930 to 1931, Andy was engaged to a beautiful hairdresser in her mid-forties, Madame Queen, who worked across the street from the taxi-cab company. Andy spent most of his engagement trying to come up with reasons to postpone his upcoming wedding. In one dialogue, Andy reads to Amos his list of reasons to postpone the wedding:

Andy Well, de fust one dat popped in my head don't mean nuthin' but I put it down. No. 1— "I don't feel like gittin' married."

Amos Yeh, dat's great. Dat ought to be enough right dere. You must-a strained yo'self thinkin' o' dat one, didn't yo'?

Andy Don't git sarcastic now, or I won't read yo' nuthin'.

Amos	Go on, read 'em to me. If dey ain't no better dan dat one though you might as well tear up de list.
Andy	No. 2——"De repression is on, an' it's gonna git bettah 'round March."
Amos	Whut else yo' got? (Correll and Gosden)

This dialogue offers some insight into the show's phenomenal popularity among white Americans. Though Amos and Andy were stereotypical African American characters in many ways, and were created in the racist climate of the early 20th-century minstrel/vaudeville era, they also had the problems of "ordinary" working-class men and women. They fell in love, fell out of love, were afraid of getting married, had difficulties adjusting to city life (just like millions of recent white immigrants from Eastern and Southern Europe), and they struggled with the economic hardship of "de repression," or the Depression. And, as historian Melvin Patrick Ely has argued, *Amos 'n' Andy* also offered a realistic, if sometimes patronizing, portrait of the tangible difficulties faced by the millions of African Americans who moved from the southern United States to northern cities like New York, Pittsburgh, and Chicago from 1914 to 1950.

Though the show had a large African American and white following, organized African American resentment began to grow. An informal protest began when a few individual African Americans wrote letters to the editor across the country, complaining that *Amos 'n' Andy* made it seem like "the Negro in every walk of life is a failure, a dead beat and above all shiftless and ignorant." Even the character of Amos, this writer complained, "plays the fool." In 1931 the editor of one of the most influential African American papers in the country, Robert L. Vann of the *Pittsburgh Courier,* vowed to collect one million signature protesting *Amos 'n' Andy*. The petition claimed that "the references made to the Negro are of such character as to prove detrimental to the self respect and general advancement of the Negro in the United States and elsewhere." Vann declared Sunday, October 25, 1931, as a national day of protest against the show and boasted that activists had collected 740,000 signatures to the *Pittsburgh Courier*'s petition against *Amos 'n' Andy* (Ely 1991, 182).

Eventually, however, Vann's protest "fizzled"—in the words of Ely. Throughout its long run *Amos 'n' Andy* remained popular with many African Americans —in part because African Americans were often hungry for any representation of African American characters in popular culture. Moreover, the appeal of the humor in *Amos 'n' Andy* was multilayered and dense. It was not simply "racist" in its depiction of the buffoonery of southern migrants. Northern African Americans enjoyed the skewering of southern naiveté, and middle-class African Americans could be assured that the farmer-cum-taxi-drivers Amos and Andy did not represent the growing class of African American professionals. And, finally, working-class African Americans enjoyed the economic humor of the burlesque tradition that Gosden and Correll had to offer; in burlesque comedy the "underdog" is king—even when he fails (repeatedly) to come out on top. Amos, Andy, Madame Queen, and characters like "Kingfish" were often united against bad bosses, unfair economic policies, middle-class respectability, and economic cycles like "de repression." For all of the racism implicit in the "blackface" performance of Gosden and Correll, *Amos 'n' Andy* still reflected certain truths about American life in the 1930s that held sway for both African Americans and whites (Ely 1991, 181–186).

Radio Advertising

Radio advertising was different from print advertising: it directly interrupted the entertainment that was underway. Print advertisements, such as those in newspapers and magazines, could be scanned quickly—or skipped all together. In magazines artists and writers worked hard to make advertisements visually appealing, and, in fact, many readers reported that they actually enjoyed reading print advertisements. Radio advertising was different. Grating jingles, "friendly" male voices that talked about bad breath and body odor, and gimmicky sounds, like whistles and fog horns, alerted listeners to their captive status as they listened to the mighty radio advertisement. If they turned down the volume to avoid the ad, they might miss the next installment of their favorite radio soap or a crucial play in a ball game. Here is an example of one of the first "standalone" radio jingles, produced by Pepsi in 1939:

> Pepsi Cola hits the spot,
> Twelve full ounces that's a lot,
> Twice as much for a nickel, too,
> Pepsi-Cola is the drink for you!
> Nickel nickel nickel . . .
> Trickle trickle trickle . . .

While this jingle went on to become a hit song, most radio advertisements were more annoying than they were popular. Advertisers knew that it could be dangerous to make annoying radio commercials because it was possible the annoyed consumer would refuse to buy Pepsi-Cola after hearing the jingle hundreds of times. On the other hand, advertisers knew that frequency was the key to brand recognition. The more times that listeners heard the Pepsi-Cola jingle, the more likely that they would be to recognize Pepsi-Cola when they saw it for sale (Newman 2004, 17–51).

Consumer Activism

Meanwhile, as radio advertisers were perfecting their craft, a movement of educators, union activists, housewives, and critics of capitalism was forming to protect consumers against dangerous products and misleading advertising campaigns. Called the "Consumer movement," this movement represented one of the first American economic movements that involved both working- and middle-class activists. The movement got its start in 1927 when an economist named Stuart Chase and an engineer named F. J. Schlink published *Your Money's Worth: A Study in the Waste of the Consumer Dollar.* With the profits from this successful book, Chase and Schlink set up a consumer testing agency in White Plains, NY, which they named Consumers' Research. Their goal was to test products and then offer unbiased and unsponsored information, directly to consumers, to help consumers navigate an increasingly complicated array of consumer choices. In 1933 Schlink and fellow consumer activist Arthur Kallet published the best-selling *100,000,000 Guinea Pigs: Dangers in Everyday Foods, Drugs, and Cosmetics.* They argued that consumers were like laboratory "guinea pigs," the unwitting creatures upon whom corporations experimented with harmful products. In 1935, after a bitter strike at the Consumers' Research testing agency, when the testers tried to form their own union, the consumer movement was split into two entities: Consumers' Research and Consumers Union. The more radical of the two, Consumers Union still publishes its popular product-testing magazine *Consumer Reports.*

One criticism levied by the Consumer movement was that many of the products that boasted that they could cure all manner of ailments actually offered no benefit to the consumer—and in some cases were extremely harmful. In one of the most important cases won by the Consumer movement in the 1930s, Fleishmann's Yeast was forced by the Federal Trade Commission to "cease representing that the product will cure or prevent constipation, bad breath, boils, acne, pimples or other manifestations of irregular digestion, and that it will 'clear' skin irritants out of the blood." Consumer movement activist Peter Morell argued that radio was especially guilty of pimping products that made these sorts of claims. In his 1936 book, *Poisons, Potions and Profits: The Anti-dote to Radio Advertising,* Morell exposed many of the low-cost, high-profit items that were frequently sold over the radio, from diet pills and toothpastes to over-the-counter headache cures and cosmetics, to show that most of what was advertised over the airwaves was worthless (Newman 2004, 52–77).

Women were crucial to the consumer movement—both as grassroots organizers and as radio listeners. In the 1930s married women did 85 percent of the family shopping and provided the largest audience for daytime radio, since women who worked at home listened to the radio throughout the day as they were cooking, cleaning, and caring for children. Women who belonged to middle-class women's organizations, like the General Federation of Women's Clubs, were often critical of mainstream radio programming. In the 1930s a women's group in Westchester, NY, organized a "We're Not Listening" campaign aimed at soap operas, the genre that dominated the daytime dial on every network. The movement eventually spread to 39 states. This was a conservative social movement that saw soap operas as harmful to "suggestible" lower-income women who were being exposed to their salacious and tragic plots. But women were also crucial to more progressive movements like the Consumers movement. Ruth Brindze, a frequent consumer advocate who wrote for the progressive magazine *The Nation,* wrote a well-received critique of radio in 1937 called *Not to Be Broadcast*. In this book she attacked the control of radio by large corporations and the censorship of free speech that resulted (Newman 2004, 52–80).

Movies of the Great Depression

Background

Going to the movies, one of the most popular forms of entertainment in the 1920s, hit an all-time low in 1933, when one-third of all movie theaters were forced to close due to low attendance. Theaters began to offer double features; they gave away dishes, offered cash prizes to lucky ticketholders, and hosted "bingo" nights in order to keep patrons coming to the movies. Theaters also began to invest in air-conditioning, which was known as "iced air." Movie attendance began to recover in 1934 and reached its peak in 1946. Many consider the mid- to late 1930s to have been a "Golden Age" for Hollywood filmmaking (Young and Young 2002, 185–186).

The other major issue plaguing Hollywood in the 1930s was the issue of censorship. William H. Hays, president of the Motion Picture Association of America (and former postmaster general), under pressure from Catholic "decency" groups, drafted a film "Production Code" in 1930. The authors of the Code argued that films, though works of art, also had a moral obligation to uphold certain standards of ethics, in part because films reached "every class of society." The Code not only restricted the use of coarse language, the use of the word *gay* for homosexual, and the word *pansy,* as well as explicit depictions of sex and violence, it also involved itself with the morality of the message of the film. Here are some of the plot guidelines set out by the Code:

1. No plot or theme should definitely side with evil and against good.
2. Comedies and farces should not make fun of good, innocence, morality, or justice.
3. No plot should be constructed so as to leave the question of right or wrong in doubt or fogged.
4. No plot should by its treatment throw the sympathy of the audience with sin, crime, wrong-doing, or evil.
5. No plot should present evil alluringly.

The period from 1930 to 1934 is often referred to as the "pre-Code" era, because the Code did not really become actively enforced until 1934, when Joseph Breen was appointed the head of the new Production Code Administration (PCA).

Greta Garbo as the androgynous Queen Christina, from the eponymous film, 1934. (Bettmann/Corbis)

Breen's office began to screen and censor films before they were distributed. For example, in the 1934 film *Tarzan and His Mate,* a brief nude scene was cut by the PCA before the film was released (Doherty 1999, 2).

During the pre-Code era, many films that violated the rules above slipped past the censors. In 1930 a Cecil B. DeMille film, *Madame Satan,* displayed the actress Kay Johnson as a sexy Satan, who dressed up in an outlandish and revealing devilish costume to win back her adulterous husband. Certainly she was the personification of, as the code would have it, "alluring evil." In the first major "gangster" film, *Little Caesar,* Edward G. Robinson played a ruthless killer. The film inspired dozens of imitators, but it also provoked social reformers to decry the new, more graphic violence of the sound film. In 1931 the openly gay British director James Whale made the infamous monster film *Frankenstein.* Today many see the isolation and pathos of the monster as a commentary on the isolation and alienation felt by gay artists who were forced to conceal their real selves. In another film that is seen as having a gay subtext, *Queen Christina* (1933), Greta Garbo stars as a real-life 17th-century Swedish queen. In the film, Garbo's Queen Christina dresses as a man and kisses one of her ladies-in-waiting on the lips.

Another pre-Code film of note is the special-effects masterpiece *King Kong.* While on the surface the film appears to be merely monster picture, a blend of early 20th-century time-travel science fiction and the popular genre of the "Congo" film, *King Kong* can also be interpreted as a reflection of the economic hard times brought on the Depression. Kong, the giant gorilla, can be seen as a metaphor of the Depression itself, wreaking havoc on the Empire State Building (which was built in 1931), and so powerful he could only be brought down by the organized forces of the U.S. military. As for its violation of the Code, the movie created a certain amount of sympathy for the monstrous monkey, despite his association with, in the words of the Code, "sin, crime and wrong-doing."

As Andrew Sarris has argued, the Hays Code enforcement helped to create the "screwball comedy" genre, or, as he called it, the "sex comedy without the sex" (Sarris 1978, 8). In screwball comedies the male and female leads, rather than having a sappy love affair, spend most of the film fighting with each other in a playful way—until the end, of course, when they realize they are in love with each other and get married. In one of the classic exemplars of the genre, *It Happened One Night* (1934), starring Clark Gable as newspaperman Peter Warne and Claudette Colbert as a millionaire's daughter, Ellie Andrews, the sexual tension is often contained beneath the surface, transformed into witty banter instead of steamy sex scenes. Of course this film was "pre-Code" so some of the dialogue is more directly sexual than it is innuendo. Here is a bit of dialogue about dunking doughnuts that seems to have some other implications:

[*Peter watches as Ellie dunks her donut*]

Peter Warne	Say, where'd you learn to dunk? In finishing school?
Ellie	Aw, now don't you start telling me I shouldn't dunk.
Peter Warne	Of course you shouldn't—you don't know how to do it. Dunking's an art. Don't let it soak so long. A dip and

[*He stuffs the donut in his mouth*]

Peter Warne	plop, in your mouth. You let it hang there too long, it'll get soft and fall off. It's all a matter of timing. Aw, I oughta write a book about it.
Ellie	[*Laughs*] Thanks, professor.
Peter Warne	Just goes to show you—twenty millions, and you don't know how to dunk.
Ellie	Oh, I'd change places with a plumber's daughter any day. (The Internet MovieDatabase, 2008)

The Gangster Film

The gangster film genre emerged quickly after the advent of synchronized sound in Hollywood. Preceded by the silent-era classics *Underworld* (1927) and *The Racket* (1928), the talking-picture gangster film began to draw crowds with *Little Caesar* (1930) starring Edward G. Robinson as a ruthless Chicago gangster who has a precipitous rise and fall; *The Public Enemy* (1931), starring James Cagney as a bootlegger who is delivered dead onto his mother's doorstep at the film's end; and *Scarface: The Shame of the Nation* (1932), starring Paul Muni as Tony Camonte, a character largely based on the nation's most famous real-life gangster, Al Capone. In part, what made these films popular was their rebellious, antiauthoritarian spirit. In addition, as film scholar Jonathan Munby has argued, audiences were drawn to their "candid dramatization of the contradictory nature of the ethnic urban working-class American experience" (Munby 1999, 20). The urban, ethnic accents employed by these new "talking film" stars made these gangster films, according to Munby, "different from anything that had come before" (Wilson 2000, 56). Ironically, the early 1930s' gangster also represented unfettered, hedonistic consumerism during a time of epic scarcity: "The gangster was someone who had thrown off the straitjacket of bourgeois moral rectitude and had set about the business of selling pleasure" (Munby 1999, 24).

Gangster films quickly became the target of the Hays Production Code, and, in part, the reason for the Code's greater entrenchment and enforcement after 1934. Religious groups and reformers worried that gangster films glorified the gangster and his crime-ridden existence. Even though the pre-Code gangster generally met a brutal ending, the overall narrative of the film, reformers argued, made the gangster life look glamorous. As a result, after 1935 many gangster films began to focus on the lawmakers rather than the lawless. Of course in one of the exemplars of this genre, *G-Men* (1935), James Cagney plays an FBI agent so violent and cold he could easily be mistaken for a gangster. Other post-Code gangster films showed that slum kids could grow up to be priests just as easily as they could grow up to be criminals. In *Angels with Dirty Faces* (1938) James Cagney plays a slum kid gone bad while Pat O'Brien plays his childhood-chum-turned-priest.

Political Films

Despite the censorship Code some mainstream Hollywood films addressed the political climate of progressive activism that characterized the 1930s. One of the most successful political filmmakers of the period was King Vidor, who was born in Galveston, Texas, in 1894. Though he had a long career he was especially prolific in the 1930s, making such classics as *Billy the Kid* (1930), Vidor's take on the Western legend; *Street Scene* (1931), an urban neighborhood drama; *The Champ* (1931), a boxing melodrama; and, perhaps Vidor's most explicitly political film, *Our Daily Bread* (1934).

Our Daily Bread starred Tom Keene as John and Karen Morley as Mary, a young city couple who are given some farmland on which they try to start a commune. They populate their land with sundry Depression-era riffraff and dropouts, and, after some conflicts with the bank, a drought, and the machinations of a young woman who hopes to break up John and Mary's marriage, the film climaxes with an exciting race to build an irrigation ditch to save the dying corn. These climactic scenes, according to film historian Raymond Durgnat, bear traces of influence from Soviet directors like Sergei Eisenstein, whose work often paid tribute to the visual beauty and rhythm of mechanization. *Our Daily Bread,* as Durgnat has argued, is "usually regarded as vaguely left wing, and at release was criticized by the Hearst Press." Interestingly, though, the left has also criticized the film for having some fascist overtones, since the main character, John, runs the farm as a benign dictator. Durgnat argues that the film's left-wing reputation comes from several plot points, including the fact that landowner John is willing "to cede ownership [of the land] to the collective," that John is willing "to abide by majority vote," and that "demagoguery" is rejected. Though the film did not win first prize at the 1935 Soviet International Exposition of Film, "it *was* awarded a certificate of merit" (Durgnat and Simmon 1988, 149).

Durgnat has argued that what made Vidor's work distinctive was his blend of Populist ideology, Emersonian transcendentalism, and rugged individualism.

The title *Our Daily Bread* may have owed something to Vidor's commitment to Christian Science. According to Durgnat, Vidor was also something of a "natural feminist." This was reflected in his choice of strong, professional women characters in many of his films, his choice of feisty women actresses for leading roles (Laurette Taylor, Lillian Gish, Marion Davies, Barbara Stanwyck, and Jennifer Jones), and the fact that he often collaborated with women writers: "No other Hollywood director of his era so often called on women collaborators—two thirds of Vidor's films not written by him alone involved women screenwriters" (Durgnat 1988, 152, 14–15).

Another landmark political filmmaker of the 1930s was Charlie Chaplin. One of his most remarkable films, *Modern Times* (1936), stars Chaplin in the role of his lovable, silent Tramp. The film opens with a shot of sheep pushing their way through a wooden chute on their way to a sheep pen, and then cuts to a shot of workers pushing each their way through a subway platform on their way to a factory. The implication is hardly subtle: this film is Chaplin's critique of industrialization, unemployment, poverty, and the penal system. And, because the film is nearly completely "silent" with only sparing use of synchronized sound, the film also offers a critique of the (then) nine-year-old takeover of American film by the "talkies."

One of the major targets of the film is automation. In one of the early scenes, the Tramp, employed in a factory, struggles to keep up with the bolt tightening on an assembly line. When the Tramp tries to take a few-seconds break to scratch his back or brush away a fly, hilarity—and chaos for the production line—ensue. In another scene a salesman comes to the factory with an automated feeding machine. Even the sales pitch is automated, since it is played on a phonograph record. When the Tramp is used to test the lunch-o-matic, the machine goes berserk and the Tramp ends up wearing his lunch rather than eating it.

The film also attacks the randomness and the brutality of the penal system for the poor. After being fired from his factory job Chaplin's Tramp looks more down and out than ever. Wandering the streets in search of a job, the Tramp picks up a red flag that has fallen off of a passing construction truck. At that same moment the Tramp is swept up in a passing parade demonstration held by Communist activists. The Tramp is mistaken for their ringleader and hauled off to jail. The intertitle reads: "Held as a communist leader, our innocent victim languishes in jail."

Eventually the Tramp gets out of jail and falls for his on-screen love (and off-screen wife), a poor gamin played by Paulette Goddard. The Tramp has several more jobs throughout the film in order to try to support his wife, including a night manager at a department store and a waiter at a restaurant. During one of the restaurant scenes the Tramp sings a song in synchronized sound, but the song is jibberish: "La spinach or la busho, Cigaretto toto bello, Ce rakish spagoletto, Ce le tu la tu la trois! Senora fila scena, voulez-vous la taximeter, Le jaunta sur la seata, Je le tu le tu le waaah!" This scene shows Chaplin's utter disregard for the filmic innovations in synchronized sound. His nearly silent film was a protest—not only against the industrial system, but against the Hollywood system as well. As one *New York Times* writer pointed out in his review of *Modern Times,* "[Chaplin] is a strange figure in a medium he did so much to popularize" (D.W.C. 1936, X4).

Modern Times was so funny that it was often embraced for its comedy as much as for its political and economic critique. But one of the most unabashedly political films of the decade was Frank Capra's *Mr. Smith Goes to Washington* (1939). It starred Jimmy Stewart as Jefferson Smith, a naïve, earnest, and determined newcomer to the U.S. Senate who tries (and only barely succeeds) to expose corruption and graft in the Senate chambers. Claude Raines brilliantly plays the corrupt Senator Paine who tries to get Smith expelled from the Senate. The dramatic climax of the film involves a marathon filibuster, organized by Smith, which ultimately results in a decision to allow the U.S. government to buy land in Smith's home state for a boys' camp. It was based on a novel titled *The Gentleman from Montana,* and it premiered in Washington, D.C., in October 1939.

Though seen today as a sentimental, feel-good drama that pitted a little man against a big system, when it premiered the film was harshly criticized in the United States and abroad for offering too negative a portrayal of American democratic institutions. Pete Harrison of *Harrison Reports,* a Hollywood trade journal, worried that the film would make it hard for other nations to admire America: "How will the people of other countries feel toward this country when they are made to believe that the United States Senate, and the entire Congress for that matter, is controlled by crooked politicians? What faith can they have in such a nation as a promoter of peace?" Frederic William Wile wrote in the *Washington Star* that *Mr. Smith Goes to Washington* "ought to go over big in Berlin, Rome and Moscow because it shows up the democratic system and our vaunted free press in exactly the colors Hitler, Mussolini and Stalin are fond of painting them" (Nugent 1939, X5).

Interestingly, though, the film was banned by the Nazis and embraced by European nations as a tribute to America's commitment to democracy. James Hilton of the *London Sunday Graphic* was surprised by the level of self-critique allowed in America: "I doubt any government in the world today would allow itself to be so freely criticized . . . in pictures . . . as does the American." A few years later, France, under Nazi occupation, would cling to *Mr. Smith Goes to Washington* as emblematic of democratic freedom. When Nazi occupiers banned English and American films many French theaters chose *Mr. Smith Goes to Washington* as the last American film to be shown before the ban. The Army News Service reported that one French village in the Vosges Mountains played *Mr. Smith Goes to Washington* every day for the last 30 days before the ban took effect ("Last Cheers of French Audience for *Smith Goes to Washington,*" 1942).

Typical visual pattern as created by Busby Berkeley. Movie still from Gold Diggers of 1933. *(Underwood & Underwood/Corbis)*

The 1930s Musical

Another important film genre of the 1930s was the Hollywood musical. Lavish, glamorous, and sometimes kooky, the musicals made by Busby Berkeley snuck abstract modernism, bizarre patterns, and plenty of exposed female legs and midriffs past the censorship of the Code. In one of the climactic scenes of *The Gold Diggers of 1933,* a backstage musical about a group of struggling musical actresses during the Depression, dancers hold violins that light up in the dark. They come together to form a giant violin made up of individual, glowing violins from the perspective of the "Berkeley top shot," a camera mounted on the ceiling of the soundstage that captured the motion below. In another scene Berkeley costumed his dancers in dresses made of plastic coins while they sang, "We're in the money." This flamboyant song-and-dance movie turned the reality of hardship into the spectacle of scantily clad women's bodies, but it still told a certain "truth" about the Depression: in the final scene of *Gold Diggers of 1933,* a group of women staring out of tenement windows sing a soulful tribute to their husbands and boyfriends, in a song called "My Forgotten Man."

Fred Astaire and Ginger Rogers were the king and queen of the Hollywood dance musical of the 1930s. While Busby Berkeley was all about the image made by the pattern of the collective, the musicals starring Astaire and Rogers were about the romance of the couple: the union not of many, but of two. According to film scholar Gary Morris, the Astaire and Rogers films also made room for a variety of "sissy" characters, the role that many gay actors were reduced to playing during the height of film censorship in Hollywood. According to Morris, "Astaire-Rogers musicals like *The Gay Divorcee* (1934) and *Top Hat* (1935) are unimaginable without mincing queens like Eric Blore, Edward Everett Horton and Franklin Pangborn demonstrating to their often clueless master (or mistress) how to act, dress and even triumph in a heterosexual love affair." The cool, sleek modernism of the Astaire-Rogers musicals provided ample opportunity for the flamboyant "sissy" to upstage the graceful dancing of the famous couple (Morris).

Race and Ethnicity in 1930s' Film

The 1930s was an important decade for the growth of African American filmmaking. The legacy of African American filmmaker Oscar Michaeux, who made dozens of all–African American films in the 1920s and 1930s, inspired more "low-brow" all–African American films in the 1930s, like *Go Down Death* and *Blood of Jesus*. The African American actresses Ethel Waters and Lena Horne, who went on to establish themselves as major film/singing stars in the 1940s, starred in 1930s' films like *The Duke Is Tops* (1938) and *Rufus Jones for President* (1933), a bizarre film in which an African American child is elected president of the United States.

But for other ethnic minorities the 1930s was not a very promising decade when it came to film. Asian characters, for example, were almost always played by white actors. In one of the most galling instances of this practice, when the best-selling novel about Chinese peasants by Pearl S. Buck, *The Good Earth* (1931), was made into a film in 1937 it was cast with all white actors and actresses. Metro-Goldwyn-Mayer paid $50,000 for the rights to the popular novel, and the Chinese American actress Anna May Wong was considered for the lead role of O-lan. But she was passed over in favor of the German-born actress Luise Rainer, in part, it was argued, because Anna May Wong did not look Chinese enough! Ironically, perhaps, Luise Rainer won the Academy Award for best actress for her portrayal of O-lan in the film.

Anna May Wong did play Asian characters in many notable films of the 1930s, including *Daughter of the Dragon* (1931) and *Shanghai Express* (1932), but she left Hollywood in the late 1930s, she said, because her characters "died too often." A tall, willowy beauty, standing sive-feet seven-inches (taller than Marlene Dietrich), she often played the tragic lover who had to be sacrificed at the end of the film. The Production Code explicitly forbade miscegenation—the representation of a mixed-race couple (Havis 2004, 67–69).

Native Americans were also employed to play stereotypical roles—usually that of the "good Indian" or "bad Indian" in the Westerns of the 1930s. As Ted Jojola has argued, "the Hollywood Indian is a mythological being who exists nowhere but within the fertile imaginations of its movie actors, producers and directors" (Jojola 1998, 12). At the start of the film era Native Americans on reservations were recruited to perform in Hollywood Westerns; though they rarely had speaking roles, in 1926 Indian actors like Chief Tahachee and Richard Davies Thunderbird formed an activist group, the "War Paint Club," to protect the rights of Native American actors and to try to control the image of Indians being portrayed. This group evolved into the Indian Actors' Association (IAA) in 1936. With these groups Indian actors tried to control the conditions of their labor, as well as the circulation of their image. As historian Nicolas G. Rosenthal has argued, "Indians working in Hollywood often confronted the stark choice between participating in these cultural productions and finding another way to make a living" (Rosenthal 2005, 330).

Politics, Art, and the Discovery of the "Folk"

People Take Center Stage

In 1936 the poet Carl Sandburg, a native of Illinois, published his epic poem, *The People, Yes*. The simple title of this poem summed up one of the core ideas of the 1930s: the idea that the "people" or the "folk" should be at the center of artistic production and political change. The discovery of the folk took place on many artistic fronts. There was a revival in folk music as well as a new interest in recording classic Anglo-American ballads, Native American Indian chants, African American work songs, and other fragments of musical culture that were perceived as dying at the very moment that recording equipment was becoming easier to use. The folk were also discovered by photographers who captured the haunting, heroic beauty of the ordinary Americans displaced by Depression-era tragedies, like Okies traveling west to escape the droughts in the Central Plains. Government-sponsored art and history projects, from the Farm Security Administration photo project to the WPA murals project, to the Federal Writers' slave narrative project, focused on the images and oral histories of ordinary people.

FSA Photographs

The discovery of the folk in the 1930s is part of what scholar William Stott has called the "documentary impulse" that artists, activists, and the federal government embraced during the Depression (Stott 1986). One of the most powerful expressions of the documentary imagination can be seen in the vast photo project that was undertaken by the Photographic Section of the Farm Security Administration (FSA). The FSA was created to help farmers and other agricultural workers who were being dislocated by natural disasters (like the midwestern drought that became known as the Dust Bowl) and the economic downturn of the era. Roy Stryker, who headed the Photographic Section, decided that one way to help the Dust Bowl migrants (nicknamed "Okies" since so many of them came from Oklahoma) would be to photograph them and, in turn, publish their images in newspapers and magazines in order to create public support for their plight. His larger goal, he explained, was to "explain America to Americans" (Shindo 1997, 75). Stryker hired a team of previously unknown photographers, including Dorothea Lange, Walker Evans, Marion Post Wolcott, Arthur Rothstein, and Ben Shahn. Together they made "seventy-seven thousand prints and nearly twice as many negatives" (Raeburn 2006, 143).

During the late 1930s Stryker was not as successful in placing photographs in popular magazines and newspapers as he had hoped. Stryker sent out between 200 and 1,400 photographs per week to news editors, most of which were

Controversy: *You Have Seen Their Faces*

One of the most popular photo-books of the era was a team effort between southern playwright/novelist Erskine Caldwell and the *Fortune/Life* magazine photographer Margaret Bourke-White. The photos and text tried to expose the hardship and poverty that characterized the American South: "The South has always been shoved around like a country cousin. It buys mill-ends and it wears hand-me-downs. It sits at second-table and is fed short-rations. It is the place where the makeshift is good enough. . . . It is the Southern Extremity of America, the Empire of the Sun, the Cotton States; it is the Deep South, Down South; it is The South" (Caldwell and Bourke-White 1937, 1).

The cover of the original edition showed a shoddily clad mother and daughter sitting at the foot of a grand, stone column, reminiscent of Greek architecture. The mother/daughter pair is dwarfed by the column and the picture seems to suggest that the once grand, Greco-Southern Empire has been reduced to squalor. Only the daughter, who is dressed in bright white, seems to represent the hope of the future. Another photograph, "Iron Mountain, Tennessee," shows a man holding the reins of a plow, two horses, an open field, and a haunting, gorgeous, cloud-filled sky above them. The man and the horses are at the base of a hill, and, like the mother/daughter pair who are dwarfed by the architecture, man, beast, and machine are dwarfed by the field and sky. If this photograph tells the story of "man against nature," man is definitely not winning the battle. In another photograph, "Hamilton, Alabama," a woman holds the handle of a piece of farm equipment and looks off in the distance. The camera angle is very low, which gives the woman, her strong hands, her worn dress, and her wide-brimmed bonnet a sense of dignity and purpose. The caption reads, "We manage to get along," though it looks like this farm woman can do much more than manage.

One of the most controversial aspects of *You Have Seen Their Faces* was the fact that the captions did not always match the photographs. In one of the most poignant examples, Bourke-White reprinted a photograph of a mother nursing a young toddler (Okefenokee Swamp, Georgia). The mother's face is lined and aged looking, though she looks down on her child with a mix of tenderness and concern. The mirror shard behind her reflects a portrait of a family member. The mother's mother, perhaps? But the caption tells a different story: "Every month the relief office gives them four cans of beef, a can of dried peas, and five dollars and the old lady generally spends a dollar and a half of it for snuff." The caption seems a jarring contrast to the photograph; it is hard to imagine this nursing mother as a snuff addict. Perhaps she was, but the quiet pain on her face undermines the harsh tone of the caption.

Ironically, perhaps, the maudlin captions may have helped to propel the successful sale of *You Have Seen Their Faces.* As journalism historian Art Hanson has argued, "Bourke-White and Caldwell destroyed their credibility by making the

Continued on next page

Controversy: You Have Seen Their Faces, *Continued*

sharecroppers seem excessively pathetic and wretched." Hanson compares *You Have Seen Their Faces* to a similar book, *An American Exodus,* by photographer Dorothea Lange and economist Paul S. Taylor. While "Lange and Taylor conveyed more information than the other authors . . . the book has little emotional impact" (Hanson 1980, 1).

You Have Seen Their Faces did raise awareness about the difficult circumstances facing so many in the South, and, especially, the plight of African American sharecroppers. Bourke-White and Caldwell convincingly argued that many southern African Americans were in a situation that was not that different from slavery. The book received much praise, such as that from Alabama author Hudson Strode: *You Have Seen Their Faces* "is a stirring and painful document, magnificently produced . . . authentic . . . fairly selected." Others, like the conservative Donald Davidson, found that *You Have Seen Their Faces* amounted to a "libelous and malicious proceedings against" the South's character (Chapin 1940, 12).

In the end, *You Have Seen Their Faces* is one of at least a dozen powerful representations of human suffering that the Depression inspired. The book should now be seen in tandem with other major photography books of the period, including Herman Clarence Nixon's *Forty Acres and Steel Mules* (1938), Archibald MacLeish's *Land of the Free* (1938), Dorothea Lange and Paul Taylor's *An American Exodus* (1939), Margaret Jarman Hagood's *Mothers of the South: Portraiture of the White Tenant Farm Woman* (1939), Oliver LaFarge's *As Long as the Grass Shall Grow* (1940), Sherwood Anderson's *Home Town* (1940) which used photographs from the FSA collection, Richard Wright's *12 Million Black Voices,* which also used FSA photographs, and Walker Evans and James Agee's *Let Us Now Praise Famous Men* (1941).

rejected by mainstream magazines, like *Life,* which was a new photo-magazine sensation in 1936. Another picture magazine, *Look,* had a more progressive editorial staff and was more receptive to publishing the FSA photos, but even *Look* did not become the outlet for social reform photography that Stryker was searching for.

Instead, the photographs found a more receptive audience in the modern art world and, later, from historians. According to historian John Raeburn, the photographs constitute "a richer, more comprehensive visual record of the era than any photographic survey before or since." "More than any other legacy," Raeburn has argued, the FSA photographs "shaped the national memory of the Great Depression" (Raeburn 2006, 145).

Romancing the Folk

In 1933 a father-and-son team, John Lomax and his son, Alan, were visiting southern prisons with a bulky sound-recording machine that made aluminum discs,

Huddy Ledbetter at Angola Prison, where he was "discovered" by Alan Lomax, 1934. (Library of Congress)

looking for folksingers they could record. When they reached Angola Prison in Louisiana they recorded Huddie Ledbetter, the only son of an African American Texas sharecropper. Ledbetter had been in prison before, and it was there that he was dubbed "Lead Belly"—a reference to his reportedly violent youth. At Angola prison the Lomaxes recorded a plea by Lead Belly to Louisiana governor O. K. Allen to pardon him, as well as a blues version of the classic tune, "Irene, Goodnight." Lead Belly was released in 1934 for good behavior, though the Lomaxes spread the rumor that it was Lead Belly's recorded plea to the governor that secured his release. The Lomaxes took Lead Belly to New York, where they advertised him as a living American legend: a human encyclopedia of pure, authentic, American folk music. Lead Belly eventually sued the Lomaxes for a share in the profits he generated with his performances and recordings, but it is also true that he might have never been "discovered" had the Lomaxes not recorded him in Angola Prison in 1933. According to historian Benjamin Filene, when Lead Belly died in 1949 he "was well known enough to generate an obituary in the *New York Times* but not popular enough to have achieved a broad-based following or any kind of financial security. Americans found Lead Belly fascinating, it seems, but they kept him at arm's length" (Filene 2000, 71).

American Slave Narratives

All quotes taken from American Slave Narrative,
Andy J. Anderson
Texas

"De Marster finished his statement asayin', 'All yous niggers can stay wid me'. I's says to myse'f, not loud 'nough fo' anyone to heah, I's thinks, but de Marster heahs me w'en I's says, 'Lak hell I's will'."

George Fleming
South Carolina

"Slaves started to work by de time dey was old enough to tote water and pick up chips to start fires wid. Some of dem started to work in de fields when dey about ten, but most of 'em was older."

James Green
Texas

"I never knew my age until after de Civil War when I was set free for de second time. Then my marster gets out a great big book and it showed dat I was twenty-five years old. It shows more too: It shows I was twelve when I was bought and $800 was paid for me. Dat $800 was stolen money, cose I was kidnapped. Dis is about how it come."

Matilda Hatchett
Arkansas

"Didn't git no chance to learn nothin' in slavery. Sometimes the children would teach the darkies 'round the house their ABC's. I've heard of folks teachin' their slaves to read the Bible. They didn't teach us to read nothin'. I've heard of it, but I've never seen it, that some folks would cut off the first finger of a nigger that could write."

Charles Williams
Louisiana

"I knows one Beauty thing erbout myself. I cin ackomplush anything I lays my mits apond." (American Slave Narratives)

Recognized as one of the leaders of the folk preservation movement, John Lomax became the folklore editor at the Federal Writers Project when the FWP was established in 1935. The Federal Writers Project was one of the most ambitious of all of the government sponsored art projects. Writers like Studs Terkel, Nelson Algren, Saul Bellow, Ralph Ellison, and Zora Neale Hurston traveled the country and recorded the stories of ethnically diverse Americans, including hundreds of former slaves. The writers themselves were paid subsistence wages, about $20 per week. In addition to collecting more than 10,000 interviews, the writers at the FWP produced beautiful, historic "guides" to each of the 48 states. The director of FWP was B. A. Botkin, whose family emigrated from Lithuania at the turn of the 20th century. An editor of a small journal called *Folk-Say* during the 1920s, Botkin was part of a movement in the 1930s that saw folklore as a legitimate part of American arts and letters.

The slave narrative project started as an ad hoc experiment when in 1936 a few of the FWP workers in southern states like Virginia and Georgia started to interview former slaves. Impressed with their efforts, Lomax created a standardized questionnaire, devised a system for transcribing the heavy southern dialect of these older speakers, and directed an 18-state slave-narrative collection project. From 1936 to 1938 the writers who worked for the FWP in each of these states conducted more than 2,000 interviews with former slaves and generated more than 10,000 pages of typescript. The project was eventually published in 17 volumes under the title: *Slave Narratives: A Folk History of Slavery in the United States from Interviews with Former Slaves.*

Federal Theater Project

The Federal Theater Project was established in 1935, and headed by the strong-willed Vassar theater graduate Hallie Flanagan. The goal of the FTP was to write plays that could be produced in as many communities as possible across the nation. It remains America's only experiment with a national theater. The largest projects were in New York, Los Angeles, and Chicago, but there were active FTP chapters in Atlanta, Boston, Buffalo, Chapel Hill, Cincinnati, Cleveland, Denver, Detroit, Gary, Hartford, Jacksonville, Manchester, Miami, New Orleans, Newark, Oklahoma City, Peoria, Philadelphia, Pittsburgh, Portland (Oregon), Raleigh, Roanoke Island, Roslyn (Long Island), Salem, San Diego, San Francisco, Seattle, Springfield, Syracuse, and Tampa. At its high point the FTP employed nearly 13,000 people.

Like other New Deal arts projects, the FTP reflected the documentary aesthetic of the 1930s. Flanagan oversaw the production of "Living Newspapers," plays that were multimedia (including film and sound recording) and that focused on contemporary social problems. But the FTP was the most controversial, and, therefore, the most short-lived of all the WPA arts projects. Flanagan was committed to experimental theater and also to racial diversity. The FTP included 16 African American theater units, including one in Harlem. In 1936 Orson Welles and John Houseman directed an all–African American production of *Macbeth* set in Haiti.

The climactic moment for the FTP came in 1938 when a New York City production of Marc Blitzstein's musical, *The Cradle Will Rock,* set in "Steeltown, USA" was halted due to budget cuts. The FTP players, however, suspected that the real reason they were being shut down is that their work was too radical,

Turpentine *was preceded by the more notorious 1936 production of* Macbeth, *directed by Orson Welles and John Houseman. (Franklin D. Roosevelt Presidential Library)*

and, as such, they were determined to go on with the show. When the production was shut down, the cast and crew moved their audience, in a parade-like format, to the adjacent Venice Theater, where they performed the musical without their lights and sets. It was, according to many who witnessed it, a very moving performance. Later, in June of 1939, after a series of heated congressional hearings, the FTP was shut down altogether.

Mural America

The artist Thomas Hart Benton deserves a certain amount of credit for bringing the aesthetic tradition of the mural to 1930s' America. Benton was born in Neosho, Missouri, into a political family. His father was a congressman, and his great-uncle, for whom he was named, was a senator. Benton, however, favored his mother's more artistic temperament; he started his art career by taking a few classes at the Chicago Art Institute in 1907. According to Henry Adams, who curated a 1989 retrospective of Benton's work, Benton rejected the abstract style of European modernists like Picasso and Duchamps for a style that bordered on "folksy" and "realist." Benton painted large-scale murals featuring oversized,

Controversy: *Turpentine*

Turpentine was produced by the Negro Unit of the Federal Theatre Project in 1936. It told the story of a rebellious collective of African American workers in the turpentine swamps of Florida. One of the play's authors, Peter Morell, was white and Jewish. The other author, J. Augustus "Gus" Smith, was African American. Smith starred in the play as "Forty Four," the leader of the African American workers. The play was melodramatic—the white bosses not only subjugated the African American male workers, they also sexually assaulted their women. But the African American workers prevailed—launching a successful strike for higher wages.

According to Hallie Flanagan, the Federal Theater Project's brash director, the writing of *Turpentine* "lacked fluency," but "the production possessed breathtaking fervor." The *New York Times* also praised the production: "As played at the Lafayette much of 'Turpentine' is exciting as melodrama and just as much is moving as a social document" (L.N. 1936, 21).

As a "social document" *Turpentine* did offer a critique of the fusion between racism and capitalism. Set in the piney woods of Florida, where turpentine is pressed from pine-tree resin, the hero of the story is the strong, angry, "Forty-Four," who is convinced by a group of "floaters" that he and his fellow workers are underpaid, and also deserve to be provided with doctors and schools. The bad guys in the drama are mostly white, including the redneck "Sheriff" and a handful of interchangeable "crackers," as they are called by the African American workers.

Interestingly, however, the critique of the turpentine industry is also voiced by some of the poor white characters who realize that their lot is tied to that of the African American workers. They know that during this strike, they will be expected to put the workers down. One white man says at the play's opening: "Ain' crazy 'nough to git mahself kilt makin' other folks rich" (Smith 1935).

Toward the end of the play an African American worker named Turtle Eyes is killed by the white turpentine bosses. This triggers the final arming and organizing of the African American workers. The play ends with a face-off in which the vicious white Sheriff corners the armed African American workers in a small church. The Sheriff shoots into the church and kills the white store owner, Dutton. The Sheriff charges into the church and says: "Drop those guns." The African American woman, Sue, the play's most outspoken radical, replies, "Not if y'all want ter keep on livin." Another African American worker shouts: "White folks, an what's gonna keep us from shootin?" Sue adds, "Dey's twelve million o' us. Whater y'all gonna do 'bout dat?" Another worker stands up: "Y'all done hang go last hand in this camp. Fightin is what y'all gits from now on" (Smith 1935).

At this juncture the white camp owner relents: "Rogers, get them back to work in the morning and give them eighty cents a barrel." One of the white characters, dismayed, exclaims: "Ah don't kno' what's gotten into dese darkies. Dey mus' be crazy." Sue gets the last line: "An Buckra, we's gitten crazier evah minute" (Smith 1935).

Continued on next page

Controversy: Turpentine, *Continued*

African American audiences gave the play mixed reviews. According to the public relations handler, "theatre going Harlem did not like to see themselves depicted in . . . 'overall plays'" (Buttitta and Witham 1982, 72). Historian Rena Fraden has shown that according to audience surveys, some Harlem theatre goers did not appreciate the "backwoods" setting: "A play about conditions in the South just wasn't sufficiently interesting to Northern Negroes living in cities; they wanted a play about 'New York Negro life and problems.' More than once, the refrain 'We want something more 'modern'" is recorded in the surveys, something that reflects 'their lives' or their idea of their lives, not in the 'backwards' South, but in Harlem, their home. A second group found all problem plays boring, too preachy. Audiences are not anxious to be preached to. . . . They want diversion, entertainment, not just morbid social problems. And a third group was embarrassed by the 'low-brow' subject matter. 'Why all this mess of backwoods. We want to improve like whites'" (Fraden 1994, 98).

But *Turpentine* still attracted enthusiastic audiences: According to one reviewer, "Judging from the warm reception given *Turpentine,* plays of protest against exploitation and oppression anywhere are welcome to Harlem's exploited, oppressed and police-ridden people" (Stevenson 1936, 18). In a similar vein, the African American intellectual Alain Locke praised the play for its working-class perspective, rating it just short of the achievement of the all-African American production of *Macbeth:* "More than any other play of the New Theatre group, [*Turpentine*] brought the thesis of labor and class struggle dramatically to life" (Locke 1937, 12).

flowing and sinewy human figures, often in agricultural settings, or in a painterly montage of humans mixed in with technology and mass culture. In 1933 he was commissioned to paint a nine-paneled mural that would represent the state of Indiana in the Chicago World's Fair of 1933. The most controversial of the panels, titled "Parks, the Circus, the Klan, the Press," today adorns a classroom at Indiana University at Bloomington. It is still such a controversial piece that every fall the university offers a class on the painting in order to diffuse students' negative reactions (Herberholz 2000, 48).

The second major influence on American mural painting in the 1930s came from Mexican artists like Diego Rivera, David Alfaro Siqueiros, and Jose Clemente Orozco. Rivera, who was active in international Communist/progressive politics for most of his adult life, was born in a silver-mining town in Mexico in 1886. His family moved to Mexico City when Rivera was five, and it was there that he became entranced by technology—and by art. By the age of 10 he was taking art classes and in the early 1900s he studied painting throughout Europe: in

Controversy: Rivera at the Crossroads

Ironically, one of the most politically radical murals painted by Diego Rivera was commissioned by industrialist Edsel Ford, son of auto manufacturer Henry Ford. Rivera was hired to paint a mural tribute to the American worker at the Detroit Institute of Arts. The resulting 27 panels, divided onto two massive walls, are considered by many to be Rivera's finest work in the United States. The murals depict shadowy naked bodies and the clenched hands of different racial groups breaking through the earth in the top panel of each wall. The bottom of each mural shows the industrial process itself in great detail, with images of (mostly male) workers straining to operate the machinery of automobile production. When the murals were unveiled in 1933 they came under immediate attack from local religious leaders who called the work "blasphemous" and conservatives who declared the work "communistic." A religious controversy was ignited by several of Rivera's panels, including one that depicted a child being vaccinated in a setting reminiscent of classical paintings of the Virgin Mary and Child. Edsel Ford, and the head of the Detroit Institute of Arts, William A. Valentiner, defended the work against all attackers, and the artwork remained at the Institute.

Rivera had more trouble when he was hired by the Rockefellers in 1933 to paint a mural in the lobby of the RCA building. Rockefeller had tried to hire Picasso and Matisse as well, but both artists declined. Rivera himself refused on first being offered the job, but agreed when the terms of payment were settled ($21,000) and Rivera was permitted to work in his favorite medium (fresco) and in color. Titled *Man at the Crossroads,* Rivera's mural included the scene of a crowded May Day demonstration and a portrait of Lenin. Here is how Rivera described some of the content of this mural.

"The center of my mural showed a worker at the controls of a large machine. In front of him, emerging from space, was a large hand holding a globe on which the dynamics of chemistry and biology, the recombination of atoms, and the division of a cell, were represented schematically. Two elongated ellipses crossed and met in the figure of the worker, one showing the wonders of the telescope and its revelation of bodies in space; the other showing the microscope and its discoveries—cells, germs, bacteria, and delicate tissues. Above the germinating soil at the bottom, I projected two visions of civilization. On the left of the crossed ellipses, I showed a night-club scene of the debauched rich, a battlefield with men in the holocaust of war, and unemployed workers in a demonstration being clubbed by the police. On the right, I painted corresponding scenes of life in a socialist country: a May Day demonstration of marching, singing workers; an athletic stadium filled with girls exercising their bodies; and a figure of Lenin, symbolically clasping the hands of a black American and a white Russian soldier and workers, as allies of the future" (Rivera 1960).

Continued on next page

Controversy: Rivera at the Crossroads, Continued

When a newspaper story about this last part of the mural appeared in the *World Telegram,* Rockefeller demanded that the portrait of Lenin be removed. Rivera refused, arguing, "hadn't every artist the right to use whatever models he wished in his painting?" Nonetheless Rivera sent a conciliatory letter to Rockefeller suggesting that he could add a portrait of Lincoln to the final painting. When he did not receive a reply from Rockefeller he asked his female assistant, Lucienne Bloch, to sneak into the lobby and photograph the mural. A few days later armed police entered the lobby and covered up the mural with canvas. Finally, after Rivera had returned to Mexico, the mural was destroyed on February 9, 1934 (Deane 1999).

Spain, Paris, and Italy. Rivera first achieved notoriety in 1924 with a mural commissioned by the Mexican Ministry of Education. In one of the 128 panels, titled *Day of the Dead,* a crowd of middle-class Mexican, peasants, and prostitutes gathers in front of a large painting of skeletons playing the guitar. The colors include muted oranges, yellows, and purples, with splashes of black and dark brown, giving the panel an earthy feel that was characteristic of Rivera's palate.

Detail of Man at the Crossroads, *by Mexican artist Diego Rivera. (Michael Freeman/ Corbis)*

The most ambitious mural project of the New Deal era was not a project initiated by the Federal Art Project under the auspices of the WPA, but rather by the Treasury Department Section of Painting and Sculpture. The head of "the Section," Edward Bruce, sponsored competitions for artists from hundreds of municipalities nationwide; artists from all backgrounds submitted sketches of potential murals for public buildings and, especially, post offices. And, since post offices were located in virtually every community, it was a plan to bring art to the masses. *Life* magazine dubbed this project "Mural America for Rural America." In her important study of the post office murals, *Wall to Wall America: Post Office Murals in the Great Depression,* Karal Ann Marling (2000) details many of the controversies that erupted over decency, politics, history, and taste when murals were selected for painting. In a controversial mural, *The Dangers of the Mail,* which has remained for many years in the building which today houses the EPA in Washington, D.C., virtually naked bodies of savage Native Americans loom over a handful of completely naked white women.

At the same time, the post office mural project itself was remarkably inclusive. While some of the murals offered racist portraits of Native American Indians, in other cases Native American Indian artists were hired to create the murals. Washington State Indian artist Julius Twohy created a mural called *Indian Village* that had a distinct, primitivist form, using two-dimensional space, geometric patterns, and images of tents and horses. A Cuban-born artist, Carlos Lopez, who was educated in Michigan, painted the mural *Plymouth Trail* for the Plymouth, Michigan, post office in 1938. Women artists were also featured, including the folk artist Doris Lee, who painted *Georgia Countryside* for the Summerville, Georgia, post office building in 1939, and Dorothy Cravath, who was hired by the Federal Artist Project to work on murals at the Coit Tower in San Francisco with fellow woman artist Helen Forbes. She remembered that Diego Rivera's style was especially influential in California: "I learned about mural technique from Diego Rivera, which is why all these WPA murals look rather Rivera-ish. I think we all learned about fresco from watching Diego Rivera do the mural in art school" (Martin 1964).

PROLETARIAN CULTURE AND THE "CULTURAL FRONT"

Politics and Entertainment

The 1930s saw the flowering of what historian Michael Denning has called the "Cultural Front"—the emergence of a left-oriented popular culture. From Earl Robinson's "Ballad for Americans," which was performed at both the Republican National Convention and the Communist Party's national convention in 1940, to the long-running union-sponsored musical review, *Pins and Needles,* to Orson Welles's movie and radio productions, to the "hot jazz" culture that surrounded performers like Billie Holiday, to the proletarian novels of authors like John Dos Passos, John Steinbeck, Mary Heaton Vorse, and Meridel Le Sueur, the 1930s was a rare decade in which progressive political values infused mainstream songs, novels, and films.

"Ballad for Americans" was originally titled "Ballad for Uncle Sam." It was composed by the Seattle-born composer Earl Robinson, with lyrics by John La-Touche. The ballad opened with a tribute to the Revolutionary War:

In seventy-six the sky was red
thunder rumbling overhead
Bad King George couldn't sleep in his bed
And on that stormy morn, Ol' Uncle Sam was born.
Some birthday!

The song continued, however, with an eye toward embracing the occupational, racial, and religious diversity of 1930s America. With a nod to Walt Whitman's *Leaves of Grass,* Robinson and lyricist LaTouche offered this litany of American working class occupations:

Well, I'm an
Engineer, musician, street cleaner, carpenter, teacher,
How about a farmer? Also. Office clerk? Yes sir!
That's right. Certainly!
Factory worker? You said it. Yes ma'am.
Absotively! Posolutely!
Truck driver? Definitely!
Miner, seamstress, ditchdigger, all of them.
I am the "etceteras" and the "and so forths" that do the work.

"Ballad for Uncle Sam" was originally written for the Federal Theater Project's musical revue, *Sing for Your Supper,* but when the FTP was shut down in 1939, Norman Corwin adapted the song for his radio series, *The Pursuit of Happiness* (Denning 1997, 115). The song, retitled "Ballad for Americans," was memorably sung by Paul Robeson, famous for his mellifluous bass voice. According to Denning, Robeson recorded the ballad with the People's Chorus, "an amateur working-class chorus directed by Earl Robinson," and the resulting Victor record was a "great success" (Denning 1997, 115).

Another success story of the Cultural Front was the musical review, *Pins and Needles,* which opened in 1937. As Denning has argued, the Cultural Front fused the energy of labor organizing by the Congress of Industrial Organizations (CIO) with the progressive values espoused by Depression-era governmental cultural agencies like the Federal Theater Project. *Pins and Needles* came out of just such a collaboration. It emerged from the drama division organized by the ILGWU and the radical wing of the Federal Theater Project. The show was sponsored by the ILGWU and "performed by New York garment workers" (Denning 1997, 295). It ran for three years, holding the title of Broadway's longest-running show until that title was usurped by the musical *Oklahoma*.

The songs, many written by a young Harold Rome, were witty, political, and satiric—often poking fun at the "Tin Pan Alley" genre of mindless love songs (Denning 1997, 300). In one example, the song "Sing Me a Song of Social Significance" combined social commentary with instructions on how to get the rhythm right:

> Sing me a song with social significance,
> All other tunes are taboo.
> I want a ditty with heat in it,
> Appealing with feeling and meat in it. . . .
> Sing me of wars, sing me of breadlines,
> Tell me of front page news,
> Sing me of strikes and last minute headlines,
> Dress your observations in syncopation.

During the long run of this popular review there were backstage tensions between pro-Communist and anti-Communist songsters and producers, between Jewish garment workers and Italian garment workers, and between shopworkers who performed in the review and full-time Broadway professionals (Denning 1997, 307–8). But, as Denning has argued, *Pins and Needles* should still be regarded as a successful celebration of working-class life—a show that reclaimed "leisure and entertainment from the leisured classes" (Denning 1997, 309).

Popular proletarian journalism and literature was another legacy of the Cultural Front. John Steinbeck, who worked as both a journalist and a novelist, penned his tribute to the hardships of the era, with novels like *In Dubious Battle* (1936) and *The Grapes of Wrath* (1939); he also wrote a series of magazine articles about migrant workers, *The Harvest Gypsies* (1936). *The Grapes of Wrath* became a best seller in 1939, and its central characters, the Joad family, became a symbol of the 1930s, especially after their tragic journey from the Dust Bowl of Oklahoma to California was made into a film by John Ford in 1940. And, while some have viewed the novel's focus on white migrants (as opposed to Mexican and Filipino migrants) as indicative of the racism of the 1930s, literary historian Charles Cunningham has argued that *The Grapes of Wrath* also offered "an appeal to middle-class readers to join forces with the working-class subjects of the story," and that Steinbeck himself was radicalized after helping the victims of Visalia, California, who had suffered a devastating flood in 1938 (Cunningham 2002).

An important nexis of Popular Front literary production during the 1930s was the literary magazine *The New Masses*. Radical novelist and literary critic Mike Gold became editor of *The New Masses* in 1928, at which point he exhorted working-class readers to send in their descriptions of working-class life, and young writers to "go left" (Denning 1997, 203). In 1935 *The New Masses* called for the formation of an American Writer's Congress. It was a call for revolutionary writers to come out of isolation and discuss the "spread of fascism" and the crumbling of the "capitalist system." It was signed by a large group of writers, including such well-known writers as Nelson Algren, Kenneth Burke, Erskine Caldwell, Malcolm Cowley, Theodore Dreiser, Josephine Herbst, Granville Hicks, Langston Hughes, Tillie Lerner, Lincoln Steffens, and Richard Wright.

Though proletarian writers are often remembered as masculine, hard-boiled types, women played an important role as journalists and novelists within the literary/popular left. Meridel Le Sueur, writing for *The New Masses* in 1932, observed that there were few federal resources for women who were down on their luck: "It's one of the great mysteries of the city where women go when they are out of work and hungry. . . . Yet there must be as many women out of jobs in cities and suffering extreme poverty as there are men. What happens to them? Where do they go?" (Kirkpatrick 1989, 144). One of Le Sueur's most powerful pieces of writing, a 1935 story titled "Annunciation," about her own pregnancy, was later anthologized in her collection of writings, *Salute to Spring* (1940). Throughout the 1930s she also published essays and stories in such mainstream magazines as *Ladies' Home Journal, Scribner's,* and *The New Republic*.

Labor Songs

One of the most important labor-song balladeers in the early 1930s was "Aunt Molly." Born Mary Magdalene Garland in Clay County, Kentucky, she was five years old when her father started working in the mines to support his family. Aunt Molly remembered that her father often brought her to union meetings when she was a young girl. Her father was also a minister: "My dad was a strong union man and good minister, so he taught me to be a strong union woman" (Lynch 2001, 52). She wrote her first song at the age of four and lost her mother at the age of six.

Between 1929 and 1931 coal production dropped precipitously. During this same period the annual earnings for coal miners dropped from $1,235 to $749 per year. According to historian Timothy Lynch, with this kind of a wage cut, miners were poised for union action: "We starve while we work; we might as well strike while we starve." During a two-year fight for a fair contract for miners, Aunt Molly composed several memorable ballads that captured the spirit of the fight. In "Kentucky Miner's Wife" (also called "Ragged Hungry Blues") she speaks to the misery that affected the entire family of the struggling miner:

> I'm sad and weary, I got those hungry ragged blues;
> I'm sad and weary, I got those hungry ragged blues;
> Not a penny in my pocket to buy one thing I need to use.

I woke up this morning with the worst blues I ever had in my life;
I woke up this morning with the worst blues I ever had in my life;
Not a bite to cook for breakfast, poor coal miner's wife.
When my husband works in the coal mine he loads a car most every trip;
When my husband works in the coal mine he loads a car most every trip;
Then he goes to the office that evening and gets denied his scrip.
All the women in this coal camp are sitting with bowed-down heads;
All the women in this coal camp are sitting with bowed-down heads;
Ragged and barefooted, and their children are a-crying for bread.

During this same struggle Aunt Molly wrote a song that was more uplifting, and which cheered the mining families on in their effort to unionize:

I am a union woman,
As brave as I can be;
I do not like the bosses,
And the bosses don't like me.
Chorus
Join the NMU,
Come join the NMU. (Aunt Molly, 1931)

The struggle in Harlan County continued, and without much success for the impoverished miners. In the meantime, their plight attracted the attention of a group of progressive writers and journalists. The "Dreiser Committee," headed by novelist Theodore Dreiser, along with John Dos Passos and Sherwood Anderson, traveled to Harlan Country to investigate the working conditions of the miners. When they heard Aunt Molly sing her ballad they were so impressed with her that they asked to come to New York to raise money for the strikers.

Over the course of the 1930s Aunt Molly became a folk legend. In 1940 and 1941 she performed at benefit concerts for the New York Committee to Aid Agricultural Workers with an impressive line-up of folksingers, including Leadbelly, Burl Ives, and Joshua White. Opera and symphony composer Elie Siegmeister described Aunt Molly as one of the true American musicians after meeting her in 1940: "There are many who speak reverently of the folk music of other countries. . . . Let them listen to Aunt Molly Jackson. Let them listen to the dance songs, the music of the prairies, the work songs, the folk music that has become part of day-to-day life of the American, for this country's music yields to no other in its richness, variety and musical quality" (Siegmeister 1940, 133).

Swing Time

Though mainstream American culture was not integrated in the 1930s, the culture of "swing band" music was. In 1938, at a swing festival on Randall's Island,

Duke Ellington at the Hurricane Club, one of the centers of the New York City swing movement. (Library of Congress)

mixed African American and white couples were among the 24,000 young people who danced to more than 25 bands for more than six hours. Swing records did $26 million worth of business in 1938, and singles sold at a "rate of 700,000 discs per month." As African American bandleader Duke Ellington said, "Jazz is music, swing is *business*" (Young and Young 2005, 143).

Duke Ellington was one of the most important bandleaders of the 1930s and, perhaps, one of the most prolific and talented American composers of all time. Born into a middle-class African American family on April 29, 1899, as Edward Kennedy Ellington, Ellington started piano lessons at the age of seven. By high school he had started writing music and had earned the nickname "Duke," as a tribute to his "elegance and regal bearing" (Bennet Kinnon 1999, 86). Though Ellington and his band started playing at the Cotton Club in 1927, their first big break came when they appeared in the Amos 'n' Andy movie *Check and Double Check* (1930), which starred the white vaudevillians Gosden and Correll in blackface. Once propelled into the spotlight, Ellington and his band played throughout the country—and around the world—during the 1930s. Ellington also wrote some of his best-known compositions in this period, including "It Don't Mean a Thing if It Ain't Got that Swing" (1932), "Sophisticated Lady" (1932), and "Caravan," which Ellington wrote with Puerto Rican trombonist Juan Tizol (George 1999, 21). In the late 1930s Ellington also began working with pianist Billy Strayhorn, with whom he worked closely for the rest of his life.

One of the most popular white bandleaders of the era was Benny Goodman. Born into a poor Hungarian Jewish family in Chicago, Goodman got his musical start on the clarinet. He took clarinet lessons when he was nine years old at the Kehelah Jacob Synagogue in Chicago. Benny Goodman's father, David Goodman, worked in the Chicago stockyards, and just as his son was starting to become successful in New York (at the tender age of 16), David Goodman was killed in a tragic streetcar accident. In 1934 Benny Goodman put together his first band; the same year he auditioned for an NBC radio show, *Let's Dance*. There were three kinds of jazz that dominated the early 1930s. One was Latin jazz. A second was called "sweet." This was relatively slow, melodic, and facilitated slower forms of ballroom dancing. Benny Goodman played the third type, "hot" jazz: it was fast, up-tempo, with aggressive rhythmic and harmonic combinations. Hot jazz featured blasting solos by trumpets, clarinets, and saxophones. West Coast teenagers, who listened to Goodman on *Let's Dance* during prime-time hours (as opposed to those on the East Coast, who probably missed the broadcast because it aired after midnight), fell in love with Goodman's "hot" jazz sound, and when Goodman and his band toured the country in 1935 the kids came out in droves to the Palomar theater in Los Angeles. Elsewhere, however, Goodman bombed. The country as a whole was not yet ready for "hot" jazz, which soon became known as "swing."

Biographies

Margaret Bourke-White, 1904–1971

Photographer

Margaret Bourke-White was one of the most important American photographers of her time. Born in the Bronx, she was the daughter of an engineer (Joseph White) and a feminist mother (Minnie Bourke) so ahead of her time that she insisted that Margaret bear both of her parents' last names as her own. She spent time at several colleges, including Rutgers, the University of Michigan, and Cornell, and graduated from Cornell in 1927. After graduation and a short, failed marriage, she moved to Cleveland where her family was living. She started her own studio and took pictures of elegant homes during the week to support herself; on the weekends took pictures of steel mills. She eventually was hired as one of the first staff photographers for Henry Luce's new business magazine, *Fortune,* and later was one of the first staff photographs for *Life* magazine. By 1933, at the age of 29, she was "the most successful photographer and one of the highest-paid women in America" (Stott 1982, 216). In the early 1930s she traveled to Russia and Germany to photograph industry, and, in 1936 she traveled the South with Erskine Caldwell for their memorable book, *You Have Seen Their Faces* (1937). In 1941, while working for *Life,* she returned to Russia, just in time to photograph the bombing of Moscow. She spent the war years in Europe taking photographs for *Life;* she flew in bombers and photographed the destruction from the air, but she also photographed the aftermath of the Nazi death camps, and the beginnings of postwar reconstruction. In 1946 *Life* sent her to India where she photographed Gandhi many times; she also took the last picture of him before he was assassinated. At the age of 50 she was diagnosed with Parkinson's disease; in 1963 she published her autobiography, *Portrait of Myself,* which became a best seller. She died in 1971.

Ruth Brindze, 1903–1984

Consumer Activist/Writer

Ruth Brindze was one of the most prolific consumer writers and consumer activists of the 1930s, and also one of the most outspoken critics of commercial radio. She was born in Harlem and spent her last two years of college at the Columbia School of Journalism. Based in Westchester County, she started her journalistic career writing for the *New Rochelle Standard Star* and the *Larchmont Times,* but by the 1930s she was a regular contributor to *The Nation.* In 1933 she was appointed by President Roosevelt's Consumer Commission to head the Westchester County Consumers Council—one of the most active Consumer Councils in the country. Then, in 1935 she published her first book, *How to Spend Money: Everybody's Practical Guide to Buying.* With the success of her first book, which was patterned after the Consumer movement best sellers like *Your Money's Worth,* Brindze started writing a regular consumer guide for *The Nation.* Then, in 1937 she published her critique of commercial radio: *Not to Be Broadcast: The Truth about Radio.* She was acutely critical of the role that pro-business radio agencies and radio monopolies played in preventing certain political viewpoints—especially those of labor—from reaching the airwaves. After the publication of a consumer guide for children in 1938, *Johnny Get Your Money's Worth,* Brindze was hailed as "one of the sanest and most successful writers of consumer guides." She spent much of the rest of her career writing children's books, though she never had children of her own. She was happily married to a lawyer, Albert Fribourg, for most of her adult life, but refused to change her name to Fribourg because she was a member of the Lucy Stone League—a feminist group started in the 1920s and dedicated to "name choice" freedom. Brindze died in 1984.

Boake Carter, 1898–1944

Radio Commentator

British-born Boake Carter was one of the most popular news commentators of the 1930s. He started his career in journalism as a reporter for the *Philadelphia Daily News* and later began creating voiceovers for the newsreels that were shown before film screenings in the Philadelphia area. This eventually led to his career as a radio commentator on the Philadelphia station WCAU. He became an overnight sensation when fans responded enthusiastically to his sensational reporting of the kidnapping of Charles Lindbergh's son. His signature sign-off was "Cheerio." In 1933 Carter signed a five-year sponsorship with Philco radio; this was a symbiotic relationship, since, as Carter's popularity grew, more of his listeners bought Philco radios with which to hear him. He also had a large, working-class audience and Philco made small, affordable, table-top radios that were perfect for this market. At the height of his popularity Carter's syndicated column appeared three days a week in dozens of newspapers across the country, and there was even a board game designed around him: "Boake Carter: Star Reporter." But Carter's working-class audience turned on him when his commentary became increasingly anti-union. And, when Carter started attacking the growing CIO movement—the union movement within which Philco workers were organized—Philco workers organized a nationwide boycott of Carter's broadcasts and even of their very own radio company, Philco. The boycott was so successful that Philco refused to sign a new contract with Carter in 1938, and, even though Carter found a new sponsor in General Mills, he never regained his former popularity. In the 1940s he joined a fringe, anti-Semitic group and died at the age of 44.

Boake Carter, who was rumored to be quite short, hated to be photographed standing up. (Library of Congress)

Irna Phillips, 1901–1973

Radio/Television Soap Opera Writer

Irna Phillips was one of the most prolific soap opera writers of the mid-century, with a career that spanned both radio and television. She was petite, just five-feet three-inches, with a plain face and flashing blue eyes. Though at first she wanted to be an actress she was quickly told that she had "neither the looks nor the stature to achieve professional success." So she tried her hand at radio writing. In 1930 she began writing a serial for WBN Chicago called *Painted Dreams*. It was successful, but she lost the rights to it, so she created another serial, *Today's Children,* for WMAQ (WBN's competition) that featured an immigrant mother much like her own. Phillips was the tenth child of German Jewish parents who ran a small grocery in Chicago. *Painted Dreams* and *Today's Children* are considered the first soap operas created for radio, and Phillips is largely credited with inventing the genre. She went on to create an additional eight radio soaps and nine television soaps, including *The Guiding Light,* which ran for 19 years on radio and from 1952 to the present on the CBS television network. Phillips, though she never married, adopted two children in her forties, and, in 1940, she was one of the highest-paid women in radio, making $250,000 a year. She was not a feminist, or a social progressive, but she was a pioneering career woman and a single mother long before either was the norm.

Earl Robinson, 1910–1991

Composer/Activist

Earl Robinson was born in Seattle, Washington. Having completed the musical composition program at the University of Washington in 1933, he was a mere 24 years old when he left Seattle to work with the Federal Theater Project. There he joined one of the more radical groups within the FTP, the "Shock Troupe of the Workers Laboratory Theatre" (Denning 1997, 115). Robinson became best known for his 1939 composition "Ballad for Americans," which he wrote with lyricist John LaTouche. Another song for which Robinson has been remembered is "The House I Live In," a song that became part of Frank Sinatra's early repertoire. In 1947 Sinatra starred in a short documentary, also titled *The House I Live In,* which featured the song; Sinatra won an Oscar. If "The House I Live In" was Robinson's most popular musical achievement, the song he wrote which was closest to the heart of the labor movement and the folk song movement was "Joe Hill," a song commemorating the leader of the Industrial Workers of the World. Hill was executed by a firing squad in Utah in 1915, but in Robinson's tribute, Hill's legacy lives on in those who organize:

> I dreamed I saw Joe Hill last night,
> Alive as you and me.
> Says I, "But, Joe, you're ten years dead,"
> "I never died," says he,
> "I never died," says he.

Robinson was blacklisted during the McCarthy era, but he was able to earn his living as the chair of the music department at Elisabeth Irwin High School in New York City. Robinson was "rediscovered" by the folk-music revival of the 1960s. He later returned to Seattle in 1989, and was killed in a car accident in 1991.

Anna May Wong, 1905–1961

Actress

Anna May Wong was born in Los Angeles, California, as Wong Liu Tsong. She is considered the most "legendary" Asian American actress of the 1920s and 1930s. She grew up watching early film crews shoot in the streets of Los Angeles's Chinatown, and had her first film role in the big budget tribute to the Boxer Rebellion, *The Red Lantern,* in 1919. Her first credited role was as Lon Chaney's long-suffering wife in *Bits of Life* (1921) and then she was cast as the star of a film based loosely on the Madame Butterfly story, *The Toll of Sea* (1922). In 1923 Douglas Fairbanks saw her in a film and was so impressed with her he cast her as the "Mongolian Slave Girl" in his Arabian Nights film *The Thief of Baghdad* (1924). She made more than 30 silent films during the 1920s, many of which have been lost forever. Her most memorable role came in 1932 when she starred with Marlene Dietrich in *Shanghai Express*. In 1937 she was rejected for the role of O-lan in *The Good Earth,* losing the role to Austrian-born actress Luise Rainer (who won an Oscar for the role). But in 1937 Wong also starred in her most significant film, *Daughter of Shanghai,* in which there were two Asian leads—Anna May Wong and her romantic interest, played by Phillip Ahn. Even today it is rare for Hollywood to cast an Asian man and an Asian woman as a romantic pair. She also made an impact with *Dangerous to Know* (1938), in which she played the vengeful lover of a gangster. After 1938 Wong left Hollywood, because, she complained, her characters were usually subjected to a tragic death. She died in 1961, leaving behind a career in which she had made more than 60 films, and is still considered one of the most successful Asian actresses Hollywood has ever seen.

Chinese American actress Anna May Wong. (Library of Congress)

References and Further Readings

American Slave Narratives. http://newdeal.feri.org/asn/asn00.html/.

Aunt Molly, 1931."Kentucky Miner's Wife (Ragged Hungry Blues)." http://xroads.virginia.edu/~MA05/luckey/amj/dreiser.htm.

Bennet-Kinnon, J. 1999. "Was Ellington America's Greatest Composer?" *Ebony* 54 (6): 86.

Bourke-White, M. 1963. *Portrait of Myself*. New York: Simon and Schuster.

Buni, A. 1974. *Robert L. Vann of the Pittsburgh Courier: Politics and Black Journalism*. Pittsburgh: University of Pittsburgh Press.

Buttitta, T., and B. Witham. 1982. *Uncle Sam Presents: A Memoir of the Federal Theatre, 1935–1939*. Philadelphia: University of Pennsylvania Press.

Caldwell, E., and M. Bourke-White. 1937. *You Have Seen Their Faces*. New York: Modern Age Books.

Cayleff, S. 1996. *Babe: The Life and Legend of Babe Didrikson Zaharias*. Urbana: University of Illinois Press.

Chapin, L. 1940. "Southern Scene," *South Atlantic Bulletin,* December, 12–13.

Coiner, C. 1998. *Better Red: The Writing and Resistance of Tillie Olsen and Meridel Le Sueur.* Urbana: University of Illinois Press.

Correll, C., and F. Gosden. 1930. *Amos and Andy,* no. 862, December 27, http://www.midcoast.com/~lizmcl/aa862.html.

Cunningham, C. 2002. "Rethinking the Politics of *The Grapes of Wrath,*" *Cultural Logic* 5. Online at http://clogic.eserver.org/2002/cunningham.html.

Currell, S. 2006. *The March of Spare Time: The Problem and Promise of Leisure in the Great Depression*. Philadelphia: University of Pennsylvania Press.

Deane, Elizabeth, Adriana Bosch, and David Ogden Stiers. 2000. *The Rockefellers* Video Recording. Arlington, VA, PBS. See also "Primary Materials" at http://www.pbs.org/wgbh/amex/rockefellers/filmmore/ps_rivera.html.

"Denies Apple Men Profit on Jobless." 1930. *New York Times,* November 14, 4.

Denning, M. 1998. *Cultural Front: The Laboring of American Culture in the Twentieth Century*. New York: Verso.

"Detroit in Furor over Rivera Art." 1933. *New York Times,* March 22, 15.

Doherty, T. 1999. *Pre-Code Hollywood: Sex, Immorality, and Insurrection in American Cinema, 1930–1934*. New York: Columbia University Press.

Downs, L. 1999. *Diego Rivera: The Detroit Industry Murals*. New York: W. W. Norton.

Durgnat, R., and S. Simmon. 1988. *King Vidor, American*. Berkeley: University of California Press.

D.W.C. 1936. "The Curious Mr. Chaplin: A Bundle of Paradoxes, the Comedian Is Still a Riddle to the Film World," *New York Times,* February 15, X4.

Earhart, A. 1937. *Last Flight*. Text arranged by George Palmer Putnam. New York: Harcourt Brace.

Ely, M. 1991. *The Adventures of Amos 'n' Andy: A Social History of an American Phenomenon*. New York: The Free Press.

Erenberg, L. 1986. "From New York to Middletown: Repeal and the Legitimization of Nightlife in the Great Depression," *American Quarterly,* 761–78.

Filene, B. 2000. *Romancing the Folk: Public Memory and American Roots Music*. Chapel Hill: University of North Carolina Press.

Fraden, R. 1994. *Blueprints for a Black Federal Theatre, 1935–1939*. New York: Cambridge University Press.

George, L. 1999. "Duke Ellington: The Man and His Music," *Music Educators Journal* 85 (6): 15–21.

Hanson, A. 1980. "A Comparison of Documentary Approaches: Margaret Bourke-White and Erskine Caldwell, Authors of *You Have Seen Their Faces,* and Dorothea Lange and Paul S. Taylor, Authors of *An American Exodus.*" Paper presented at the sixty-third annual meeting of the Association for Education in Journalism, Boston, August 9–13.

Havis, R. 2004. "Anna May Wong: From Laundryman's Daughter to Hollywood Legend," *Cineaste* 30:67–69.

Herberholz, B. 2000. "Thomas Hart Benton's Home and Studio," *Art and Activities* 127 (2): 38–40, 48–49.

Hurlburt, L. 1989. *The Mexican Muralists in the United States.* Albuquerque: University of New Mexico Press.

Jojola, T. 1998. "Absurd Reality II: Hollywood Goes to the Indians." In *Hollywood's Indian: The Portrayal of the Native American in Film,* ed. P. Rollins and J. O'Connor. Lexington: University of Kentucky Press, 1998.

Kennedy, R. 2004. *Monopoly: The Story Behind the World's Best Selling Game.* Layton, UT: Gibbs Smith.

Kirkpatrick, K. 1989. "Women Writers in the Proletarian Collection, McFarlin Library," *Tulsa Studies in Women's Literature* 8 (1): 143–48.

"Last Cheers of French Audience for *Smith Goes to Washington.*" 1942. *Hollywood Reporter,* November 4. Online at http://xroads.virginia.edu/~ma97/halnon/capra/smithrev.html.

Leong, K. 2005. *The China Mystique: Pearl S. Buck, Anna May Wong, Mayling Soong and the Transformation of American Orientalism.* Berkeley: University of California Press.

L. N. 1936. "The Play: Pine Forest," *New York Times,* June 27, 21.

Locke, A. 1937. "God Save Reality! Retrospective Review of the Literature of the Negro: 1936," *Opportunity* 15 (1): 12.

Lynch, T. 2001. *Strike Songs of the Depression.* Jackson: University Press of Mississippi.

"'A Lynching' in Broadway." 1933. *Guardian Unlimited,* 6 December. http://century.guardian.co.uk/1930–1939/Story/0,,126964,00.html.

Marling, K. 2000. *Wall-to-Wall America: Post-Office Murals in the Great Depression.* Minneapolis: University of Minnesota Press.

Martin, M. 1964. "Interview with Dorothy Cravath." Smithsonian Archives of American Art. http://www.aaa.si.edu/collections/oralhistories/transcripts/cravat64.htm.

Morris, G. N.d. "A Brief History of Queer Cinema." Greencine Web site. http://www.greencine.com/static/primers/queer.jsp.

Munby, J. 1999. *Public Enemies, Public Heroes. Screening the Gangster from* Little Caesar *to* Touch of Evil. Chicago: University of Chicago Press.

Newman, K. 2004. *Radio Active: Advertising and Consumer Activism, 1935–1947.* Berkeley: University of California Press.

Nugent, F. 1939. "Capra's Capitol Offense," *New York Times,* October 29, X5.

"Police to Bar Apple Vendors from Midtown." 1931. *New York Times,* April 3, 26

Raeburn, John. 2006. *A Staggering Revolution: A Cultural History of Thirties Photography.* Urbana: University of Illinois Press.

Reider, R. 1999. "Robinson, Earl Hawley." HistoryLink.org, Essay 2029. http://www.historylink.org/essays/output.cfm?file_id=2029.

Rivera, D., with G. March. 1960. *My Art, My Life: An Autobiography [by] Diego Rivera.* New York: Citadel Press. Republished by Dover Publications 1991.

Robinson, E., and J. LaTouche. International Lyrics Playground. http://lyrics playground.com/alpha/songs/b/balladforamericans.shtml.

Robinson, E., with Erica A. Gordon. 1998. *Ballad of an American: Autobiography of Earl Robinson.* Lanham, MD: Scarecrow Press.

Rosenthal, N. 2005. "Representing Indians: Native American Actors on Hollywood's Frontier," *Western Historical Quarterly* 6 (3): 329–52.

Sarris, A. 1978. "The Sex Comedy Without the Sex," *American Film* (March): 8–15.

Shindo, C. 1997. *Dust Bowl Migrants in the American Imagination.* Lawrence: University Press of Kansas.

Siegmeister, E. 1940. "America's Folksongs," *New York Times,* February 11, 133.

Smith, J., with P. Morell. 1935. *Turpentine.* Electronic eition by Alexander Street Press, L.L.C., 2005. http://www.alexanderstreet4.com/cgi-bin/asp/bldr/navigate?/projects/artfla/databases/asp/bldr/fulltext/IMAGE/.155.

Stevenson, P. 1936. "Turpentine Workers," *New Theatre* (August): 18.

Stott, W. 1986. *Documentary Expression and Thirties America.* Chicago: University of Chicago Press.

Wilson, R. 2000. Review of "Public Enemies, Public Heroes: Screening the Gangster from *Little Caesar* to *Touch of Evil,*" *Film Quarterly,* 54–56.

Young, W., and N. Young. 2002. *The 1930s.* Westport, CT: Greenwood Press.

Young, W., and N. Young. 2005. *Music of the Great Depression.* Westport, CT: Greenwood Press.

Private Lives

By Alice L. George

Overview

Even when a calamity such as the Great Depression strikes a nation, everyday life goes on. Individuals adapt to the crises reshaping their society as they proceed from day to day in their private lives. The Great Depression had little impact on a wealthy few, but it touched the lives of the majority of Americans. Whether they were struggling to regain lost fortunes or merely trying to protect their families from the further ravages of financial decline, most Americans lived within the shadow of this great economic disaster. Many lived each day like a drowning man struggling to keep his head above water amid the assault of pounding waves. For some, what had once been small concerns—feeding and clothing their families—became burdensome tasks.

Some families tightened their bonds to provide mutual support during the darkest days of the 1930s. Even keeping a roof over a family's head was a challenge in a decade when there were more than 1.5 million nonfarm home foreclosures (U.S. Bureau of the Census 1949, 174). Some extended families crowded into shabby tenements to save money. The ravages of desperation, shame, and neediness shattered many households, and families disintegrated, unable to face the pressures of achieving economic survival. Thousands of boys joined men who hit the rails and became migrant workers, following an erratic path toward the promise of self-preservation. Other unemployed men haunted their homes, ghosts of their former selves, now shrouded in self-pity and disgrace. Women strained to maintain the family, sometimes as the lone wage earner and often as the administrator of the household budget. Women without jobs sometimes found small ways to earn money at home, and many became experts at living cheaply. For many Americans, from children to senior citizens, hunger and malnutrition became a part of daily existence, and troublesome medical problems among the poor led to greater government involvement in health care. In their time of need, some Americans turned to religion; others found that church membership was one more thing they could not afford. At school, formerly middle-class children faced humiliation as they struggled to maintain their social status in the face of poverty. Adolescents found fewer available jobs and consequently remained in public school longer than they might have in more prosperous times.

While the government spawned New Deal programs in the public sector to counteract the effects of the economic disaster gripping the nation, individuals fought privately to maintain their identities, their families, and their way of life. Driven by the fear of losing their privileged status, many anxious middle-class Americans shared a frenetic existence just beyond poverty's grasp. Insecure about their future standing, they tried to stay one step ahead of impending disaster and loss. Among the poor, frustrated men queued up in breadlines, and resourceful mothers mixed ketchup and water to create tomato soup for their children. This era became a benchmark in the lives of its survivors and a source of life lessons. For many children of the 1930s, the period's most memorable moments occurred behind closed doors as they watched their parents' personal battle to survive.

Timeline

1930 Only 20.4 percent of Americans in the 14- to 19-year-old age group have jobs. This represents a considerable drop from a level of 31 percent 10 years earlier. This figure continued to drop through the 1930s, hitting 13.2 percent in 1940.

The percentage of 10- to 15-year-olds in the workforce drops to 4.7 percent, down from 8.5 percent in 1920.

Children's portion of the population, which stood at 56 percent 100 years earlier, now is only 38 percent. It will drop to 36 percent over the next decade.

In Harlem, African American men in the 35 to 44 age group are three times as likely to be single as their counterparts in South Carolina because the New York neighborhood offers a refuge for gay men, according to historian George Chauncey.

1931 Adults and children reportedly forage for food in the garbage dumps of New York and St. Louis.

New York newspapers launch a crusade against clubs where female impersonators perform and where emcees "boast of a lavender tinge in their makeup."

1932 An estimated 1 to 2 million men are roaming the country looking for work.

The marriage rate stands at 7.87 per 1,000 persons, a significant decline from 1929, when the same rate was 10.14. There are 250,000 fewer weddings than there had been three years earlier.

The Public Health Service starts a 40-year Tuskegee study of the impact of syphilis on untreated African American men in Macon County, Alabama.

1933 Average family income is 40 percent less than it was in 1929.

The divorce rate in Muncie, Indiana, shows a 43 percent drop over the last five years.

Fewer than 17 million telephones are in service, a drop from more than 20 million in 1930.

The nation's infant mortality rate ends a steady drop and begins to rise.

1934 Spending on public schools is down 34 percent from pre-Depression years.

1935 The average southern girl leaves school at 14 or 15, Nora Miller's *The Girl in the Rural South* reports.

St. Jude's National Shrine begins publishing the *Voice of St. Jude*. Thousands of Americans start writing to the shrine asking for favors from the saint.

1936 Presbyterian churches record a 5 percent drop in membership over 10 years;

Episcopalians report a 6.7 percent decline over the same period. Meanwhile, membership in fundamentalist churches is mushrooming.

The Moody Bible Institute conducts nearly 500 Bible conferences nationwide.

Sixty-three percent of Americans support teaching and using birth control, according to a Gallup poll.

1938 The number of Americans paying for products with installment plans exceeds the number of Americans who approve of buying on credit, according to a *Ladies' Home Journal* survey.

About 1.5 million people have postponed marriage because of economic hardship, according to one expert.

Life magazine concludes that young people in this era of economic upheaval "are a sober lot."

1939 Margaret Jarman Hagood's *Mothers of the South* shows that the fertility rate among southern farm women is 6.4 live births per married woman, compared to an average of 2.4 births per married woman nationwide.

Family

Unemployment and wage slashing had dramatic effects on many families during the 1930s. In 1932 only 72 percent of American households included an employed wage earner (Mintz and Kellogg 1988, 134). A year later, Americans' overall income was about 55 percent of what it had been in 1929, according to U.S. Census data. Some unemployed Americans left their homes every day in search of work and after giving up on the day's quest passed the time by reading in public libraries. Selling surplus products became an occasional occupation for many of the unemployed. The International Apple Shippers Association kicked off this process by allowing individuals to buy a case of apples and then sell them on the street at a profit. After repaying the distributor for the crate of fruit, a person could make a little over $1 a day. In addition to other produce items, the unemployed sometimes sold neckties under a similar arrangement. Others went door to door selling brushes or Bibles, and some set up makeshift shoeshine operations on sidewalks.

Lack of employment affected the state of the American family. Some couples chose to delay marriages until their financial position improved, although the marriage rate stopped its decline and began to rise in 1934. Others decided not to have children or to minimize the number of children in their household. Married women increasingly entered the workforce on at least a part-time basis, reducing their ability to provide child care. Male breadwinners sometimes suffered psychological problems after losing their jobs and quickly spending their entire life savings on necessities like housing and food. If these men felt compelled to apply for relief, their suffering was greater, particularly if they had previously

Members of a South Texas farm family halt their quest for work long enough to repair a tire on their truck. The penniless parents are taking their three children to the Arkansas Delta, where they hope to find work in the cotton fields. "It's tough," the father says, "but life's tough any way you take it." (Library of Congress)

belonged to the middle class. Unemployment also put husbands and wives in close proximity all day long—and that could lead to marital strife. Alcoholism offered one escape from the harsh realities of daily life. Desertion rates also were high as many men drifted away from their wives and children. While some fathers hit the rails or hitchhiked to find jobs to support their families, others set out to start new lives. Sons also joined the transient community as they sought work and independence. And entire farm families became migratory, following crops to earn enough money to survive.

Over the course of the Great Depression, families developed as economic units and demonstrated differences based on race, class, and gender. African Americans made up a disproportionately large percent of the unemployed in many urban areas and in the rural South. Many African American women, who worked as domestic servants in middle-class white homes, lost jobs as their employers struggled to maintain their standard of living despite unemployment or shrinking paychecks. Men and women sometimes found themselves cast in new and unfamiliar roles; others struggled to maintain the living status they had enjoyed before hard times arrived. The Depression era also witnessed more open homosexual lifestyles in places like New York, where diversity in the population had become common.

Family Ties

Dependence on extended families was a natural outgrowth of the Great Depression, with housing frequently serving as the focal point for interdependence. Many families could not afford rent or mortgage payments. Foreclosures or evictions forced families to find innovative solutions to their housing woes. A significant number of families shared housing units with relatives or with neighbors. In some cases, severe crowding made it necessary for residents to sleep in shifts. A survey of workers who had lost their jobs at U.S. Rubber Company in two Connecticut towns showed that 15 percent of the unemployed workers' households included members besides parents and children. Such "superfamilies," which sometimes included multiple wage earners, eased housing problems and sometimes provided loans for family members as well as gifts of food or clothing. The Emergency Work Bureau of Philadelphia surveyed almost 1,500 applicants and discovered that 12.9 percent had received some form of aid other than loans from family members, and 10 percent lived in shared housing (Wandersee 1981, 30, 31).

In many cases, extended family households included two groups with declining employability—teenagers and senior citizens. In 1931, when overall unemployment stood at 15 percent, a survey showed that 35 percent of workers between the ages of 16 and 25 were jobless (Kyvig 2002, 221). Teenaged boys sometimes could find part-time work that generated a small amount of income. Typically, they worked as janitors, assisted clerks in retail establishments, or delivered newspapers. Fewer jobs were open to young girls, so they commonly worked at home to help their mothers make wise use of the limited household budget. At the same time, many employers forced workers over 60 into retirement or part-time status. The 1930 Census showed that Americans over 65 made up 5.5 percent of the overall population, but by 1940 that percentage had grown to almost 7 percent. Because Americans were living longer, the issue of care for the elderly gained new importance. Traditionally, old people on farms had worked up until the day they died; however, factory jobs could be too strenuous for elderly workers. Not surprisingly, employers favored workers who were more mature than teenagers but young enough to handle a heavy workload.

With both young and old family members unable to find full-time jobs, the burden on wage earners was onerous. In crowded tenements where two or more families lived together, dependency strengthened some family ties while the psychological effects of unemployment and poverty placed great strain on others. Thousands of the poorest Americans settled in tarpaper shacks in "Hoovervilles,"

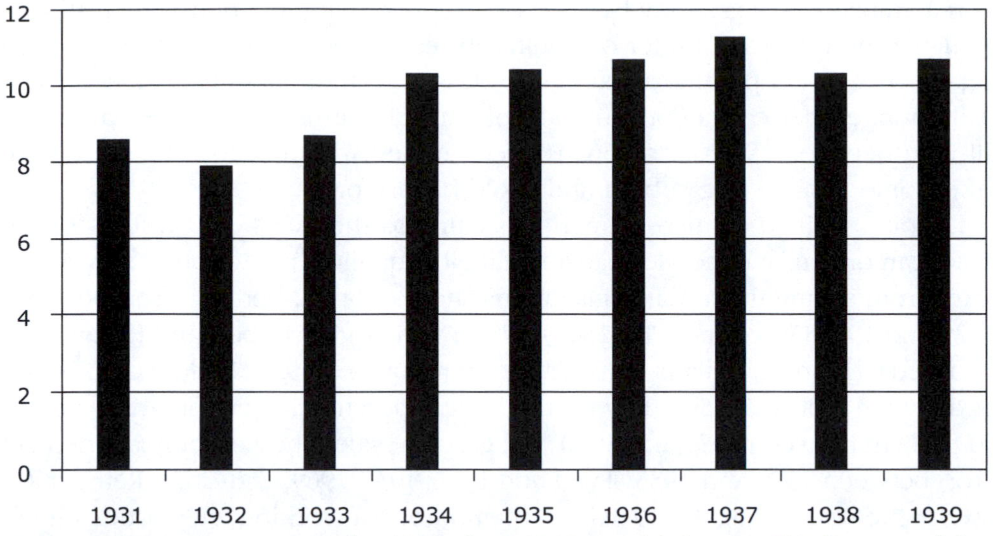

Figure 7.1 *Marriage rate in the 1930s (per 1,000 people).* Source: *U.S. Bureau of the Census, 1949.*

which typically formed on the fringe of urban areas. Housing was more expensive for African Americans, who routinely devoted almost half of their earnings to rent, leaving insufficient savings for other living expenses such as food, running water, and electricity. In the face of these circumstances, hundreds of thousands of Americans watched their families come apart.

The Family as Consumer Unit

The typical Depression-era family had an annual income of $1,100 to $1,200, which provided $20 to $25 a week for household expenses. Weekly expenses included food, clothing, and housing (Ware 1982, 3). Faced with the challenge of living on a small budget, families adapted in a variety of ways. Those who lost their jobs generally exhausted their savings quickly. More than half of those applying for work at the Emergency Work Bureau in Philadelphia had some savings when the economic catastrophe began. When savings had been drained, many applicants' families found themselves in debt. More than half were behind schedule in paying rent. Twenty-six percent borrowed money, and almost as many obtained credit from grocers (Wandersee 1981, 31). Clothes and food became cheaper and that reduced expenses; however, spending on housing, which included rent, fuel, electricity, and refrigeration, rose during the same period. Plumbing upgrades and the addition of electrical service were responsible for most of that increase. When household resources had been stretched to the limit, women, who usually controlled the budget, developed new ways of maximizing savings. They became experts at finding inexpensive substitutes —margarine instead of butter or poultry instead of beef. Jell-O, a fruit-flavored gelatin, became a popular inexpensive dessert. Although some families faced daily hunger, per capita consumption of spinach, citrus fruits, juices, and milk all rose between 1917 and 1936. To save money without reducing calorie intake, some families began buying day-old bakery products.

Despite strained finances, Americans clung to their cars. As symbols of the American dream, automobiles had an intangible quality that stopped many Americans from selling them. Car registrations show only a 2 percent drop between 1929 and 1935 (Wandersee 1981, 41). When sociologists Robert and Helen Lynd returned to Muncie, Indiana, to update their renowned 1929 "Middletown" study of daily life in a small city, they found that car purchases were down by almost 50 percent between 1929 and 1930, but gasoline sales showed only a 4 percent drop between 1929 and 1933 (Lynd and Lynd 1937/1969, 266–267). Refrigerator ownership rose during the 1930s, but the number of working telephones shrank in the decade's first four years. Despite a drop in prices, new clothes remained too expensive for some. As a result, many women used sewing tricks to make children's clothes last longer and repaired shoes with strips of cardboard. Some lined coats with old blankets to provide better protection from the cold. With little money to spend on outside entertainment, many families spent leisure time gathered around the radio, listening to their favorite shows. Playing cards and board games also were popular pastimes. Monopoly, which was introduced in the middle of the decade, became a fad, and with its prime properties for sale, the game provided an ironic counterpoint to the real lives of most Americans during the Great Depression.

How Classes Were Affected

The Depression affected Americans of all classes, but it probably took the greatest psychological toll on newly minted members of the middle class. Living cheaply was common for working-class families, but members of the middle class, which expanded significantly in the 1920s, had become accustomed to certain luxuries. Working-class urban families were the most likely to seek relief, although agricultural families frequently had smaller incomes, according to a 1941 Indianapolis study. Researchers also found that very few white-collar families sought relief despite economic hardships. Pride apparently motivated this trend. At the same time, middle-class women struggled to maintain the external trappings of their former status. Generally, the hardest-hit white-collar workers were young employees who had not worked long enough to establish a safety net against economic catastrophe (Modell 1985, 408). Interviews with Oakland, California, families showed that middle-class mothers with jobless spouses demonstrated greater fatigue, less security, and deeper dissatisfaction

Aviator Charles Lindbergh testifies about the disappearance of his infant son from the family's home. The child's death became one of the most notorious crimes of the decade. (Library of Congress)

than other women. A follow-up study in 1958 showed that daughters of parents who had lost status during the Depression were less likely to remember either their father or mother as a "good" parent (Elder 1974/1999, 54–55, 109)

Many wealthy Americans avoided economic collapse, but they were nevertheless affected. For example, prices of premium products dropped. One jeweler offered a $50,000 emerald ring for just $37,500, while Bergdorf Goodman reduced the prices of sable products by 40 percent. The Pullman Company also slashed the cost of upper berths in railroad passenger cars by one-fifth (Leuchtenburg 1958/1993, 248). Affluent Americans who typically donated to charities reduced their contributions during the 1930s—and as a result, private agencies had fewer resources to help to the poor. Some contributors reneged on pledges, and the United Hospital Fund reported that some sought refunds. Although hunger and homelessness were distant threats to these Americans, they, too, felt the need to tighten their belts as the economy faltered.

The decade's most notorious crime seemed to suggest that no amount of success could guarantee a family's safety. The infant son of aviator Charles Lindbergh and his wife, writer Anne Morrow Lindbergh, was reported missing March 1, 1932. *Editor and Publisher,* a journalistic trade publication, proclaimed, "With news more important because more heart-rending than any in the last decade, facing them, more than 150 reporters[,] photographers, motion picture men, and broadcasters crowded around the Lindbergh house on that first day" (Hughes 1936, 34). The media frenzy surrounding the apparent kidnapping extended through most of the decade, providing a distraction from daily household worries. H. L. Mencken wrote that the case was "the greatest story since the Resurrection" (*Famous American Trials*). The Lindberghs paid a $50,000 ransom, but the baby's body was found buried near their home about two months after his disappearance. Convincing evidence against a convicted burglar, Richard "Bruno" Hauptmann, led to a conviction and execution. Speculation that the baby was killed accidentally within the Lindbergh household has never been proven.

Alternative Lifestyles: The Gay Community

American culture frowned upon open homosexuality during this era; nevertheless, New York, with its huge and diverse population, offered one environment in which gays could gather in their own communities within neighborhoods. During the Prohibition years, 1920–1933, the city experienced a "pansy craze." It began when gay men became prominent figures in the Times Square amusement district, where they appeared in nightclubs and on stage. These shows, which were most popular in 1930–1931, received attention in *Variety* and other mainstream publications. The Times Square shows continued throughout the decade, although there was a major crackdown in 1939 just before the World's Fair.

Although church leaders campaigned against public acknowledgment of Harlem's gay community, the annual Hamilton Lodge Ball had become a gay-dominated event in the previous decade when many drag queens began to attend. The ball's popularity climbed in the 1930s. In 1934 the *Amsterdam News* reported 4,000 people attended the ball as participants or spectators. The level of attendance was about the same through the rest of the decade, except in 1937 when the crowd skyrocketed to 8,000. Among the attendees were both African Americans and whites, including socialites, prostitutes, cutting-edge literary figures, and neighborhood families. The event, commonly known as "the Fairies' Ball," attracted attention in conventional publications. Historian George Chauncey has argued that drag queens became an accepted part of Harlem's black community because their femininity helped to accentuate the perceived masculinity of most African American men (Chauncey 1994, 256–60).

Historians, sociologists, and doctors who studied gay culture uncovered a separate culture within Manhattan. "I have no contact with heterosexual people," one man reported to a physician in the late 1930s. If homosexuals wanted to secede from heterosexual culture, they could live, work, and socialize solely with members of gay culture. Discreet gay men faced relatively little harassment as long as they frequented bathhouses and bars that catered to them. Social historian Caroline Ware, who made a study of Greenwich Village's gay community, found that "by 1930, promiscuity was tame and homosexuality had become the expected thing." She found examples of heterosexual people apparently pretending to be gay to develop an avant garde reputation (Chauncey 1994, 235).

The Depression Touches Many Lives

The Great Depression had an impact on the family lives of millions of Americans. In some families, it weakened the position of fathers as heads of families. In others, it led to combining households with friends or relatives. Tough times also led both individuals and entire families to leave their homes and travel in search of work. The fact that so many Americans drastically altered their living arrangements for economic survival affected a generation of children, who lacked the pleasant security their parents had enjoyed during the century's first three decades. Middle-class families experienced a period of unusual insecurity that was addressed by New Deal programs such as Social Security. The federal government's Rural Electrification program also transformed the lives of families in rural areas by making electricity available to a significant minority of rural households, allowing farmers access to the blossoming national culture driven by the power of radio. Before 1935 only 10 percent of farms had electrical power; by 1941 40 percent were electrified (Ware 1982, 9). Moreover, the Public Works Administration built schools and cultural institutions.

At the same time, labor unions, which usually excluded or discouraged female membership, reached out to women as the budget masters of American families. Organized labor urged shoppers to buy only products made by union workers. Viewing families as consumer units enhanced the perceived power of wives and mothers.

The Congress of Industrial Organizations also made the maintenance of family life a high priority by organizing social events intended to bolster family connections.

Women

When aviatrix Amelia Earhart disappeared during an effort to fly around the world, people worldwide were tantalized by the mystery. For Earhart, the 1930s had provided an opportunity to overcome gender barriers and partake in a great adventure. Most American women faced serious challenges during the decade, but the typical woman, unlike Earhart, found her life defined by the necessity to preserve her family in difficult times. Because women lacked a national organization to promote their goals and because 90 percent of married women did not pursue long-term careers outside the home, they typically functioned in isolation, struggling to make the most of a tight family budget. Consequently, women were more likely than men to maintain strong ties to their extended kinship circle.

In this era, new attitudes about sex, marriage, and birth control affected women's lives, but there were also more mundane changes in their work at home. Women continued to perform the household work long allocated to females—cooking, cleaning, and caring for children. A study done in 1929 showed that the amount of time a woman invested in housework ranged from 44.3 hours to 87.5 hours per week (Wandersee 1981, 58). In the 1930s, women had access to new products that affected how they approached their labors. Grocery stores offered an ever-broadening array of packaged foods that required little preparation, like 21 varieties of Campbell's soups, six kinds of Jello-O, Van Camp pork and beans, Del Monte fruits, Heinz spaghetti, and a variety of breakfast foods, including Post Grape Nuts Flakes, Cream of Wheat, and Kellogg's Corn Flakes. In addition, gas stoves had replaced wood- and coal-burning stoves in many households. They made cooking easier and reduced the amount of time necessary to clean up. Telephone shopping and newly developed supermarkets offered more efficient ways for women to get the products they needed. For those who could afford them, vacuum cleaners also simplified housework.

Even on more primitive farms, there was a sharp division of labor based on gender. Women cooked, sewed, and washed clothes, while men were busy maintaining the farm. Clothes washing was the most difficult task as women cleaned everything from men's overalls to babies' dirty diapers. Men and women shared responsibility for tending to livestock. Rural women were both geographically and psychologically isolated, and most of them lacked modern conveniences like gas ovens and electric lighting.

Women's Work

Women of this era found societal pressure to stay at home and pursue traditional domestic tasks; however, the family budget forced some women to find work outside the home. Fewer than 20 percent of families at the lowest income level had more than one wage earner, but the number of families with multiple wage earners grew among those with $800 to $1,600 in annual income and was even higher for those with annual incomes of more than $1,600. Sometimes, these extra workers were male relatives, but by 1940 working wives contributed to the household economy more than teenaged children. Nevertheless, most of the married women who worked were not the sole wage earner in their homes.

Many women found ways to earn money while staying at home. Taking in boarders who slept or ate in the house was one means of generating income. These guests were able to enjoy home cooking and other amenities for much less than a hotel or restaurant would charge. In houses with boarders, women and children worked to make their guests comfortable. Typically, the guests ate first, and then the family dined on whatever was left.

Some skills, such as sewing, baking, and pickling, could be used to make a small profit or to save money for the family by avoiding the need to buy food. Some women offered their services as seamstresses to private customers. At the same time, many used their sewing talents to bolster the family budget by making clothes last longer or by producing new clothing. However, as clothing prices declined, women found that many ready-made items could be purchased so cheaply that sewing at home was unnecessary. Pickled goods or bakery items could be used to expand the family's food supply or to bring in a bit of extra income. Sales of glass jars rose as demands for packaged foods in cans and jars dropped in 1931.

Changing Attitudes about Sex and Marriage

Young adults in the United States married at a slower than average rate in the 1930s, and at the same time, surveys showed less restrictive attitudes among young people about premarital sex. Faced with economic uncertainties, many couples chose to postpone weddings for months or years, and when couples did marry, weddings tended to be modest affairs held at home with only family members present. The marriage rate stood at 7.87 per 1,000 persons by 1932, a plunge from 10.14 in 1929. One source estimated that as many as 1.5 million Americans postponed their marriages because couples did not earn enough to finance a separate household. Sometimes, temporary postponements led to permanent cancellations. After the Depression ended, women who had been between 25 and 30 in 1935 made up a much larger proportion of the single female population than those who were five years older. One schoolteacher recalled. "I was going with someone when the Depression hit. We probably would have gotten married. . . . Suddenly, he was laid off. It hit him like a ton of bricks. And he just disappeared" (Ware 1982, 6–7).

While promiscuity did not run rampant through the growing single population as some commentators had predicted, premarital sexual activity was fairly common on college campuses. In fact, *Fortune* reported, "Sex is no longer news." Just as it was then acceptable for college women to wear makeup and smoke, new sexual mores changed anticipated behavior. Dorothy Dunbar Bromley and Florence Britten opened their 1938 study, "Youth and Sex," by asserting, "Joe and Jane petting on the back seat of an automobile are unimportant. Five million boys and girls petting on public highways have national significance." Their interviews showed that 50 percent of male college students and 25 percent of female students had engaged in premarital sex. In most cases, women did not take part in sex until they were engaged or believed that their partner was a future husband (Ware 1982, 62, 63). Two-thirds said they would have sex with a

A car stops to take advantage of a designated "lovers' lane" near Camden, New Jersey, in 1933. At this time, the proliferation of automobiles provided young people with a new private venue for kissing and sexual experimentation. In one evening, more than fifty drivers parked on this particular site, owned by farmer Lewis B. Simon. (Bettmann/Corbis)

man "for true love" (Parrish 1992, 117). If sexual activity caused pregnancy, Bromley and Britten found, it was relatively easy for college students to obtain illegal abortions, and up to 10,000 American women died as a result of illegal abortions each year (Ware 1982, 63). Popular culture reflected contemporary attitudes toward premarital sex. *Esquire* debuted as a men's magazine in 1935, and *True Confessions* magazine enjoyed a circulation of more than 17 million by that time. *Photoplay* also offered readers steamy Hollywood gossip and illustrations. Tamer radio soap operas traced the efforts of hard-working Americans to see their children married to wealthy and desirable members of the opposite sex.

The Birth Rate and Birth Control

During the 1930s, American birthrates plummeted to their lowest point in history. As a result, the nation's population growth rate, which stood at 16 percent in the 1920s and 15 percent in the 1940s, was a mere 7 percent (Kyvig 2002, 228). The actual number of births dropped from 21.3 live births per 1,000 people in 1930 to 18.4 three years later (Ware 1982, 7). This statistical phenomenon, no doubt, was tied to the decline in the marriage rate; however, many married couples also chose not to have children or to limit the family's size.

As the Great Depression began, American periodicals demonstrated growing public interest in birth control by increasing the number of articles that ad-

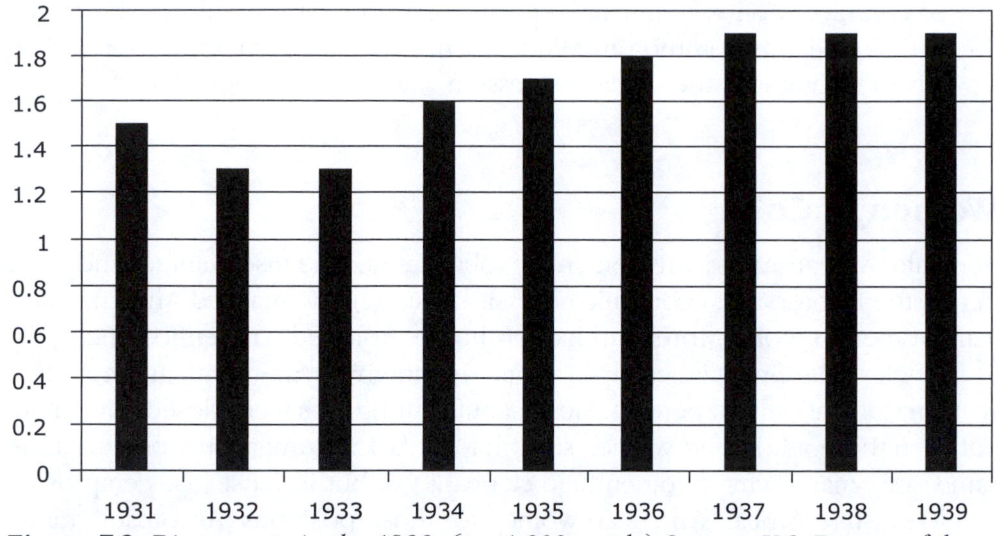

Figure 7.2 *Divorce rate in the 1930s (per 1,000 people).* Source: *U.S. Bureau of the Census, 1949.*

dressed birth control. Liberal publications such as *The Nation* and *The New Republic* had backed birth control for years, but in the 1930s discussion of the issue also appeared in mainstream magazines like *Time* and *Newsweek*. The *American Journal of Public Health* also explored the topic, raising questions about whether public health agencies should provide birth-control assistance. Contraceptive advocates formed the Birth Control Federation of America in 1937 to put birth control on the agenda of "public-health programs of every state in the United States" (Hart 1994, 162). Birth control as a part of public health services was a contentious issue within the African American community. Many physicians and intellectuals argued that it would be in the best interests of African Americans if wealthier African Americans had larger families and the poor had greater access to birth control so that fewer children were born into poverty. Some blamed white society for the failure to provide birth-control information to poor African Americans. They argued that smaller working-class families would have a better chance of moving up into the middle class.

The Catholic Church strongly opposed the use of contraceptives, and the American Medical Association withheld its support from birth control until 1937. However, by the beginning of the next decade, distribution of birth-control literature to married couples had been legalized in every state except Connecticut and Massachusetts. A 1936 Gallup poll showed more than three-fifths of Americans supported birth-control education as well as the practice of birth control (Ware 1982, 7). The Sears, Roebuck Catalog offered contraceptives for sale, and condoms were available in public restrooms at service stations. Furthermore, use of contraception was not limited to urbane big-city dwellers: The Lynds found their use was common in Middletown. In fact, the contraception industry thrived throughout the Great Depression as other businesses failed.

Women of Color

As a rule, African American women did jobs that no one else wanted, and even before the Depression, economic necessity forced many married African American women to work. More than half of those employed women lost their jobs as a result of the financial collapse, while the unemployment rate among white women stood at only 30 percent. Most manufacturing jobs were closed to women, but even those who hired women seldom took African American women. At the same time, many white women held clerical jobs, but in most cases employers would not hire African American women for those positions. As a result, many worked as domestics in the homes of white Americans and earned as little as 10 cents for an hour's work. In some cities, African American women got up every morning and went to a street corner where they stood in hopes that a white person would drive up and offer them a day's work.

Because most African American men in urban areas were unemployed, they were much more dependent on their wives' income than white men were. Several New Deal employment programs did not allow African American women or women in other minority groups, especially in southern states, to participate. By offering aid to only the poorest families, the Aid to Dependent Children program, which was initiated by the Social Security Act of 1935, tended to discourage maintenance of two-income families. As a result, aid programs may have contributed to the splintering of the nuclear family. Mexican and Mexican American women, on the other hand, found that New Deal relief programs made it easier for them to find work. Because of a strong patriarchal tradition, these women typically did not work outside the home until the Great Depression. Many Chicanas were forced to look for work in the 1930s, and government programs eased their way into the workforce. Frequently, these working women were forced to turn over every penny they earned to their fathers.

Children and Teenagers

The Great Depression affected the lives of children and adolescents in significant ways. A drop in the birth rate had reduced children's percentage of the overall population, and the nation's median age, which stood at 25.3 in 1920, rose from 26.5 to 29.0 during the 1930s, according to Census data. The presence of fewer children lowered family size, which theoretically lessened expenses,

Historians' Perspective: Changing Gender Roles in Homes with Male Unemployment

The Great Depression's impact on American women and on gender roles has been the topic of great debate. What seems clear is that there is no universal answer. An individual's class and her specific experiences during this period of economic collapse shaped the extent to which her own life was altered. Among the wealthy who avoided serious financial woes, there was little reason for gender roles to change—and in many ways, the poorest of the poor similarly experienced nothing that would lead to radical changes in family structure. Those who have studied migrant farm families such as the Okies who roamed in the Far West found no pattern of change in gender roles.

However, for some, unemployment among men carried the biggest impetus for change. Without a job, some men had difficulty fulfilling their responsibilities as titular head of the family. If a wife became the family breadwinner, a shift in power was likely, although it may not have been obvious. Many marriages suffered under these circumstances. In homes where both a man and a wife were jobless, the constant presence of both spouses at home sometimes led to angry exchanges. A husband's unwillingness to help around the house by doing what he identified as women's work could worsen conflict. In the workplace, women faced a culture that maintained a general hostility to the idea of working wives. Many institutions and New Deal programs gave women short shrift by arguing that working wives were taking men's jobs. Consequently, a woman who supported her family out of necessity commonly was viewed as a threat to other workers rather than an honorable breadwinner. While many women provided the sole support or much-needed additional income for their families, women's magazines continued to steer female college graduates to "appropriately female" jobs, such as merchandising, catering, and writing, and they perpetuated the idea that working at home as a wife and mother was proper.

In their return to Middletown, the Lynds commented on how roles had been affected by the economic downturn: "Men's and women's roles have in some cases been reversed, with the woman taking a job at whatever money she could earn and the man caring for the household and children." They argued that men were under the greatest pressure to change and described men "adrift from their usual routine, [who] lost much of their sense of time and dawdled helplessly and dully about the streets" (Lynd and Lynd 1937/1969, 179). Others, such as Glen H. Elder Jr. in his *Children of the Great Depression,* have argued that boys' wish to be like their fathers hung on a single issue—perceived success in the community, a prize that seemed unattainable to unemployed men in the 1930s. However, sociologist Mirra Komarovsky found in her 1940 study, *The Unemployed Man and His Family,* that most jobless fathers maintained their position as authority figure within the family when they enjoyed a good marriage. When the marriage was weak, husbands were more likely to suffer a decline in status.

A teacher at a small country school near Sunflower, Mississippi, distributes grapefruit from the Red Cross to her students. (Library of Congress)

but lower family size meant that household chores were likely to fall more heavily upon fewer children, especially in working-class families with both parents working. Even when wives did not work outside the home, their efforts to save money frequently required more work on tasks like sewing and canning, which diverted their attention from more mundane housework, which children could handle. Many teenagers had part-time jobs, but most had difficulty finding full-time work. The percent of teenagers in the labor force decreased among both sexes in the 14–15, 16–17, and 18–19 age groups (Wandersee 1981, 62). Nevertheless, 50 percent of male teens in California and 25 percent of females had a part-time job (Mintz and Kellogg 1988, 140). Children also earned small amounts of money by babysitting, shoveling snow, and mowing lawns.

Elementary school enrollments sagged late in the decade as a result of a drop in the birth rate. Children in deprived households were most likely to drop out of school during the junior high years because even part-time jobs or household work could significantly enhance the family's ability to meet the economic challenges of the Great Depression. High school enrollments, on the other hand, increased because fewer full-time jobs were available for adolescents. Most of the additional high school students were not desperately poor, and they attended classes to prepare for jobs, not for college. For very poor children, schools offered niceties absent from their homes. In school facilities, they could take hot showers and enjoy hot meals. Teachers sometimes contributed part of their hard-earned salaries to buy eyeglasses, meals, and clothing for these youngsters. Impoverished Milwaukee students benefited from fundraising drives to buy textbooks for children, and some school organizations provided no-interest loans so that students could buy supplies.

Thousands of adolescents found a new opportunity for independence. Although finding work was not easy, a boy who was able to land a full-time job experienced new freedom from parental control. Other workers became their peer group, and they saw less reason to defer to their parents' judgment. Among adults, there was an ongoing debate about how schools should prepare children for life on their own. Some claimed that the existence of the Great Depression offered evidence that the old ideals of capitalism had failed, and they believed that schools should open students' minds to economic alternatives. On the opposing side, conservatives urged educators to reinforce long-held ideals and traditional American values. A third group rejected using schools as instruments of propaganda. There was no clear-cut winner among these opposing ideas. Many teens relished newfound freedom without analyzing which values would hasten their success.

Educational Prospects Decline

The economic imperatives faced by school systems adversely affected the public school environment. Declines in tax revenue meant that less money was available to maintain buildings and to pay teachers. This led to reductions in faculty size, pay cuts for teachers, and cancellation of building projects. As a result, many children found themselves squeezed into outmoded classrooms with overwhelmed teachers. More often than not, school supplies and equipment were inadequate. Some crowded schools operated on triple shifts, and high student-teacher ratios became the norm.

Spending dropped $500 million in one three-year period, and construction expenditures sank more than 80 percent. Nearly 25 percent of city school systems canceled summer programs from 1931 through 1933, and night classes for adults were slashed. About 11 percent of cities closed kindergarten classes, and more than 15 percent ended classes for the handicapped. A 1934 report estimated that 1 million students could not attend schools because none was open in their neighborhood or town. And in 1936, an estimated 1.4 million students attended classes in buildings that were unsanitary or unsafe (Sears 1936, 417–418). African

American schools in the South were especially hard hit by spending cuts, with many counties offering no high school education for those students. In Macon County, Alabama, the school system spent $65.18 a day for each white student in 1934 and only $6.58 a day for each African American student (Gray 2002, 33).

The severity of budget problems varied. For instance, the vast majority of Alabama schools were closed in March 1933 when Franklin D. Roosevelt became president, and the few teachers who still had jobs were paid with a combination of cash and scrip, which many businesses refused to accept. Teachers in both New York and Seattle were required to "donate" part of their pay to their school system. And in Chicago, where thousands of unpaid teachers took their protests to the streets, they found that there simply was no money to pay them. By the middle of 1932, foreclosures had been executed on the homes of more than 750 Chicago teachers who had worked without pay and used up their savings. Some had turned to loan sharks, who charged a 42 percent annual rate of interest (Leuchtenburg 1993, 247).

High School Attendance Climbs

High school attendance among 14- to 18-year-olds rose from about 50 percent in 1930 to 75 percent in 1940. The high school graduation rate for enrolled students rose from 9 percent in 1910 to 51 percent in 1940 (Wandersee 1981, 56). Outside the South, the median 17-year-old had a high school diploma in 1935, a huge jump from 1920, when a youth of that age had only a 20 percent likelihood of high school graduation (Goldin 1998, 358). In Middletown, high school students composed 15.2 percent of the entire school population in 1930 and 18.7 percent in 1933. The number of high school graduates in the overall population climbed from a 1920 level of one in 320 residents to one in 154 residents in 1930, and to one in 120 in 1934 (Lynd and Lynd 1937/1969, 206, 208).

High schools increasingly gave greater emphasis to vocational training instead of promoting a classical education. For example, while 51 percent of students in 1900 took Latin classes, only 16 percent of their counterparts in 1934 learned the language. Ten percent of students in 1934 were studying bookkeeping, 17 percent typing, and 9 percent shorthand (Goldin 1998, 352). As high school began to play a bigger part in the lives of young Americans, peer pressure became a bigger factor in their attitudes and behavior. Teens who came from formerly middle-class families that now were deprived found it difficult to meet the appearance standards set by their peer group. Based on the judgments of other students, these newly deprived pupils failed to measure up in junior high school, according to an Oakland study. This remained a problem for girls throughout adolescence;, however, appearance was a smaller factor in the status of high school boys. As a consequence of this problem, girls from newly deprived families experienced sadness and a sense of social rejection (Elder 1999, 130).

College Attendance

The number of public high school students aiming to attend college declined during the 1930s. While the number of high school graduates grew, most did not set their sights on college. Moreover, many middle-class students whose parents might have financed a college education 10 years earlier now found that higher education was out of their reach. The percent of public school graduates who intended to go to college stood at 31 percent in 1923. That figure dropped to 21 percent in 1933 and registered a slight increase to 24 percent in 1937 (Goldin 1998, 351). Author Caroline Bird wrote that the United States "lost a generation of college graduates in the classes of the early thirties. Almost everyone knew someone who couldn't go to college" (Ware 1982, 56).

Private colleges, which suffered from the loss of endowment funds invested in the stock market and from a decline in donations, needed high tuitions to survive. However, at comparatively inexpensive land grant colleges, the National Youth Administration's student aid program helped increase enrollments and allowed many students to remain in college and earn a diploma. Among young women, between 10.5 and 12.2 percent enrolled in higher education. At the same time, women's portion of college students declined from 43.7 percent in 1930 to 40.2 percent in 1940 (Ware 1982, 57). However, in Middletown, the number of girls who had their high school transcripts sent to colleges actually exceeded the number of boys in 1932–1934 (Lynd and Lynd 1937/1969, 211).

Migrant Youths

During the Great Depression, at least 250,000 children and adolescents joined the older men who were riding the rails in search of work (Ware 1982, 55). Most of these young hobos were male. Some had searched for work in their hometowns for years before jumping on a boxcar and entering the hard-scrabble life of nomads. Many young men began their quest in the winter of 1931–1932. Small southwestern towns reported the arrival of about 200 transients per day on the Southern Pacific Company's trains, and 40 to 50 out of each group were adolescents. In January 1933 the executive director of the Child Welfare League of America testified before a Senate committee that at least 200,000 and perhaps as many as a million children already were riding in freight cars or hitchhiking across the country and hoping to find a better life (Uys 1999, 13).

In the late 1920s, most hoboes had been middle-aged men, but by 1932 three-quarters of these transients were believed to be between the ages of 16 and 25. The Interstate Commerce Commission recorded the deaths or injuries of 5,962 railroad trespassers in the first 10 months of 1932. About one-fifth of the casualties were under 21. Gen. Pelham D. Glassford, superintendent of police in the nation's capital, credited these youngsters with being more resourceful than those who remained at home without work. "The more venturesome take

Children of agricultural day laborers spend their hours in a roadside camp near Spiro, Oklahoma, in 1939. (Library of Congress)

to the road," he observed. Some Americans viewed these young travelers with trepidation. In Buffalo, Herman Shubert explored the lives of 20,000 transients and concluded, "These men and women, or perhaps even better, these boys and girls are close to becoming gypsies, if not bandits and criminals." Others feared a massing of dissatisfied young men could be a prelude to revolution. The chief of the federal Children's Bureau, Grace Abbott, warned that young transients "make a game of beating the authorities" (Uys 1999, 13–17).

Young migrants also were among hundreds of thousands of farm workers from the midwestern states and Mexico who traveled through the Far West with their families. Setting aside separate classes for migrant children became a widely accepted means of providing their education. Both Mexicans and midwestern migrants, frequently called Okies, were judged to be mentally inferior. As a result, they were segregated from children whose families had permanent homes in the area. A 1939 California study showed that 10 percent of migrant youngsters were four years behind typical California students (Theobald and Donato 1990, 34).

Youths Experience Economic Change

The 1930s' impact on young people had many facets. The Great Depression increased small children's dependence on the family unit, but it also diminished the family's ability to fulfill those needs. For teenagers who entered the working world, the decade provided new liberties. Unemployed fathers, in particular, found that they had a declining influence on older children, especially sons. "One of the most common things—and it certainly happened to me—was the feeling of your father's failure," one child of that era said. "Sure things were tough, but why should I be the kid who had to put a piece of cardboard into the sole of my shoe to go to school?" Another commented, "Children develop doubts about their parents. They leave home out of necessity. They must find jobs quicker and quicker." Employed adolescents from deprived middle-class families and working-class families were most likely to exhibit adult-oriented behavior, as the natural adolescent tendency to push parents away received an economic sanction. Work roles reinforced a sense of self-direction, but these youths lost the benefits of valuable social or leisure activities that might have helped them if they had remained children a bit longer. Greater interaction with adults (other than their parents) led these young people toward increased respect for dependability and maturity about spending practices (Elder 1999, 80).

Many children of the Depression experienced changes for the better as a result of New Deal programs. The Works Progress Administration constructed new schools so that youngsters could receive safer and longer public school educations, the National Youth Administration loaned money to help more young adults complete college, and the Social Security Act provided a wide array of assistance ranging from food to health care. Unfortunately, the poorest families sometimes profited least from these programs. Segregated schools in the South continued to provide inferior educations for African American children. Children of single mothers could receive aid, but because the Social Security Act offered no money for single mothers themselves, their households had little chance of escaping poverty.

Health Patterns

The health of the American people reflected advances in medical science, expanded efforts to provide public health care, and the physical and psychological stresses of the Great Depression. Malnutrition among the poor was common. At the same time, strain related to economic deprivation caused intensified incidents of emotional and mental instability. Both domestic violence and child abuse increased. As poverty spread, infant mortality rates, which had fallen during the 1920s, began to rise again in 1933, but after two years rates again began to decline.

Most of those who were sick could not afford health care, according to estimates made in 1934. Many of the poorest Americans, such as African American tenant farmers in the South, lacked medical practitioners and hospitals as well

Table 7.1. Reportable Diseases: Annual Rate per 1,000 People

Year	*Diphtheria*	*Smallpox*	*Typhoid Fever*	*Scarlet Fever*	*Poliomyelitis*	*Whooping Cough*
1930	54	39.7	22.1	141.4	7.9	135.5
1931	57.2	24.4	21.4	162.4	14.6	137
1932	48.1	9	21.4	168.9	3.2	172.4
1933	40.1	5.2	18.6	169	4.3	142.5
1934	34.1	4.2	17.6	174.1	5.9	209.8
1935	30.8	6.2	14.4	204.6	8.5	141.6
1936	23.4	6.1	12.4	190.2	3.5	114.6
1937	22.1	9	12.4	177.1	7.4	166.1
1938	23.4	11.5	11.4	145.6	1.3	174.6
1939	18.4	7.6	10	124.6	5.6	140.1

Source: U.S. Bureau of the Census, 1949.

as access to information that would have steered them away from dangerous behavior or guided them toward greater health. On the positive side, scientific advances in warding off and treating common diseases reduced occurrences in all reported diseases except whooping cough. In addition, because most states had established mandatory school attendance laws by 1930, fewer children were working at early ages, and therefore fewer youngsters fell victim to the dangers of industrial employment.

At the same time, fewer Americans were purchasing once-popular patent medicines. A druggist in Middletown reported, "At the bottom of the Depression our sales of patent medicines fell to about one-third of their pre-depression volume" (Lynd and Lynd 1969, 398). Some patent medicines were totally ineffective; however, others offered treatments drawn from herbs and other natural sources. All in all, Americans probably needed medical care more than in preceding decades, but they had a lower capacity to pay for it.

Government Expands Role in Preserving Public Health

Charities and federal, state, and local governments embraced the public health issue. This new attention played a vital role in avoiding and controlling the kind of health threats that sometimes accompany economic collapses. Although Americans of all ages received attention from health-care professionals, the health of children garnered the greatest attention. On October 6, 1933, a Child Health Recovery Conference hosted by the U.S. Children's Bureau recommended dramatic action to assist young people, especially the millions whose families were re-

The Tuskegee Syphilis Study and Race

The most notorious public health study of the 1930s occurred in a rural area of the South without attracting public attention, but when the details of the study became known 40 years later, outrage followed. The U.S. Public Health Service began a Macon County, Alabama, study of syphilis victims in 1932. The project followed the lives of roughly 600 African American men to document the progressive damage that syphilis caused. The majority of participants actually suffered from syphilis, while approximately 200 syphilis-free individuals were used as a control group to measure the relative decline of the diseased men. Although the patients were told that a spinal tap intended to diagnose their condition was "treatment," no effort was made to treat the disease (Reverby 2001, 22).

Macon County's population in 1930 was 27,103—22,320 of whom were African American. According to 1940 Census figures, the county contained 5,205 farm dwelling units, and 4,500 were in need of repair. In this era, almost every part of daily life occurred in a racially segregated society. Lynching and other violence against African Americans were not uncommon. As a result, the county offered a virtually powerless and poor African American community with little access to health care. In addition, Macon County was home to the Tuskegee Institute, which owned a hospital that served African Americans. This combination of factors made the county perfect for the kind of study doctors mapped out (Gray 2002, 28).

Members of the elite—government officials and physicians—apparently saw no moral issue that would preclude launching a study of this type. In that era, many members of their class believed that poor African American tenant farmers were unlikely to get medical assistance and unlikely to enjoy long life anyway. As a result, the decision to merely watch their deterioration rather than trying to prevent it seemed scientifically sound. And at the time the study began, there was no proven treatment for syphilis. A decade later, when penicillin became available, those involved in the study apparently were so locked into their original plan that no change was made. African American doctors at the Tuskegee Institute encouraged African American men to participate, but historians have conjectured that they made this appeal solely because they could not afford to turn down a federal program. Also, as part of an elite African American community that developed around the institute, they may have been affected by class prejudices against the impoverished test subjects.

ceiving state and federal relief. Among the conference's proposals were dispersal of food to those on relief, an increase in the number of public nurses, and school lunch programs. The attendees also favored establishing arrangements to pay private doctors who treated indigent patients. After the conference, the Children's Bureau joined the Federal Emergency Relief Administration in initiating the Child Health Recovery Program, a two-year program aimed at feeding and caring for poor children, with a special emphasis on those isolated in rural areas.

Unfortunately, budget pressures led some schools to reduce funding for supplemental food programs, and in Middletown the results were clear in medical exams showing that most of the students in one school were anemic. Schools were vital to health services because they offered a good opportunity to help many children simultaneously. A 1935 school lunch program in Utah was aimed at helping young children on relief; however, the project's backers quickly realized that they would have to extend their reach because hunger was a daily factor in the lives of many older children as well as children whose families did not receive relief. In Colorado a survey revealed that half of students were not getting enough food, and in some counties 80 percent of youngsters were 15 percent underweight. Consequently, with the help of the Works Progress Administration, local groups established countywide lunch programs (Wandersee 1981, 29).

County public health departments across the nation began to intensify immunization programs and sanitation education, and in many areas, free clinics offered care for the poor. Another important factor in the expansion of public health efforts was broadening the role of nurses, especially to rural areas. When the Great Depression began, there were estimates that 2,500 of the nation's 3,000 counties were predominantly rural and offered little health care. This was especially true in the South, where many suffered from diseases related to poor nutrition, such as scurvy and pellagra, and where infant mortality and communicable diseases were more common. Many private-duty nurses had lost their jobs, and thousands participated in New Deal programs. Many of these women traveled through rural areas attending to health problems that otherwise would not have been treated.

Starvation and Malnutrition

One common sight in the 1930s was the long breadline or the queue outside a "soup kitchen" where shabbily dressed Americans awaited an allotment that would spare them from starvation. Desperation about food ran high among the poor between 1930 and 1935. There were food riots in Detroit and demonstrations in New York City and Chicago. Horror stories spread about mothers who had little beyond flour to feed their families, about people who ate food intended for animals, about households that survived on a diet of only bananas. In city dumps, men, women, and children were seen digging for food. Chicago's poor stood at the back doors of restaurants waiting for scraps; others looked for spoiled produce in outdoor markets. In rural areas, hungry families devoured roots and weeds.

New York hospitals admitted 238 patients in 1931 for starvation or malnutrition. The city reported 29 starvation deaths in 1933 and 110 a year later. Some Americans had to make tough choices, such as holding down funeral costs so that they could afford food. In Middletown a newspaper editorial cited the com-

A soup kitchen sponsored by Chicago gangster Al Capone offers food to the unemployed. (National Archives)

mon belief that no one in town was suffering from a lack of food, and urged readers to "ask the schoolteachers on the South Side about their undernourished children." One junior high school principal reported that many of the boys in his school stole to fill their bellies. Because "virtually no one in Middletown" had actually starved, the Lynds argued that "the debits of rachitic [rickets-stricken] children, abscessed teeth, and tuberculosis are readily overlooked in this go-as-you-please culture in which the onus for keeping healthy is placed traditionally on the individual" (Lynd and Lynd 1937/1969, 137, 400). Migrant farm workers knew hunger, too. The winter months were lean with little harvesting work to do. Adults and children suffered side by side. Among about 1,000 children in California labor camps, a 1938 study showed that 17 percent suffered from malnutrition, while others displayed the symptoms of rickets, a dietary deficiency that caused defective bone growth. Another study of the San Joaquin Valley found 28 percent of all of the migrant children lived off an inadequate diet (Gregory 1989, 64).

Despite Problems, American Lives Grow Longer

Despite all of the bad health news during the Great Depression, the typical American actually had a longer life expectancy by the decade's end. Scientific

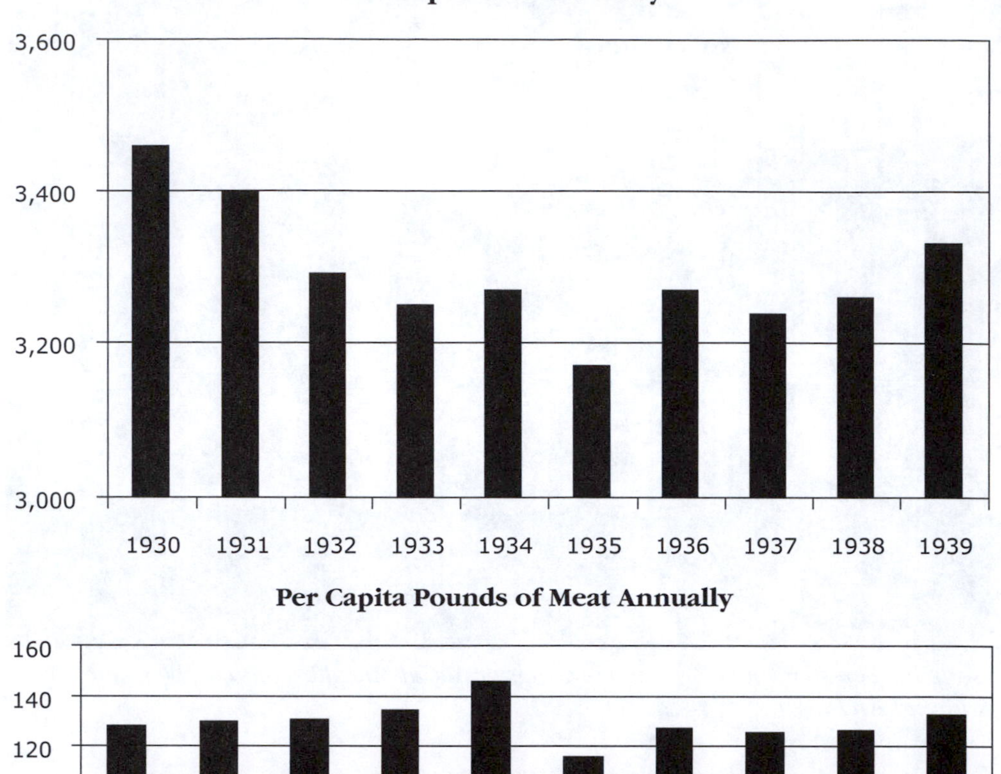

Figure 7.3 *Food consumption data.*
Note: *Data for meat skewed by 1934–1935 slaughter under Emergency Government Relief Purchase Program*. Source: *U.S. Bureau of the Census, 1949.*

advancements and increased attention to public health contributed to this achievement. Census data shows that the life expectancy for a male born in 1939–1941 was 62.81, for a female, 67.29. This was a significant increase over 1929–1931, when male babies had a projected lifespan of 59.12 and females' life expectancy was 62.67. And despite evidence of malnutrition among the poor, per capita food consumption remained relatively stable during the 1930s. Those lucky enough to have money obviously did not hesitate to buy food. Census figures show that per capita calorie intake changed very little; however, consumption of meat did plummet from a high of 147.3 pounds in 1924 to 128.3 in 1930.

One product of the 1930s' efforts to make health care more efficient was the introduction of health insurance. Insurance developed to address hospitals' need for a steady income flow and to eliminate price competition between medical facilities. Increased use of technology in health care and rising costs of medical care also bolstered the movement toward a new insurance system. Government agencies supported the idea of tying health insurance to employment.

During this decade, the concept of industrial diseases also gained visibility when thousands of jobless workers turned their frustrations toward their former employers by filing lawsuits demanding compensation for acute silicosis and other respiratory illnesses that diminished their ability to work. Those who claimed disabilities typically were miners, construction workers, and laborers in foundries or steel factories. New technology in the 20th century had exposed many workers to the dangers of silica dust, which led to chronic illnesses. In 1936 it was declared "the most serious occupational disease hazard in existence today" (Markowitz and Rosner 1989, 230). The silicosis lawsuits led insurers and industries to push the states to incorporate silicosis in existing programs providing workers compensation, and that is how the situation was resolved. This was the first time that illness caused by industrial hazards received widespread attention rather than simply being the focus of affected labor unions. Negotiating on the issue led to the concept of reimbursing employees for lost income rather than putting a dollar value on their impaired ability to function.

Religion

The 1930s witnessed a decline in many facets of traditional religious worship, but at the same time, desperate times heightened the religiosity of some Americans. Two conflicting forces—the move toward a more secular culture and the belief that faith would save those in suffering—affected Americans during this decade. These forces brought changes to American religion, some of which would have lasting effects. Mainstream liberal and moderate Protestant denominations—Methodists, Congregationalists, Presbyterians, Episcopalians, and Lutherans—lost members during the Great Depression and often were constrained by debt and high operating expenses at a time of diminished giving by their members. When Robert and Helen Lynd returned to Middletown in the 1930s, they noted that the city had become more secular over the years since their mid-1920s study. Sundays now seemed more like Saturdays. A new city swimming pool attracted many children and adolescents on Sundays. The annual horse show reached its climax on Sunday, and some prosperous men played golf on Sunday instead of going to church. A local radio station reported heavy fan mail after it switched from religious music to popular music on Sunday. A new state law even forbade citizens from asking political candidates to fill out questionnaires saying where they stood on religious issues. In many ways, the pattern in Middletown reflected what was happening across the nation. Many traditionally religious Americans found little time or money to devote to their church. Instead of going to church each Sunday, many of those with money took a drive or visited a resort. And for many of the poor, Sunday became a day to catch up on chores.

At the same time, desperation and a need for hope led some to pray for miracles and to turn toward beliefs that seemed to offer a more direct connection with God. While some Catholics asked Saint Jude to intercede in their lives, fundamentalists celebrated their intimate link to God through their study of the Bible. Among many Americans, these emotionally driven efforts attracted more attention than mainstream churches. "The religious life of a great many men and women has been quickened," a sociologist reported in 1935; however, he pointed out that many among the newly devout sought economic rather than spiritual security (Groves 1935, 776). By the end of the decade, the ranks of fundamentalists and other true believers had grown significantly.

Religious Interpretations of Economic Decline

Religious groups interpreted the Great Depression in varying ways. Millenarians —fundamentalist Christians who believed that the past world war had been one sign that the end of the world was near—characterized the economic collapse as just one more piece of evidence that life as they knew it was about to conclude, to be replaced by 1,000 years of rule by Jesus and his true followers. Catholics, on the other hand, were likely to see this period as a taste of purgatory in which the living must now suffer to win their eventual place in heaven. Some Catholic clergymen also preached that the Great Depression was God's retaliation for the excesses of materialistic life. Many mainstream Protestant ministers blamed man's selfish and sinful behavior for the economic hardships that now shackled the nation.

A multitude of ministers predicted that this era of suffering would return Americans to religious piety; however, the nation's churches lost almost 3 million members between 1930 and 1940. A 1939 Gallup poll showed that about 50 percent of respondents attended religious services less often than their parents, and only 20 percent exceeded their parents' record. The editor of one religious periodical asserted that many Americans did not attend church because they believed that economic problems were manmade and not subject to prayer or demonstrations of piety. While most young Americans were nominal church members, it was estimated that only about one-third were truly religious. A 1934 college survey demonstrated that lowerclassmen were more likely to believe in

God than juniors and seniors who had been exposed to more of the college curriculum (Wector 1948, 213–214).

At various times in the nation's history, Americans have identified the United States as God's favored nation, but in the 1930s there was little evidence to bolster that contention. With young Americans admitting to premarital sexual activity and gays coming out of the closet and onto the stages of the nation's most populous city, it was easy for some clergymen to visualize a nation filled with temptation and sin. Catholic leaders bemoaned birth control usage as a sign of human interference with God's work, and fundamentalists warned against those who interpreted the Bible loosely and through the lens of contemporary practices. As millions suffered the effects of the Great Depression, so did long-established churches. The turmoil of daily life shook the foundations of many mainstream institutions, while providing a new impetus for those seeking something different.

Bible School, Fundamentalist Boom

Conservative and evangelical fundamentalist Protestantism experienced great growth during this period. Many of its congregants awaited the millennium of Jesus' rule, as promised in the Book of Revelations. Membership in the fundamentalist Assemblies of God quadrupled between 1926 and 1940, while the Church of the Nazarene grew more than 100 percent. The Southern Baptists gained nearly 1.5 million members in the same time period and claimed a total membership of almost 5 million (Carpenter 1980, 74).

One sign of fundamentalist strength was the development of Bible institutes across the nation. These schools appealed to fundamentalist groups and to fundamentalist members of more liberal denominations. Their initial goal was to train laymen and laywomen to serve as missionaries or Sunday school superintendents; however, attendees encouraged expanding them to educate ministers and to provide other services that would spread fundamentalist beliefs. Two powerful fundamentalist organizations, the Moody Bible Institute in Chicago and the Philadelphia School of the Bible, planned a series of seven-day conferences in summertime as well as shorter sessions. They also helped to spread the Word outside their cities by providing guest preachers for weekly services and evangelists for revival meetings.

Some schools sprouted publishing branches that reinforced their message in writing. The Moody Bible Institute organized weekend conferences at almost 500 churches across the country in 1936. The following year, it received donations from more than 15,000 people, and about the same number were enrolled in its correspondence school. The *Moody Monthly* listed 88 conferences at 27 sites when it began publishing a nationwide calendar of events in 1930. Eleven years later, the same schedule included more than 200 events at more than 50 sites. As Bible schools blossomed into colleges, their impact grew. Gordon College of Theology and Missions near Boston had a profound effect on Baptist congregations in New England. By the mid-1930s, the school had trained 48 Boston pastors and half of all Baptist pastors in New Hampshire. In Minnesota 75 pastors were alumni of the Northwestern Bible and Missionary Training School (Carpenter 1980, 67–68). Although more liberal denominations reduced missionary work abroad during the Great Depression, fundamentalist efforts expanded, and their funding grew, too. The fundamentalist China Inland Mission employed almost 1,400 missionaries in the 1930s. Fundamentalists also took their message to radio on shows with titles like *Radio Bible Class* or *Bible Study Hour*. Evangelists like Charles E. Fuller reached out to large audiences in the United States and eventually to Christians around the globe.

Prior to the 1930s, evangelists focused much of their attention on individual issues in which their beliefs conflicted with those of more liberal Christians. For instance, fundamentalists in the previous decade had rallied around opposition to teaching evolution in school. In this decade, according to historian Joel A. Carpenter, they shifted their focus to "the evangelical gospel" and found an eager audience. Evangelist Aimee Semple McPherson drew two million people —one in every 50 Americans—during a nationwide tour (Sutton 2005, 308). However, the spread of fundamentalism was not evident in every city. The Lynds wrote that in Middletown, "the bottom had dropped out of the revival movement which flourished in 1925" (Lynd and Lynd 1937/1969, 302).

St. Jude

Many American Catholics turned to saints for help in their time of crisis. Some sought aid from Saint Jude, the patron saint of desperate causes. The Our Lady of Guadalupe congregation, which had begun as a mission to the poor Mexican community in Chicago, began its first novena (nine consecutive days of prayers and devotions) to Saint Jude on October 28, 1929, Black Monday of the stock-market crash. The church, under the leadership of Father Jaime Tort, soon began to set a new course. Tort began the League of St. Jude in November 1929, and the church became Saint Jude's national shrine. By 1935, the newly created shrine's publication, *Voice of St. Jude,* began receiving thousands of pleas each year for the saint's intercession in the letter writers' lives. Two years later, the number of letters rose to thousands per day. When the shrine held a novena in the spring of 1937, 4,000 worshipers attempted to attend each service. Later, a different sort of letter began to arrive: Individuals wrote to thank Saint Jude for answering their prayers. One woman had written earlier about her husband's problems in competing with younger workers, and the problem apparently had been resolved because she proclaimed, "I am so thankful to Saint Jude that I feel like shouting from the rooftops." Some Catholic clergymen considered such devotions to a saint as a cult and discouraged Catholics from taking part in this kind of devotionalism.

Jewish Culture

American Judaism underwent a period of change during the 1930s. Since a flood of Eastern European Jews entered the United States between 1890 and 1920, there had been a persistent separation between the late arrivals, who were primarily Orthodox Jews, and the native-born American Jews, whose ancestors had come to America as immigrants from Central Europe primarily in the mid-19th century. Most of the American-born Jews whose roots were planted in an earlier migration embraced Reform or Conservative Judaism, and because of their ancestry they were labeled as "German Jews." However, in the 1930s these groups began interacting to a greater extent. They met outside the synagogue in social service programs and rapidly expanding Zionist organizations. Some Jews began holding joint membership in two synagogues, thus enhancing their interactions with other Jews. (The rituals of the Orthodox held a lingering appeal for the more modern Reform Jews, and at the same time the freedoms available outside Orthodoxy led some Jews to consider joining a Reform or Conservative synagogue.)

During the Great Depression, many synagogues raised membership fees in an effort to make ends meet, but this often led members to withdraw from synagogues. While continuing anti-Semitism in the United States and the rise of Nazism in Germany added to Jewish feelings of insecurity, the liberal vision of the New Deal carried a certain resonance with the left-leaning traditions of more recent immigrants, who were closely tied to labor unions. At the same time, the role of women in American Judaism was changing. New York City's Jewish school enrollment was one-third female in the 1930s and even higher in Reform Sunday schools (Pratt 1978, 697). Although Orthodox Jews involved girls in educational training only reluctantly, some of their traditionally all-male schools accepted girls with restrictions on the range of their studies. Women also played a growing role in the mutual aid society, B'nai B'rith.

African Americans and Native Americans

African Americans who migrated to the nation's urban areas during and after World War I helped to bolster African American churches in cities such as Chicago. Two of the nation's largest Protestant congregations in the 1930s were the city's Olivet Baptist Church and Pilgrim Baptist, both of which were African American. Catholic churches and schools in Chicago were racially segregated, and all–African American parish schools prospered during this era. In New York, evangelist Father Divine led huge events, where he attempted to spread optimism among his followers and defined himself as the Second Coming of Christ. In many locales, African American congregations suffered financial woes. With costs rising and donations sinking, some congregations abandoned all missionary efforts. In places, when impoverished churches tried to serve their impoverished

Evangelist Father Divine, who preaches optimism to Depression-weary African Americans, takes part in a parade marking the acquisition of Heavens, a New York communal gathering place. (Bettmann/Corbis)

congregations, hope often was all they had to offer. Some African Americans turned their backs on Christianity and explored Islam, which had been the religion of some of their ancestors in Africa; however, disagreements between congregations limited unity among these groups.

Following the appointment of John Collier as commissioner of Indian affairs in 1933, Native Americans experienced greater freedom to worship as they wanted. In what he called the "Indian New Deal," Collier ordered that Native Americans be allowed to perform their traditional rituals without interference from outsiders. Collier's motives have been questioned by scholars who believe that he, too, wanted to remake Native Americans in his own image; however, he did initiate significant changes in the treatment of Native Americans while helping them to survive the Great Depression. Almost since the first white men arrived in America, Christian missionaries had tried to convert Native Americans, but Collier brought an end to required Christian instruction in schools for Indian children and opened the door to classes that focused on Native American beliefs and traditions. The Native American Church, an intertwining of Indian traditions and Christian beliefs, won approval to operate on Indian reservations during his tenure (see "Social Movements" chapter).

Churches Reach Out to the Suffering

Early in the Great Depression, the nation's churches took an active and prominent role in offering food and clothing to those Americans who were suffering the most. However, as the New Deal took hold and other governmental programs began to take the lead in providing relief to the poor, many religious organizations retreated behind the church walls rather than opening their doors and reaching out to the poor. Many destitute churches struggled to maintain operations, and many urban ministers suffered significant salary cuts. The Catholic Church had the greatest success in maintaining a link with needy members—and this may well have sprung from the natural interaction that occurred as a result of Catholics' belief that missing Sunday services was a sin. Among other denominations, the Church of the Latter-Day Saints (LDS, or Mormons) in Utah established the most direct aid program. They rejected federal handouts and made each ward of the LDS responsible for the impoverished. When a ward became overwhelmed, money would pour in from higher levels of the church. The Mormons sought ways to make families self-sufficient through the adoption of money-saving schemes and the establishment of church employment bureaus.

Despite the financial woes of many religious institutions, religious leaders realized that they needed to make a connection with people who were not attending services. As a result, national radio broadcasts became an attractive forum for religious sentiments. The *National Radio Pulpit* put the spotlight on three Protestant ministers. *The Message of Israel* appealed to Jewish listeners, and Bishop Fulton J. Sheen starred on the *Catholic Hour.* These programs offered a message from the viewpoint of the mainstream churches to which most prominent Americans belonged. Fundamentalists, who often appealed to working-class believers, also showed that they could master the relatively new medium. Charles E. Fuller's *Old Fashioned Revival Hour* drew listeners with a more impassioned appeal.

The continued growth of conservative, Protestant fundamentalism in the 1930s helped to lay the groundwork for a shift that would cross the country and eventually become a powerful force in American politics. Okies and other migrants helped to spread this message to the West Coast in the 1930s. Revivals, radio broadcasts, and Bible conferences helped to strengthen this movement and created new links between Americans in different regions of the country. Fundamentalist growth would continue through the rest of the 20th century, eventually returning to the issue-oriented political role that had guided attacks on the teaching of evolution in the 1920s (see "Social Movements" chapter).

Biographies

Eugene Dibble, 1893–1968

Physician at Tuskegee Institute

Eugene Dibble directed John Andrew Hospital at the Tuskegee Institute during the 1930s. Dibble, who was African American, encouraged other African Americans to participate in the controversial U.S. Public Health Service program chronicling the physical deterioration of African American men with syphilis. The study became controversial because the syphilis victims, in most cases, were not treated for their illness: The decline in their health was merely studied and recorded. Dibble assisted with some portions of the study's work, including a required spinal tap for each of about 600 men in the project, most of whom had syphilis. Over the years, there has been debate about whether Dibble shared in culpability for the suffering of men who were not treated. His defenders have argued that no African American institution in the 1930s could afford to alienate the federal government. It is known that Dibble prescribed penicillin for some study participants; however, it is unclear whether he was knowingly treating their syphilis or prescribing the drug to address other ailments.

Charles E. Fuller, 1887–1968

Fundamentalist Leader and Evangelist

Charles E. Fuller became a prominent figure in radio evangelism when he launched the *Old Fashioned Revival Hour* in October 1937. The show initially aired on 13 stations of the Mutual Network. Fuller began the 1930s as pastor of Calvary Church in Placentia, California, a church he had helped to form as an evangelical body just five years earlier. Fuller was a strong supporter of the Bible schools and conferences that spread rapidly during the 1930s, and despite roots in the Presbyterian Church, he favored a more fundamentalist approach to Christianity. Fuller had delivered radio messages at various times during the 1920s, but it was in February 1930 that he decided to broadcast all of his church's Sunday services. The church initially paid $180 per month to put its message on the airwaves. By the spring of 1931 he broadcast three services each Sunday. In 1933 he resigned from Calvary to devote his attention to a radio ministry. He experimented with various formats before establishing the *Old Fashioned Revival Hour.* By 1951 his show was broadcast by the ABC network on about 650 stations around the world. The program continued to air until 1968.

Lorena Hickok, 1893–1968

Journalist and Beloved Friend to Eleanor Roosevelt

Lorena Hickok was a pioneering journalist, a political progressive, and an intimate friend of Eleanor Roosevelt. Although she began her journalistic career as society editor of the *Milwaukee Sentinel,* Hickok pushed through doors previously closed to female reporters. Beginning in the World War I years, she reported on political news, crime stories, and even sports. She met Eleanor Roosevelt in 1932 after convincing her editors at the Associated Press to assign her to cover the Democratic presidential candidate's wife. A year later, Hickok gave up her job at the Associated Press because she realized that her objectivity had been compromised by her relationship with Eleanor. Subsequently, she was employed by Harry Hopkins, chief of the Federal Emergency Relief Administration, to examine the conditions faced by average Americans. Hickok also served as Eleanor's mentor when she began writing a daily newspaper column, *My Day.*

Roosevelt biographer Blanche Wiesen Cook's documentation of correspondence from the First Lady to Hickok has revealed Eleanor's open expressions of what most would categorize as romantic love for Hickok. In 1936 Hickok moved from Washington to Long Island to work for a public relations company, but in 1940 she returned to Washington and lived in the White House while working as executive secretary of the Women's Division of the Democratic National Committee. After Franklin Roosevelt's death, Hickok worked for the New York State Democratic Committee and eventually moved to Hyde Park to be closer to Eleanor. Despite Hickok's declining health, the two women collaborated on *Ladies of Courage,* a book about female political leaders, in 1954. Hickok also wrote *Reluctant First Lady,* published in 1962.

Eleanor Roosevelt, right, and her intimate friend Lorena Hickok share time together in St. Thomas, Virgin Islands, in 1934. Standing between them is the governor of the Virgin Islands, Paul Martin Pearson. (Corbis)

Meridel Le Sueur, 1900–1996

Writer

In both journalism and fiction, Meridel Le Sueur became a prominent chronicler of women's lives during the Great Depression. She spent much of the decade traveling across America talking to women who were typically members of the working class. She interviewed women in many settings, including farms, factories, picket lines, relief sites, and unemployment offices. From the information she gained, she gave these women greater visibility on the pages of literary magazines, such as *Scribner's* and *Partisan Review.* Her story, "Women in the Bread Lines," published in January 1932 by *New Masses,* offered the viewpoint of women waiting for nonexistent jobs in quiet unemployment offices. Her autobiographical 1935 story, "Annunciation," described her decision to become pregnant as an affirmation of life in 1927, the same year in which she mourned what she considered to be the unjust executions of anarchists Nicola Sacco and Bartolomeo Vanzetti for armed robbery and murder in Massachusetts. She also provided voices to women in organized labor, when she wrote about women's contribution to a 1934 Teamsters' strike in "I Was Marching." Her 1934 *American Mercury* article, "Cows and Horses Are Hungry," described a desolate drive through the drought-stricken midwestern states. As both a feminist and a Communist, Le Sueur placed the spotlight on the unseen suffering of women in rural and urban America. She was among those writers who called for and led the 1935 American Writers Congress at the peak of the Communist Party's influence on American literary figures. Her 1939 book, *The Girl,* which was not published until 1978, revealed the ugly realities of women's lives, including hunger and sexual abuse. Her writing career and political activism spanned 60 years.

Gene/Jean Malin, 1908–1933

Performer

Female impersonator Gene/Jean Malin was the biggest nightclub star to take part in the "pansy craze" in midtown Manhattan during the late 1920s and 1930s. After growing up in Brooklyn, he performed in the chorus lines of several Broadway shows; however, after frequent complaints that he was too effeminate, he decided to make his career as a female impersonator. He took the name Jean when he entered the gay community and began competing in drag balls. In his twenties, he became a well-known celebrity after moving his act from Greenwich Village to the Times Square district. He served as a witty master of ceremonies, introducing performers and moving throughout the Club Abbey talking to patrons. One newspaper reported that he "wore men's clothes, but talked and acted like a woman." He personified the "pansy" figure that sophisticated New Yorkers expected to see in these clubs. Like all of the "pansy" performers, he sometimes faced heckling, but he typically used biting wit to ridicule audience members. For a few years, he was the highest-paid performer on Broadway. Many of his fans were surprised when he married a woman in 1931, but when the marriage quickly ended, audiences returned to their assumption that he was gay. His success led other clubs to showcase "pansy" performers. When the Club Abbey closed its doors, Malin took his act to Boston, and by 1933 he performed in a Hollywood club that carried his name. He drowned that year when he lost control of his car and it flew off a pier into deep water.

Thomas Parran, 1892–1968

Public Health Official

As a physician with a background in rural sanitation, Thomas Parran became New York's state health commissioner in 1930 at the request of then-governor Franklin Roosevelt. In that position, he led the Special Health Commission, which produced findings in 1932 that offered a blueprint for the operation of county health departments during the Great Depression. Although the state of New York failed to enact many of the commission's proposals, Parran gained notoriety after the

Columbia Radio System told him that he could not use the term *syphilis control* in a planned address. As a result, he canceled the speech, and his undelivered address reached a wide audience when newspapers shattered taboos by printing it in uncensored form. In 1934 President Roosevelt named Parran to serve on the Committee on Economic Security, which drew up the Social Security Act. Two years later, Parran became the nation's surgeon general. His antisyphilis campaign blossomed in the late 1930s when New Deal initiatives enabled the government to identify and treat syphilis victims. His 1937 book, *Shadow of the Land,* explained his strategy for attacking the potentially deadly disease. During his service as surgeon general during World War II, he helped to define the growing role of public health officials at home and abroad.

Thomas Parran, a physician, worked closely with Franklin Roosevelt, first as New York's state health commissioner, and later as surgeon general of the United States. He did pioneering work in defining the public health role of county governments and in promoting aggressive action against the spread of syphilis. (Bettmann/Corbis)

Caroline Ware, 1899–1990

Social Historian

Caroline Farrar Ware was an early advocate of directing historical research away from the records of institutions and into the lives of ordinary people. Greatly affected by Helen and Robert Lynd's Middletown study of the late 1920s, she left her job as a professor at Vassar College in 1935 and accepted the task of leading a community study supported by Columbia University's Council in Research. The project—*Greenwich Village 1920–1930: A Comment on American Civilization in the Post War Years*—was important because it re-emphasized the importance of understanding ordinary lives and because it provided new insights into the lives of people within Greenwich Village's gay community. Ware reported expanding evidence of the homosexual community's role in the neighborhood. "The Village became noted as the home of 'pansies' and 'Lesbians,' and dives of all sorts featured this type," she wrote. Ware, who considered homosexuality to be a fad, indicated that the neighborhood's residents "pass on from free love to homosexuality . . . to mark the outposts of revolt" (Chauncey 1984, 235). Although she did not expect homosexuality to have lasting effects in Greenwich Village, she did demonstrate that the area's gay residents had managed to achieve autonomy and acceptance. A Vassar alumna, Ware edited the 1940 work, *The Cultural Approach to History,* which featured essays from a broad array of historians who advocated changes in the study of history.

References and Further Readings

Carpenter, J. 1980. "Fundamentalist Institutions and the Rise of Evangelical Protestantism, 1929–1942," *Church History* 49 (1): 62–75.

Chauncey, G. 1994. *Gay New York: Gender, Urban Culture, and the Making of the Gay Male World 1890–1940.* New York: Basic Books.

Cowdry, H. V. 1945. "Shall They Survive?" *Science* 101 (2634): 625–29.

Elder, G. 1974/1999. *Children of the Great Depression: Social Change in Life Experience.* Boulder, CO: Westview Press.

Fass, P. 1989. *Outside In: Minorities and the Transformation of American Education.* New York: Oxford University Press.

Foley, B. 1990. "Women and the Left in the 1930s," *American Literary History* 2 (1): 150–69.

Goldin, C. 1998. "America's Graduation from High School: The Evolution and Spread of Secondary Schooling in the Twentieth Century," *Journal of Economic History* 58 (2): 345–74.

Gray, F. D. 2002. *The Tuskegee Syphilis Study: The Real Story and Beyond.* Montgomery, AL: New South Books.

Gregory, J. 1989. *American Exodus: The Dust Bowl Migration and Okie Culture in California.* New York: Oxford University Press.

Groves, E. 1935. "Adaptations of Family Life," *American Journal of Sociology* 40 (6): 772–79.

Hapke, L. 1995. *Daughters of the Great Depression: Women, Work, and Fiction in the American 1930s.* Athens: University of Georgia Press.

Hart, J. 1994. "Who Should Have the Children? Discussions of Birth Control Among African-American Intellectuals, 1920–1939," *Journal of Negro History* 79 (1): 71–84.

Hughes, H. 1936. "The Lindbergh Case: A Study of Human Interest and Politics," *American Journal of Sociology* 42 (1): 32–54.

Kaiser, C. 1997. *The Gay Metropolis, 1940–1996.* Boston: Houghton Mifflin.

Komarovsky, M. 1940. *The Unemployed Man and His Family.* New York: Columbia University Press.

Kyvig, D. 2002. *Daily Life in the United States, 1920–1940.* Chicago: Ivan R. Dee.

LaGrand, J. 1996. "The Changing 'Jesus Road': Protestants Reappraise American Indian Missions in the 1920s and 1930s," *Western Historical Quarterly* 27 (4): 479–504.

Leuchtenburg, W. 1958/1993. *The Perils of Prosperity, 1914–1932.* 2nd ed. Chicago: University of Chicago Press.

Lynd, R., and H. Lynd. 1937/1969. *Middletown in Transition.* New York: Harcourt, Brace.

Markowitz, G., and D. Rosner. 1989. "The Illusion of Medical Certainty: Silicosis and the Politics of Industrial Disability, 1930–1960," *Milbank Quarterly* 67, supp. 2 (pt. 1): 228–53.

Mintz, S., and S. Kellogg. 1988. *Domestic Revolutions: A Social History of American Family Life.* New York: The Free Press.

Modell, J. 1985. "Public Griefs and Personal Problems: An Empirical Inquiry into the Impact of the Great Depression," *Social Science History* 9 (4): 399–427.

Orsi, R. 1996. *Thank You, St. Jude: Women's Devotion to the Patron Saint of Hopeless Causes.* New Haven: Yale University Press.

Parrish, M. 1992. *Anxious Decades: America in Prosperity and Depression, 1920–1941.* New York: W. W. Norton.

Pratt, N. 1978. "Transition in Judaism: The Jewish American Women through the 1930s," *American Quarterly* 30 (5): 681–702.

Reverby, S. 2001. "More than Fact and Fiction: Cultural Memory and the Tuskegee Syphilis Study," *Hastings Center Report* 31 (5): 22–28.

Satter, B. 1996. "Marcus Garvey, Father Divine and the Gender Politics of Race Difference and Race Neutrality," *American Quarterly* 48 (1): 43–76.

Scharf, L. 1980. *To Work and to Wed: Female Employment, Feminism, and the Great Depression.* Westport, CT: Greenwood Press.

Sears, J. "Getting the Schools Out of the Depression," *Elementary School Journal* 36 (6): 417–23.

Sutton, M. 2005. "Clutching to 'Christian' America: Aimee Semple McPherson, the Great Depression, and the Origins of Pentecostal Political Activism," *Journal of Policy History* 17 (5): 308–38.

Theobald, P., and R. Donato. 1995. "A Look at Rural Education in the United States." *Peabody Journal of Education* 67 (3): 29–45.

Thomasson, M. 2000. "From Sickness to Health: The Twentieth-Century Development of the Demand for Health Insurance," *Journal of Economic History* 60 (2): 504–8.

U.S. Bureau of the Census. 1949. *Historical Statistics of the United States 1789–1945.* Washington, DC: Department of Commerce.

U.S. Bureau of the Census. 1975. *Bicentennial Edition Historical Statistics of the United States Colonial Times to 1970, Part 1*. Washington: Government Printing Office. Also available at http://www2.census.gov/prod2/statcomp/documents/CT1970p1-.01.pdf (accessed September 5, 2006).

Uys, E. 1999. *Riding the Rails: Teenagers on the Move during the Great Depression*. New York: TV Books.

Violas, P. 1971. "The Indoctrination Debate and the Great Depression," *The History Teacher* 4 (4): 25–35.

Wandersee, W. 1981. *Women's Work and Family Values, 1920–1940*. Cambridge, MA: Harvard University Press.

Ware, S. 1982. *Holding Their Own: American Women in the 1930s*. Boston: Twayne Publishers.

Wector, D. 1948. *The Age of the Great Depression, 1929–1941*. New York: Macmillan.

People and Events in the 20th Century

The 1900s

THE 1910s

The 1920s

The 1930s

THE 1940s

THE 1950s

The 1960s

The 1970s

The 1980s

The 1990s

1930s Index

About the Author and the Contributors

Cecelia Bucki is an associate professor of history at Fairfield University in Fairfield, Connecticut. Dr. Bucki has published articles in *International Labor and Working-Class History, Labor History, Social Science History,* and *Labor Histories: Class, Politics, and the Working-Class Experience*. Her book, *Bridgeport's Socialist New Deal, 1915–1936* (University of Illinois Press, 2001), won the 2002 Homer D. Babbidge Jr. Award for Best Book on Connecticut history.

Alice L. George received her PhD in history from Temple University in 2001, after 20 years as an editor at newspapers including the *Detroit Free Press* and the *Philadelphia Daily News*. She is the author of *Awaiting Armageddon: How Americans Faced the Cuban Missle Crisis* and works as an independent historian in Philadelphia, Pennsylvania.

Catherine McNicol Stock is professor and chair of the Department of History at Connecticut College. She is the author of *Main Street in Crisis: The Great Depression and the Old Middle Class on the Northern Plains* (University of North Carolina Press, 1991) and *Rural Radicals: From Bacon's Rebellion to the Oklahoma City Bombing* (Cornell University Press, 1997). With Robert D. Johnston, she is the editor of *The Countryside in the Age of the Modern State* (Cornell University Press, 2001).

Kathy M. Newman is an associate professor of English at Carnegie-Mellon University in Pittsburgh, Pennsylvania. She has published *Radio-Active: Advertising and Activism 1935–1947* (University of California Press, 2004), and also writes a bi-weekly media column for *The Pittsburgh City Paper*.